ÆTHELRED

LEVI ROACH is lecturer in medieval history at
He was educated at Trinity College, Cambridge, and the Ruprecht-Karls-Universität Heidelberg, and is a past winner of the Royal Historical Society's Alexander Prize (2011).

ÆTHELRED
THE UNREADY

LEVI ROACH

YALE UNIVERSITY PRESS
NEW HAVEN AND LONDON

For information about this and other Yale University Press publications, please contact:
U.S. Office: sales.press@yale.edu   yalebooks.com
Europe Office: sales@yaleup.co.uk   yalebooks.co.uk

Typeset in Adobe Garamond Pro by IDSUK (DataConnection) Ltd
Printed and bound in Great Britain by CPI Group (UK) Ltd, Croydon, CR0 4YY

Library of Congress Cataloging-in-Publication Data

Names: Roach, Levi, 1985- author.
Title: Æthelred the unready / Levi Roach.
Other titles: Ethelred the Unready
Description: New Haven : Yale University Press, [2016]
Identifiers: LCCN 2016019938 | ISBN 9780300196290 (alk. paper)
    Subjects: LCSH: Ethelred II, King of England, 968?-1016. | Great Britain—History—
    Ethelred II, 979-1016. | Great Britain—Kings and rulers—Biography.
Classification: LCC DA154.7 .R63 2016 | DDC 942.01/74092 [B]—dc23
LC record available at https://lccn.loc.gov/2016019938

A catalogue record for this book is available from the British Library.

ISBN 978-0-300-22972-1 (pbk)

10 9 8 7 6 5 4 3 2

CONTENTS

PLATES, MAPS AND FIGURES

Plates

1. Frontispiece of the New Minster Refoundation Charter (S 745): Edgar presents the charter to Christ. © The British Library Board (MS Cotton Vespasian A. viii, fol. 2v).
2. Post-reform coinage of Edgar, Edward the Martyr and Æthelred. © *The Sylloge of Coins from the British Isles* (SCBI), 66 vols. (1958–).
   a) Edgar, *Reform/Small Cross* (*SCBI*, L, no. 264): mint place – Lewes; moneyer – Theodgar.
   b) Edward, *Small Cross* (*SCBI*, II, no. 753): mint place – Northampton; moneyer – Cylm.
   c) Æthelred, *First Small Cross* (*SCBI*, LI, no. 1): mint place – Lincoln; moneyer – Swerting.
   d) Æthelred, *First Hand* (*SCBI*, LXV, no. 102): mint place – London; moneyer – Cyn(e)sige.
   e) Æthelred, *Second Hand* (*SCBI*, LXV, no. 124): mint place – Exeter; moneyer – Luoda.
   f) Æthelred, *Benediction Hand* (*SCBI*, II, no. 825): mint place – Worcester; moneyer – Durand.
   g) Æthelred, *Crux* (*SCBI*, LXV, no. 313): mint place – Malmesbury; moneyer – Leofwine.
   h) Æthelred, *Intermediate Small Cross* (*SCBI*, LI, no. 134): mint place – Malmesbury; moneyer – Ealdred.
   i) Æthelred, *Long Cross* (*SCBI*, LXV, no. 683): mint place – London; moneyer – Godwine.
   j) Æthelred, *Helmet* (*SCBI*, LXV, no. 1016): mint place – Theford; moneyer – Osulf.
   k) Æthelred, *Agnus Dei* (*SCBI*, LXV, no. 1095): mint place – Derby; moneyer – Blacaman.

Maps

Figures

A NOTE ON NAME FORMS AND REFERENCES

As those who have read any amount of scholarship on Anglo-Saxon England will be aware, early English personal names can be modernized in a variety of fashions. The attempt here has been to conform to standard scholarly practice at present. Thus, the Old English vowel æ (pronounced as a sharp 'a', rather like that in 'cat' or 'hat') is kept, but ð and þ are replaced by their modern equivalent 'th' and ƿ by 'w'. The attempt has otherwise been to keep as close as possible to the original (thus, Æthelstan not Athelstan, Eadwig not Edwy, etc.); however, where there are good modern equivalents of the name in question, these have been preferred (e.g. Alfred not Ælfred, Edgar not Eadgar). With non-English names the approach has been less systematic and more impressionistic. Here I generally follow the forms used in the *Wiley Blackwell Encyclopedia of Anglo-Saxon England* (Swein rather than Swegen or Sveinn, Olaf rather than Olav or Oláfr); otherwise, I seek to render them in the form best known to Anglophone students and scholars. Doubtless many inconsistencies remain, but hopefully it will be clear enough who is intended. When rulers are first mentioned in the main text, their reigns are given in parentheses; likewise, the episcopates and abbacies of important prelates are often given when they are first encountered.

My approach to referencing has been similarly pragmatic: I have attempted to cite all the most recent and relevant secondary literature, without seeking to be exhaustive. In order to avoid overburdening an already long text, articles are cited from their most recent place of appearance (or at least the most recent one known to me), except when this is in a rare or hard-to-find volume. Likewise, citations of sources are to the most recent edition; guidance on other editions and translations (if available) can generally be found there. Readers wishing to delve more fully into the sources of the period are pointed in the first instance towards Dorothy Whitelock's invaluable *English Historical Documents*. When sources are first mentioned, their date of composition is given (if known). For these purposes I follow standard scholarly convention in using '×' to designate an unknown point during a span and '–' to designate the span itself: 997 × 1002 thus means 'written/completed at some point between 997 and 1002', whereas 997–1002 would mean 'written continuously between 997 and 1002'.

ACKNOWLEDGEMENTS

This book has been a long time in the planning, but a short time in the writing. That this should be so is thanks in no small measure to the help and support of many friends and colleagues. On the Exeter end of things, the Department of History and broader community of medievalists have made the last three years of writing and research immensely enjoyable. A timely spell of research leave in the first half of 2015 facilitated the drafting of the main text. I am particularly grateful to Sarah Hamilton, who made time out of her busy schedule to discuss aspects of tenth- and eleventh-century European history, and Helen Birkett, whose office has been a welcome sanctuary during the storm of term. Thanks also go to the first group of students on my Æthelred Special Subject; their interest and enthusiasm for all things Æthelredian helped sustain me through the final stages of revision. Friends and colleagues elsewhere in the UK and beyond have likewise been a source of sage counsel and constructive criticism. I am especially beholden to Charlie Insley, Emily Ward, Andrew Rabin, Alban Gautier, Eric Denton, Courtney Konshuh and Hendrik Mäkeler, who have shared thoughts, work-in-progress and copies of hard-to-find publications. An even greater debt is owed to those kind souls who read through the book (or sections thereof) in draft form: Megan Welton, who went through Chapter 1 with an eye to the treatment of queens; Alison Hudson, who read Chapters 1–4, offering guidance on all matters monastic; and Rory Naismith, who read the entire manuscript, making many helpful suggestions, particularly regarding the treatment of coinage. Similar thanks are owed to the Press's two anonymous readers, whose comments and criticisms greatly improved the text. On a more personal note, it would not have been possible to write this book without the support and encouragement of many good friends both within and beyond the academy; in the place of many, I should like to thank Matthias Ammon, Ronni Phillips, Erik Niblaeus, Danica Summerlin and Johanna Dale.

The staff at the London office of Yale University Press have been a model of professionalism and efficiency throughout. I am particularly grateful to Heather McCallum, who was willing to entrust such a major project to a young and relatively untested scholar, and to Rachael Lonsdale and Melissa Bond (and their team), who saw the text through production. I have also been fortunate to receive a great deal of help from within the family. As ever, my parents and their spouses have been a source of much-needed support, encouragement and distraction along the way. Likewise, my in-laws have repeatedly opened their doors to me on holidays and research trips to London; it is no exaggeration to say that Hampton has come to feel like a second home. My wife, Cathy, has inevitably borne the greatest burden of all: throughout our married life she has had to share my time with Æthelred (the 'third person' in our relationship, as it must have felt); that she has done so with such equanimity is a credit to her love, patience and care. Last, but certainly not least, I owe an immeasurable debt – both personal and intellectual – to Simon Keynes. It was his teaching which first inspired me to become a medieval historian (and steered me towards the subject of Æthelred) and his scholarly example continues to guide my work. I dedicate this book to him.

Levi Roach
University of Exeter
St George's Day, 2016

ABBREVIATIONS AND SHORT TITLES

General abbreviations

Ælfric, *CH: FS*	Ælfric of Eynsham, *Catholic Homilies: The First Series*, ed. P. Clemoes, EETS s.s. 17 (Oxford, 1997)
Ælfric, *CH: SS*	Ælfric of Eynsham, *Catholic Homilies: The Second Series*, ed. M. Godden, EETS s.s. 5 (Oxford, 1979)
Ælfric, *LS*	Ælfric of Eynsham, *Lives of Saints*, ed. W.W. Skeat, 4 pts, EETS o.s. 76, 82, 94, 114 (Oxford, 1881–1900; repr. as 2 vols., Oxford, 1966)
Ælfric, *Supplementary Homilies*	*Homilies of Ælfric: A Supplementary Collection*, ed. J.C. Pope, 2 pts, EETS o.s. 259–60 (London, 1967–8)
ANS	*Anglo-Norman Studies*
ASC	*Anglo-Saxon Chronicle*
ASE	*Anglo-Saxon England*
BL	London, British Library
BNJ	*British Numismatic Journal*
CCCM	Corpus Christianorum Continuatio Mediaevalis
CCSL	Corpus Christianorum Series Latina

DA	*Deutsches Archiv für Erforschung des Mittelalters*
EEMF	Early English Manuscripts in Facsimile
EETS	Early English Text Society
Whitelock, *EHD*	*English Historical Documents c. 500–1042*, ed. D. Whitelock, 2nd edn (London, 1979)
EHR	*English Historical Review*
EME	*Early Medieval Europe*
FMSt	*Frühmittelalterliche Studien*
HBS	Henry Bradshaw Society
HSJ	*Haskins Society Journal*
HZ	*Historische Zeitschrift*
JEGP	*Journal of English and Germanic Philology*
MGH:	Monumenta Germaniae Historica:
Cap. n.s.	Capitularia regum Francorum: nova series
Conc.	Concilia
Epp.	Epistolae
SS	Scriptores
SS rer. Germ.	Scriptores rerum Germanicarum in usum scholarum
SS rer. Germ. n.s.	Scriptores rerum Germanicarum: nova series
NC	*Numismatic Chronicle*
ODNB	*Oxford Dictionary of National Biography*, ed. H.C.G. Matthew and B. Harrison, 60 vols. (Oxford, 2004)
PL	*Patrologia Cursus Completus. Series (Latina) Prima*, ed. J.-P. Migne, 221 vols. (Paris, 1844–64)
P & P	*Past and Present*
SCH	*Studies in Church History*
Scriftboc	*Scriftboc*, ed. A. Frantzen, 'The Anglo-Saxon Penitentials: A Cultural Database' (http://www.anglo-saxon.net/penance/, accessed 13 January 2016)
TRHS	*Transactions of the Royal Historical Society*

Abbreviations for Anglo-Saxon charters

Anglo-Saxon charters are cited by their 'S number' from P.H. Sawyer, *Anglo-Saxon Charters: An Annotated List and Bibliography*, rev. S.E. Kelly and R. Rushforth (http://www.esawyer.org.uk/) with an edition given in parentheses. For these purposes the following abbreviations are used:

BCS	W. de G. Birch, ed., *Cartularium Saxonicum: A Collection of Charters Relating to Anglo-Saxon History*, 3 vols. (London, 1885–93)
KCD	J.M. Kemble, ed., *Codex Diplomaticus Aevi Saxonici*, 6 vols. (London, 1839–48)
Abing	S.E. Kelly, ed., *Charters of Abingdon Abbey*, 2 pts, Anglo-Saxon Charters 7–8 (Oxford, 2000–1)
Bath	S.E. Kelly, ed., *Charters of Bath and Wells*, Anglo-Saxon Charters 13 (Oxford, 2007)
Burt	P.H. Sawyer, ed., *Charters of Burton Abbey*, Anglo-Saxon Charters 2 (Oxford, 1979)
CantCC	N. Brooks and S.E. Kelly, ed., *Charters of Christ Church, Canterbury*, 2 pts, Anglo-Saxon Charters 17–18 (Oxford, 2013)
CantStA	S.E. Kelly, ed., *Charters of St Augustine's Abbey, Canterbury, and Minster-in-Thanet*, Anglo-Saxon Charters 4 (Oxford, 1995)
Glast	S.E. Kelly, ed., *Charters of Glastonbury Abbey*, Anglo-Saxon Charters 15 (Oxford, 2012)
LondStP	S.E. Kelly, ed., *Charters of St Paul's, London*, Anglo-Saxon Charters 10 (Oxford, 2004)
Malm	S.E. Kelly, ed., *Charters of Malmesbury Abbey*, Anglo-Saxon Charters 11 (Oxford, 2005)
Pet	S.E. Kelly, ed., *Charters of Peterborough Abbey*, Anglo-Saxon Charters 14 (Oxford, 2009)

Roch	A. Campbell, ed., *Charters of Rochester*, Anglo-Saxon Charters 1 (London, 1973)
Sel	S.E. Kelly, ed., *Charters of Selsey*, Anglo-Saxon Charters 6 (Oxford, 1996)
Shaft	S.E. Kelly, ed., *Charters of Shaftesbury Abbey*, Anglo-Saxon Charters 5 (Oxford, 1995)
Sherb	M.A. O'Donovan, ed., *Charters of Sherborne*, Anglo-Saxon Charters 3 (Oxford, 1988)
StAlb	J. Crick, ed., *Charters of St Albans*, Anglo-Saxon Charters 12 (Oxford, 2007)
Wells	S.E. Kelly, ed., *Charters of Bath and Wells*, Anglo-Saxon Charters 13 (Oxford, 2007)
WinchNM	S. Miller, ed., *Charters of the New Minster, Winchester*, Anglo-Saxon Charters 9 (Oxford, 2001)

Map 1 England in the reign of Æthelred II.

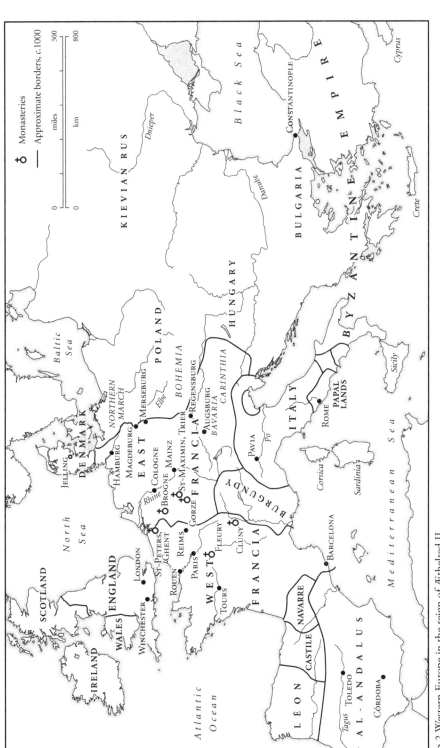

Map 2 Western Europe in the reign of Æthelred II.

Figure 1 The West Saxon Royal Family, 871–1016 (simplified).

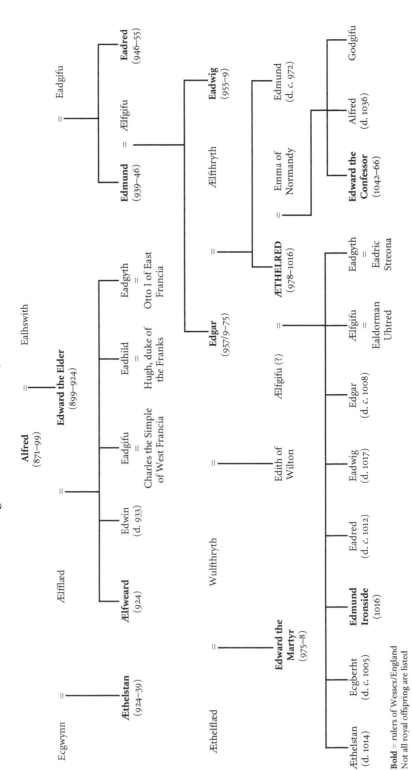

Bold = rulers of Wessex/England
Not all royal offspring are listed

AN UNREADY AND ILL-COUNSELLED KING?

It is fair to say that Æthelred II of England (978–1016), better known to posterity as 'the Unready', has received something of a bad press. The only Anglo-Saxon monarch to bear a mocking moniker, he is one of England's archetypal 'bad kings', frequently mentioned in the same breath as John 'Lackland' (1199–1216), whose ill rule famously led to Magna Carta, and Richard III (1483–5), who is generally held responsible for the death of the 'Princes in the Tower', the rightful heirs to the throne. At a glance, Æthelred would seem to be in the right company here: he came to the throne under a cloud following the assassination of his half-brother, Edward the Martyr (d. 978), and his reign witnessed a rising tide of viking attacks, culminating in two successive conquests of England by Swein Forkbeard (1013–14) and his son Cnut (1015–16). The latter went on to establish an Anglo-Danish regime that would rule for a quarter century, and it was only the chance death of Cnut's sons without heirs which enabled the native English dynasty to reassert itself in 1042 (temporarily, as it would prove). Æthelred's failure could thus scarcely be clearer, and it is all too easy to see the events of 1013–14 and 1015–16 as a prelude to that more famous conquest of England half a century later. To compound matters, there are signs that Æthelred's actions did not meet with general approval in his own lifetime: he spent much of his later years restoring lands and rights taken from the church in his youth, and in 1014 he was

1

forced to promise that he would rule his people 'better than he had before'. It is, therefore, unsurprising that posterity has been unkind to Æthelred; his failings would seem to have been many and grievous.

W.C. Sellar and R.J. Yeatman, in their humorous take on English history, gave Æthelred the dubious honour of being the 'first Weak King of England' who caused a 'wave of Danes', and in so doing stood in a venerable tradition.[1] Edward Augustus Freeman, the great nineteenth-century Oxford don, had asserted that Æthelred was 'the only ruler of the male line of Ecgberht whom we can unhesitatingly set down as a bad man and a bad King'.[2] Though willing to concede him 'a certain amount of energy', Freeman insisted that 'it was an energy utterly unregulated and misapplied', and in the final measure Æthelred's reign saw 'little but the neglect of kingly duty, little but weakness, impolicy, cowardice, blind trust in unworthy friends and even detected traitors'.[3] Of course, Freeman wrote during the heyday of the so-called 'Whig Interpretation of History', which Sellar and Yeatman were to mock so mercilessly; like many historians of the era, he was swift to make sweeping moral judgements of a kind later scholars would eschew. Nevertheless, despite the eclipse of this approach to historical writing in the twentieth century, opinions about Æthelred remained largely unchanged. Thus, while Sir Frank Stenton, writing in the early 1940s, was prepared to acknowledge that there were signs in Æthelred's reign 'of a trouble which lies deeper than a mere incapacity for government' (note the 'mere'!), he still branded him 'a weak king', characterizing this period as one of 'national degeneracy'.[4] Stenton was not alone; his younger contemporary, Dorothy Whitelock, similarly wrote of 'general disorder' and 'bad government' in connection with Æthelred, and as late as 1982 Eric John could assert that Æthelred's reign was a period 'of almost unremitting disaster' (though John was quick to add that 'there is more than incapacity to Aethelred').[5]

---

[1] W.C. Sellar and R.J. Yeatman, *1066 and All That* (London, 1931), 12.

[2] E.A. Freeman, *The History of the Norman Conquest of England*, I, *The Preliminary History to the Election of Eadward the Confessor*, 3rd edn (Oxford, 1877), 260–1.

[3] *Ibid.*, 261–2.

[4] F.M. Stenton, *Anglo-Saxon England*, 3rd edn (Oxford, 1971), 374 and 394. These remarks are to be found in the first edition of 1943.

[5] Whitelock, *EHD*, 47; E. John, 'The Return of the Vikings', in *The Anglo-Saxons*, ed. J. Campbell (London, 1982), 192–213, at 193.

It was only as the millennium of Æthelred's accession approached that opinions began to change. Already in 1967 David Kirby had expressed the opinion that 'there must have been more to the Danish conquest of England than the incompetence of one ruler', and this line of thought was taken up by Pauline Stafford in her University of Oxford DPhil thesis of 1973, in which she presented the first dedicated reassessment of Æthelred's reign.[6] Such opinions started to reach a wider audience with the publication of the papers given at the millenary conference in honour of Æthelred's accession (1978), which included an important piece by Stafford, elaborating upon the findings of her doctoral dissertation, and seminal articles by two other young scholars, Patrick Wormald and Simon Keynes.[7] The publication of a revised version of Keynes's own doctoral dissertation, *The Diplomas of King Æthelred 'the Unready'*, two years later marked another important milestone in Æthelred scholarship: far more wide-ranging than the title suggests, this offered the first systematic treatment of the period in print.[8] Both Stafford and Keynes argued that Æthelred was a much misunderstood figure: though ultimately unsuccessful, he was far from incompetent and his reign witnessed many important political and administrative developments. Although this revisionist angle did not immediately convince all, it has slowly won the field: the most recent biographies of the king take their lead from such work and these arguments have found their way into textbook form in Nicholas Higham and Martin Ryan's *Anglo-Saxon World*.[9] There are even signs of change within popular culture. Thus, while in 1977 Christopher Logue could include the mischievous refrain 'Ethelred! Ethelred! / spent his royal life in bed: / one shoe off, and one shoe on, / greatly loved by everyone', in his poem on the king, Patricia

---

[6] D.P. Kirby, *The Making of Early England* (London, 1967), 116; P. Stafford, 'Royal Government in the Reign of Æthelred II, A.D. 979–1016' (DPhil diss., Univ. of Oxford, 1973).

[7] *Ethelred the Unready: Papers from the Millenary Conference*, ed. D.H. Hill (London, 1978).

[8] S. Keynes, *The Diplomas of King Æthelred 'the Unready', 978–1016: A Study in their Use as Historical Evidence* (Cambridge, 1980).

[9] R. Lavelle, *Aethelred II: King of the English*, 2nd edn (Stroud, 2008); A. Williams, *Æthelred the Unready: The Ill-Counselled King* (London, 2003); N.J. Higham and M. Ryan, *The Anglo-Saxon World* (New Haven, CT, 2013), 335–86. Cf. I. Howard, *The Reign of Æthelred II: The King of the English, Emperor of All the Peoples of Britain, 978–1016* (Oxford, 2010).

Bracewell's ongoing trilogy on the life of Æthelred's second wife, Emma, presents a more nuanced view, taking her cue from the work of Stafford.[10]

The present study is written in the same spirit, as part of the ongoing reassessment of this most maligned of Anglo-Saxon monarchs. At the same time, it attempts to go beyond simple revisionism. Whether Æthelred was a 'Bad King' (or, indeed, a 'Bad Thing') will always be a matter of personal judgement, one which detracts from the more interesting and important question of why it is that he behaved the way he did. Indeed, though there has been no shortage of studies of Æthelred's reign, surprisingly little has been written about the king himself. The two most recent scholarly biographies, by Ryan Lavelle and Ann Williams, are a case in point: these are not so much studies of Æthelred, as studies of his reign, political narratives of a high quality, but ones in which the monarch himself rarely emerges from the shadows. Yet Æthelred was at the heart of developments during these years and there are, as we shall see, a number of points at which we can get a sense of his thoughts and feelings. The aim is, therefore, to understand Æthelred rather than to judge him, to put flesh and bones on the scanty sources for these years and present a more nuanced and rounded picture of developments than can be found in traditional caricatures.

Of course, there are major source-critical problems which confront this endeavour. As Keynes already demonstrated in his contribution to the 1978 millenary conference, our main narrative for Æthelred's reign, preserved in the C, D and E versions of the composite work known as the *Anglo-Saxon Chronicle*, was written after Æthelred's death with the benefit of hindsight: it telescopes events, presenting the Danish conquest of 1016 as the inevitable result of English cowardice and incompetence. Though divided into separate entries for each year, the author went about his work systematically: there are numerous cross-references and the effect is cumulative – he presents a woeful tale of decline and decomposition. The result makes riveting reading, but can only be used with caution to reconstruct the events of the period: though the chronicler had access to earlier sources,

---

[10] C. Logue, 'An Archaic Jingle', *Times* (17 Nov. 1977), 14; P. Bracewell, *Shadow on the Crown* (New York, 2013), and *The Price of Blood* (New York, 2015). See also J. Woods, *Eadric the Grasper* (Scotts Valley, CA, 2009), for another broadly revisionist (albeit rather more idiosyncratic) take on these years.

foreknowledge of the eventual English defeat haunts his writing at every turn.[11] His main villain, however, is not Æthelred himself: though veiled criticism of the king can be detected at a few points, the real scapegoats are Æthelred's generals and advisers, above all Ælfric of Hampshire and Eadric Streona, who fail their king and nation repeatedly in their hour of need. Like any good tale, this soon grew in the telling. When, following the Norman Conquest, a new generation of reform-minded churchmen came to write the history of the Anglo-Saxon period, they made extensive use of the *Chronicle*-account of these years. From this, it was easy to construct a narrative in which Æthelred's own incompetence began to take centre stage. In an age in which divine providence was thought to guide historical developments (what historians often call 'salvation history' or *Heilsgeschichte*), Æthelred's sticky end was felt to speak for itself: he *must* have done something to deserve this. The circumstances of Æthelred's accession played into this: his predecessor, Edward the Martyr (975–8), had been murdered by Æthelred's supporters and, though contemporary reports do not implicate the king or his family directly, later accounts were quick to make the connection, placing the blame above all on Æthelred's mother Ælfthryth, who became the archetypal evil stepmother, a scheming Jezebel who orchestrated the accession of her son over the dead body of his elder half-brother.[12] As Æthelred's and Ælfthryth's star fell, that of Dunstan was on the rise. Dunstan had been archbishop of Canterbury during Æthelred's early years and soon after his death in 988 came to be venerated as a saint. The earliest account of his life, written by the elusive figure

---

[11] S. Keynes, 'The Declining Reputation of Æthelred the Unready' (1978), rev. and repr. in *Anglo-Saxon History: Basic Readings*, ed. D. Pelteret (New York, 2000), 157–90, at 158–68. See also C. Clark, 'The Narrative Mode of *The Anglo-Saxon Chronicle* before the Conquest' (1971), repr. in and cited from her *Words, Names, and History: Selected Writings of Cecily Clark* (Cambridge, 1995), 3–19, at 10–15; A. Sheppard, *Families of the King: Writing Identity in the Anglo-Saxon Chronicle* (Toronto, 2004), 71–120; N. Brooks, 'Why is the *Anglo-Saxon Chronicle* about Kings?', *ASE* 39 (2010), 43–70, at 51–2; and C. Konshuh, '*Anraed* in their *Unraed*: The Æthelredian Annals (983–1016) and their Presentation of King and Advisors', *English Studies* 97 (2016), 140–62.

[12] P. Stafford, 'Queens, Nunneries and Reforming Churchmen: Gender, Religious Status and Reform in Tenth- and Eleventh-Century England' (1999), repr. in and cited from her *Gender, Family and the Legitimation of Power: England from the Ninth to the Early Twelfth Century* (Aldershot, 2006), no. XI, 24–30; K.A. Fenton, *Gender, Nation and Conquest in the Works of William of Malmesbury* (Woodbridge, 2008), 106–14.

known by the initial 'B.' (995 × 1004, probably 997 × 1002), already ascribed Dunstan the ability to predict the future, and by the time Adelard of Ghent came to rework this into twelve shorter readings (1006 × 1011) the archbishop was credited with having prophesied the viking invasions which England was suffering at the time. This seed would also grow following the Conquest, when it combined with the bad impression made by the *Chronicle*-account of the period: Dunstan became the sage prelate, whose good counsel the incorrigible young Æthelred scorned to the detriment of himself and his nation.[13] Thus, while posterity was kind to Dunstan, it was hard on Æthelred in equal measure, and it is no accident that the first systematically negative portrayal of the king was written by William of Malmesbury, who had an active interest in Dunstan's cult and would later write a *Life* of the archbishop. William's Æthelred is almost comic: a baby who soiled the font at his baptism, who developed a life-long fear of candles from repeated beatings by his mother with candle-sticks, and whose ultimate failure had already been prophesied by Dunstan at the moment of his coronation.[14] This account was to set the tone for later writers – and, indeed, many modern scholars. Inviting though such narratives frequently are, their authors rarely had access to more information than did William, and in most cases they had less to hand. Even William largely adds colour to the *Chronicle*-account, supplementing this with oral tales circulating in his day.[15] It was as a result of his growing notoriety that Æthelred seems to have acquired his immortal epithet: *unræd*. This is first attested by Walter Map, writing in the 1180s, who renders it into Latin as *[nullum] consilium* ('lacking in counsel'), and the earliest reference to it in something approximating its vernacular form comes in the early thirteenth-century 'Laws of the English' (*Leges*

---

[13] C. Cubitt, 'Archbishop Dunstan: A Prophet in Politics', in *Myth, Rulership, Church and Charters: Essays in Honour of Nicholas Brooks*, ed. J. Barrow and A. Wareham (Aldershot, 2008), 145–66.

[14] William of Malmesbury, *Gesta regum Anglorum* II.161–180, ed. R.A.B. Mynors with R.M. Thomson and M. Winterbottom (Oxford, 1998), 268–320; with Keynes, 'Declining Reputation', 168–73.

[15] E.A. Winkler, 'England's Defending Kings in Twelfth-Century Historical Writing', *HSJ* 25 (2013), 147–163, esp. 150–6. See also A. Williams, 'The Dangers of Invention: The Sack of Canterbury, 1011, and the Theft of Dunstan's Relics', in *Cathedrals, Communities and Conflict in the Anglo-Norman World*, ed. P. Dalton, C. Insley and L.J. Wilkinson (Woodbridge, 2011), 27–40, esp. 38–40.

Anglorum).[16] The sobriquet is, of course, a clever pun on the king's name, which means 'noble counsel' and by extension 'good counsel'. Æthelred thus becomes 'good counsel, ill counsel'; or more colloquially perhaps something like 'noble counsel – my hat!' Though the designation probably predates its first attestation, there is no particular reason to believe that it was contemporary – writers remained conversant with Old English long after 1066 and the twelfth century, when Æthelred's reputation entered terminal decline, provides the natural context for the coinage.[17] Indeed, it is interesting to note that the epithet is an addition in the 'Laws of the English' and is not found in this work's source, the twelfth-century 'Laws of Edward' (*Leges Edwardi*) (*c.* 1130); it would seem that it had been popularized in the intervening years.[18] As the term *unræd* fell out of use in the fifteenth and sixteenth centuries, it came to be misinterpreted as alluding to the ill-preparedness for which Æthelred was also accused by William of Malmesbury – out of the ill-advised king was made the unready one.[19]

Such accounts must be put to one side if we are to understand Æthelred's reign on its own terms. As a near-contemporary narrative the *Chronicle* retains much value, but even it must be used with caution. More immediate interest accrues to the strictly contemporary evidence, above all the charters, decrees and coinage issued in Æthelred's name. These do not tell a coherent story, but that is part of their appeal: unlike later narratives, they were not produced with an eye to Æthelred's sticky end. Nevertheless, because they do not present us with a coherent account, we must piece one together on the basis of the scattered insights they furnish. This is no easy task, since the surviving documentary and material record represents but a fraction of what once existed – it is rather like trying to complete a jigsaw

---

[16] Walter Map, *De nugis curialum*, Dist. 5, ch. 3, ed. M.R. James, rev. C.N.L. Brooke and R.A.B. Mynors (Oxford, 1983), 412; *Die Gesetze der Angelsachsen*, ed. F. Liebermann, 3 vols. (Halle, 1903–16), I, 62, n. **; with Keynes, 'Declining Reputation', 173–4. For a possible earlier case, see Herman, *De miraculis S. Edmundi*, ch. 4, ed. T. Licence, *Herman the Archdeacon and Goscelin of Saint-Bertin: Miracles of St Edmund* (Oxford, 2014), 14 (with the editor's observations at n. 73).

[17] On post-Conquest knowledge of English, see E. Treharne, *Living Through Conquest: The Politics of Early English, 1020–1220* (Oxford, 2012), 91–187.

[18] *Leges Eadwardi Confessoris*, ch. 34.2, ed. B. O'Brien, *God's Peace and King's Peace: The Laws of Edward the Confessor* (Philadelphia, PA, 1999), 192.

[19] Keynes, 'Declining Reputation', 174–5.

puzzle with only a tiny proportion of the original pieces. Still, as work over the last four decades has shown, progress is possible. The greatest difficulty lies in establishing how and when we can infer information regarding the king and his regime from such superficially dry records, which by their nature shed light only on particular moments in Æthelred's life and reign. Keynes's doctoral work made him keenly aware of the limitations of these sources and in the preface to his book he commented that

> having passed five years with Æthelred the Unready never far from mind, I naturally wondered from time to time whether he deserved the censure he received from posterity for manifold weaknesses of character; but far from experiencing a deepening awareness of his personal qualities as work progressed, I experienced only a deepening frustration that one has hardly the faintest idea of what he was really like.[20]

Keynes's caution is understandable. Æthelred never speaks directly in the surviving sources and certainty regarding his character – like that of any medieval ruler – is rarely possible. Nevertheless, this book is written in the belief that we can reconstruct aspects of Æthelred's personality. The key is to provide close and contextualized readings of contemporary sources, which offer windows into the thoughts and concerns of the king and his closest advisers.[21]

Perhaps the most important sources in this respect are royal charters (or diplomas, as they are also known). These are documents issued by the king, granting or confirming legal rights (generally over land).[22] They survive in good numbers and therefore offer a relatively stable source base. In total, some eighty-four diplomas are preserved in Æthelred's name which have

---

[20] Keynes, *Diplomas*, xviii.

[21] See, e.g., P. Stafford, 'Political Ideas in Late Tenth-Century England: Charters as Evidence' (2001), repr. in and cited from her *Gender, Family and the Legitimation of Power: England from the Ninth to the Early Twelfth Century* (Aldershot, 2006), no. VII; and C. Cubitt, 'The Politics of Remorse: Penance and Royal Piety in the Reign of Æthelred the Unready', *Historical Research* 85 (2012), 179–92.

[22] Technically a charter is any document relating to the holding or transfer of legal rights, while a diploma is a charter issued in the name of public authority (a 'royal/sovereign charter').

good claims to authenticity, while another ten may be partly or substantially authentic. The distribution is fairly even, with an average of two to three documents a year, though there are a few spikes and troughs, with some years seeing the production of up to six diplomas (983, 1002) and others not represented at all (991–2, 1006 and 1010).[23] In part, this is a product of patchy rates of survival. As a general rule, charters only survive if they made their way into the archive of a religious house, and even then preservation can be decidedly hit and miss: some archives suffered significant losses in the Middle Ages (St Paul's, for example, was struck by fire in 1087), while others were badly hit by the dissolution of the monasteries (Glastonbury, for example). As a result, the surviving records are significantly skewed in favour of major religious centres, particularly those with stable institutional histories. Still, enough survive for this to be a relatively representative sample and when we do see major gaps, as in 991–2, 1006 and 1010, there may be other grounds for these.

Broadly speaking, charters survive in two forms: originals and copies. 'Originals' are those preserved as first produced in Æthelred's reign: written in contemporary script and showing signs of their later preservation (such as folding, archival marks and annotations), they are historical records of the highest standing. Only ten of these survive for Æthelred's reign. The rest of the documents are later copies. These take many forms, the most common being the cartulary copy. Cartularies are collections of charters, presented as a single text (or series of texts), generally comprising the documents of an individual religious house. Most of these were produced in the twelfth and thirteenth centuries, when church archives across western Europe underwent a degree of reorganization and rationalization.[24] Whatever the form, copies stand at a remove from the original and thus pose particular source-critical problems: scribes sometimes made errors when transcribing texts; moreover, it was tempting to 'improve' documents in the process of copying, adjusting their texts to conform to the present needs and interests of the religious house in question. As a

[23] Keynes, *Diplomas*, 47. For an invaluable overview of the corpus, see *ibid.*, 237–68.
[24] P.J. Geary, *Phantoms of Remembrance: Memory and Oblivion at the End of the First Millennium* (Princeton, NJ, 1994), 81–114; C.B. Bouchard, *Rewriting Saints and Ancestors: Memory and Forgetting in France, 500–1200* (Philadelphia, PA, 2015), 9–37.

general rule only originals are unimpeachable; any other document may have been tampered with in some way. Nevertheless, we should not be too critical. Many diplomas which survive in later copies have good claims to authenticity; moreover, by working from originals to copies, a fairly clear picture emerges as to what kinds of formulation were current. The value of originals goes considerably beyond offering a benchmark for judging other texts, however: their appearance itself often throws salient light on to the historical context in which they were issued, providing precious insights into court politics in these years.

Diplomas are written in Latin and generally conform to a standard format and layout. The core constituent parts comprise the preamble (or proem), presenting the pious motives of the donor; the dispositive section (or *dispositio*), recording the legal transaction and any conditions on this; the sanction, threatening divine wrath on any who infringe its terms; the boundary clause (or bounds), describing the estates involved (the one part of the document in Old English); the dating clause, specifying when (and occasionally also where) the document was produced; and finally the witness-list, encompassing those present at the time of the document's production. Occasionally, more complex diplomas also contain a narrative section (or *narratio*) presenting the background to the transaction; this normally follows the preamble and prefaces the dispositive section. The issuing of diplomas was reserved for large-scale assemblies of the realm, which took place some three to five times a year. The precise mechanisms behind their production have been the subject of much debate. Some believe that they were drawn up at court by a royal writing office, while others think that they were produced locally by interested priests and religious houses.[25] There is some

---

[25] Centralized production: Keynes, *Diplomas*, 14–153, and 'Regenbald the Chancellor (*sic*)', *ANS* 10 (1988), 185–222. Localized production: P. Chaplais, 'The Origin and Authenticity of the Royal Anglo-Saxon Diploma' (1965), repr. in and cited from *Prisca Munimenta: Studies in Archival and Administrative History Presented to Dr. A.E.J. Hollander*, ed. F. Ranger (London, 1973), 28–42, and 'The Royal Anglo-Saxon "Chancery" of the Tenth Century Revisited', in *Studies in Medieval History Presented to R.H.C. Davis*, ed. H. Mayr-Harting and R.I. Moore (London, 1985), 41–51. See also C. Insley, 'Charters and Episcopal Scriptoria in the Anglo-Saxon South-West', *EME* 7 (1998), 173–97; *Charters of Abingdon Abbey*, ed. S.E. Kelly, 2 pts, Anglo-Saxon Charters 7–8 (Oxford, 2000–1), lxxi–cxxxi; and B. Snook, *The Anglo-Saxon Chancery: The History, Language and Production of Anglo-Saxon Charters from Alfred to Edgar* (Woodbridge, 2015).

middle ground, insofar as those who argue for centralized production acknowledge that religious houses might occasionally be charged with drawing up such documents (often in their own favour), while those who see localized production as the norm admit that there must have been some 'central' influence on aspects of form and formulation. The balance of probability seems to favour a degree of centralization, at least insofar as diplomas were issued in the king's presence at royal assemblies; nevertheless, the key thing is that whoever was involved – and variety is likely to have been the order of the day here – they were in close contact with king and court: if not always 'royal scribes' in the strict sense, they were figures who enjoyed the ruler's trust.[26] In fact, the very dichotomy between 'centralized' and 'localized' production is perhaps unhelpful: arrangements must have been flexible, and one imagines that both the king and the recipients had some say in the resulting texts. Diplomas were thus one of the means by which rulers communicated with their subjects, taking us to the heart of contemporary politics. Indeed, recent studies emphasize the symbolic and performative nature of these documents: they are not just records of legal transactions, but active participants in power politics; they served to enact and announce new programmes.[27]

After charters, the next most important sources are the decrees issued in Æthelred's name. Often somewhat anachronistically called 'law-codes', these texts comprise a diverse group of exhortations and injunctions to be observed throughout the realm (or large portions thereof). Written in Old English and presented as lists of instructions (generally with an opening preface), they too stem from major assemblies of the realm. Yet their audience went considerably further, as they were intended for public declamation at more local assemblies throughout the kingdom. At least six law-making gatherings are known from these years, which led to some

[26] S. Keynes, 'Church Councils, Royal Assemblies, and Anglo-Saxon Royal Diplomas', in *Kingship, Legislation and Power in Anglo-Saxon England*, ed. G.R. Owen-Crocker and B.W. Schneider (Woodbridge, 2013), 17–182, esp. 102–26; L. Roach, *Kingship and Consent in Anglo-Saxon England, 871–978: Assemblies and the State in the Early Middle Ages* (Cambridge, 2013), 78–89.

[27] G. Koziol, *The Politics of Memory and Identity in Carolingian Royal Diplomas: The West Frankish Kingdom (840–987)* (Turnhout, 2012). See also L. Roach, 'Public Rites and Public Wrongs: Ritual Aspects of Diplomas in Tenth- and Eleventh-Century England', *EME* 19 (2011), 182–203.

seven or eight distinct texts. Some of these assemblies are not represented by any written ordinances, however, while others spawned as many as three sets. Later losses may account for some of this variation, but cannot do so entirely, and the impression is that the recording of such details was decidedly *ad hoc*: sometimes discussions led to written decrees, while in other cases matters were simply dealt with orally. In any case, none of these texts survives in anything like its 'original' format: they are all copies, often of a much later date. Not only were they sometimes adjusted in transmission (some only survive in post-Conquest Latin translations), but in the absence of originals we can only speculate as to how such texts circulated in Æthelred's reign. Here opinion divides between those who see them as fundamentally pragmatic, reaching a relatively wide audience (often in written form), and those who see them as largely ideological works, whose precise textual form stands in at best a loose relationship with the original proclamation by the king.[28] Particular problems attach to the decrees of Æthelred's later years, all of which were drafted by one individual: Archbishop Wulfstan II of York (1002–23). Since these are written in the archbishop's distinctive style and often preserved in manuscripts associated with him, it is hard to know how far they represent the king's own desires. Behind these stand broader questions about how far we can use such 'normative' texts to reconstruct social realities; because they describe society as it ought to be, royal ordinances are often unreliable guides to how it actually was. Still, one should not exaggerate the resulting difficulties. It has been cogently argued that the decrees of this period were indeed widely read and applied; moreover, if these texts cannot be taken as direct windows into social realities, they still tell us much about the ambitions of

---

[28] Pragmatic texts: S. Keynes, 'Royal Government and the Written Word in Late Anglo-Saxon England', in *The Uses of Literacy in Early Medieval Europe*, ed. R. McKitterick (Cambridge, 1990), 226–57, at 231–44; D. Pratt, 'Written Law and the Communication of Authority in Tenth-Century England', in *England and the Continent in the Tenth Century: Studies in Honour of Wilhelm Levison (1876–1947)*, ed. D. Rollason, C. Leyser and H. Williams (Turnhout, 2010), 331–50. Ideological exercises: P. Wormald, '*Lex scripta* and *verbum regis*: Legislation and Germanic Kingship from Euric to Cnut' (1977), repr. in and cited from his *Legal Culture in the Early Medieval West: Law as Text, Image and Experience* (London, 1999), 1–43, and *The Making of English Law: King Alfred to the Twelfth Century*, I, *Legislation and its Limits* (Oxford, 1998). See also J. Hudson, 'L'écrit, les archives et le droit en Angleterre (IXᵉ–XIIᵉ siècle)', *Revue historique* 308 (2006), 3–35.

law-makers and the means by which they sought to realize these.[29] Even the 'Wulfstan problem' may be more apparent than real, as we shall see: while the venerable prelate certainly exercised a significant influence over the style and content of Æthelred's later ordinances, this should be viewed in the context of his high standing at court. Or, put differently: the image of Wulfstan madly fabricating decrees in the king's name sits awkwardly with other evidence of the archbishop's active involvement in the regime.[30] Thus, like the draftsmen of Æthelred's diplomas, those charged with composing his decrees seem for the most part to have been intimates of the king, and the resulting texts thus provide further windows into debate and discussion at and around court.

On the face of it, Æthelred's coinage presents us with fewer problems. Produced by the many moneyers dotted throughout his realm, it would seem to represent the source *par excellence* for the ruler's ambitions. At some level, this is doubtless true: the coins of this period share a common design which was periodically changed, and we can be confident that Æthelred and his advisers had significant input here; they are thus statements of the regime. Nevertheless, because changes in type are common, it is not always clear how much we can read into them. For example, when in the late 980s or early 990s the Hand of God is replaced by the cross on the reverse (or 'tails') of Æthelred's coins, it is hard to know whether this is symbolic of a break with the past, or simply reflects the need to distinguish the new coins from the preceding ones.[31] Likewise, while it was once thought that Æthelred's regime oversaw recoinages on a strict six-year (or 'sexennial') cycle, with new types being introduced in 985, 991, 997, 1003 and 1009, recent work has raised significant doubts about this.[32] Shorn of such certainties, it becomes much harder to link individual types to political programmes. Still, provided due caution is exercised, coins remain a most valuable source, often enriching the picture furnished by charters and decrees. To these 'core' sources we may add the rich literary

---

[29] C. Cubitt, ' "As the Lawbook Teaches": Reeves, Lawbooks and Urban Life in the Anonymous Old English Legend of the Seven Sleepers', *EHR* 124 (2009), 1021–49.

[30] See below, Chapter 5, pp. 227–35.

[31] See below, Chapter 4, pp. 182–3.

[32] See below, Chapter 1, pp. 27–8, and Chapter 2, pp. 88–9.

production of the period, above all the works written for or by members of the court, such as Archbishop Wulfstan: these years saw much writing both in Latin and Old English, which often throws significant oblique light on the king and his regime. The resulting source base is not always rich enough to permit fine-grained insights into the workings of Æthelredian politics, and we should often like to know more; nevertheless, the broad contours which emerge are clear enough.

The importance of such sources lies above all in their proximity to the ruler: they all emanate from within or were produced by members of his court. The court itself is something of an elusive entity, however: unlike its early modern and modern counterpart, the medieval court was not a physical location with set boundaries, but rather consisted of those who were with the king at any given time as he traversed the realm. Because its makeup changed significantly over the course of the year and the ruler's reign, the court was something of a microcosm of the polity, a symbol of the broader body politic.[33] By tracing the composition and operation of the court we can therefore gain an impression of Æthelred's interests and concerns, as well as seeing who was calling the shots at any given moment. Indeed, while it might be objected that I at times use 'court' as a cipher for the king, inferring royal initiative where there need not have been any,[34] we must bear in mind that royal politics *were* court politics in the Middle Ages. Kings and their counsellors were in the proverbial thick of it and we should no more expect Æthelred to have made decisions in a vacuum than did any other ruler, nor should we mistake his reliance on counsel for a lack of personal initiative. Some have, of course, expressed doubts as to whether we can speak of royal 'policies' at all in the Middle Ages, since monarchs of the period were more reactive than proactive, often making it up as they went along rather than pursuing long-term plans.[35] But the evidence from Æthelred's reign suggests that the term is not entirely out of place, provided it is defined sufficiently broadly. While there is ample

---

[33] See below, Chapter 3, pp. 96–100.

[34] Cf. the remarks of T. Reuter, 'The Ottonians and the Carolingian Tradition', in his *Medieval Polities and Modern Mentalities*, ed. J.L. Nelson (Cambridge 2006), 268–83, at 268–9.

[35] See, e.g., K. Görich, 'Versuch zur Rettung von Kontingenz – Oder: Über Schwierigkeiten beim Schreiben einer Biographie Friedrich Barbarossas', *FMSt* 43 (2009), 179–97.

evidence of improvization, certain core aims can be detected behind many of the king's actions, and it is the contention of this book that if we listen carefully to the strictly contemporary sources – and above all the royal charters – we can often catch echoes of the debates and discussions going on around the king. From these it is clear that Æthelred was anything but a passive bystander. Further insights are offered by the king's personal relationships; how he interacted with his mother, (half-)siblings and sons, not to mention friends and associates, can also tell us much about Æthelred's interests and how these developed over time.[36] In the end, we cannot expect to reconstruct all aspects of Æthelred's personality and the gaps which remain are immense; nonetheless, the effort is worthwhile.

Comparison with other rulers of the early and central Middle Ages offers further means of approaching Æthelred. The focus here has tended to be on the king's English ancestors, above all his great-great-grandfather Alfred the Great (871–99). The attempt is therefore to cast the net wider, considering not only Æthelred's Anglo-Norman and Angevin successors in the British Isles, but also his immediate counterparts in what were to become France and Germany. That Æthelred shared a great deal with these figures should not be doubted: not only did he face similar structural challenges to many of them, but he was related to most by blood or marriage, numbering amongst his great-aunts queens of both France and Germany (i.e. West and East Francia).[37] The picture painted is thus one of a rather more 'European' Æthelred, a ruler who not only enjoyed close contacts with the continent, but also can be compared with other continental monarchs of the early and central Middle Ages.[38] Particular attention is given to those monarchs who faced similar structural challenges to Æthelred, such as Charles the Bald of West Francia (840–77) and Henry I

---

[36] See G. Tellenbach, 'Der Charakter Kaiser Heinrichs IV. Zugleich ein Versuch über die Erkennbarkeit menschlicher Individualität im hohen Mittelalter', in *Person und Gemeinschaft im Mittelalter. Festschrift für Karl Schmid zum fünfundsechzigsten Geburtstag*, ed. G. Althoff *et al.* (Sigmaringen, 1988), 345–68; and J.L. Nelson, 'Writing Early Medieval Biography', *History Workshop Journal* 50 (2000), 129–36.

[37] S. Foot, 'Dynastic Strategies: The West Saxon Royal Family in Europe', in *England and the Continent in the Tenth Century: Studies in Honour of Wilhelm Levison (1876–1947)*, ed. D. Rollason, C. Leyser and H. Williams (Turnhout, 2010), 237–53.

[38] See also J. Campbell, 'England, France, Flanders and Germany in the Reign of Ethelred II' (1978), repr. in and cited from his *Essays in Anglo-Saxon History* (London, 1986), 191–207.

of East Francia (919–36), who were confronted with foreign invasion, or Otto III of Germany (983–1001) and Louis IX of France (1214–70), who came to the throne as boys. Particular points of similarity emerge with the ninth-century Frankish emperor Louis the Pious (814–40) and the eleventh-century Salian ruler Henry IV of Germany (1056–1106). However, like all good foils, these serve not only to identify similarities, but also to reveal differences; they point to both the general and the specific.

We must also bear in mind the challenges posed by the biographical endeavour itself. Pierre Bourdieu has warned of what he calls the 'biographical illusion', that is, the illusion created by the biographer, who structures and gives meaning to his subject's life, presupposing the individual lifespan to be a natural and coherent entity.[39] In doing so, he raises fundamental issues: do we remain the same person across the entire span of our lives (is the child Æthelred in any meaningful sense the same individual as the adult?); and, if not, is a human lifespan itself a meaningful division of time? More to the point, he notes the common conceit of biographers, who place their subject at the centre of developments, shaping the narrative around this figure. Though Bourdieu has modern biographers in mind, similar charges can be laid at the door of their more historically minded counterparts, who also find themselves in cahoots with their subjects, trying to shape the past around these figures' activities. The medieval biographer faces particular challenges here: the perennial paucity of source material and the formulaic nature of much of what survives make it especially tempting to infer personal involvement where there need have been none.[40] Be that as it may, one hesitates to designate an individual lifespan an arbitrary period of study, at least when the individual in question is a king and the period in question is the Middle Ages. If modern historians are at times guilty of ascribing too great a coherence to their historical actors, they are certainly not alone in doing so: in the Middle

[39] P. Bourdieu, 'The Biographical Illusion', in *Identity: A Reader*, ed. P. du Gay, J. Evans and P. Redman (London, 2000), 297–303.

[40] S. Hamilton, 'Early Medieval Rulers and their Modern Biographers', *EME* 9 (2000), 247–60; M. Prestwich, 'Medieval Biography', *Journal of Interdisciplinary History* 40 (2010), 325–346.

Ages, as in the antique world before, the lives of powerful rulers were the points around which narratives were formed. In this respect, focusing on the individual need not involve overlooking context; as Jacques Le Goff notes, biography can itself be a means of examining broader themes of government, economy and society.[41] That the biographer's subject is, in the end, partly a product of his own contrivance should not be denied; the same is, of course, true of all historical writing.[42] The picture presented in what follows is therefore very much that of 'my' Æthelred; others can and will produce different pictures, ones no less valid for being based on different presumptions and conjectures. Nevertheless, it remains my conviction – old-fashioned though it may sound to some – that real progress can be made by close engagement with the evidence for the life of an individual such as Æthelred. Indeed, though the Æthelred presented in what follows is on one level emphatically 'mine', he is at the same time deeply embedded in the sources of the time and thus not entirely the product of my (or anyone else's) contrivance. Hence if, by some miracle of modern science, Æthelred were able to look down upon these pages, I should like to think that he would be able to recognize elements of himself therein – warts and all.

I have, in short, attempted to be sympathetic to the king without whitewashing him, producing an analysis in which error and defeat have a part to play, but one alongside chance, contingency and sheer bad luck. The account proceeds chronologically. The reasons for this are threefold. First, for Æthelred, unlike many rulers of the earlier Middle Ages, we are fortunate enough to have a sufficient density of source material to sustain such treatment.[43] Second, since Æthelred reigned for some thirty-eight years (longer, that is, than any of his immediate predecessors or successors), approaching his life thematically risks presenting too static a picture; breaks and changes of direction can be seen at many points, as we shall see,

[41] J. Le Goff, 'The Whys and Ways of Writing a Biography: The Case of Saint Louis', *Exemplaria* 1 (1989), 207–25. See also J. Le Goff, *Saint Louis*, trans. G.E. Gollrad (Notre Dame, IN, 2009), xx–xxxii.

[42] J. Fried, 'Wissenschaft und Phantasie. Das Beispiel der Geschichte', *HZ* 263 (1996), 291–316.

[43] Cf. S. Foot, *Æthelstan: The First King of England* (New Haven, CT, 2011), 7–8, explaining why this is not possible for Æthelred's great-uncle, Æthelstan.

and must be given their due. Finally, precisely because we can discern such changes and developments, a chronological approach promises the clearest insights into how the king's thoughts and feelings evolved over the various stages of his life and reign. Still, thematic treatment is not entirely eschewed and at times specific issues are handled separately, either in asides to the main text or in dedicated sub-chapters.

The first chapter deals with Æthelred's youth and the reign of his father, Edgar, describing the world into which the prince was born (*c.* 966×9–75). Particular attention is given to social and political developments in these years – the growth and institutionalization of royal authority; monastic reform – and the role of his mother Ælfthryth. The second takes the story from Edgar's death through the reign of Æthelred's elder half-brother, Edward the Martyr (975–8), to his own earliest years on the throne (978– 84), when a *de facto* regency ruled on his behalf. Here the focus is on the succession dispute between Edward and Æthelred and the death of Edward at the hands of the latter's sympathizers, events which were to cast a long shadow. The third chapter then details the first years of Æthelred's majority rule (984–93), when the king struck out against the politics of his erstwhile regents, despoiling churches and promoting new favourites. These actions clearly upset the balance and Chapter 4 examines their legacy (993–1002), tracing how in the face of escalating viking raids in the 990s Æthelred came to interpret these as divine punishment for his earlier misdeeds. The king's solution was to re-embrace the teachings of his father, mother and the reformers, restoring church rights and promoting the cult of his half-brother Edward. The fifth chapter reveals how the concerns visible in the 990s became desperation in the years following the turning of the millennium (1002–9). In the face of mounting attacks, the king and his advisers were now forced to attempt ever more drastic solutions to the 'viking problem': first, in 1002, they ordered the execution of 'all Danish men' within the realm (probably those mercenaries who had recently entered into royal employ); then, in 1005–6, the king undertook a dramatic purge of his court. Finally, the last years of Æthelred's life, the subject of Chapter 6 (1009–16), offer a tale of decomposition: during this time matters went from bad to worse, and if there is any period of Æthelred's reign for which traditional clichés hold, it is this one. Like the audience to a Shakespearean tragedy, we thus know where the story is going; however, we must bear in mind that Æthelred and his contemporaries did not. Every effort is taken to adopt their standpoint, appreciating how events unfolded without presupposing the king's eventual failure. The result is a picture of a ruler who, for all his failings, tried hard in the face of what were often overwhelming odds; a king who was neither unready nor ill-counselled, but certainly ill-fated.

CHAPTER I

BIRTH AND CHILDHOOD
The court of King Edgar, *c.* 966×9–75

We know remarkably little about the earliest years of Æthelred's life. He was the son of King Edgar 'the Peacemaker' (957/9–78) with his third wife, Ælfthryth. We know neither the date nor the precise circumstances of his birth: he cannot have been born before 966, since he is not included in the witness-list of the New Minster refoundation charter (which otherwise covers all immediate members of the royal family as of that year), but must have been alive by 969, when he is listed amongst the royal offspring in a genealogical tract.[1] That we do not know more is partly a product of the slim source base for these years: the only continuous narrative, that furnished by the various versions of the *Anglo-Saxon Chronicle*, is extremely laconic, and the information supplied by other sources does little to fill the gaps, at least where the young prince is concerned. But even if we were to have richer sources, we would not necessarily expect to hear much more about Æthelred's early years; detailed knowledge about a royal youth is the exception, not the rule, in the earlier Middle Ages. This is partly down to differing attitudes towards birth and childhood: death dates were more important than birth dates, since these

---

[1] S 745 (*WinchNM* 23); D.N. Dumville, 'The Anglian Collection of Royal Genealogies and Regnal Lists', *ASE* 5 (1976), 23–50, at 43.

determined when masses and prayers were said for one's soul.[2] High rates of infant mortality also had a part to play: one could rarely be sure that any given son would live to succeed his father (at least one of Æthelred's elder brothers, Edmund, was indeed to predecease Edgar). It was, therefore, only as teens that princes started to become noteworthy individuals, around the time when according to Isidore of Seville (d. 636), the great medieval encyclopaedist, boyhood (*pueritia*, covering the ages seven to fourteen) gave way to adolescence (*adolescentia*, ranging from fourteen to twenty-eight).[3] However, while there may be little we can say about the specific circumstances of Æthelred's birth and youth, there is much to be said about the period into which he was born.

In what follows we shall first examine the historical background to Edgar's reign, considering the kingdom he inherited; then we will discuss three core themes in these years, all of which were to have a significant bearing on Æthelred's upbringing and subsequent reign: administrative and institutional centralization; monastic reform; and the development of the office of queen.

England between Alfred the Great and Edgar 'the Peacemaker' (871–957/9)

Æthelred was born at an eventful time, both for England and for the rest of western Europe. As mentioned, he was the third son of Edgar, the great-grandson of Alfred the Great (871–99). The period between Alfred's accession in the late ninth century and Æthelred's birth in the mid-tenth had seen striking and enduring changes in England's political landscape. Before Alfred's time the region had been divided into many different kingdoms of varying size and influence, the most important being Wessex to the south and west of the Thames (Alfred's own realm), Kent in the south-east (incorporated into Wessex by Alfred's immediate predecessors), Mercia in the Midlands, East Anglia to the east and Northumbria in the north (Map 1).

---

[2] O.-G. Oexle, 'Memoria und Memorialüberlieferung im früheren Mittelalter', *FMSt* 10 (1976), 70–95; K. Schmid and J. Wollasch, ed., *Memoria. Der geschichtliche Zeugniswert des liturgischen Gedenkens im Mittelalter* (Munich, 1984). Specifically on England, see H. Foxhall Forbes, *Heaven and Earth in Anglo-Saxon England: Theology and Society in an Age of Faith* (Farnham, 2013), 201–64.

[3] Isidore of Seville, *Etymologiae* XI.2, ed. W.M. Lindsay (Oxford, 1911) (unpaginated).

Although in the eighth and ninth centuries there had been a trend towards larger and more powerful realms which could exert a degree of influence over their immediate neighbours, there was no attempt to unify all (or even most) of the English-speaking peoples.[4] This all changed upon the arrival of the major viking force known as the 'Great Army' (Old English: *micel here*) in 865. Although Scandinavian raiders had been making their influence felt in the British Isles for some time, this army was something new: larger and better organized than earlier forces, it represented a different kind of threat.[5] It overran Northumbria (867), East Anglia (869–70) and much of Mercia (874) in quick succession; and, though Wessex under Alfred was able to halt its advance, the political geography of southern Britain had been indelibly changed as a result. When, following a decisive victory at Edington in 878, the West Saxons went on the offensive, the number of potential rivals had been significantly reduced: Mercia was but a shadow of its former self (and now dependent on its West Saxon allies), while the new Scandinavian rulers to the east and north, dangerous though they might be, seem to have operated on a smaller scale than had their Anglo-Saxon predecessors. The exception, the powerful viking kingdom of York, lay a safe distance away from Alfred and his successors in Wessex. Moreover, its rulers maintained active interests in Dublin, which often served to distract them from more southerly affairs.[6] The years between Alfred the Great's accession and Æthelred's birth can thus be characterized as ones of steady – though not inexorable – expansion. The first move came soon after the victory at Edington, when Alfred incorporated Mercia into his realm, establishing the local nobleman Æthelred as ealdorman – that is, a royal functionary, rather like a continental count or duke – to rule the region on his behalf. This sudden expansion is reflected in the king's titles: whereas his predecessors had styled

[4] S. Keynes, 'England, 700–900', in *The New Cambridge Medieval History*, II, *c.700–c. 900*, ed. R. McKitterick (Cambridge, 1995), 18–42, provides a good introductory sketch.

[5] N. Brooks, 'England in the Ninth Century: The Crucible of Defeat' (1978), repr. in and cited from his *Communities and Warfare, 700–1400* (London, 2000), 48–68, esp. 48–59.

[6] A. Smyth, *Scandinavian York and Dublin: The History and Archaeology of Two Related Viking Kingdoms*, 2 vols. (Dublin, 1975–9); C. Downham, *Viking Kings of Britain and Ireland: The Dynasty of Ívarr to A.D. 1014* (Edinburgh, 2007).

themselves 'king of the West Saxons' or 'king of the West Saxons and men of Kent', Alfred is henceforth called 'king of the Angles and Saxons' or 'king of the Anglo-Saxons' (*rex Anglorum et Saxonum* or *rex Angulsaxonum*), titles which give expression to the new union between the Saxon kingdom of Wessex and its Anglian neighbours to the north in Mercia.[7] This new 'Anglo-Saxon' identity was fostered at court and works such as the *Anglo-Saxon Chronicle* bear witness to it, illustrating the common heritage of the English-speaking peoples in their common tongue.[8] Alfred's son, Edward the Elder (899–924), inherited this 'Kingdom of the Anglo-Saxons' and expanded it further, incorporating East Anglia and the 'Five Boroughs' of the northern Midlands (Leicester, Stamford, Derby, Nottingham and Lincoln). Edward also took over direct control of Mercia, which had hitherto been ruled by the quasi-regal Æthelred (*c.* 881–911) and his wife and successor Æthelflæd (911–18).[9] More fundamental change, however, was first to come under Edward's son, Æthelstan (924–39). Although in his earliest years Æthelstan too was styled 'king of the Anglo-Saxons', after his conquest of York in 927 he consistently bears more ambitious titles, generally variations on 'king of the English' (*rex Anglorum*) or 'king of all Britain' (*rex totius Britanniae*). This change in styles reflects a sea change in how the realm was conceived: whereas the 'Kingdom of the Anglo-Saxons' was a product of a West Saxon–Mercian alliance, this now gave way to a more unified vision of the kingdom as being constituted by a single people, 'the English' (*Angli*).[10]

However, if it was at Æthelstan's court that the concept of a coherent 'Kingdom of the English' was born, it was his successors' reigns which saw this idea transformed into reality. Following Æthelstan's death most of his and his father's gains in the Midlands and East Anglia – those regions later known as the 'Danelaw' after Scandinavian settlement there – were lost

---

[7] S. Keynes, 'King Alfred and the Mercians', in *Kings, Currency and Alliances: History and Coinage of Southern England in the Ninth Century*, ed. M.A.S. Blackburn and D.N. Dumville (Woodbridge, 1998), 1–45.

[8] S. Foot, 'The Making of *Angelcynn*: English Identity before the Norman Conquest', *TRHS* 6th ser. 6 (1996), 25–49, esp. 35–6.

[9] S. Keynes, 'Edward, King of the Anglo-Saxons', in *Edward the Elder, 899–924*, ed. N.J. Higham and D.H. Hill (London, 2001), 40–66.

[10] S. Foot, *Æthelstan: The First King of England* (New Haven, CT, 2011), esp. 10–28.

to Olaf Guthfrithson, the leader of the York (and Dublin) vikings. The fortuitous death of Olaf in 941 allowed Æthelstan's half-brother and successor Edmund (939–46) to re-establish the 'Kingdom of the English'; however, York remained something of a sticking point and it was only in 954 that Eadred (946–55), Edmund's brother and successor, definitively integrated this region into the English realm. Following the death of Eadred and accession of Eadwig (955–9), the elder son of Edmund, what had been a story of conquest became one of consolidation. Eadwig's reign saw the division of the kingdom between the king and his younger brother, Edgar, who took up rule north of the Thames in 957. Although this move has earned Eadwig censure from medieval and modern commentators alike, there may have been good grounds for it. Fraternal succession was fairly common in this period and dividing the realm was an expedient way of ensuring that Edgar had sufficient experience of rule before his own accession. Such a division was not without precedent: when Alfred the Great's father, Æthelwulf, departed to Rome in 855, he divided the West Saxon kingdom between his two eldest sons, one of whom took over Wessex proper while the other was established in Kent; and following the death of Edward the Elder in 924 the realm seems to have been temporarily divided between Æthelstan north of the Thames and his half-brother Ælfweard to the south (though whether this had been planned is not entirely clear).[11] The benefit of such a division in 957 presumably lay in pleasing local sentiment: it made for a more accessible ruler in the north, where the inhabitants of Mercia and the Danelaw still harboured memories of earlier glories. Indeed, it is probably no accident that Edgar, who had been fostered by the powerful ealdorman of East Anglia, Æthelstan Half-King, was the one appointed to these regions.[12] In any case, the arrangement was not to last long, since Eadwig died in 959, leaving the entire kingdom in the hands of his younger brother.

[11] See J.L. Nelson, 'Æthelwulf (d. 858)', in *ODNB*, I, 438–41; and Foot, *Æthelstan*, 17–18.

[12] There is a parallel here to Æthelstan, who was raised in Mercia: P. Stafford, *Unification and Conquest: A Political and Social History of the Tenth and Eleventh Centuries* (London, 1989), 42–4.

The reign of King Edgar: administrative consolidation

Edgar's reign presents something of a paradox. We know that important developments were afoot, but we are often ill-informed as to their course and nature, a fact which famously led Sir Frank Stenton to assert that 'it is a sign of Edgar's competence as ruler that his reign is singularly devoid of recorded incident.'[13] This was a key moment in the formation of a consolidated realm, during which the aspirations of Edgar's predecessors started to become something approximating reality. These developments were no doubt in part a product of the period's famed peacefulness; with the Scandinavian rulers of Dublin otherwise occupied, the integration of York, first attempted in 927 (and finally settled in 954), could step up apace. Signs of greater interest in the region can already be seen during Edgar's reign north of the Thames (957–9), during which a number of figures bearing Scandinavian names appear as witnesses to his charters.[14] Later on these individuals largely disappear from sight, but the officer charged with overseeing York (whose title is generally 'earl' rather than 'ealdorman', as was common further south) remains a regular presence. Edgar's involvement in the affairs of the northern parts of his realm is also reflected in the ordinances issued at *Wihtbordesstan* (precise location unknown), known as *IV Edgar*, in which he became the first ruler to acknowledge the different legal customs governing the region.[15]

Edgar's reign is also significant from an administrative standpoint. Although under Alfred, Edward and Æthelstan we have hints of important institutional developments, these first come fully to light under Edgar.[16] The key challenge faced by these rulers was how to govern a rapidly expanding realm: Alfred the Great's 'Kingdom of the Anglo-Saxons' was already almost twice the size of his father's 'Kingdom of the West Saxons', while Æthelstan's

---

[13] Stenton, *Anglo-Saxon England*, 368.

[14] L. Abrams, 'King Edgar and the Men of the Danelaw', in *Edgar, King of the English 959–75: New Interpretations*, ed. D. Scragg (Woodbridge, 2008), 171–91. See also D. Whitelock, 'The Dealings of the Kings of England with Northumbria in the Tenth and Eleventh Centuries' (1959), repr. in and cited from her *History, Law and Literature in 10th–11th Century England* (London, 1981), no. III.

[15] *IV Eg* 12, 15 (ed. Liebermann, I, 212–15); with Wormald, *Making of English Law*, 317–20.

[16] G. Molyneaux, *The Formation of the English Kingdom in the Tenth Century* (Oxford, 2015).

'Kingdom of the English' was more than twice that of Alfred's again. In order to overcome this challenge, kings delegated greater authority to local representatives while also seeking to create new administrative networks in which these figures could operate. The most important and enduring of the resulting divisions was the shire (or county), which remains the cornerstone of British local government to this day. The early history of the shire is hard to trace. Already in the ninth century it seems to have been the core administrative division within Wessex. Originally each shire was overseen by an ealdorman, who was charged with raising levies and perhaps also overseeing the local court (though the evidence is scant on the latter point). At the heart of the shire lay the local assembly (the 'shire court'), at which such business was conducted. As the kingdom grew, it became necessary to entrust ever larger areas to ealdormen, however, severing the link between these officers and the shire. The expanding realm also posed other problems: since the shire was a West Saxon phenomenon, it had to be instituted in newly conquered regions in order to ensure that justice could be administered there in the same manner.[17] As a part of this process we start to see a new kind of royal officer appear: the shire reeve (or sheriff, as he would later be known), who plugged the gap between the ealdorman and shire, taking over partial responsibility for local administration (though ealdormen continued to play a role here). How swiftly this process proceeded is a matter of debate: traditionally the shiring of England is thought to have been the work of Edward the Elder and Æthelstan, and the appearance of the shire reeve is placed somewhat later; but recent work suggests that developments may have been more gradual, with shiring first becoming systematic under Edgar and his successors and the shire reeve emerging as part of this process.[18]

It is not only shires and shire reeves that begin to appear at this point. Tougher to trace, but no less important, are two smaller administrative divisions: the hundred and the tithing. Like the shire, the origins of the hundred lie in earlier governmental arrangements. As it appears in the later

[17] S. Keynes, 'Shire', in *The Wiley Blackwell Encyclopedia of Anglo-Saxon England*, ed. M. Lapidge *et al.*, 2nd edn (Chichester, 2013), 434–5.

[18] D.H. Hill, 'The Shiring of Mercia – Again', in *Edward the Elder, 899–924*, ed. N.J. Higham and D.H. Hill (London, 2001), 144–59; L. Marten, 'The Shiring of East Anglia: An Alternative Hypothesis', *Historical Research* 81 (2008), 1–27; Molyneaux, *Formation*, 155–72.

Anglo-Saxon period, however, the hundred is a product of tenth-century developments. It is, in essence, a subdivision of the shire, designed to allow access to justice at a more local level. The hundred – or wapentake (Old Norse *vápnatak*, referring to the taking of weapons), as its northern Danelaw equivalent was known – was administered by the local leading men and, like its larger counterpart, was characterized by assemblies: each hundred had one or more meeting sites, at which various legal and administrative matters were overseen. This was the forum to which most people would appeal in cases of wrongdoing – the shire court was only to be consulted if it proved impossible to find justice here.[19] The tithing, on the other hand, sat alongside the hundred. It took the form of a group of ten (or possibly as many as twelve or more) free men who swore not to undertake any act of theft and to accept mutual responsibility for the others if they were to do so.[20] The tithing thus made local communities responsible for the acts of their own malefactors. Since tithings and hundreds operated on a smaller scale and a more local level than shires, it is harder to trace their evolution and operation. Nevertheless, as with the shire, there are both tantalizing hints of early developments (particularly in the reign of Æthelstan), and signs that these first started to become systematic under Edgar. Thus, while the first reference to a hundred comes from decrees in the name of Edmund, the first works to discuss the operation of the hundred court in any detail date from Edgar's reign. These ordinances are also amongst the first to discuss tithings, illustrating the close relationship between the two.[21]

Similar developments toward a greater standardization can be seen in the coinage of the period. Since the pioneering work of Michael Dolley and David Metcalf, it has become clear that Edgar oversaw an important overhaul of the monetary system towards the end of his reign (probably *c.* 973).[22] Whereas the coins of earlier tenth-century rulers reveal various

[19] H.R. Loyn, 'The Hundred in England in the Tenth and Early Eleventh Centuries' (1974), repr. in and cited from his *Society and Peoples: Studies in the History of England and Wales, c. 600–1200* (London, 1992), 111–34; Molyneaux, *Formation*, 141–55.

[20] Pratt, 'Written Law'; Molyneaux, *Formation*, 113–15, 150 and 195–7.

[21] Molyneaux, *Formation*, 143–6 and 166–7.

[22] R.H.M. Dolley and D.M. Metcalf, 'The Reform of the English Coinage under Edgar', in *Anglo-Saxon Coins: Studies Presented to F.M. Stenton on the Occasion of his 80th Birthday, 17 May 1960*, ed. R.H.M. Dolley (London, 1961), 136–68.

signs of regionalization – different types were minted in different areas and circulated largely (though not exclusively) within these – Edgar for the first time established that only one type would be in circulation at a time throughout his realm. Subsequently it became common to have recoinages every six or seven years, in which the previous type would be recalled and replaced by a new one. Whether this was the plan from the start, as Dolley believed, is doubtful, however, and the impression is that variation was the order of the day in these early years – certain basic principles were observed, but the approach was more experimental than systematic.[23] Such measures certainly presuppose a high degree of royal oversight and it is not without reason that Edgar's reform has been seen as one of the crowning achievements of late Anglo-Saxon kingship. Nevertheless, the reform built on a long-standing tradition of royal control over coinage and more recent work has relativized some of the more extreme claims of Dolley and others.[24] Indeed, though the degree of standardization achieved by Edgar is impressive, there continued to be regional variation in die-cutting and it is unlikely that a strict scheme of recoinages every six years was ever enforced (if, indeed, this had been the intention).

Edgar thus took existing traditions forward in novel and important fashions. Yet as important as these pragmatic measures was the ideological contribution of his reign. As George Molyneaux notes, it was in this period that English rulers finally settled on 'king of the English' as their standard title, dropping the claims to dominion over all Britain which had been a periodic feature of royal titulature since the time of Æthelstan. Molyneaux argues that this was a product of the administrative developments sketched above: as kingship became more intensive within the English realm, the distinction between this direct form of rule and the loose overlordship exerted over the other regions of Britain became unmistakable; for Edgar or

---

[23] P. Grierson, 'Numismatics and the Historian', *NC* 7th ser. 2 (1962), i–xiv, at viii–xiv; B.H.I.H. Stewart, 'Coinage and Recoinage after Edgar's Reform', in *Studies in Late Anglo-Saxon Coinage in Memory of Bror Emil Hildebrand*, ed. K. Jonsson (Stockholm, 1990), 455–85.

[24] R. Naismith, 'Prelude to Reform: Tenth-Century English Coinage in Perspective', in *Early Medieval Monetary History: Studies in Memory of Mark Blackburn*, ed. M. Allen, R. Naismith and E. Screen (Farnham, 2014), 39–84; D.M. O'Gorman, '*Unius regulae ac unius patriae*: A Standardizing Process in Anglo-Saxon England' (PhD diss., Loyola University, 2015), 68–136.

Æthelred to claim to rule Wales and northern Britain in the same manner as they did Wessex or Mercia was no longer possible. Though claims to broader insular domination were not dropped as swiftly as Molyneaux implies – both Edgar and Æthelred were often styled rulers of 'all Britain' or 'Albion' – there is certainly something to these arguments, which explain why later rulers are generally known as 'kings of the English' (or even 'of England'), even when, as was frequently the case, they continued to exert a degree of influence over their immediate neighbours.[25]

Perhaps the most classic expression of Edgar's power and influence came in 973, when the king underwent a second coronation at Bath at Pentecost, followed by a meeting with the rulers of Wales and northern Britain at Chester. This was clearly a show of strength: Bath's Roman ruins and waters – the latter perhaps reminiscent of Aachen, the symbolic centre of the Carolingian realms on the continent – were redolent of 'imperial' status, while the presence of the neighbouring Welsh and northern British rulers at Chester (on English ground, that is) served to underline Edgar's claims to insular dominion further.[26] This act reveals an important further aspect of Edgar's regime: the role of pomp and ceremony. Though his predecessors were clearly alive to the political potential of ritual and display, Edgar's reign also seems to represent something of a watershed here: accounts of the period are replete with descriptions of ritualized activity, much of which is associated with the royal court.[27] Edgar was probably learning lessons from his continental counterparts: such ceremonial played a central role at the Ottonian court in Germany (and northern Italy), where it began to take on new dimensions following the imperial coronation of Otto I in 962, while in France too a heightened interest in demonstrative behaviour can be seen in these years (perhaps in response to

[25] G. Molyneaux, 'Why were Some Tenth-Century English Kings Presented as Rulers of Britain?', *TRHS* 6th ser. 21 (2011), 59–91.

[26] J.L. Nelson, 'Inauguration Rituals' (1977), repr. in and cited from her *Politics and Ritual in Early Medieval Europe* (London, 1986), 283–307, at 296–303; Keynes, 'Edgar', 48–51. For a different perspective: J. Barrow, 'Chester's Earliest Regatta? Edgar's Dee-Rowing Revisited', *EME* 10 (2001), 81–93; D.E. Thornton, 'Edgar and the Eight Kings, AD 973: *textus et dramatis personae*', *EME* 10 (2001), 49–79; and A. Williams, 'An Outing on the Dee: King Edgar at Chester, A.D. 973', *Mediaeval Scandinavia* 14 (2004), 229–43.

[27] Roach, *Kingship and Consent*, 161–211, esp. 202–8.

developments east of the Rhine).[28] The importance of ritual and display lay above all in its ability to project an image of the king and his regime; as the realm expanded, it helped bridge the gap between monarch and people. There was a religious undertone to much of this symbolic activity and it sat alongside other efforts to emphasize the sacrality and inviolability of royal office in these years. Indeed, there is reason to believe that much of this interest in pomp and show was cultivated within the circles of monastic reform, and it is to this that we must turn if we are to gain a fuller understanding of Edgar's regime.

King Edgar and the church: monastic reform

One of the most striking features of Edgar's reign was the king's support for monastic reform. This movement – or more accurately: series of movements – swept across Europe in the tenth century and the English took inspiration here from their continental neighbours. In order to appreciate the importance of these events, we must, however, briefly consider the broader history of monasticism.

Although born in the deserts of Egypt in the third and fourth centuries, by the fifth and sixth monasticism had spread throughout the provinces and former provinces of the Roman Empire. The original holy men of North Africa and the Middle East had lived a solitary life as hermits, but it was communal (or coenobitic) monasticism which was to prove popular in the Latin-speaking west. The model was provided by Martin of Tours (d. 397), the Roman soldier-cum-bishop (and monk) who was instrumental in bringing monastic life to the west. Early communal tendencies derived further impetus from the rules for monastic life drawn up in the sixth century, the most influential being that of Benedict of Nursia (the so-called Benedictine Rule), which places great emphasis on community

[28] K.J. Leyser, 'Ritual, Ceremony and Gesture: Ottonian Germany', in his *Communications and Power in Medieval Europe*, ed. T. Reuter, 2 vols. (London, 1994), I, 189–213; T. Reuter, '*Regemque, quem in Francia pene perdidit, in patria magnifice recepit:* Ottonian Ruler Representation in Synchronic and Diachronic Comparison' (1998), repr. in and cited from his *Medieval Polities and Modern Mentalities*, ed. J.L. Nelson (Cambridge, 2006), 127–46; G. Koziol, *Begging Pardon and Favor: Ritual and Political Order in Early Medieval France* (Ithaca, NY, 1992), esp. 109–37.

and stability, singling out monks who lead a peripatetic lifestyle ('gyro-vagues') for particular censure.[29] However, while the basic principle of coenobitic life came to be accepted across the former Western Empire, variety continued to characterize monasticism. Indeed, though Benedict's Rule circulated widely, there was little attempt to apply it beyond the abbot's own foundation at Monte Cassino; other houses tended to follow 'mixed rules', which combined elements of various authoritative texts (of which Benedict's was but one) with local traditions.[30] Under such circumstances the very distinction between monastic and clerical life often blurred and the Latin term *monasterium* ('monastery') could be used to describe what we would now call cathedral chapters or houses of canons, a fact which has left its mark on Modern English usage, in which 'minster' – derived from *monasterium* – can describe any important church.[31]

The first serious attempts to impose greater unity came in the ninth century, when, under the influence of Benedict of Aniane (whose vocational name was a conscious homage to Benedict of Nursia), Louis the Pious (814–40) set out to impose Benedictine observance throughout the monasteries of his empire, which stretched across much of modern France, Switzerland and the Low Countries, as well as large parts of Italy, Germany and Austria. In order to achieve this, Louis called together a series of reforming councils at Aachen (816–19), at which he and Benedict called for greater standardization of monastic practice in line with the Rule. These efforts built on the initiatives of Louis's father, the great Frankish ruler Charlemagne (768–814), who had sought to achieve greater consistency in other aspects of religious life; what was new was the specifically monastic focus. Behind these endeavours stood a new imperial ideology, one which took the monastery as a model for empire: just as Louis ruled over only one realm, so too there was to be only one form of monastic observance within

---

[29] *Regula Benedicti*, ch. 1.10–11, ed. J. Neufville with notes and an introduction by A. de Vogüé, 2 pts, Sources Chrétiennes 181–2 (Paris, 1972), 438–40. In general, see M. Dunn, *The Emergence of Monasticism: From the Desert Fathers to the Early Middle Ages* (Oxford, 2003), 59–137.

[30] S. Foot, *Monastic Life in Anglo-Saxon England, c. 600–900* (Cambridge, 2006), 48–60.

[31] S. Foot, 'Anglo-Saxon Minsters: A Review of Terminology', in *Pastoral Care before the Parish*, ed. J. Blair and R. Sharpe (Leicester, 1992), 212–25.

this.[32] Although the emperor's calls for conformity were never fully realized and a degree of variety was always accepted in practice, they left a strong legacy and would be echoed by many later reformers. Indeed, by establishing the Benedictine Rule as the ultimate measure of monastic practice, Louis created a yardstick for judging the successes and (more often) failings of individual monastic houses.

The reform movements of the tenth century in many respects represent a continuation of those of the ninth; they hark back to the efforts of Louis and Benedict, and in a number of cases direct lines of continuity can be traced. Traditionally, these new undertakings have been seen as a reaction against abuses within once reformed centres, which had crept in during the later ninth century when viking, Muslim and Magyar (Hungarian) raids wreaked havoc across large swathes of the Carolingian empire. However, more recent studies have significantly modified this picture, demonstrating that though monastic life suffered notably in some places, in many others there are signs of continuity and even vitality throughout this period, which belie the later tales of destruction and negligence painted by the reformers.[33] We are not, therefore, dealing with a sharp break, but a gradual development out of the ninth century. To understand why we see such 'waves' of reform we must appreciate the rhetoric employed by the reformers. Benedict of Aniane and his associates called upon a deep-seated sense of decline within the Christian tradition – decline since man had been expelled from the Garden of Eden, decline since Christ and his apostles had set an example for the gentiles, and decline since the time of the desert fathers and Benedict of Nursia, when monasticism had first been placed on a firm footing.[34] The reformers thus looked back to a semi-mythical past and in doing so set the bar impossibly

---

[32] T.F.X. Noble, 'The Monastic Ideal as a Model for Empire: The Case of Louis the Pious', *Revue Bénédictine* 86 (1976), 235–50. Cf. M. de Jong, 'Carolingian Monasticism: The Power of Prayer', in *The New Cambridge Medieval History*, II, *c.700–c.900*, ed. R. McKitterick (Cambridge, 1995), 622–53.

[33] A. Dierkens, *Abbayes et chapitres entre Sambre et Meuse (VIIᵉ–XIᵉ siècles). Contribution à l'histoire religieuse des campagnes du Haut Moyen Âge* (Sigmaringen, 1985); J. Nightingale, *Monasteries and Patrons in the Gorze Reform: Lotharingia c. 850–1000* (Oxford, 2001); S. Vanderputten, *Monastic Reform as Process: Realities and Representations in Medieval Flanders, 900–1100* (Ithaca, NY, 2013).

[34] Cf. R.A. Markus, *The End of Ancient Christianity* (Cambridge, 1990), 227–8.

high; since perfection could neither be achieved nor maintained, there was always room for improvement (or, as a senior colleague once remarked, 'monks are always in need of reform!'). This is what gave monasticism its 'volcanic' character, explaining why from the ninth century to the fifteenth (and, indeed, beyond) there is scarcely a period of European history which did not witness the eruption of some form of monastic reform or another.[35] A modern parallel is perhaps offered by debates about educational reform, which periodically make headlines across the western world: these too feed upon a deep-set perception that standards are slipping (education 'is not what it used to be'). Thus, medieval monks – like many modern educational reformers – were striving for the unobtainable, seeking to re-establish an ideal that never was. The contribution of the Carolingians was not so much this mind-set, as the establishment of the Rule of St Benedict as the means by which to measure it. Hence when, within the span of a single generation in the 930s and 940s, reform once again became the order of the day across much of the former Carolingian empire, it was to the Rule and texts produced by Louis and Benedict which reformers turned.[36]

It is against this background that the English and continental reforms of the period must be judged. Although it was once common to speak of 'monastic reform' in the singular, it has become clear that there was great variety amongst these movements. Nevertheless, the reformers shared certain characteristics, some of which may be the result of direct contact and mutual influence, but many of which are a product of common traditions (above all a shared Carolingian heritage). The central ambition of these movements was to improve monastic life through a stricter dedication to the Rule. Particular causes for concern were secular influence on monastic life and (in particular) the election of abbots; the loss of church lands (often related to such secular interference); and laxity in monastic observance (itself frequently a consequence of the former issues). Reform sprang up largely independently in a number of different centres in France, Germany and the Low Countries and spread outward from these. The

[35] A. Murray, *Reason and Society in the Middle Ages* (Oxford, 1978), 7.

[36] J. Semmler, 'Das Erbe der karolingischen Klosterreform im 10. Jahrhundert', in *Monastische Reformen im 9. und 10. Jahrhundert*, ed. R. Kottje and H. Maurer (Sigmaringen, 1989), 29–77.

most important in this respect were Cluny in Burgundy; Fleury in the Loire Valley (which had been reformed by Odo of Cluny); the circles of Gerard of Brogne in the Low Countries (centred on Brogne itself and St-Peter's, Ghent); and the 'Gorzian' houses of the Rhineland, particularly Gorze and St-Maximin in Trier.[37] Although each of these movements displays certain distinctive features – 'Gorzian' reform, for example, is often held to have been more open to secular influence – they were far from homogenous and the labels used to designate them ('Cluniac', 'Fleuriac' and 'Gorzian') are but modern terms of convenience. Indeed, if there was a single common denominator behind them it tended to be the activity of one or more charismatic leaders.

From the very earliest days of these reforms such ideas began to make themselves felt in England. In the 930s Æthelstan's court acted as a magnet for political, cultural and religious contacts with continental Europe: Dunstan and Æthelwold, two of the leading later reformers, met there, and their mentors Bishop Ælfheah 'the Bald' of Winchester and Bishop Coenwald of Worcester helped open the way for such influences.[38] Ideas about monastic renewal could call upon existing traditions in England: already Alfred the Great had shown an interest in improving religious standards, fostering a tradition of royally sponsored piety which can be traced through the tenth century. In the years following Æthelstan's reign reforming ideals started to take firmer root: under Edmund and Eadred a number of grants was made to 'religious women', which David Dumville sees as a sign of growing interest in religious life amongst the laity.[39] It was in these years too that Oda, a relative of the later reformer Oswald and another early patron of reforming ideals, was appointed archbishop of Canterbury (941–58).[40] Eadred himself is reported to have held Dunstan in high esteem, charging him with important administrative duties

[37] See J. Wollasch, 'The First Wave of Reform', in *The New Cambridge Medieval History*, III, *c. 900–1024*, ed. T. Reuter (Cambridge, 1999), 163–85, for a synthesis.

[38] Foot, *Æthelstan*, 107–9; M. Gretsch, *The Intellectual Foundations of the English Benedictine Reform* (Cambridge, 1999). Cf. C. Cubitt, 'The Tenth-Century Benedictine Reform in England', *EME* 6 (1997), 77–94.

[39] D.N. Dumville, *Wessex and England from Alfred to Edgar: Six Essays on Political, Cultural, and Ecclesiastical Revival* (Woodbridge, 1992), 173–84. Cf. *ibid.*, 185–205.

[40] C. Cubitt and M. Costambeys, 'Oda (*d.* 958)', in *ODNB*, XLI, 484–7.

(apparently including the production of royal charters) during his later years, when the king was incapacitated by illness.[41] Of more lasting importance was the emergence of the first reformed houses at Glastonbury and Abingdon. Glastonbury was entrusted to Dunstan by Edmund and, though secular clerics may have continued to live alongside monks there, its importance for the dissemination of ideas about reform is clear: it is here that many later reformers, including Æthelwold, are said to have received their training in monastic life, and it is through Glastonbury that many reforming texts seem to have been transmitted. At Abingdon, which Eadred granted to Æthelwold in order to prevent the holy man seeking his vocation on the continent, these developments were taken further: of all the reformers Æthelwold was to prove the strictest when it came to applying the stipulations of the Rule, and it was with monks trained at this centre that he was later able to spread reform to Winchester and beyond. Indeed, it may be at Abingdon that reforming ideals began to take on their characteristically monastic focus. Nevertheless, for all the signs that the material and intellectual foundations of the reform were laid in the reigns of Æthelstan, Edmund and Eadred (and perhaps also Eadwig, though he was later to receive something of a bad press at the hands of the reformers), it is important to emphasize the limits of these early initiatives: at the time of Edgar's accession in 959 there were only two reformed houses and little sign that this number was likely to rise quickly. Moreover, while earlier tenth-century rulers took their religious duties seriously, there is no indication that monastic reform *per se* was a priority – indeed, when a group of clerics expelled from St-Bertin by the continental reformer Gerard of Brogne sought refuge in England in 944, they were welcomed with open arms and settled at Bath.[42]

When Edgar came to the throne the groundwork had thus been laid for a more thorough-going reform of English monasticism: there was a

---

[41] B., *Vita S. Dunstani*, ch. 20, ed. M. Winterbottom and M. Lapidge, *The Early Lives of St Dunstan* (Oxford, 2012), 64; with S. Keynes, 'The "Dunstan B" Charters', *ASE* 23 (1994), 165–93, esp. 185–6.

[42] Folcuin of St-Bertin, *Gesta abbatum S. Bertini Sithiensium*, ch. 107, ed. O. Holder-Egger, MGH: SS 13 (Hannover, 1881), 629; with D. Misonne, 'Gérard de Brogne, moine et réformateur (†959)' (1984), repr. in and cited from *Revue Bénédictine* 111 (2001), 25–49, at 34–6.

growing body of reform-minded monks at Glastonbury and (in particular) Abingdon, and there were figures such as Dunstan, Æthelwold and Oswald, who had an acquaintance with continental reforming traditions (in the former and latter cases at first hand) and were ready to take on the task of fronting the movement. Still, it was far from certain that reform would proceed as rapidly and successfully as it did. That within the span of little more than a decade it was implemented throughout much of England is thanks to the active support of Edgar, who showed a deep interest in and concern for monastic life. Already as king north of the Thames he had recalled Dunstan from exile (the latter having fallen foul of Eadwig and taken refuge at St-Peter's, Ghent). Upon his return, Dunstan was immediately appointed bishop (957/8); for a brief time he may have operated as 'bishop without portfolio' (perhaps as a so-called *chorepiscpous* or 'auxiliary bishop'), but upon the death of Coenwald of Worcester (958) he was appointed successor to this early proponent of reform. Shortly thereafter, he was promoted further, succeeding Brihthelm at the strategic see of London, which he may have held alongside Worcester.[43] Yet Dunstan's rise did not stop here: when Edgar took control of the south following Eadwig's death in October 959, he drove the recently appointed Byrhthelm from Canterbury and installed Dunstan in his stead; whether the former had been formally anointed into his office or not is a moot point, but either way Dunstan's instalment was evidently a matter of some urgency.[44] Elsewhere Edgar proceeded more cautiously, but his priority was clearly to populate the most important sees of his kingdom with supporters of reform. Thus, when Worcester, the wealthiest diocese north of the Thames, became free in 961 the king appointed Oswald to this post (reportedly at Dunstan's behest). As a relative of Oda of Canterbury, who had done much to pave the way for the later reform, Oswald was a

---

[43] N. Brooks, 'The Career of St Dunstan' (1992), repr. in and cited from his *Anglo-Saxon Myths: State and Church 400–1066* (London, 2000), 154–80, at 177–8; S. Keynes, 'Edgar, *rex admirabilis*', in *Edgar, King of the English 959–75: New Interpretations*, ed. D. Scragg (Woodbridge, 2008), 1–58, at 8, n. 28. Cf. *Early Lives*, ed. Winterbottom and Lapidge, xxxv–xxxvii.

[44] D. Whitelock, 'The Appointment of Dunstan as Archbishop of Canterbury' (1973), repr. in and cited from her *History, Law and Literature in 10th–11th Century England* (London, 1981), no. IV; *Early Lives*, ed. Winterbottom and Lapidge, xxxvii–xxxviii.

natural choice; moreover, like Dunstan, he had first-hand experience of reformed monasticism on the continent, having spent time at Fleury in the earlier 950s.[45] Two years later Winchester, the most important southern bishopric after Canterbury, became free, and this time it was Æthelwold who was appointed.

With these three bishoprics in the hands of reform-minded prelates, the way was open for more ambitious undertakings. Our accounts of the reform are all retrospective, in most cases written around the turn of the first millennium; nevertheless, it is clear that with royal support the movement was able to make rapid progress. Perhaps the most dramatic event came with the expulsion of secular clerics from the Old and New Minsters in Winchester – that is, the traditional chapter house and the adjacent monastery founded by Edward the Elder – undertaken by Æthelwold under royal fiat in 964.[46] This was commemorated a few years later with the production of the lavish New Minster refoundation charter: probably drafted by Æthelwold and presented as a codex, rather than a single sheet of parchment, this is a programmatic statement of the reformers' aims. It opens with a portrait of Edgar, flanked by St Mary and St Peter, granting the charter to Christ (Plate 1). The following text is written throughout in gold and begins with a lengthy preamble reflecting upon the origin of sin and Fall of Man (the expulsion of Adam and Eve from the Garden of Eden), likening this to the fate of monasticism in England, which has also fallen from earlier heights.[47] The reformers' role is thus presented as one of cleansing and purifying, restoring monastic life to its former glory.[48] It was probably around this time (*c.* 966) that Edgar gave instructions to Æthelwold, Oswald and Dunstan to reform and refound monasteries

---

[45] D.A. Bullough, 'St Oswald: Monk, Bishop and Archbishop', in *St Oswald of Worcester: Life and Influence*, ed. N. Brooks and C. Cubitt (London, 1996), 1–22.

[46] *ASC* 964 A (ed. Bately, 75–6); Wulfstan Cantor, *Vita S. Æthelwoldi*, ch. 16, ed. M. Lapidge and M. Winterbottom, *Wulfstan of Winchester: Life of St Æthelwold* (Oxford, 1991), 28–30.

[47] S 745 (*WinchNM* 23). See M. Lapidge, 'Æthelwold as Scholar and Teacher' (1988), repr. in and cited from his *Anglo-Latin Literature 900–1066* (London, 1993), 183–211, at 189–90.

[48] J. Barrow, 'The Ideology of the Tenth-Century English Benedictine "Reform"', in *Challenging the Boundaries of Medieval History: The Legacy of Timothy Reuter*, ed. P. Skinner (Turnhout, 2009), 141–54.

throughout the rest of his realm.[49] Æthelwold seems to have been the most active in this regard: in addition to Abingdon and the Old and New Minsters, he oversaw the reform (or refoundation) of Ely, Peterborough and Thorney in the east Midlands and East Anglia, and probably also Chertsey and Milton south of the Thames. Oswald, for his part, is reported to have introduced monks to Westbury-on-Trym, Winchcombe, Pershore and the cathedral chapter of Worcester within his own diocese, as well as Ramsey in the fenlands. Dunstan apparently introduced monastic observance to Glastonbury, Malmesbury and Westminster, and perhaps also Bath and centres in Kent (though the evidence here is slight). Many further houses were touched by reform, though the precise chronology and nature of developments is frequently unclear. The reformers took different approaches to their task: Æthelwold was reportedly the most stringent, tolerating nothing less than the strictest observance of the Rule; Oswald seems to have been more measured, allowing secular clerics to live alongside monks for a time at Worcester; while Dunstan was less actively involved – indeed, the degree of reforming activity undertaken at Canterbury and beyond is not entirely clear.

Reform was thus introduced by individuals with close contacts with the continent and one of its most striking contributions was the promotion of a new system of writing: Caroline minuscule, the script used elsewhere in Europe. Elements of Caroline writing may have been adopted earlier, but it was only in reformed houses that this came to be employed systematically.[50] Another characteristic of reform was the popularization of the so-called 'hermeneutic style', a bombastic approach to Latin prose composition which had its roots in the writings of the Englishman Aldhelm of Malmesbury (d. 709/10), but was modelled more immediately on contemporary continental trends. Though this style too started to gain ground before the heyday of the reform, it was avidly adopted by the reformers and came to be some-

---

[49] Byrhtferth of Ramsey, *Vita S. Oswaldi* III.9–12, ed. M. Lapidge, *Byrhtferth of Ramsey: The Lives of St Oswald and St Ecgwine* (Oxford, 2009), 70–80.

[50] R. Rushforth, 'English Caroline Minuscule', in *The Cambridge History of the Book in Britain*, I, *c. 400–1100*, ed. R. Gameson (Cambridge, 2012), 197–210. Important further work is to be anticipated from Julia Crick and Colleen Curran.

thing of a badge of pride amongst them.[51] However, for all it owed to the continent, the English reform was distinctive in many respects. It not only drew on earlier traditions within the British Isles (above all the writings of the eighth-century Northumbrian scholar Bede, which presented an earlier 'Golden Age' to which the reformers could aspire), but also enjoyed more direct royal patronage; whereas elsewhere reform was driven primarily by local prelates and magnates, such as Count Arnulf of Flanders (d. 965), Bishop Adalbero of Metz (d. 962) and Duke Giselbert of Lotharingia (d. 939), in England it was the king who took the lead.[52] This is not to say that lay aristocrats did not contribute to developments in England, nor that continental rulers were unreceptive to reforming impulses; the balance was simply different. In this respect, Edgar looks more like Louis the Pious than his immediate French and German counterparts, and it would be the early eleventh century before the latter started to take similar initiatives.[53] The importance of such royal patronage is reflected in the place given to prayers for the king and queen in the *Regularis concordia*, the key document of the reform, promulgated at Edgar's behest at the Council of Winchester in order to regularize monastic customs within the realm (probably *c.* 970).[54]

---

[51] M. Lapidge, 'The Hermeneutic Style in Tenth-Century Anglo-Latin Literature' (1975), repr. in and cited from his *Anglo-Latin Literature 900–1066* (London, 1993), 105–49; R. Stephenson, 'Scapegoating the Secular Clergy: The Hermeneutic Style as a Form of Monastic Self-Definition', *ASE* 38 (2010), 101–36.

[52] P. Wormald, 'Æthelwold and his Continental Counterparts: Contact, Comparison, Contrast' (1988), repr. in and cited from his *The Times of Bede: Studies in Early English Christian Society and its Historian*, ed. S. Baxter (Oxford, 2006), 169–206; Nightingale, *Monasteries and Patrons*; F. Mazel, 'Monachisme et aristocratie aux Xe–XIe siècles. Un regard sur l'historiographie récente', in *Ecclesia in medio nationis: Reflections on the Study of Monasticism in the Central Middle Ages*, ed. S. Vanderputten and B. Meijns (Leuven, 2011), 47–75.

[53] See H. Hoffmann, *Mönchskönig und rex idiota. Studien zur Kirchenpolitik Heinrichs II. und Konrads II.*, MGH: Studien und Texte 8 (Hannover, 1993); and G. Koziol, 'The Conquest of Burgundy, the Peace of God, and the Diplomas of Robert the Pious', *French Historical Studies* 37 (2014), 173–214.

[54] *Regularis concordia*, chs. 8, 17, 19, 21, 24, 31, 33–5, ed. T. Symons and S. Spath, *Consuetudinem saeculi X/XI/XII monumenta non-cluniacensa*, ed. K. Hallinger, Corpus Consuetudinum Monasticarum vii.3 (Siegburg, 1984), 74, 81–2, 83, 84, 86, 90, 91–2. See J. Barrow, 'The Chronology of the Benedictine "Reform"', in *Edgar, King of the English 959–75: New Interpretations*, ed. D. Scragg (Woodbridge, 2008), 211–23, who suggests an earlier date (*c.* 966); and D. Pratt, 'The Voice of the King in "King Edgar's Establishment of Monasteries"', *ASE* 41 (2012), 145–204, at 170–2, for the reassertion of traditional orthodoxy.

Related to more direct (and assertive) royal patronage is another distinctive feature of the English reform: the emphasis on unity of practice. As the *Regularis concordia* states, it was promulgated because the king had observed that English monks were 'of one faith, but not of one manner of observance' (*una fide, non tamen uno consuetudinis usu*) and therefore urged them to be 'of one mind regarding the manner of observance' (*concordes aequali consuetudinis usu*), settling on appropriate practices to be followed throughout the realm.[55] Such sentiments owe much to the texts promulgated by Louis the Pious in the early ninth century, but find little immediate echo elsewhere in Europe. Indeed, though reformers on the continent valued unity of practice in conformity with the Rule (as the presence of monks from Ghent at the Council of Winchester demonstrates), this apparently came second to the restitution of lost estates and the resistance of lay lordship. To appreciate the full significance of such regularization and standardization to Edgar and his monastic advisers (above all Æthelwold), we must look not only to Carolingian precedent, but also to the context in which the English reforms were nurtured. Unlike West and East Francia, the English kingdom was a recent creation and in his youth Edgar had seen it divided between himself and his elder half-brother. Reform offered a blueprint for unity: it provided an ideological underpinning for administrative centralization, sending the powerful message – as it had under Louis the Pious – that within one realm there was to be only one form of monastic usage. Yet the potential of reform was not purely ideological: by removing monasteries from secular oversight (except, of course, that of king and queen), Edgar also secured greater influence over the religious houses of his realm, centres which thanks to royal patronage were now increasingly wealthy and politically active.[56] That so many reformed houses lay in the fenlands of the East Midlands and East Anglia may therefore be significant; reform seems to have been part and parcel of how royal authority was asserted within the region.[57]

---

[55] *Regularis concordia*, ch. 4 (ed. Symons and Spath, 70–1).

[56] N. Banton, 'Monastic Reform and the Unification of Tenth-Century England', *SCH* 18 (1982), 71–86; O'Gorman, 'Standardizing Process', 179–260. See also E. John, *Orbis Britanniae and Other Studies* (Leicester, 1966), 154–80; with the caveats of Cubitt, 'Reform', 85–6.

[57] T. Pestell, *Landscapes of Monastic Foundation: The Establishment of Religious Houses in East Anglia, c. 650–1200* (Woodbridge, 2004), 127–31.

Still, one should not reduce Edgar's aims to *Realpolitik*. More important than any immediate practical gains were the religious rewards which might accrue. Already Alfred the Great had expressed the conviction that the ravages of the viking 'Great Army' were a product of neglect for learning amongst the English, and this belief that the well-being of the realm depended upon national wisdom and piety was maintained and developed by his successors, whose active religious patronage forms a bridge between Alfredian educational renewal and Edgarian monastic reform.[58] Indeed, the connection Alfred had drawn between the material well-being of the realm and the devotion of its ruler and people was taken to new heights by the tenth-century reformers. Æthelwold's account of 'Edgar's Establishment of Monasteries', which was written as a preface to his translation of the Rule of St Benedict (*c.* 966 × 970) – itself designed to make this work accessible 'to laymen' (*woroldmonnum*, a term also used for the secular clergy) – explicitly associates the king's political success with his support for reform.[59] A similar association between national well-being and royal piety had been drawn in the seventh-century Irish tract 'The Twelve Abuses of the Age' (*De duodecim abusivis saeculi*), which was popular in these years, especially within reforming circles.[60] Edgar's own decrees reveal that the king thought likewise: the *Wihtbordesstan* ordinances (*IV Edgar*), issued in the aftermath of a natural disaster (perhaps the 'great mortality' reported by the *Chronicle* under 962), frame themselves as an act of repentance, an attempt to restore order to the realm by returning to pious ways.[61] (It may, incidentally, be more than a coincidence that Edgar's first reforming acts came only two years after this plague, with the expulsion of clerics from the Old and New Minsters.)

---

[58] Dumville, *Wessex and England*, 185–205. See also Pratt, 'Voice of the King', 153–4 and 162–8.

[59] 'Edgar's Establishment of Monasteries', ed. D. Whitelock, *Councils and Synods with Other Documents Relating to the English Church, I, A.D. 871–1204*, ed. D. Whitelock, M. Brett and C.N.L. Brooke (Oxford, 1981), no. 33, 143–54. See most recently Pratt, 'Voice of the King'.

[60] M. Clayton, '*De Duodecim Abusiuis*, Lordship and Kingship in Anglo-Saxon England', in *Saints and Scholars: New Perspectives on Anglo-Saxon Literature and Culture in Honour of Hugh Magennis*, ed. S. McWilliams (Woodbridge, 2012), 141–63. See further below, Chapter 3, pp. 113–14.

[61] *IV Eg*, prol. (ed. Liebermann, I, 206–7). See Whitelock, *EHD*, 434; Keynes, 'Edgar', 11–12; and Pratt, 'Voice of the King', 169–70; and cf. Wormald, *English Law*, 441–2, who prefers a later date.

Reform evidently sat well alongside Edgar's other endeavours. He was a powerful monarch and his later epithet, *pacificus*, is best rendered 'peace-maker', not 'the peaceable' (as has become conventional): it implies the ability to ensure peace by means of force. At the same time, Edgar was a deeply religious king, who believed that his successes were owed in no small part to piety and support for reform. He bears comparison with the great Carolingian ruler Charlemagne, who dominated much of western Europe in the late eighth and early ninth centuries: a powerful, at times overbearing monarch, one who centralized administration but also patronized learning and renewed religion.[62]

Family and faction: Æthelred at the court of King Edgar

Edgar's reign not only provides the context for Æthelred's birth and youth, but also sets the scene for his later reign: administrative centralization and monastic reform were the order of the day and these must have informed the young prince's understanding and expectations of royal rule. As noted, the English kingdom had been divided in the later 950s and it was only the chance death of Eadwig which enabled unity to be re-established in 959. While recent studies have done much to rehabilitate Eadwig's brief reign, the division of the realm at this point reflects fundamental fault-lines within England's ruling elite. Nowhere are these clearer than in the career of the later archbishop Dunstan, who was driven from Eadwig's court in 956, only to be welcomed back with open arms by Edgar just over a year later. Further signs of tension come from the property transactions undertaken by Eadwig, many of which overturned acts of his predecessors; a changing of the guard was taking place, with new favourites emerging and being rewarded with the lands and rights of old associates.[63] Edgar may have initially found support amongst the families of the dispossessed, but it would be misleading

[62] R. McKitterick, *Charlemagne: The Formation of a European Identity* (Cambridge, 2008).

[63] S. Keynes, 'Eadwig (*c.* 940–959)', in *ODNB*, XVII, 539–42. See also P. Wormald, 'The Strange Affair of the Selsey Bishopric, 953–963', in *Belief and Culture in the Middle Ages: Studies Presented to Henry Mayr-Harting*, ed. R. Gameson and H. Leyser (Oxford, 2001), 128–41; and R. Lavelle, 'Royal Control and the Disposition of Estates in Tenth-Century England: Reflections on the Charters of King Eadwig (955–959)', *HSJ* 23 (2014), 23–49.

to see his accession in 959 as a simple return to the *status quo ante*; there is little evidence of direct hostility between Edgar and his elder brother, and most of the latter's favourites found acceptance (and continued patronage) at Edgar's court. Still, there can be little doubt that beneath the calm façade of Edgar's reign lurked lingering tensions, tensions which found expression in part through the king's complex marital politics.

Edgar is associated with at least three different women – Æthelflæd, Wulfthryth and Ælfthryth – and the reasons behind this serial monogamy have been the subject of much speculation.[64] These matches were presumably contracted with political benefits in mind and it is noteworthy that they come towards the start of Edgar's reign, when the king was in greatest need of support. Æthelflæd, who is thought to have been Edgar's first consort, is reported by post-Conquest sources to have been the daughter 'of the most powerful Ealdorman Ordmær' (*Ordmeri ducis potentissimi*), apparently a man of some substance, perhaps in those regions first ruled by Edgar in 957–9.[65] It has been suggested that this individual was an associate of Ealdorman Æthelstan Half-King and his family, who had enjoyed a dominant position in East Anglia since the 930s. An East Anglian nobleman of this name is indeed mentioned in the *Libellus Æthelwoldi* – a post-Conquest Latin text, based on an earlier vernacular work written in Ely (perhaps *c.* 986 × 996) – and this has been taken as confirmation of the identification.[66] Plausible though this may be, it is not without problems: the Ordmær mentioned in the *Libellus* is clearly not an ealdorman, and it may be that later writers confused traditions relating to Æthelflæd with those concerning Edgar's more famous third wife, Ælfthryth, whose father was indeed an ealdorman and bore the similar name Ordgar. In any case, Æthelflæd was certainly of noble stock and it was with her that Edgar's first son, Edward, was born, probably in the late 950s or early 960s. What became of her is unclear: it is conceivable that Edgar dissolved the marriage

---

[64] S. Jayakumar, 'The Politics of the English Kingdom, *c.* 955–*c.* 978' (DPhil diss., Univ. of Oxford, 2001), 174–228. See also B. Yorke, 'The Women in Edgar's Life', in *Edgar, King of the English 959–75: New Interpretations*, ed. D. Scragg (Woodbridge, 2008), 143–57.

[65] William of Malmesbury, *Gesta regum Anglorum* II.159 (ed. Mynors, 258–60); John of Worcester, *Chronicon, s.a.* 964, ed. R.R. Darlington and P. McGurk (Oxford, 1995), 416.

[66] *Libellus Æthelwoldi episcopi*, ch. 5 (= *Liber Eliensis* II.7, ed. E.O. Blake, Camden Society 3rd ser. 92 [London, 1962], 79–80); with Jayakumar, 'Politics', 199–208, esp. 202–3.

in favour of a more advantageous match (perhaps soon after acceding to the southern part of the kingdom in 959); however, it is equally possible that she passed away in the early 960s (perhaps in childbirth, as Cyril Hart has suggested).[67] Edgar's other early consort, Wulfthryth, was raised at Wilton and later retired there. Her background is obscure, but her association with one of the kingdom's most important nunneries indicates elevated status and it has been suggested that she belonged to a local noble family, perhaps that of the Wihtbord who makes an appearance in the Fonthill Letter, an earlier document pertaining to a dispute in the reign of Edward the Elder (c. 910).[68] Wulfthryth certainly enjoyed close connections with Wilton, where her daughter with Edgar, Edith, went on to be abbess. How and when this match was contracted and broken off is unclear – indeed, it is not entirely certain that it constituted a formal marriage (certainly, later writers saw herein a stain upon the king).[69] There would be nothing unusual in this: marriage was not yet a formal institution and it was common for noblemen to enter and dissolve matches swiftly.[70] The political implications of marriage encouraged such serial monogamy; since unions amongst the nobility were political acts, they naturally shifted alongside other political constellations. This can be seen amongst Edgar's continental counterparts: Henry I of East Francia (Germany) (919–36) famously repudiated his first wife once it became clear that he would be sole heir to his father (as a third son, there was little reason to anticipate this), meanwhile Robert the Pious of France (996–1031) went through no fewer than three wives in his quest for an heir.[71] It may, therefore, be that as Edgar's star began to rise

---

[67] C.[R.] Hart, 'Edward (c.962–978)', in *ODNB*, XVII, 783–5.

[68] Jayakumar, 'Politics', 189–98. See also York, 'Women', 144–5.

[69] Osbern of Canterbury, *Vita S. Dunstani*, ch. 35, ed. W. Stubbs, *Memorials of Saint Dunstan*, Rolls Series (London, 1874), 111–12; Eadmer of Canterbury, *Vita S. Dunstani*, ch. 56, ed. A.J. Turner and B.J. Muir, *Eadmer of Canterbury: Lives and Miracles of Saints Oda, Dunstan, and Oswald* (Oxford, 2006), 134–6; William of Malmesbury, *Gesta regum Anglorum* II.158 (ed. Mynors, 258). However, see B. Yorke, 'The Legitimacy of St Edith', *HSJ* 11 (1998), 97–113.

[70] D.L. d'Avray, *Medieval Marriage: Symbolism and Society* (Oxford, 2005), 74–99; R.M. Karras, *Unmarriages: Women, Men, and Sexual Unions in the Middle Ages* (Philadelphia, PA, 2012), esp. 25–67.

[71] M. Becher, *Otto der Große. Kaiser und Reich: Eine Biographie* (Munich, 2012), 69–71; G. Duby, *The Knight, the Lady and the Priest: The Making of Marriage in Medieval France*, trans. B. Bray (New York, 1983), 75–85.

his earlier matches were no longer deemed appropriate; certainly, his third wife, Ælfthryth, was cut from a different cloth.

That we know so much more about Ælfthryth is no accident: she was clearly a force to be reckoned with and her legacy casts a long shadow over Æthelred's reign. Her family was amongst the most powerful in southern England. Her father, Ordgar, hailed from the south-west and appears as ealdorman of the region from 964 (a promotion he perhaps owed to his daughter's marriage in this year). Ælfthryth herself had earlier been married to Ealdorman Æthelwold of East Anglia, the eldest son of the formidable Half-King, whose family enjoyed a key position in the eastern Danelaw.[72] From the start Ælfthryth's actions suggest a degree of confidence unusual in a royal wife and her reign has been identified as a decisive moment in the development of the office of queen.[73] Before this, royal consorts had not wielded much power in England. Asser, the Welsh biographer of Alfred the Great, famously wrote of the 'wrongful' tradition of the West Saxons, according to which royal consorts were denied the title 'queen', being styled 'the king's wife' (*regis coniunx*) instead. The reason was reportedly that the wife of Beorhtric, who had ruled Wessex in the late eighth century (786–802), had behaved tyrannically, eventually killing her own husband by mistake (the poison he imbibed was actually intended for another, who also died as a result of her machinations); his successors had therefore sought to curtail their wives' influence in order to prevent a repeat. While this story contains legendary elements, it speaks volumes of the ambiguous position of the royal consort at Alfred's court – she was not an office-holder in her own right and owed what influence she enjoyed to her husband.[74] Indeed, as Pauline Stafford has shown, queenship was slow to evolve in England and throughout the ninth and early tenth centuries few royal spouses made a real mark on the historical record. The relatively low standing of these figures is reflected in the documentary record: they rarely appear as witnesses

---

[72] C.R. Hart, 'Athelstan "Half King" and his Family' (1973), rev. and repr. in his *The Danelaw* (London, 1992), 569–604.

[73] P. Stafford, *Queen Emma and Queen Edith: Queenship and Women's Power in Eleventh-Century England* (Oxford, 1997), 162–4.

[74] Asser, *Vita Alfredi regis*, chs. 13–14, ed. W.H. Stevenson with an introduction by D. Whitelock, *Asser's Life of King Alfred* (Oxford, 1959), 10–13.

to royal diplomas, and when they do they are invariably styled the 'king's wife' or 'king's mother', titles which underline their dependence on male relatives.[75] The partial exception, Eadgifu, the third wife of Edward the Elder, is telling: though she exerted great influence in the mid-tenth century, it was as a mother of kings, not as the wife of one – indeed, she may have owed much of her influence to her unusual longevity.[76]

As noted, Ælfthryth's reign represents something of a watershed in this regard. Why this should be so is a good question. In part, she was building on existing foundations: Eadgifu had cut quite a figure in the first half of the tenth century and may have helped prepare the ground for her later granddaughter-in-law. At least as important, however, were changing attitudes towards marriage. So long as it was possible to marry and discard consorts more or less at will, it was hard for the queen to establish any real purchase at court; her position was simply too fragile. As church teachings about the indissolubility of marriage began to make themselves felt, however, this played into the hands of aspiring royal wives. This process can be seen on the continent in the ninth century, when Lothar II (855–69), the grandson of Louis the Pious, who ruled over the region later known as Lotharingia ('the kingdom of Lothar': *regnum Hlotharii*) (Map 2), ran into major difficulties in his attempt to leave a childless union with Theutberga in favour of a match with his previous mistress Waldrada (with whom he already had a son); despite many years of trying, Lothar failed to gain ecclesiastical approval and eventually died without an heir in 869. Lothar's position was, admittedly, somewhat unusual, insofar as his uncles, who ruled the kingdoms to his immediate west and east, took every opportunity to undermine his position; nevertheless, his case illustrates how church regulations began to win ground, and how queens might benefit from this.[77] It is

---

[75] P. Stafford, 'The King's Wife in Wessex 800–1066' (1981), repr. in and cited from her *Gender, Family and the Legitimation of Power: England from the Ninth to the Early Twelfth Century* (Aldershot, 2006), no. IX. See also S. Keynes, *An Atlas of Attestations in Anglo-Saxon Charters, c. 670–1066*, rev. edn (Cambridge, 2002), tables XXXIa–XXXIc; and Stafford, *Queen Emma*, 162–206.

[76] However, our evidence for Edward's later years is scant and the foundations of Eadgifu's later prominence may lie here. Further discussion is to be anticipated from Megan Welton.

[77] K. Heidecker, *The Divorce of Lothar II: Christian Marriage and Political Power in the Carolingian World*, trans. T.M. Guest (Ithaca, NY, 2010).

probably no accident that the Ottonians, who ruled the remnants of Lothar's realm from the 920s onwards, held themselves to higher standards in this respect: they avoided illicit unions and only allowed legitimate heirs to succeed to royal office.[78] Their West Frankish (French) counterparts generally did likewise, though slightly more wiggle room remained here.[79] In England, which was not directly touched by the Carolingian reforms of the eighth and ninth centuries, such teachings took longer to take root, but by the mid-tenth we see signs of them doing so. Edgar's brother Eadwig had faced stern opposition to his marriage with the noblewoman Ælfgifu on grounds of consanguinity (that is, that the two were too closely related) and was eventually forced to give up the match.[80] This was the first time that such regulations had been imposed upon an English monarch and it is significant that it was Dunstan and Oda, the two great reformers, who headed the opposition. Marriage regulations seem to have been a particular concern of these prelates: prohibitions on incest are included amongst the 'Constitutions of Oda', a short selection of church regulations drawn up by the archbishop, and Adelard of Ghent reports that during his later pontificate Dunstan excommunicated a leading nobleman for an illicit union.[81] Such concepts thus seem to have come across the Channel along with reforming ideas. On the continent, queens and noblewomen had seen a steady rise in standing since the ninth century; tenth-century England was now moving in the same direction. We must, however, be wary of exaggerating the scale and pace of change; in his early years Edgar does not seem to have shied away from the serial monogamy characteristic of his West Saxon

---

[78] P. Corbet, *Autour de Burchard de Worms. L'Église allemande et les interdits de parenté (IXème–XIIème siècle)* (Frankfurt, 2001), 70 and 222–3; K. Ubl, 'Der kinderlose König. Ein Testfall für die Ausdifferenzierung des Politischen im 11. Jahrhundert', *HZ* 292 (2011), 323–63, at 343–4.

[79] K. Ubl, *Inzestverbot und Gesetzgebung. Die Konstruktion eines Verbrechens (300–1100)* (Berlin, 2008), 387–402. See further *ibid.*, 373–83 and 402–40; and C.B. Bouchard, *'Those of My Blood': Constructing Noble Families in Medieval Francia* (Philadelphia, PA, 2001), 39–58.

[80] *Early Lives*, ed. Winterbottom and Lapidge, xxx–xxxiii. See also C. Cubitt, 'Bishops and Succession Crises in Tenth- and Eleventh-Century England', in *Patterns of Episcopal Power: Bishops in Tenth and Eleventh Century Western Europe*, ed. L. Körntgen and D. Waßenhoven (Berlin, 2011), 111–26, at 114–15.

[81] 'Constitutions of Oda', ch. 7, ed. Whitelock, *Councils*, no. 20, 72–3; Adelard of Ghent, *Lectiones in depositione S. Dunstani*, ch. 12, ed. Winterbottom and Lapidge, *Early Lives*, 142–4.

forebears, indicating that there was some way to go yet. Still, this flurry of marriages predates the reform's greatest successes and it is probably no accident that Edgar's successors were more restrained in their marital politics (the Danish conqueror Cnut notwithstanding).

Ælfthryth's elevated position at court finds expression in a number of contemporary sources. Though neither of Edgar's earlier consorts had appeared in his diplomas, already in 964 Ælfthryth surfaces as the recipient of an estate at Aston Upthorpe (Berks.). The charter recording this grant only survives in the thirteenth-century Abingdon cartulary, but there is no reason to doubt its authenticity: the text's formulation finds broad parallels in other authentic acts of the period and there would have been little obvious reason to concoct such a document at a later date (it concerns a grant to a queen, not to Abingdon, and the estate in question is not listed amongst the abbey's later holdings). Though Ælfthryth's marriage is elsewhere placed in 965, this need not speak against the charter: the source in question is the 'Northern Recension' of the *Anglo-Saxon Chronicle*, which was drawn up in the early eleventh century at some remove from court.[82] Moreover, John of Worcester places the match in 964 (on what authority, we know not) and the promotion of Ordgar to ealdorman in this year would also seem to speak in favour of the date.[83] Indeed, the Aston Upthorpe charter is amongst the first – perhaps *the* first – which Ordgar attests in his new role, raising the possibility that his promotion coincided with the wedding itself. In any case, the diploma's text opens with a unique preamble reflecting upon the transitory nature of life, then noting that the king has undertaken this grant 'in praise of Christ, who said "they two shall be one flesh" [Matthew XIX.5, Mark X.8]' (*in laude Christi dicentis 'Erunt duo in carne una'*). This line is evidently an allusion to the couple's married status and the quotation itself is taken from Christ's meditation on the indissolubility of marriage (which itself echoes the language of Genesis II, the story of the making of Eve). In the main (or 'dispositive') section of the document Edgar

---

[82] *ASC* 965 D (ed. Cubbin, 46). See S. Keynes, 'Manuscripts of the *Anglo-Saxon Chronicle*', in *The Cambridge History of the Book in Britain*, I, *c.400–1100*, ed. R. Gameson (Cambridge, 2012), 537–52, at 545.

[83] John of Worcester, *Chronicon*, *s.a.* 964 (ed. Darlington and McGurk, 416); Keynes, *Atlas*, table LVI.

then goes on to address Ælfthryth as 'my consort' (*lateranea mea*), referring to her as his 'beloved' (*dilecta*) and associating the grant with 'my kingdom' (*regnum meum*) – all unmistakable signs of favour.[84] What is more, he emphasizes that he has undertaken this act 'at the advice of my followers, bishops, ealdormen and thegns' (*meorum consilio satellitum, pontificum, comitum, militum*); the new queen's elevation is thus explicitly sanctioned by the kingdom's great and good. It would not be going too far to see this diploma as a first expression of Ælfthryth's new position at court, something of a material and documentary corollary to her marriage. The queen's power and influence is revealed less by the grant itself (though the lands in question are not insignificant) than by the manner in which she is addressed: the biblical language of marriage frames the act, placing her legitimacy and association with the affairs of the realm beyond doubt.

There may be deeper resonances to this act. The charter's most recent editor, Susan Kelly, notes how 'appropriate' the opening quotation from Matthew is, suggesting that it may have been issued on the very occasion of the wedding.[85] This is a tempting proposition and it may be significant that a particularly large number of lay potentates attest the document, suggesting that it stems from an unusually large gathering. The biblical quotation with which it opens is, as noted, taken from Christ's meditation on the indissolubility of marriage (Matthew XIX.3–9), a fact which can hardly have escaped the notice of our draftsman – even if, as Kelly suggests, he drew these details from Gregory the Great's letter to Queen Bertha of Kent (as preserved in Bede's *Ecclesiastical History*).[86] Interestingly enough, the line in question is also found in Gregory's treatment of incest in the 'Little Book of Responses' (*Libellus responsionum*) he sent to Augustine of Canterbury (d. 604), which is also preserved in Bede's *Ecclesiastical History* (as well as independently) and was to form the basis of much early medieval canon (i.e. church) law on marriage.[87] In the aftermath of

---

[84] S 725 (*Abing* 101). On the estate itself, see M. Gelling, *Signposts to the Past: Place Names and the History of England*, 2ⁿᵈ edn (Chichester, 1988), 196–201.

[85] *Charters of Abingdon*, ed. Kelly, 405–6. See also Stafford, *Queen Emma*, 70–2.

[86] Bede, *Historia ecclesiastica gentis Anglorum* II.11, ed. B. Colgrave and R.A.B. Mynors (Oxford, 1969), 172–4.

[87] Bede, *Historia ecclesiastica* I.27 (ed. Colgrave and Mynors, 84); with Ubl, *Inzestverbot*, 220–7.

Eadwig's incestuous union, it would seem that such regulations were being more rigorously applied. What is more, given the diploma's immediate context, issued on the occasion of (or soon after) the king's third marriage in no more than five or six years (and the queen's second marriage in the same timespan), it is hard not to see herein a veiled allusion to Edgar's (and possibly also his new consort's) previous liaisons. If so, the message could hardly have been clearer: this union really was to last, even if the king's track record was not the best in this regard. It is hard to know whether to give credence to post-Conquest tales implicating Edgar in the death of Ælfthryth's first husband, Ealdorman Æthelwold – these smack suspiciously of the biblical story of David and Uriah – but if these do preserve genuine traditions, then there would have been all the more reason to emphasize the union's solemnity.[88] Indeed, though we do not know the fate of Edgar's first wife, his second was certainly still alive at this point and issues of legitimacy and indissolubility were therefore most topical. This diploma thus bears witness to a key moment in the development of the office of queen; it not only mirrors Ælfthryth's rise, but may also have contributed to this. It is a powerful public affirmation of her new role at court.

Given what we have already observed, it is tempting to suggest that the leaders of the monastic reform played a part in Ælfthryth's rise, and perhaps even lay behind this unique document. Simon MacLean argues that the queen and her associates derived some of their ideas about queenship from the continent, where since the 950s Gerberga had exerted a similar kind of influence in West Francia, above all as a patron of reform.[89] A key player in this respect must have been Æthelwold of Winchester: although he is not

[88] William of Malmesbury, *Gesta regum Anglorum* II.157 (ed. Mynors, 256–8). Though Jayakumar, 'Eadwig and Edgar', 96–8, is prepared to accept the tale, I would urge caution. Certainly, Ælfric's *De oatione Moysi*, which Jayakumar reads as a critique of Edgar, seems more likely to represent a commentary on Æthelred's actions in the 980s: see below, Chapter 4, p. 165.

[89] S. MacLean, 'Monastic Reform and Royal Ideology in the Late Tenth Century: Ælfthryth and Edgar in Continental Perspective', in *England and the Continent in the Tenth Century: Studies in Honour of Wilhelm Levison (1876–1947)*, ed. D.[W.] Rollason, C. Leyser and H. Williams (Turnhout, 2010), 255–74. See also S. MacLean, 'Reform, Queenship and the End of the World in Tenth-Century France: Adso's "Letter on the Origin and Time of the Antichrist" Reconsidered', *Revue belge de philologie et d'histoire* 86 (2008), 645–75.

amongst those known to have objected to Eadwig's marriage, he had been Edgar's tutor and was to be one of Ælfthryth's closest associates. Æthelwold himself was in close contact with reformers elsewhere, including Abbot Womar of St-Peter's, Ghent (953–80), who was an associate of Queen Gerberga. Another model may have been the Ottonian court, where Adelheid had risen to prominence in the 950s and enjoyed imperial consecration in Rome alongside her husband in 962, only two years before these events. Adelheid herself was in close contact with the continental reformers and her stepson Liudolf (d. 957) was Edgar's cousin.[90] It is, therefore, interesting to note that the document survives in the archive of Æthelwold's first foundation, Abingdon, with which the bishop maintained close ties following his elevation to Winchester; if he had indeed had a hand in its production, it would make sense that it should later find its way to this centre (possibly along with the estate in question). In the diploma itself the queen is given the title *lateranea*, a rare variant of *conlateranea* ('consort'), which may also point in this direction: such recherché vocabulary is characteristic of the hermeneutic style promoted by Æthelwold and the reformers and the term *conlateranea* is used to describe Eve in the so-called *Orthodoxorum* charters, a group of forgeries produced at Abingdon and related houses in the late tenth and early eleventh centuries.[91] Æthelwold's own first-person (or 'subjective') subscription to the charter, which immediately follows those of Edgar and Archbishop Dunstan, is suggestive of a particular involvement in the transaction, reinforcing the impression that he stands behind it.[92] Though such indications hardly amount to certainty, they point tantalizingly towards Æthelwold and his circle. It would, therefore, not be surprising if this extraordinary document had been drawn up by someone with close ties to the prelate (though conceivably also in royal employ).

The first charter issued by the newly married Edgar thus sends a powerful message: it establishes Ælfthryth's position at court beyond all

---

[90] S. Weinfurter, 'Kaiserin Adelheid und das ottonische Kaisertum' (1999), repr. in and cited from his *Gelebte Ordnung, gedachte Ordnung. Ausgewählte Beiträge zu König, Kirche und Reich* (Sigmaringen, 2005), 189–212.

[91] S 658 (*Abing*), S 673 (*Abing* 84), S 786 (BCS 1282), S 812 (BCS 1187), S 876 (*Abing* 124). Of these, only the last is likely to be authentic: see below, Chapter 4, pp. 143–5.

[92] On such statements, which must be taken with a pinch of salt, see Keynes, *Diplomas*, 26–8.

doubt and distinguishes this implicitly (but unmistakably) from that of the king's previous consorts. This is not the only evidence that Ælfthryth's position differed from that of her predecessors. Alone of Edgar's marriages this match warranted inclusion in the 'Northern Recension' of the *Anglo-Saxon Chronicle*, compiled some years later under the oversight of Wulfstan II of York. The provision for the consecration of a queen alongside the king in the revised version of the 'Second English *Ordo*', produced around this time and designed to provide instructions for royal coronations, suggests that Ælfthryth may have been the first royal consort anointed into her office (perhaps even on two separate occasions, like her husband).[93] Indeed, given the close association between marriage and consecration where queens were concerned (the former frequently paved the way for the latter), it is tempting to suggest that Ælfthryth underwent these rites at this point. This might explain why whereas Edgar's previous wives did not attest his diplomas, Ælfthryth does so quite often, frequently subscribing as 'queen' (*regina*) (rather than 'the king's wife').[94] Further signs of elevated standing come from her judicial activity: unlike most other royal consorts, Ælfthryth was active in the role of legal advocate (*forespeca*), intervening on behalf of associates and (in particular) noblewomen.[95] Echoes of her new-found status can even be detected in the writings of Ælfric of Eynsham, who studied under Æthelwold at Winchester in these years: as Stacy Klein notes, the homilist shows a pronounced interest in queens and queenship.[96]

Ælfthryth's power and influence was doubtless helped by the fact that she soon produced prospective heirs: by 966 at the latest she had born Edgar a first son, Edmund, and a second soon followed, Æthelred (966 × 969). Given the preference for fraternal succession in this period, it is likely that both were envisaged as throne-worthy heirs and their names

[93] J.L. Nelson, 'The Second English *Ordo*', in her *Politics and Ritual in Early Medieval Europe* (London, 1986), 361–74, at 372–4; Stafford, *Queen Emma*, 62–3 and 162–4.

[94] Keynes, *Atlas of Attestations*, tables XXXIa–XXXIc. The only royal woman to be granted the title of queen before this point is Eadgifu, and then only in a blatant forgery: S 477 (*CantCC* 111).

[95] A. Rabin, 'Female Advocacy and Royal Protection in Tenth-Century England: The Career of Queen Ælfthryth', *Speculum* 84 (2009), 261–88.

[96] S. Klein, *Ruling Women: Queenship and Gender in Anglo-Saxon Literature* (Notre Dame, IN, 2006), 125–90.

suggest as much: the former received the name of his paternal grandfather, Edmund (939–46), while the latter was apparently named after Alfred the Great's elder brother (and immediate predecessor), Æthelred I (866–71). There is, however, no mistaking the relative hierarchy: as the second son of this union (and Edgar's third in all), Æthelred received the more obscure designation, that of a scion of the family which had lost out to Alfred and his heirs in the early tenth century. While male offspring may have strengthened the queen's hand, they are likely to have intensified any tensions arising from her rise. Indeed, when medieval rulers married a second or third time, the offspring of previous unions often felt threatened, and understandably so; though their chances of succession were not immediately undermined, the existence of alternative heirs could weaken their position, as could the presence of an influential stepmother at court whose interests lay in the succession of her own children. The kind of difficulties which might result are revealed by Louis the Pious's reign in the early ninth century: soon after his accession Louis took a second wife, Judith, with whom he went on to have a son, the future Charles the Bald (840–77). Yet when the emperor sought to carve out an inheritance for Charles, his other sons led a serious uprising and Louis's final decade on the throne was dominated by speculation over the succession.[97] Similar trends can be seen in the reign of Edgar's East Frankish counterpart, Otto I (936–73). Otto first married an English princess, Eadgyth (Edith) c. 928/9, with whom he had a son, Liudolf; however, following the queen's death in 946, Otto married the wealthy Burgundian heiress Adelheid (952), with whom he had another son, the future Otto II (973–83). Liudolf, who had been designated his father's heir shortly before this marriage, clearly felt threatened by these developments – as well as by the rising star of his uncle, Duke Henry of Bavaria, who was an associate of Adelheid – and his response was to lead an uprising which shook the Ottonian realm to its very foundations.[98] That Edgar's eldest son, Edward (probably born

[97] J.L. Nelson, *Charles the Bald* (London, 1992), 75–104; B. Schneidmüller, *Die Welfen. Herrschaft und Erinnerung* (Stuttgart, 2000), 51–8. Issues of succession were, however, only one of many factors; see M. de Jong, *The Penitential State: Authority and Atonement in the Age of Louis the Pious*, 814–40 (Cambridge, 2009), for a masterful account.

[98] Becher, *Otto der Große*, 158–85. See also K.J. Leyser, *Rule and Conflict in an Early Medieval Society: Ottonian Saxony* (London, 1979), 9–31.

c. 959 × 962), watched such developments with unease therefore stands to reason. He certainly had grounds for concern. As we have seen, Ælfthryth periodically attests her husband's charters as *regina*, a title which may have been felt to convey a greater degree of legitimacy on her and her offspring. That in some eyes this was so is suggested by the New Minster refoundation charter of 966. The witness-list of this document, which as we have noted was probably drafted by Æthelwold, opens with the king, followed by Archbishop Dunstan and then the royal family: the young princes (or æthelings, to use the Old English term),[99] followed by the queen and Edgar's grandmother Eadgifu. This ordering is in itself interesting, since royal kin normally attest either above or below the archbishops and bishops (rather than between them). More significant, however, is the order of attestation within this group: Ælfthryth's son, Edmund, subscribes first, ahead of his elder half-brother Edward; moreover, Edmund is styled 'legitimate son of the aforementioned king' (*legitimus prefati regis filius*), whereas Edward is simply said to be 'begotten by the same king' (*eodem rege . . . procreatus*). Ælfthryth's own attestation, which immediately follows, is similarly revealing: she is styled 'legitimate wife of the king' (*legitima prefati regis coniunx*). The implied deficit in Edward's lineage is palpable and his belittlement even takes on a visual guise: alone amongst the members of the royal family the gold cross next to Edward's name is not filled in.[100]

The witness-list of the New Minster charter is thus suggestive of an ongoing effort to emphasize the legitimacy of Ælfthryth and her offspring to the detriment of Edward. In this respect, it is significant that the document is associated with Æthelwold, one of Ælfthryth's closest allies.[101] The prominence given to Ælfthryth in the *Regularis concordia*, another key document of the reform whose text has been attributed to Æthelwold, should be viewed in this light: here the queen is given oversight of all female monastic houses and the kingdom's monks (and nuns) are requested to pray for her alongside

---

[99] D.N. Dumville, 'The Ætheling: A Study in Anglo-Saxon Constitutional History', *ASE* 8 (1979), 1–33.

[100] BL Cotton Vespasian A. viii, fol. 30v; with Williams, *Æthelred*, 2.

[101] B. Yorke, 'Æthelwold and the Politics of the Tenth Century', in *Bishop Æthelwold: His Career and Influence*, ed. B. Yorke (Woodbridge, 1988), 65–88, at 81–6.

her husband.[102] The association between Æthelwold and the queen can also be seen in the *Libellus Æthelwoldi*, which records Ælfthryth making and petitioning a number of grants on Æthelwold's and Ely's behalf.[103] That the queen was indeed seeking to pave the way for her sons' accession may also be suggested by the will of Ealdorman Ælfheah of Wessex (the elder brother of Ælfhere of Mercia), which makes bequests to Edmund and Æthelred, but omits all reference to their elder half-brother.[104] Though Æthelred was probably too young to have been entirely aware of these developments, the passing of Edmund in 971 or 972 would have changed this; it catapulted the young prince into consideration for the succession. Before this point he had been the king's third son and at best second in line for the throne (after Edmund); now he was one of only two contenders, and one with a powerful backer at court at that. Æthelred would have been between two and six at this time and this may have been one of his formative memories: the moment the hopes and dreams of his mother came to rest on his shoulders alone. Certainly, Ælfthryth is unlikely to have given up her plans easily and, as we shall see, a party did indeed support Æthelred's candidacy come 975. How the young prince felt about this is hard to say; perhaps he resented the pressure, perhaps he revelled in it. Either way, strong bonds were formed with his mother, bonds which would be of great moment in future years. Still, not all shared Ælfthryth's vision for the future: Edward – whose name is also unmistakably royal, recalling that of his great-grandfather – is given precedence over his younger brothers in all other contemporary charters, suggesting that most – probably including the king – continued to see him as Edgar's natural heir. The compiler of a royal genealogy in the later 960s clearly felt likewise, since he states baldly that 'Edward and Edmund and Æthelred the æthelings are the sons of King Edgar' (*Eadweard 7 Eadmund 7 Æðelred æðelingas syndon Eadgares suna cyninges*); here Edward is accorded precedence and no distinction is acknowledged between the two branches of the family.[105]

---

[102] *Regularis concordia*, ch. 3 (ed. Symons and Spath, 70). See also above, n. XXX.

[103] *Libellus Æthelwoldi episcopi*, chs. 41, 49, 51, 58 (*Liber Eliensis* II.31, 37, 39, 47, ed. Blake, 105, 111–12, 116).

[104] S 1485 (*Anglo-Saxon Wills*, ed. D. Whitelock [Cambridge, 1930], no. 9).

[105] BL Cotton Tiberius B. v, vol. 1, fol. 23r. See Dumville, 'The Ætheling', 4–5.

One imagines, therefore, that Edward had his own supporters. If later events are anything to go by, Dunstan is likely to have been amongst these, as may have been the sons of Æthelstan Half-King, who since the rise of Ælfhere of Mercia had been forced to take something of a back seat in national politics. Many of these factions go back to Eadwig's reign, as Shashi Jayakumar notes: Ælfthryth was backed primarily by individuals who had risen to prominence under Eadwig, whereas Edward's allies seem to have been recruited from amongst the 'old guard' which had run the realm under Edmund and Eadred.[106] Thus, while some were busy advancing Æthelred's cause, others stood against him, and one imagines that the atmosphere at court was tense during the prince's early years: different groups were jostling for power and influence and no-one was certain which way the succession would go. We know nothing concrete about Æthelred's relationship with his half-brother, but it must have been strained, and probably became more so with every passing year: the older Æthelred was, the more viable his candidacy. It would, however, be misleading to present the factions of this period in monolithic terms; although Dunstan's and Æthelwold's political allegiances were apparently at odds, their biographers present them as close friends and there is no reason to doubt this.[107] Furthermore, Ælfthryth's rise need not have been directly to the detriment of the family of the Half-King (as is often presumed) – while she was a close associate of Ælfhere of Mercia and his family, who in some respects replaced that of Æthelstan, her first husband had been a son of the East Anglian ealdorman and it may be that she remained on good terms with the family thereafter (whatever post-Conquest historians would have us believe). Even the evidence of tensions between Ælfhere and the sons of the Half-King, though suggestive, is hardly iron-clad, and we must allow for the possibility that these figures were sometimes on cordial or even amicable terms; factions were fluid and Edgarian politics were more than a story of two opposing camps.[108] There was doubt-

---

[106] Jayakumar, 'Politics', 187–212 and 301–3.

[107] Wulfstan Cantor, *Vita S. Æthelwoldi*, ch. 14 (ed. Lapidge and Winterbottom, 24–6); Adelard of Ghent, *Lectiones in depositione S. Dunstan*, ch. 7 (ed. Winterbottom and Lapidge, 130–2). Cf. Yorke, 'Æthelwold', 86–8.

[108] S. Ashley, 'The Lay Intellectual in Anglo-Saxon England: Ealdorman Æthelweard and the Politics of History', in *Lay Intellectuals in the Carolingian World*, ed. P. Wormald and J.L. Nelson (Cambridge, 2007), 218–44, at 224–30.

less some speculation as to who would succeed Edgar, and Ælfthryth clearly tried to improve the chances of her sons whenever she could; nevertheless, there must often have been more pressing matters for which co-operation across factional lines was required. Indeed, Edgar acceded as a young man and there was every reason to believe that he would go on to enjoy a long and fruitful reign; his death in 975 at the age of only thirty-two must have come as something of an unpleasant surprise.

This was the world into which Æthelred was born. We hear little of the young prince in these early years – even the witness-lists of charters fall silent where he and his half-brother are concerned. As noted, this is not surprising: we have relatively few sources for this period, and in any case we scarcely know more about the youth of any other Anglo-Saxon monarch (save perhaps Alfred the Great, for whom we have the singular good fortune of possessing a contemporary biography). However, what we lack in certain knowledge can be compensated for with prudent specula-tion. We can be certain that Æthelred was influenced by the political and intellectual atmosphere at Edgar's court. Monastic reform must have been a major factor here: as a movement supported by Æthelred's father and mother, we can safely presume that the prince was raised to respect and value reformed monks. In fact, it is possible that he was tutored by Æthelwold of Winchester: as the leading reformer and a close associate of Ælfthryth, not to mention Edgar's own sometime tutor, he would have been the ideal candidate.[109] It was common for queens to take a leading role in their sons' education – Alfred the Great was to remember his own mother fondly in this guise[110] – and all indications are that Ælfthryth did likewise: the close, at times fraught relationship between her and Æthelred in future years speaks of genuine intimacy, one presumably borne of expe-riences in these early years. Æthelred would later entrust her with raising his own sons, a decision which further suggests that she played a part in

---

[109] Interestingly, Æthelwold is recorded as having brought Æthelred to Ely during Edward the Martyr's reign (975–8), perhaps indicating a degree of responsibility for the young prince: see below, Chapter 2, p. 71. Cf. *Regularis concordia*, ch. 1 (ed. Symons and Spath, 69); 'Edgar's Establishment of Monasteries' (ed. Whitelock, 146).

[110] Asser, *Vita Ælfredi regis*, ch. 23 (ed. Stevenson, 20).

his upbringing. Certainly, the young prince will have received a sound education and it stands to reason that he acquired some level of literacy in Old English and perhaps also Latin: there was a dynastic tradition where learning was concerned – Alfred the Great is said to have translated a number of works into Old English, and many of his successors are known to have owned or donated books – and we know that the nobleman (and royal relative) Æthelweard (d. 998) achieved an impressive command of the complex hermeneutic Latin preferred by the reformers in these years.[111] His core education, however, will have taken place outside the classroom: as with other noblemen, training in arms, hunting and riding would have begun at a young age and continued into Æthelred's teenage years. Where this education took place is hard to say. His earliest years would have been spent largely with his mother. They presumably spent much time at and around the royal court as it traversed the West Saxon heartlands of Wiltshire, Hampshire, Somerset and Dorset. Queens were, however, not always with their husbands, and there will have been periods of time which Ælfthryth and Æthelred spent apart from the king, probably on the queen's own lands. Interestingly, Ælfthryth is later recorded as possessing a large estate called *Æthelingadene*, i.e. 'the valley of the princes' (probably now Dean in Sussex). This name suggests an association with royal offspring, and while the estate is generally identified as where Ælfthryth raised her grandchildren, the 'princes' in question could just as well have been Æthelred and his brother Edmund.[112] In any case, as he grew older, Æthelred may have been fostered out to one of the kingdom's leading noble families to complete his education (as his father had been to Æthelstan Half-King); in fact, it may be such a relationship that

---

[111] D. Pratt, 'Kings and Books in Anglo-Saxon England', *ASE* 43 (2014), 297–377, esp. 322–33; M. Gretsch, 'Historiography and Literary Patronage in Late Anglo-Saxon England: The Evidence of Æthelweard's *Chronicon*', *ASE* 41 (2012), 205–48. See further D. Pratt, *The Political Thought of King Alfred the Great* (Cambridge, 2007). Though questions have been raised as to the degree of 'Alfredian' involvement in the translations ascribed to the king, he was certainly remembered as a learned ruler in Æthelred's day: M. Godden, 'Did King Alfred Write Anything?', *Medium Ævum* 76 (2007), 1–23; J. Bately, 'Did King Alfred Actually Translate Anything? The Integrity of the Alfredian Canon Revisited', *Medium Ævum* 78 (2009), 189–215.

[112] S 904 (KCD 707); with Keynes, *Diplomas*, 187, n. 117; and Stafford, *Queen Emma*, 130, n. 173.

underpinned the alliance between his mother and the family of Ælfhere, whose brother Ælfheah is recorded as the queen's 'co-parent' and may thus have been Æthelred's or Edmund's godfather.[113]

Other influences on the young Æthelred will have been more overtly 'political' in nature: the pomp and circumstance of Edgar's court, particularly in its later years, must have made an impact on the boy, as too must the administrative developments of the age. The growing sense of Englishness which can be discerned from the time of Æthelstan onwards will also have had its part to play. Finally, we should imagine that the world of faction and intrigue traced over the last few pages left its mark. Indeed, though we should not exaggerate the degree of tension in these years, it would be equally foolish to deny it; medieval courts were places of intrigue and death often struck unexpectedly (none of Edgar's immediate male relatives had lived past their early thirties). There was, therefore, all to play for and anything could happen once 'the hungry athelings began to prowl' (as Kenneth Harrison memorably put it).[114]

[113] See below, Chapter 2, p. 62.
[114] K. Harrison, *The Framework of Anglo-Saxon History to AD 900* (Cambridge, 1976), 92.

'WOE TO THEE, OH LAND, WHEN THY KING IS A CHILD'

Succession and dispute, 975–84

Edgar's later years saw the apogee of his reign: he oversaw a growing number of reformed monastic houses (a responsibility formalized in the *Regularis concordia*), he overhauled the kingdom's coinage, and in 973 he held an exalted 'second coronation' at Bath followed by a meeting at Chester with the neighbouring rulers of Wales and northern Britain. It must, therefore, have come as something of a surprise when he died only two years later. That this was not foreseen is suggested by the consequences: England descended into the first major succession crisis in half a century. The parties which emerged owed much to earlier factions, though, as we have seen, these may not have been as stable as is sometimes presumed. Royal successions were the flashpoints of medieval politics: since rulership depended heavily on inter-personal bonds, the kingdom's power structures were subject to sudden and substantial change following the death of a monarch. Such tensions were exacerbated when there was more than one contender for the crown, as was the case in 975.

This chapter examines the fall-out of this. The first section is dedicated to the succession dispute itself, while the second deals with the attacks on monasteries visible in these years. Further sections then consider the core events of Edward's reign (975–8), ending in his tragic martyrdom, and the earliest years of Æthelred's own reign (978–84), which were dominated by a *de facto* regency led by Ælfthryth and her associates.

Crisis and consolidation, 975

Our main sources for the years following Edgar's death are a few laconic entries in the various different versions of the *Anglo-Saxon Chronicle*, supplemented with the more detailed description of events in Byrhtferth of Ramsey's *Life* of Oswald of York and the testimony of a handful of surviving authentic charters. The *Chronicle* entries for 975 vary in length and detail, but not in gist. They report the death of Edgar and succession of Edward, along with the sighting of a comet and other disturbances.[1] Cosmic phenomena attracted great interest from medieval chroniclers, who saw them as portents. The great Northumbrian scholar Bede (d. 735) and following him Byrhtferth of Ramsey (d. *c.* 1016) associated comets with pestilence, famine, war or a change of regime, and the relevance of this to the events of 975, which saw Edgar's death, famine and other tribulations should be clear.[2] Paramount amongst these troubles were the expulsion of Oslac, earl of York, and attacks on monastic houses. This is all highly suggestive, and it is not hard to read between the lines into the broader political divisions visible at this point. Nevertheless, no mention is made of a succession dispute *per se*, a fact which is all the more striking in the light of Byrhtferth's testimony in which this looms large. It may be that these events were simply too raw: the main *Chronicle*-account takes the form of a verse eulogy for Edgar, composed before Edward's death (975 × 978); at this point it may have seemed politic to pass over the rival claims of the ruler's half-brother in silence.[3] As noted, more detail is provided by Byrhtferth of Ramsey's *Life* of Oswald, written a quarter of a century later (995 × 1005, probably 997 × 1002).[4] This reports that following Edgar's death there was uncertainty as to who should accede, with many supporting Edward but others preferring his younger half-brother due to Æthelred's

---

[1] *ASC* 975 ABC (ed. Bately, 76–8), 975 DE (ed. Cubbin, 47).

[2] Bede, *De natura rerum*, ch. 24, ed. C.W. Jones, CCSL 123A (Turnhout, 1975), 216; Byrhtferth, *Enchiridion* II.3, ed. P.S. Baker and M. Lapidge, EETS s.s. 15 (Oxford, 1995), 120–1.

[3] On the dating, see S.T. Scott, 'The Edgar Poems and the Poetics of Failure in the *Anglo-Saxon Chronicle*', *ASE* 39 (2010), 105–37, at 107–8; and cf. M. Salvador-Bello, 'The Edgar Panegyrics in the Anglo-Saxon Chronicle', in *Edgar, King of the English 959–75: New Interpretations*, ed. D. Scragg (Woodbridge, 2008), 252–72, at 254–5.

[4] *Byrhtferth of Ramsey*, ed. Lapidge, xxxvi–xxxviii.

more gentle nature.[5] Byrhtferth's testimony is telling. It indicates that Edward was indeed seen as Edgar's natural successor, since Æthelred's claim had to be justified. What is more, it preserves some of the arguments adduced in Æthelred's favour. Suitability for office, emphasized in this account, was certainly a serious consideration: rules of succession had yet to be formalized and a combination of seniority, legitimacy and suitability could all play an important part in choosing a king.[6] That issues of legitimacy were indeed at stake is likely, despite Byrhtferth's silence on the subject (perhaps out of respect for Edward, who by the 990s had come to be venerated as a saint): the post-Conquest accounts of Osbern and Eadmer make this the main bone of contention and, as we have seen, Ælfthryth had been angling for the succession of her sons for some time.[7]

Byrhtferth does not identify the leaders of the different factions, but we can make informed guesses. As we have seen, Æthelwold of Winchester was sympathetic to the claims of Ælfthryth's sons and we would not go far wrong in seeing in him one of the leading advocates of Æthelred's cause. Other likely supporters include the family of Ealdorman Ælfhere, whose brother Ælfheah had left bequests to Ælfthryth and her sons in his will and who is said to have been the queen's 'co-parent' (Old English: gefæðeran), a term indicating that either Ælfthryth was godparent to one of Ælfheah's children, or vice-versa.[8] Ælfhere himself had been the leading ealdorman in Edgar's later years, controlling all of Mercia and perhaps also parts of central Wessex, and the ill reputation he later acquired amongst Oswald's circles may be a product of his support for Æthelred's candidacy.[9] Despite such exalted backing, Æthelred faced an uphill battle: he was but a boy – no more than nine (and perhaps only six or seven) to his half-brother's

[5] Byrhtferth of Ramsey, Vita S. Oswaldi IV.18 (ed. Lapidge, 136–8).

[6] A. Williams, 'Some Notes and Considerations on Problems Connected with the English Royal Succession, 860–1066', ANS 1 (1979), 144–67 and 225–33; Roach, Kingship and Consent, 149–52.

[7] Osbern, Vita S. Dunstani, ch. 35 (ed. Stubbs, 111–12); Eadmer, Vita S. Dunstani, ch. 59 (ed. Turner and Muir, 144–6). Note that Osbern and Eadmer differ in matters of detail: Keynes, Diplomas, 163–5.

[8] S 1485 (Wills, ed. Whitelock, no. 9); with J.H. Lynch, Christianizing Kinship: Ritual Sponsorship in Anglo-Saxon England (Ithaca, NY, 1998), 245–6.

[9] A. Williams, 'Princeps Merciorum gentis: The Family, Career and Connections of Ælfhere, Ealdorman of Mercia, 956–83', ASE 10 (1981), 143–72, at 160–1.

thirteen to sixteen – and Edward could also call upon prominent backers. Later accounts give Dunstan a leading role in the king's accession and they are probably not far wrong, since as archbishop it would have fallen on him to anoint Edward.[10] There are, moreover, scattered hints that Dunstan's politics were frequently at odds with those of Æthelwold, for all their shared reforming interests: whereas the latter had maintained good relations with Eadwig in the later 950s, forging bonds with newly appointed figures such as Ælfheah and Ælfhere and acknowledging the king's marriage to Ælfgifu, Dunstan was exiled for his opposition to this match and later conducted a campaign of *damnatio memoriae* (what we might now call a 'smear campaign') against the king.[11] Other backers of Edward probably included Bishop Sideman of Crediton, who Byrhtferth states had been his tutor, and Archbishop Oswald, whose kinsman Oda had also opposed Eadwig's marriage to Ælfgifu and whose Midlands houses suffered a number of reprisals from Ælfhere at this point. Amongst the aristocracy Edward may have also received support from Ealdorman Æthelwine of East Anglia, one of the sons and successors of the Half-King and an associate of Oswald.[12]

Although Æthelred was not to prevail, the fact that there was a succession dispute at all indicates that his mother's efforts had not been in vain – in spite of Edward's greater age, seeds of doubt had evidently been sown as to his legitimacy (and perhaps also suitability). It is interesting to note that a division of the realm, as implemented in 924 and 957–9, was not on the cards; following developments in the intervening years, it would seem that England, like its counterparts elsewhere in western Europe, had become

---

[10] *Passio S. Eadwardi regis et martyris*, ed. C.E. Fell, *Edward, King and Martyr* (Leeds, 1971), 2; Osbern, *Vita S. Dunstani*, ch. 37 (ed. Stubbs, 114); Eadmer, *Vita S. Dunstani*, ch. 59 (ed. Turner and Muir, 144); William of Malmesbury, *Vita S. Dunstani* II.18, ed. M. Winterbottom and R.M. Thomson, *William of Malmesbury: Saints' Lives* (Oxford, 2002), 268.

[11] Yorke, 'Æthelwold', esp. 87–8.

[12] Byrhtferth, *Vita S. Oswaldi* IV.8 (ed. Lapidge, 138); S. Jayakumar, 'Reform and Retribution: The "Anti-Monastic Reaction" in the Reign of Edward the Martyr', in *Early Medieval Studies in Memory of Patrick Wormald*, ed. S. Baxter *et al.* (Farnham, 2009), 337–52, at 348–9; D. Waßenhoven, 'The Role of Bishops in Anglo-Saxon Succession Struggles, 955–978', in *Leaders of the Anglo-Saxon Church from Bede to Stigand*, ed. A.R. Rumble (Woodbridge, 2012), 97–108, at 103–6; Williams, '*Princeps Merciorum*', 167–8.

'indivisible', a single realm for which only one ruler was conceivable.[13] Still, while tempers may have flared in 975, following Edward's victory peace was swiftly made: all of the likely supporters of Æthelred's candidacy appear as witnesses to Edward's charters and there is every reason to believe that they were reconciled to his regime.[14] How this was achieved is unknown, and a degree of resentment may have lingered; nevertheless, Edward and his supporters had won the day. For Æthelred and his mother, this must have come as a sore disappointment: their lofty hopes and dreams, not to mention careful political manoeuvring, had come to naught.

The 'anti-monastic reaction'

Though, as mentioned, the various versions of the *Anglo-Saxon Chronicle* do not speak explicitly of a succession dispute, they do mention a number of attacks on monasteries in Mercia at this point, where monks were reportedly driven out and replaced by clerics. Byrhtferth mentions similar incidents and on this basis historians have frequently spoken of an 'anti-monastic reaction' in these years. Originally seen as an active rejection of reform on the part of the laity, a more nuanced picture of developments has now emerged. Already in 1952 D.J.V. Fisher questioned whether the attacks of these years were truly 'anti-monastic' in nature, and subsequent work has both extended and modified his arguments.[15] In particular, the idea that secular aristocrats should be inherently hostile to reform has been questioned, and it has been noted that aristocratic patronage was actually one of the motors behind this movement; there can, in other words, have been no exclusively 'monastic' and 'lay' factions.[16] The putative leader of

---

[13] G. Tellenbach, 'Die Unteilbarkeit des Reiches. Ein Beitrag zur Entstehungsgeschichte Deutschlands und Frankreichs', *HZ* 163 (1941), 20–42; Scheidmüller, *Welfen*, 81–2 and 88.

[14] Keynes, *Atlas*, table LVIII.

[15] D.J.V. Fisher, 'The Anti-Monastic Reaction in the Reign of Edward the Martyr', *Cambridge Historical Journal* 10 (1952), 254–70.

[16] J.M. Pope, 'Monks and Nobles in the Anglo-Saxon Monastic Reform', *ANS* 17 (1995), 165–80; A.R. Rumble, 'Laity and the Monastic Reform in the Reign of Edgar', in *Edgar, King of the English 959–75: New Interpretations*, ed. D. Scragg (Woodbridge, 2008), 242–51; F. Tinti, 'Benedictine Reform and Pastoral Care in Late Anglo-Saxon England', *EME* 23 (2015), 229–51. Cf. J. Howe, 'The Laity's Reform of the Church', *American Historical Review* 93 (1988), 317–39.

the anti-monastic group, Ealdorman Ælfhere of Mercia, is a case in point: Ælfhere is recorded as a patron of Abingdon and Glastonbury, while his brother left bequests to the Old Minster – these were certainly not straightforward 'enemies of the monks'![17]

How we are to explain the attacks on monasteries at this point is therefore a good question. That these might be related to the succession dispute, as Fisher argued, is an attractive proposition. As he noted, Ælfhere struck at the foundations of Archbishop Oswald, who seems to have been in Edward's camp; these could thus be construed as targeted moves against a political opponent, rather than an expression of fundamental opposition to monastic life. We should, however, not ignore the possibility that a degree of frustration towards the monks played a part. One did not have to be an enemy of reform *per se* to object to the accumulation of land and power by a local monastic neighbour, and it is significant that lay aristocrats are often recorded as patrons of centres outside (or on the borders of) their immediate spheres of influence: Ælfheah and Ælfhere, who hailed from Mercia and oversaw central Wessex and (western) Mercia respectively, are recorded as benefactors at Abingdon, Glastonbury and the Old Minster; Æthelstan Half-King and his sons, whose power base lay in East Anglia, were patrons of Glastonbury and Ramsey; and Ealdorman Byrhtnoth of Essex was a patron of Ely. Under these circumstances it is not surprising that one centre's supporter was frequently another's detractor. Thus, while Ælfhere was a benefactor of Glastonbury and Abingdon, he was clearly an enemy of Oswald's foundations in the west Midlands. Likewise, while Æthelwine and Ælfwold, the sons of the Half-King, were remembered as the leaders of the pro-monastic faction at Ramsey, at Ely the former enjoyed a decidedly mixed reputation: he is recalled as having raised unjustified pleas, broken promises and opposed donations – all at around the same time that Ælfhere was despoiling Oswald's foundations in Mercia.[18]

---

[17] Williams, '*Princeps Merciorum*', 166–7; *Charters of Glastonbury Abbey*, ed. S.E. Kelly, Anglo-Saxon Charters 15 (Oxford, 2012), 153–4. See also S 1216 (*Abing* 115).

[18] *Libellus Æthelwoldi*, chs. 5, 38, 46, 58 (*Liber Eliensis* II.7, 27, 35, 47, ed. Baker, 79–80, 100–1, 110, 116). See S. Keynes, 'Ely Abbey 672–1109', in *A History of Ely Cathedral*, ed. P. Meadows and N. Ramsay (Woodbridge, 2003), 3–58, at 26–7.

In part, these actions point to the divisions amongst the reformers; as we have seen, 'reform' was not a homogenous programme and there were important differences between the circles of Æthelwold, Oswald and Dunstan (and doubtless also within each of these).[19] Ælfhere and Æthelwine may therefore have been less 'anti-' and 'pro-monastic' than patrons of different strands of reform: the former of Æthelwold's and the latter of Oswald's. Yet even this equation is probably too simple, since Æthelwine is also attested as a supporter of Æthelwold's foundation at Peterborough, whose core estate he helped secure.[20] Indeed, 'Æthelwoldian' and 'Oswaldian' circles were only informal groupings, a far cry from the eleventh-century 'Cluniac church' (*ecclesia Cluniacensis*) or the later monastic orders of the central Middle Ages, and there was much scope for variation and even tension within them. Lay loyalties, on the other hand, were above all to individual churches and therefore criss-crossed factional divides. Thus, though the succession dispute of 975 may at times have found expression through these divisions – Æthelwold and Oswald do seem to have been on different sides at this point, as we have seen – we should not overlook the local dynamics of these attacks. Indeed, neither Byrhtferth nor the author of the *Libellus Æthelwoldi* associates them with the succession dispute and the latter, in particular, makes it clear that the claims raised against Ely were a product of local tensions and conflicts, not epiphenomena of a broader succession dispute. In this connection we must bear in mind that 'patron' and 'detractor' are not always distinct categories: many of those who came into conflict with Ely were disputing bequests of their own kin and we seem to be observing dynamics similar to those identified by Barbara Rosenwein on the continent, where those who clashed with monastic houses were frequently benefactors of the same centres.[21] Moreover, the *Libellus* reveals that it was not only exalted individuals such

[19] Cubitt, 'Benedictine Reform', 83–4. Cf. S. Patzold, *Konflikte im Kloster. Studien zu Auseinandersetzungen in monastischen Gemeinschaften des ottonisch-salischen Reichs*, Historische Studien 463 (Husum, 2000).

[20] A. Hudson, 'Æthelwold's Circle, Saints' Cults, and Monastic Reform, *c.* 956–1006' (DPhil diss., Univ. of Oxford, 2014), 182–3. Cf. *Charters of Peterborough Abbey*, ed. S.E. Kelly, Anglo-Saxon Charters 14 (Oxford, 2009), 43–4 and 50–1.

[21] B.H. Rosenwein, *To Be the Neighbor of Saint Peter: The Social Meaning of Cluny's Property, 909–1049* (Ithaca, NY, 1989), esp. 49–77. See also Nightingale, *Monasteries and Patrons*.

as Ælfhere and Æthelwine who took advantage of the uncertainty of these years to claim lands and rights from monasteries – many other more local figures were involved. A rare episode recorded in both the *Libellus* and Byrhtferth's *Life* of Oswald neatly illustrates the complexity of these events. According to these accounts a man called Leofsige (only named in the *Libellus*) sought to appropriate estates from Peterborough but was opposed by Ealdorman Æthelwine and his brother Ælfwold, the latter of whom was eventually forced to kill the nobleman in order to prevent his usurpations.[22] While on the face of it this might look like the kind of factional violence postulated by Fisher, the details do not quite fit: Peterborough was an Æthelwoldian foundation, yet Æthelwine and Ælfwold are believed to have been supporters of Edward and thus opponents of Æthelwold – indeed, as we have seen, they enjoyed a decidedly mixed reputation at the bishop's larger fenland foundation at Ely. Leofsige's appropriations, like most of those recorded in the *Libellus* (and doubtless also those taking place in Mercia, though Byrhtferth is vague on the details), were thus a local affair in which national politics were at best secondary. There was, therefore, something of a reaction – or, perhaps more accurately: a series of local reactions – against reformed monastic houses at this point, whose power and influence had been a cause of jealousy amongst their lay neighbours.[23] Many of these were new foundations (or refoundations) and the scale of their endowments must have caused major shifts in local land-holding patterns, shifts which cannot have been in the interests of all. That within the upper echelons of society such tensions were sometimes refracted through the lens of other political constellations is natural, but should not lead us to ignore the broader pattern of expropriations. Nevertheless, these attacks are not indicative of an outright rejection of reform amongst the secular aristocracy; rather, they represent the growing pains of the reform movement, revealing how a new generation of laymen and ecclesiastics sought to renegotiate the terms of their relationship. We can only speculate

[22] *Libellus Æthelwoldi*, chs. 10–11 (*Liber Eliensis* II.11, ed. Blake, 84–6); Byrhtferth, *Vita S. Oswaldi* IV.14 (ed. Lapidge, 128–30); with D. Whitelock, 'Foreword', in *Liber Eliensis*, ed. E.O. Blake, Camden Society 3rd ser. 92 (London, 1962), ix–xviii, at xii–xiii.

[23] Keynes, 'Edgar', 54–6; Jayakumar, 'Reform and Retribution'; Hudson, 'Æthelwold's Circle', 171–3. See also A. Rabin, 'Holy Bodies, Legal Matters: Reaction and Reform in Ælfric's *Eugenia* and the Ely Privilege', *Studies in Philology* 110 (2013), 220–65.

as to Æthelred's own feelings about this. His main supporters were all known patrons of reform and Æthelwold himself had been the leading figure of this movement, so one hardly imagines that he enjoyed seeing such houses suffer. Nevertheless, one of his main backers, Ælfhere, happens to be the straw man in Byrhtferth's account, so we must also allow for a degree of pragmatism here: while certainly not 'anti-monastic', Æthelred presumably appreciated that under certain circumstances such appropriations were justifiable.

The life and death of a 'holy innocent': Edward II as king and martyr, 975–8

Little is known about Edward's reign save what can be gleaned from a few short notices in the *Chronicle* and the three authentic charters in his name. The general impression is of a tentative start; like Æthelstan in his early years, for which few charters are preserved and relatively little activity is recorded, it would seem that Edward struggled to find his feet.[24] This is not unusual: most monarchs took some time to settle into the job, and it was Edward's singular misfortune that he never had the opportunity to do so properly. Indeed, he was probably no more than sixteen (and perhaps only twelve or thirteen) at the time of his accession and still a youth at his time of death.

What Edward's charters reveal is that by 976 he had achieved the acknowledgement of a broad cross-section of the kingdom's ruling elite. His first act, which survives in what may be its original format, is a grant to a royal thegn (i.e. retainer) in Devon. This is attested by almost all of the kingdom's leading magnates, including Æthelwold and Ælfhere. Two ealdormen make their first appearances at this point and presumably owed their promotion to Edward: Æthelweard and Leofwine.[25] The former was appointed to the 'western shires' (roughly the modern West Country) and

---

[24] Roach, *Kingship and Consent*, 57–9 and 97–8; G.R. Little, 'Dynastic Strategies and Regional Loyalties: Wessex, Mercia and Kent, *c.* 802–939' (PhD diss., Univ. of Sheffield, 2007), 309–11.

[25] S 830 (ed. F. Rose-Troup, 'Crediton Charters of the Tenth Century', *Transactions of the Devonshire Association* 74 [1942], 237–61, at 255–6).

went on to play a prominent part at Æthelred's court; the latter is a some-what shadowy figure, who only attests during Edward's reign and whose regional and familial associations are unknown. If the witness-list of a somewhat suspect diploma from the Abingdon cartulary is to be trusted, then a third appointee soon followed: Eadwine, whose career can also be traced into the early years of Æthelred's reign.[26] The ranks of the ealdormen had been thinned during Edgar's later years, when the king frequently did not replace deceased office-holders; these appointments reversed this policy.[27] They were presumably designed to shore up Edward's fledgling regime: new kings were always in need of support and by appointing figures to vacant posts Edward might hope to curry favour. These promo-tions may also have been a move against some of the king's erstwhile opponents: if, as has been suggested, Ælfhere of Mercia had inherited over-sight over much of Wessex in Edgar's later years (which is, however, by no means certain), then the appointment of Æthelweard might have been intended to curtail his authority.[28] In any case, his first grant certainly indicates that Edward was firmly established by 976. It may also point towards his support base. The recipient, Ælfsige, was apparently a local Devonian aristocrat and there are signs that this region formed the core of his support – it was from here that his tutor Sideman hailed, and it was also here that the newly appointed Ealdorman Æthelweard's jurisdiction lay. The diploma itself was issued at an assembly at *Pydelan*, which has been identified as Puddletown in Dorset, and may have been written by a West Country scribe (perhaps an associate of Sideman from Crediton) – further signs of a distinctly 'south-western' orientation.[29] Geoffrey Koziol has noted that the first documents issued by new rulers were often symbolic of their regimes and this diploma is no exception: it presents Edward's kingship to his followers and showers favour on those who had backed him in recent months.[30] It opens with a preamble meditating upon how worldly patrimonies (*seculorum patrimonia*) will be left to known and

---

[26] S 828 (*Abing* 117). Eadwine was apparently ealdorman of Sussex.

[27] Keynes, *Atlas*, table XXXII; with Keynes, 'Edgar', 31–2.

[28] Hart, 'Athelstan', 591–2; Williams, '*Princeps Merciorum*', 158.

[29] Insley, 'Episcopal Scriptoria', 186–7. See also Jayakumar, 'Reform and Retribution', 348–9.

[30] Koziol, *Politics of Memory*, 63–118.

unknown successors, and all earthly glory will likewise eventually come to an end. Though these are common thoughts – the same preamble is found in a number of earlier grants[31] – one cannot help but feel that the message was particularly appropriate here: in the wake of the recent succession dispute (a dispute, as it were, over *seculorum patrimonia*) questions of patrimony and inheritance were certainly topical.

In any case, Edward's next two diplomas, issued in 977, show the king continuing to assert his authority. The first is a grant to another thegn, Ælfric, of land at Wylye in Wiltshire. Like the document of the previous year, this is attested by a range of bishops, ealdormen and thegns, including Æthelwold, Ælfhere and the newly promoted Æthelweard (but excluding the other new appointee, Leofwine).[32] The second records a grant of estates in Cornwall to Æthelweard. As with the first diploma in the king's name, this latter document may have been drafted by an individual associated with the cathedral chapter at Crediton, and the impression once more is that this is where Edward's position was strongest.[33] One feature of all three of these documents deserves mention: the absence of Ælfthryth and Æthelred. The attestations of queens and æthelings were only periodic in these years and one must therefore be careful not to read too much into what one scholar has called the 'sounds of medieval silence'.[34] Nevertheless, there were good grounds for tension between these figures, as we have seen, and Æthelred's only known contact with his half-brother is particularly interesting in this light: in a later charter in favour of Abingdon Æthelred recalls how, during his youth, his brother Edward had granted him a series of estates traditionally belonging to the king's sons.[35] On the face of it, this would seem to suggest cordial relations – and perhaps it does. However, there is more than meets the eye to this transaction: the lands in question had previously been granted by Edgar to Abingdon; in

---

[31] Cf. Insley, 'Episcopal Scriptoria', 187, n. 76.

[32] S 831 (KCD 611).

[33] S 832 (ed. J. Earle, *A Hand-Book of the Land-Charters and Other Saxonic Documents* [Oxford, 1888], 295–7). See P. Chaplais, 'The Authenticity of the Royal Anglo-Saxon Diplomas of Exeter' (1966), repr. in and cited from his *Essays in Medieval Diplomacy and Administration* (London, 1981), no. XV, 16.

[34] Cf. Geary, *Phantoms of Remembrance*, xiii–xiv.

[35] S 937 (*Abing* 129). See further below, Chapter 4, pp. 149–50.

favouring his younger brother Edward was thus also despoiling the most prized foundation of one of Æthelred's main supporters (Æthelwold). The grant may have been intended to sow seeds of dissension amongst Æthelred's allies, and it is interesting to note that he was later to express uncertainty as to whether this had been done 'justly or unjustly' (*iuste aut iniuste*). It is, therefore, by no means certain that Æthelred was a willing participant here and the impression certainly is one of distance between the two half-brothers. Ælfthryth herself was probably also *persona non grata* at court and the only record of her activities in these years is similarly revealing: the *Libellus Æthelwoldi* records that Æthelwold brought both Æthelred and his mother to his fenland foundation at Ely during Edward's reign, at which point a major local gathering saw the resolution of a number of local property disputes. While one should very much like to know whether this event preceded Edward's reallocation of lands from Abingdon to his brother, it indicates that for a time at least the nexus between Æthelred, Ælfthryth and Æthelwold remained unbroken. Indeed, it is probably no coincidence that the one other figure whose presence is mentioned at this point, Ælfric Cild, was a kinsman of Ælfhere, whom he later succeeded as ealdorman of Mercia; he too was a member of this faction.[36]

The *Chronicle* has a little to add to this. Under 977 the C and B versions, which were probably written shortly after these events, record that a 'great assembly' (*myccle gemot*) took place in Kirtlington (Oxon.) after Easter at which Bishop Sideman died. Although the prelate had wished to be buried at Crediton, the king and Dunstan now arranged for his interment at Abingdon.[37] Given Æthelwold's apparent sympathy for Æthelred in 975 and his continued contact with the ætheling and his mother thereafter, this is an interesting choice; perhaps the abbot of Abingdon, Osgar, did not share his mentor's politics (particularly if his centre had come to suffer for these); or perhaps earlier wounds had now been healed. In any case, the notice confirms that Bishop Sideman was amongst Edward's leading advisers, and that he and Dunstan were on good terms. Otherwise, there

---

[36] *Libellus Æthelwoldi*, ch. 12 (*Liber Eliensis* II.11, ed. Blake, 86).
[37] *ASC* 977 CB (ed. O'Brien O'Keeffe, 83–4).

is little that we can say about the gathering, save that it might have seen the production of either (or both) of the diplomas of this year. The D and E versions of the *Chronicle*, on the other hand, which are rather more distant from the events they describe, mention an assembly at Calne in western Wiltshire (not far from Chippenham), at which the upper floor of the building fell through, leaving Dunstan standing miraculously on a beam and leading to the death and injury of many of the others present.[38] This report was clearly composed after Dunstan's death (988) and reflects the subsequent growth of his cult; it reads like the sort of miracle story frequently found in a saint's *Life*. There is, therefore, reason to doubt the strict veracity of the account, and if we look for the effects of this event upon the kingdom's ruling elite, we do so in vain: Æthelred's earliest diplomas are attested by almost all the same figures who had been prominent under his half-brother.[39] Still, that Edward held an assembly at Calne in 977 or 978 should not be doubted: it fits well with his known interest in the West Country and Calne is attested elsewhere as a royal residence.[40]

Otherwise, Edward's coinage reveals that Edgar's reforms were maintained.[41] Regional die production seems to have become more common in these years, but this need not be a sign of weakness – it was probably just a pragmatic response to the demands of supplying the kingdom's many mint places and moneyers (iconographic consistency was in any case maintained). However, it is not Edward's life, but his death which was to earn him a place in posterity: the young king was killed after only two or three years on the throne, apparently by supporters of his younger half-brother. There has been some confusion over the date of this event. The slightly later (and closely related) D and E versions of the *Chronicle* place the killing and Æthelred's coronation in quick succession in 979 and two (possibly also related) regnal lists give Edward a reign of three and a half years (i.e. ending in 979), which has led to the proposition that Edward

---

[38] *ASC* 978 DE (= ?977) (ed. Cubbin, 49–50). On the D and E versions (the 'Northern Recension'), see Whitelock, *EHD*, 113–16; and Keynes, 'Manuscripts', 545.

[39] Keynes, *Atlas*, tables LVIII–LXVI.

[40] Cf. Keynes, 'Church Councils', 143.

[41] K. Jonsson, *Viking-Age Hoards and Late Anglo-Saxon Coins: A Study in Honour of Bror Emil Hildebrand's Anglosachsiska mynt* (Stockholm, 1987), 50–7.

actually died on 18 March 979 (rather than 978, as has generally been presumed).[42] Be that as it may, many of Æthelred's diplomas – including an undisputed original of 993 – calculate the start of his reign from 978, and the contemporary A and near-contemporary C versions of the *Chronicle* also give this as the year of his accession; there can be little doubt that they are right. The confusion we later see regarding this date would seem to have emerged from the fact that though Edward died on 18 March 978, Æthelred was not actually crowned until over a year later on 4 May 979: the D and E versions of the *Chronicle* are thus conflating events from two separate years under 979. This is also why some of Æthelred's other diplomas date his reign from 979 rather than 978 – there were, in effect, two dates from which to choose: that of his accession (18 March 978) and that of his consecration (4 May 979).[43]

The earliest account of Edward's death comes from a short Latin poem included in a manuscript written at Canterbury *c.* 1000 and probably composed in the 990s. This presents the event as an act of betrayal, perpetrated by the king's 'own people' (*propria gens*), and reports that some time thereafter the body was taken from its original resting place and brought to Shaftesbury in a procession led by Ealdorman Ælfhere.[44] More detail is provided by Byrhtferth of Ramsey, whose account follows on from his description of the succession dispute between Æthelred and Edward in the *Life* of Oswald. According to this, two years after his election Edward fell victim to a plot: as the king came to visit his brother and stepmother at Corfe (Dorset), he was met by their thegns, who took it upon themselves to kill the young king. The killing itself is described in biblical terms: the responsible parties greeted Edward amicably, then turned upon him just as Judas had Christ. He was then buried in haste and without the appropriate obsequies, but a year later the body was discovered uncorrupted and Ælfhere then oversaw its translation – the ceremonial transfer of a body,

---

[42] Stafford, 'Royal Government', 85–9; D.N. Dumville, 'The Death of King Edward the Martyr – 18 March, 979?', *Anglo-Saxon* 1 (2007), 269–83. Cf. *Councils*, ed. Whitelock, 183–4, n. 3.

[43] Keynes, *Diplomas*, 232–3, esp. 233, n. 7. See further S. Keynes, 'The Diplomas of King Æðelred II (978–1016)' (PhD diss., Univ. of Cambridge, 1978), 323–35.

[44] *Omnibus est recolenda*, ed. Dumville, 'Death', 281.

often that of a saint – to a more appropriate resting place (unspecified by Byrhtferth).[45] The *Chronicle* adds relatively little to this. The A version simply records the fact of Edward's death and Æthelred's accession, while the C version describes this event in terms of martyrdom, also adding some confusion by recording Æthelred's consecration both under this year and the following one. The first of these is clearly a contemporary account, possibly written before the Latin poem and the *Life* of Oswald; the latter would seem to have been composed once Edward's cult had started to develop in the early 990s.[46] The so-called 'Northern Recension' of the *Chronicle*, on the other hand, which was also written once Edward's cult had been established (probably in the early eleventh century), reports that the king was martyred at Corfe and then buried 'without any royal dignity' (*butan ælcum cynelicum wurðscipe*) at Wareham before Ælfhere oversaw his translation to Shaftesbury; this represents a further elaboration of the tale, though probably one drawing on authentic traditions.[47] It is noteworthy that in all of these reports the guilty parties remain anonymous. Later writers were not so reserved, however. The first to implicate the queen is the Latin *Passion* of Edward, written in the late eleventh century, perhaps by the prolific Goscelin of St-Bertin, and this set the tone for most later narratives.[48] Though there is little contemporary evidence to implicate Ælfthryth and her son, this event was clearly very troubling. Medieval kings were felt to be touched by divinity; not only had they been chosen by God, but like bishops they were anointed into their office with holy oil. Royal consecration was a well-established tradition and the reformers had done much to emphasize the God-given nature of royal authority further: writers such as Byrhtferth presented the monarch as God's 'vice-regent on

---

[45] Byrhtferth, *Vita S. Oswaldi* IV.18–19 (ed. Lapidge, 136–42). See M. Lapidge, 'Byrhtferth and Oswald', in *St Oswald of Worcester: Life and Influence*, ed. N. Brooks and C. Cubitt (London, 1996), 64–83, at 79–80.

[46] *ASC* 978 A (ed. Bately, 78), 978 C (ed. O'Brien O'Keeffe, 84).

[47] *ASC* 979–80 DE (= 978–9) (ed. Cubbin, 47); with Clark, 'Narrative Mode', 11.

[48] *Passio S. Eadward regis et martyris* (ed. Fell, 5–8). On the date of composition, see J.E. Denton, 'Late Tenth-Century Anglo-Saxon Hagiography: Ramsey and the Old Minster, Winchester' (PhD diss., Univ. of Cambridge, 2012), 35–62. See also P.A. Hayward, 'Translation-Narratives in Post-Conquest Hagiography and English Resistance to the Norman Conquest', *ANS* 21 (1999), 67–93, at 85–9.

Earth' (*vice sui regiminis in terra*), while artwork of the Winchester school presents him in a Christ-like guise.[49] To kill a king was, therefore, more than a crime – it was a sin of the first order. Such thoughts find expression in Ælfric the homilist's famous observation that 'no man can make himself king, but the people has a choice to choose as king whom they please; but after he is consecrated as king, he then has dominion over the people, and they cannot shake his yoke from their necks'.[50] The fruits of these teachings can be seen in the differing responses to deaths of King Edmund, who was killed under obscure circumstances in 944, and Edward: while the former attracted surprisingly little notice, the latter became a veritable *cause célèbre*. Though the circumstances were quite different, it is hard to escape the impression that English kingship was starting to take on something of the numinous quality it enjoyed elsewhere in Europe.[51]

Æthelred was clearly too young to have orchestrated this event, but much uncertainty surrounds his mother's involvement. Post-Conquest narratives almost invariably present her as the guilty party, the archetypal evil stepmother who plotted Edward's demise, and modern historians have often been inclined to follow suit: since she had much to gain from Edward's death, and since this transpired on a royal estate at which she was residing, it is presumed that Ælfthryth must have played a part therein. Signs of her involvement have been identified in the fact that the body's

[49] Byrhtferth, *Vita S. Oswaldi* IV.19 (ed. Lapidge, 140); R. Deshman, '*Christus rex et magi reges*: Kingship and Christology in Ottonian and Anglo-Saxon Art' (1976), and '*Benedictus monarcha et monachus*: Early Medieval Ruler Theology and the Anglo-Saxon Reform' (1988), both repr. in and cited from his *Eye and Mind: Collected Essays in Anglo-Saxon and Early Medieval Art*, ed. A. Cohen (Kalamazoo, MI, 2010), 104–71. See also Pratt, *Political Thought*, 72–8.

[50] Ælfric of Eynsham, *CH: FS* XIV.111–15 (ed. Clemoes, 294): 'Ne mæg man hin sylfne to cynge gedon ac þæt folc hæfð cyre to ceasenne þone to cyning þe him sylfum licað; Ac syððan he to cyninge gehalgod415 bið. Þonne hæfð he anweald ofer þam folce. 7 hi ne magon his geoc. of heoran swyran asceacan.' Although this line is a close translation of Ælfric's source, he clearly thought it appropriate to an English context: K.R. Kritsch, 'Fragments and Reflexes of Kingship Theory in Ælfric's Comments on Royal Authority', *English Studies* 97 (2016), 163–85; cf. M. Godden, 'Ælfric and Anglo-Saxon Kingship', *EHR* 102 (1987), 911–15, for words of caution.

[51] See Leyser, *Rule and Conflict*, 75–108 (though note the rather dismissive treatment of England at 106–7); and cf. L. Körntgen, *Königsherrschaft und Gottes Gnade. Zu Kontext und Funktion sakraler Vorstellungen in Historiographie und Bildzeugnissen der ottonisch-frühsalischen Zeit* (Berlin, 2001), for important caveats.

translation was overseen by the queen's close associate (and relative) Ælfhere, which might be seen as a form of belated amends. The fact that Edward's bones were translated a second time at Shaftesbury in 1001, perhaps shortly after Ælfthryth's death (999 × 1001), has been seen as pointing in a similar direction: according to this line of thought the queen blocked the formal acknowledgement of Edward's cult and only her death finally allowed this to flourish. That Æthelred eventually embraced his half-brother's sanctity has itself been seen as a sign of his complicity (albeit at second hand); as with Ælfhere in 979, this is presumed to have been a form of compensation.[52] Fascinating though such speculation may be, it must be emphasized that not a single contemporary source implicates Ælfthryth, Ælfhere or Æthelred. While Ælfthryth would hardly have been the first queen to resort to violence to place her son on the throne, we must be careful of seeing conspiracy where there was none.[53] Indeed, if Ælfhere really were one of the guilty parties, then it is surprising that Byrhtferth, who was no friend of the Mercian ealdorman, does not make more of this; instead he uncharacteristically praises him for his role in Edward's translation. The very silence of our sources may itself be significant: it would seem that contemporaries were as uncertain as modern historians as to who was to blame. Parallels can be seen with the mysterious death of William Rufus (1087–1100) while out hunting in the New Forest or the demise of Thomas Becket at the hands of Henry II's knights in 1170: in both cases there have been no shortage of modern conspiracy theories, a fact which reflects contemporary uncertainties as to where the blame lay.[54] If there is a hint of criticism regarding Æthelred and his mother, it lies in

[52] D.W. Rollason, 'The Cults of Murdered Royal Saints in Anglo-Saxon England', *ASE* 11 (1982), 1–22, at 17–19; A. Thacker, 'Cults at Canterbury: Relics and Reform under Dunstan and his Successors', in *St Dunstan: His Life, Times and Cult*, ed. N. Ramsay, M. Sparks and T. Tatton-Brown (Woodbridge, 1992), 221–44, at 248; B. Yorke, 'Edward, King and Martyr: A Saxon Murder Mystery', in *Studies in the Early History of Shaftesbury Abbey*, ed. L. Keen (Dorchester, 1999), 99–116; Lavelle, *Aethelred II*, 46–7 and 90–1.

[53] S. Keynes, 'The Cult of King Edward the Martyr', in *Gender and Historiography: Studies in the Earlier Middle Ages in Honour of Pauline Stafford*, ed. J.L. Nelson, S. Reynolds and S.M. Johns (London, 2012), 115–25; S.J. Ridyard, *The Royal Saints of Anglo-Saxon England: A Study of West Saxon and East Anglian Cults* (Cambridge, 1988), 154–71; N. Marafioti, *The King's Body: Burial and Succession in Late Anglo-Saxon England* (Toronto, 2014), 161–91.

[54] F. Barlow, *William Rufus*, rev. edn (New Haven, CT, 2000), 420–32, and *Thomas Becket*, rev. edn (London, 1997), 251–75; A. Duggan, *Thomas Becket* (London, 2004), 201–23.

the fact that they did not pursue Edward's killers more successfully.[55] That individuals beyond the queen and prince wished to see Edward dead should not come as a surprise. The succession dispute clearly still rancoured in many circles and if Byrhtferth is to be trusted (and, for all his literary flourishes, there is little reason why he should not be) then Edward was by no means universally loved: he was a rather petulant young man, less suited to royal dignity than his younger half-brother.

It is hard to know how Æthelred and his mother reacted to this event. On one level, it must have come as welcome news: Edward and his followers had stymied their earlier efforts and now, finally, the path to the throne was free. Nevertheless, the manner in which this had transpired must have given grounds for pause: just as Henry II felt uncomfortable about the death of Becket, who had been a close friend as well as mortal enemy, so too one imagines that Æthelred had decidedly mixed feelings about the death of a blood relative (and an anointed one at that) – gratification, perhaps, that his hopes and dreams of rule would be fulfilled, but a gratification tarnished by the underhand manner in which this had come to pass. Indeed, the English realm must have seemed something of a poisoned chalice; if Edward had been a suitable target for an assassin's blade, there was little to say that Æthelred could not be.

Regency rule: Ælfthryth and Æthelwold, 978–84

Regardless of who was to blame, Edward's death cast a shadow over Æthelred's accession; not only did it set a dangerous precedent, but it placed Æthelred and Ælfthryth in the awkward position of being the beneficiaries of such a nefarious act. One of the factors which had stood against Æthelred's candidacy two and a half years earlier must still have been a concern: his youth. He was no more than twelve and perhaps only eight or nine at this point. Royal minorities presented a major challenge in the Middle Ages; since a boy could not command the same kind of authority as a grown man, these tended to be periods of political weakness, in which

---

[55] The 'Northern Recension' of the *Chronicle* emphasizes that 'his earthly kinsmen did not wish to avenge him' (*Hyne noldon his eorðlican magas wrecan*): *ASC* 979 DE (= ?978) (ed. Cubbin, 47).

magnates could have their own way.[56] Writings on kingship reflect these concerns. The influential Irish tract known as 'The Twelve Abuses of the Age' quotes Ecclesiastes X.16, 'Woe to thee, oh land, when thy king is a child and thy princes dine in the morning!' (*Vae enium terrae, cuius rex est puer et cuius principes mane comedunt*), in its discussion of the 'unjust king' (*rex iniquus*); child kingship and bad kingship are thus equated.[57] The *Chronicle*-poem on the death of Edgar does much the same: it underlines Edward's youth in 975, implying that this was one of the causes of unrest. One imagines, therefore, that many were apprehensive at the prospect of another child ascending the throne less than three years later.

This air of apprehension may explain the hesitancy of Æthelred's regime. Though Edward died on 18 March 978 it was over a year before Æthelred himself was inaugurated at Kingston-upon-Thames in Surrey on 4 May 979. What transpired in the interim is a matter of speculation. It may be that some magnates were hesitant to accept Æthelred and had to be won over with threats and promises. There were also other matters which required attention. The one recorded act between Edward's death and Æthelred's consecration takes on particular significance here: the translation of the former's body. This was clearly intended to bring closure. One of the most shocking aspects of Edward's death had been the treatment of his body, and this now needed to be made good; the previous king had to be buried with appropriate dignity before a new one could take his place. If early accounts are right in reporting that Edward's body had been disposed of secretly – years later Wulfstan of York was to express the belief that it had been burnt[58] – then this would have further complicated matters: the body had to be found before it could be reburied. The bones discovered in the north transept of Shaftesbury Abbey in 1931 are of particular interest here. These have been carbon dated to the period in

---

[56] T. Offerfeld, *Reges pueri. Das Königtum Minderjähriger im frühen Mittelalter*, MGH: Schriften 50 (Hannover, 2001). See also J. Le Goff, 'Le roi enfant dans l'idéologie monarchique de l'Occident médiéval', in *Historicité de l'enfance et de la jeunesse* (Athens, 1986), 231–50; and T. Vogtherr, ' "Weh Dir, Land, dessen König ein Kind ist." Minderjährige Könige um 1200 im europäischen Vergleich', *FMSt* 37 (2003), 291–314.

[57] Pseudo-Cyprian, *De XII abusivis saeculi*, abusio 9, ed. S. Hellmann (Leipzig, 1910), 51–3.

[58] Wulfstan, *Sermo Lupi ad Anglos*, (EI) ll. 77–8, ed. D. Bethurum, *The Homilies of Wulfstan* (Oxford, 1957), 270.

question and, though medical examinations have revealed them to belong to a man in his late twenties or early thirties (and thus not to the teenage Edward), they may well once have been revered as the martyred king's relics.[59] Indeed, in the tense atmosphere of early 979, Edward's remains may have had to be invented if they were not to be found. In any case, there is no need to see this act as an expression of guilt on the part of the new king's guardians; promoting regicide was not in anyone's interests, and Ælfhere and Ælfthryth would have wished to do all they could to underscore the inviolability of royal office at this juncture. The choice of Shaftesbury for the body reveals the standing in which Edward was held: the centre had been founded by Æthelgifu, a daughter of Alfred the Great, and was one of the kingdom's wealthiest nunneries at the time of the Conquest.[60] As a female monastic house, it also stood under Ælfthryth's protection, reducing the danger of the body becoming a rallying-point for opposition to the regime.

What other business was conducted between Edward's death and the inauguration of Æthelred is anyone's guess. As noted, successions placed the kingdom under particular strain and in this case the most important business must have been establishing who would rule in the young king's stead. As a boy of no more than twelve, there can have been no question of Æthelred ruling on his own. Nevertheless, there were no fixed conventions for minority rule in the earlier Middle Ages. The fiction was generally maintained that the child was head of state: pronouncements were made by others, but issued in his name, and when it came time for the boy to take over control this made little mark in the documentary record.[61] What we

---

[59] S. Keynes, 'King Alfred the Great and Shaftesbury Abbey', in *Studies in the Early History of Shaftesbury Abbey*, ed. L. Keen (Dorchester, 1999), 17–72, at 54–5. Cf. P. Rahtz, 'The Bones of St Edward the Martyr', *British Archaeological News* 4.ii (March, 1989), 17–18. The purported bones of Edward are now cared for and venerated by the small Russian Orthodox Saint Edward Brotherhood in Brookwood (Surrey).

[60] Marafioti, *King's Body*, 161–74; J. Crick, 'The Wealth, Patronage, and Connections of Women's Houses in Late Anglo-Saxon England', *Revue Bénédictine* 109 (1999), 154–85, esp. 177–8; B. Yorke, 'The Burial of Kings in Anglo-Saxon England', in *Kingship, Legislation and Power in Anglo-Saxon England*, ed. G.R. Owen-Crocker and B.W. Schneider (Woodbridge, 2013), 237–57, at 254–5.

[61] T. Kölzer, 'Das Königtum Minderjähriger im fränkisch-deutschen Mittelalter. Eine Skizze', *HZ* 251 (1990), 291–332; Offergeld, *Reges pueri, passim*.

are dealing with, therefore, is a *de facto* regency not a *de iure* one. The absence of an appointed regent made the question of who would govern, if anything, more pressing. The danger, as noted, was that unscrupulous magnates would exploit the king's youth to their advantage. The famous line from Ecclesiastes X.16 underscores this threat, the implication being that the kingdom's leading nobles will run riot if not kept in check; they will dine in the morning (rather than evening), perverting the natural order of things. That this was a real danger is shown by the minority of Henry IV of Germany (1056–1106), who acceded at the tender age of six: initially his mother Agnes was the power behind the throne, but since she was felt to be exerting undue influence, the young monarch was kidnapped at Kaiserswerth in 1062 by the kingdom's leading bishops, who agreed to share the business of ruling the realm thereafter. However, this too proved a fragile arrangement, which Archbishop Adalbert of Hamburg-Bremen was able to exploit to his benefit, convincing Henry to act in the prelate's own interests; the result was further strife and eventually Adalbert's expulsion from court in 1066.[62] As this example reveals, the key to successful minority rule lay in compromise and consensus: the balance of power had to be maintained if the realm's great and good were to accept the rule of a queen-mother or any other leading magnate on the boy's behalf.

In Æthelred's case the leading figures during his youth seem to have been Ælfthryth, Æthelwold and Ælfhere. As we have seen, the latter two had been the queen's closest allies in previous years and it was only natural that she would call upon them now. Still, this was not simply a case of 'out with the old and in with the new': with the exception of Ælfthryth herself, these figures had all featured in Edward's charters, while those identified as Edward's leading supporters are also found amongst the subscriptions to Æthelred's early diplomas, suggesting that they too were incorporated into the regime.[63] Every effort was apparently made to heal old wounds and the reburial of Edward's remains must have played a key role here. That Æthelred's mother should be at the forefront of the minority may seem

---

[62] I.S. Robinson, *Henry IV of Germany, 1056–1106* (Cambridge, 1999), 19–62; G. Althoff, *Heinrich IV.* (Darmstadt, 2006), 41–66 (cf. also *ibid.*, 288–302); Offergeld, *Reges pueri*, 785–97.

[63] Keynes, *Atlas*, tables LVIII, LX, LXII.

natural in light of her prominence at Edgar's court; nevertheless, this was far from inevitable. The position of the king's wife was an ambiguous one in Wessex, as we have seen, and the royal mother was not the only conceivable regent, as the experiences of other medieval child monarchs reveal. During the minority of Louis the Child in East Francia (Germany) (899–911) it was not the king's mother Uota, but a group of prominent lay and ecclesiastical magnates led by the so-called 'Conradines' (*Konradiner*) who oversaw the realm on his behalf.[64] This is, admittedly, something of a special case – Uota had faced charges of adultery only shortly before her husband's death, weakening her position at court – but it does not stand alone: Agnes was removed from the regency over Henry IV in 1062, as we have seen, and similar efforts were made to oust Otto III's mother and grandmother at the start of his reign in East Francia (983).[65] Such trends are also visible in France and Spain: the regency of Gerberga for the thirteen-year-old Lothar IV (954–86) had to be bought by concessions to Hugh the Great, West Francia's leading magnate, while the next French queen-regent, Anne of Kiev, relied upon the support of her brother-in-law, Baldwin V of Flanders, who eventually took over this role following Anne's remarriage to Raoul III of Valois (1062); meanwhile in Spain the regency of Elvira García for the five-year-old Alfonso V of Asturias-León (999–1027) was apparently ousted by a palace coup led by the Galician count Menendo González in 1003.[66] Even Blanche of Castile, the most successful French queen-regent of the Middle Ages, faced stern opposition to her influence during the early years of Louis IX (1226–70).[67] By the end of the tenth century the

---

[64] Offergeld, *Reges pueri*, 518–641. Cf. T. Reuter, 'Sex, Lies and Oath-Helpers: The Trial of Queen Uota' (2002), trans. in his *Medieval Polities and Modern Mentalities*, ed. J.L. Nelson (Cambridge, 2006), 217–30.

[65] F.-R. Erkens, '. . . *more Grecorum conregnantem instituere vultis?* Zur Legitimation der Regentschaft Heinrichs des Zänkers im Thronstreit von 984', *FMSt* 27 (1993), 273–89.

[66] MacLean, 'Reform', 263–6; F.-R. Erkens, ' "Sicut Esther regina". Die westfränkische Königin als consors regni', *Francia* 20.i (1993), 15–38, at 19–21; R.-H. Bautier, 'Anne de Kiev, reine de France, et la politique royale au XIᵉ siècle' (1985), repr. in and cited from his *Recherches sur l'histoire de la France médiévale: Des Mérovingiens aux premiers Capétiens* (Aldershot, 1991), no. X, esp. 552–8; E.J. Ward, 'Anne of Kiev (*c.*1024–*c.*1075) and a Reassessment of Maternal Power in the Minority Kingship of Philip I of France', *Historical Research* (forthcoming); J.M. Fernández del Pozo, 'Alfonso V, rey de León. Estudio histórico-documental', in *León y su historia. Miscelánea histórica*, V (León, 1984), 11–262, at 78–81.

[67] Le Goff, *Saint Louis*, 60–3 and 579–81.

queen-regent had thus become a common figure in western Europe, but her rights rarely went unchallenged and when England faced its next royal minority following the death of King John in 1216, it was not the young Henry III's mother, Isabella of Angoulême, but the powerful earl William Marshal who was to play this role.[68] Ælfthryth's prominence in Æthelred's early years should therefore not be taken for granted and the willingness of the kingdom's leading magnates – including many of those who had backed Edward in 975 – to accept her speaks strongly against her involvement in Edward's murder; as the experiences of Uota show, a tarnished queen made an improbable regent.

Æthelred's consecration on 4 May 979 publicly enacted his succession. This took place at the symbolic residence at Kingston-upon-Thames, which had been the favoured site of inauguration for some time. Its significance lay in its association with previous monarchs: Æthelstan (925) and Eadred (946) had certainly been consecrated there, and it is very likely that Edmund (939), Eadwig (late 955 or early 956), Edgar (c. 960) and Edward the Martyr (975) had also been.[69] The choice of Kingston itself was a reflection of the broader English body politic: located on the border between Wessex and Mercia (and between these and the Danelaw), at a site used for negotiations between the West Saxon kings and the archbishop of Canterbury (and men of Kent) in the early ninth century, it straddled the main fault-lines of the realm. No accounts of Æthelred's consecration survive, but it is possible to reconstruct the rough details from reports of other inaugurations along with the evidence of the surviving liturgical *ordines*, which describe how these events were meant to be conducted.[70] The first act would have been Æthelred's election. Early medieval elections were very different from their modern counterparts; less a means of

[68] D.A. Carpenter, *The Minority of Henry III* (Berkeley, CA, 1990), 13–19.

[69] Keynes, 'Church Councils', 147–50.

[70] The earliest surviving text of the revised B-version of the Second English *Ordo*, with which Æthelred was probably consecrated, is preserved in the Dunstan (or Sherborne) Pontifical: Paris, Bibliothèque nationale, MS lat. 943, fols. 67r–75v. See M.A. Conn, 'The Dunstan and Brodie (Anderson) Pontificals: An Edition and Study' (PhD diss., Univ. of Notre Dame, 1993), 113–126, for an edition; and cf. *The Claudius Pontificals (from Cotton MS. Claudius A.iii in the British Museum)*, ed. D.H. Turner, HBS 97 (Chichester, 1971), 89–95, for a more readily available one (from the slightly later Claudius Pontifical II). See Nelson, 'Second English *Ordo*'; and Conn, 'Pontificals', 386–428, for discussion.

decision-making than of announcing a decision once it had been made, they were more celebratory than deliberative (though no less important for this fact). What the act of 'election' actually involved is rarely stated, but a reasonable guess is an acclamation led by the kingdom's senior magnates, perhaps accompanied by an oath of fidelity, by which they pledged support to the new monarch. Once this had been completed, action will have moved inside the church. Here the archbishop of Canterbury presided. In Æthelred's case, as in that of Edward almost four years earlier, this would have been Dunstan. He will have led the young king into the church and up through the nave to the main altar, where Æthelred then prostrated himself and those present sang the *Te Deum* ('Thee, O God', an antiphonal prayer – or hymn, as we would now call it). Thereafter, the king would have been raised up and made his three-fold coronation oath – to protect and preserve the church, to forbid theft and other crimes and to show justice and mercy in his judgements – the text of which was laid upon the altar, symbolizing his commitment to the vows.[71] Whether the oath itself was given in Latin, as recorded in the relevant liturgical *ordines*, or in the vernacular, as it is found in the text known as the *Promissio regis* (a translation of the oath, with accompanying commentary), is not entirely certain. Latin was generally the language of the liturgy, but since this promise was made not only to God, but also to the assembled people, it is conceivable that the common tongue was preferred. The relative youth of Æthelred may also have called for the vernacular; even if adult monarchs swore in Latin, we cannot be sure whether the young prince would have been up to this.[72] In any case, once the promise had been made, benedictions (blessings) were said over the king before further antiphons were sung. The ceremony then reached its high point with the anointing of the new monarch, when he was consecrated on the head with holy oil, after which further antiphons were sung. Æthelred was then invested with the symbols of his office, each with accompanying instructions from the archbishop: the ring, as a symbol of sacred faith; the sword, with which to overcome his own enemies and adversaries of the church; the crown of

[71] M. Clayton, 'The Old English *Promissio regis*', *ASE* 37 (2008), 90–150, at 107–8 and 112–13.
[72] *Ibid.*, 92–3, 113.

glory and justice, that he might come to earn the crown of the Eternal Kingdom; the sceptre of royal authority, to protect his people from the impious, correct the wicked and bring peace to the righteous; and the rod of virtue and justice, that he might teach the erring, humiliate the proud and exalt the humble. Further benedictions then followed, wishing the king a long and fruitful reign, after which he was finally enthroned and received instructions to stand and retain his newly acquired realm, which he should rule as 'mediator between clergy and people' (*mediator cleri et plebis*). A final benediction brought the service to an end, after which those present proceeded to the ensuing coronation feast. Though not described in the surviving *ordines*, this event attracted much interest from contemporary writers and was in some ways the highlight of the day: feasting was an important demonstrative act, which served to create lasting bonds of association, bonds which were particularly important for a new monarch.[73] The entire event was an elaborate rite of passage, rich in symbolism: it was through this that the heir-apparent became king, one of the Lord's anointed (*Christus domini*).[74] In the case of Æthelred, whose accession had been anything but smooth and whose age meant that serious questions could be raised about his suitability for office, this must have been especially important. What the young boy made of all this pageantry is a good question. Was he impressed by the pomp and spectacle? Or did the crown sit heavily on his head? Perhaps both – certainly, in his later years Æthelred was to show a rather introspective tendency, one perhaps born of too much pressure too young. For Dunstan, on the other hand, the ceremony offered a welcome opportunity to instruct the new monarch in his duties; the entire rite with its prayers, benedictions and hymns was nothing less than an object lesson in righteous rule. Though this was in a sense a triumph for those who had supported Æthelred in 975, the involvement of Dunstan and many others who had been on the opposing side would have made

[73] A. Gautier, *Le festin dans l'Angleterre anglo-saxonne (V^e–XIe siècle)* (Rennes, 2006); G. Althoff, 'Der frieden-, bündnis-, und gemeinschaftsstiftende Charakter des Mahles im frühen Mittelalter', in *Essen und Trinken in Mittelalter und Neuzeit*, ed. I. Bitsch, T. Ehlert and X. von Ertzdorff (Sigmaringen, 1990), 13–25.

[74] J.L. Nelson, 'Inauguration Rituals', 283–307; J. Dale, *Kingship in Comparison: Inauguration and Liturgical Kingship in England, France and the Empire c.1050–c.1250* (Woodbridge, forthcoming).

this less an act of retribution than one of reconciliation; just as Ælfhere and Æthelwold had acquiesced to Edward's succession, so now others gave way.

Successful regency rule was inevitably something of a balancing act. A good regent was one who did not rock the boat and this was why queens were popular: they offered the most direct continuity with the previous regime. In Æthelred's case, matters were doubtless complicated by recent events and Ælfthryth proceeded with care: as we have seen, there was a gap of over a year between Edward's death and the consecration of his younger brother, during which one imagines that she, Ælfhere and Æthelwold were busy generating the support necessary for Æthelred's succession, a process involving concessions to erstwhile opponents, promises of future favour and much else besides. That in the end Æthelred's minority passed remarkably quietly speaks of their success. Not surprisingly, Ælfthryth figures prominently in the early diplomas in his name, attesting over half of those issued before 984. What is more, whereas previously she had attested after the kingdom's archbishops and bishops, now she often subscribes before them and immediately after the king (her son).[75] Her heightened involvement in politics is hard to miss and her hand can be detected behind many of the transactions conducted in these years. Thus, the first two surviving diplomas in Æthelred's name are in favour of Ælfthryth's most prominent supporters: Ælfhere and Æthelwold. The first grants the Mercian ealdorman ten hides – the hide being the standard Anglo-Saxon measure of land, representing the amount theoretically needed to support a single peasant family – at Olney (Bucks.) and the draftsman addresses Ælfhere as 'a certain companion most faithful to me and also joined to me by blood' (*cuidam mihi oppido fideli comitate atque consanguinitate coniuncto*) thus drawing attention to the familial bonds between the two.[76] The second, on the other hand, is a sign of things to come: it grants Æthelwold and the

---

[75] Keynes, *Diplomas*, 174–5, n. 82. See also Stafford, *Queen Emma*, 200.

[76] S 834 (*Pet* 18). See P. Stafford, 'The Reign of Æthelred II: A Study in the Limits of Royal Policy and Action' (1978), repr. in and cited from her *Gender, Family and the Legitimation of Power: England from the Ninth to the Early Twelfth Century* (Aldershot, 2006), no. IV, 26; and Williams, '*Princeps Merciorum*', 170.

Old Minster an estate in Hampshire.[77] This is followed by a number of further charters in favour of Æthelwold and his foundations: a year later (980) the Old Minster received two further diplomas; in 982 a bequest by Ealdorman Æthelmær to the New Minster was confirmed; and in the following year donations were made to both Abingdon and Æthelwold himself.[78] In the light of these documents it is hard not to conclude that Æthelwold and Ælfhere were the ones calling the shots alongside Ælfthryth, a conclusion which finds support in their prominent attestations to these and other charters.[79] Indeed, since there was no formal regent, one suspects that these three were very much equal partners. The role played by Ælfhere in the translation of Edward also points in this direction – he would seem to have acted as a 'representative of the regime'. Moreover, it was only after the deaths of Ælfhere (983) and Æthelwold (984) that the king began to strike out on his own. That these two should stand out so prominently at this juncture is surely no coincidence. As we have noted, the first documents issued by a new regime were often symbolic of its ambitions and the message here could scarcely have been clearer: Ælfthryth, Æthelwold and Ælfhere were now back at the helm.[80] It would be misleading, however, to see herein simple venality: though the donation to Ælfhere is quite generous, it is not unprecedented, while the privileges for Æthelwold and his houses are actually rather modest. Indeed, in these same years Æthelmær, the son of the Ealdorman Æthelweard who had been appointed by Edward, also received a grant at Thames Ditton (Surrey), suggesting that it was not only old allies who were being rewarded.[81] The charters of this period thus show Æthelwold and Ælfhere to have been in the thick of it, but they do not speak of unbridled generosity; old friends were being rewarded, but not at the cost of alienating former enemies.

Beyond this clutch of privileges for Ælfhere and Æthelwold, these years witnessed a conscious effort to maintain the status quo. The ruling

---

[77] S 835 (KCD 622).

[78] S 836 (KCD 626), S 837 (KCD 624), S 842 (*WinchNM* 26), S 843 (*Abing* 119), S 849 (KCD 640).

[79] Keynes, *Atlas*, tables LX and LXII. Cf. Keynes, *Diplomas*, 174–5.

[80] See above, p. 69; and cf. Koziol, *Politics of Memory*, 63–118.

[81] S 847 (ed. C.R. Hart, *The Early Charters of Eastern England* [Leicester, 1966], 186–7).

personnel remained much the same as it had been under Edward: after the succession dispute and local reprisals against monastic houses, peace and stability were in the interests of all concerned. Indeed, it is around this time that Byrhtferth and the *Libellus Æthelwoldi* stop mentioning attacks on monasteries; the reformers were evidently once again in a position to withstand opportunistic strikes. In the case of Æthelwold, in particular, it would seem that after a brief period on the political side-lines, the bishop was now once again at the height of his powers. It therefore comes as no surprise that his opponents sought to make amends. According to Wulfstan Cantor, writing at Winchester in the late 990s (*c.* 997), this took place on the occasion of the rededication of the Old Minster in 980. During this event Æthelwold's adversaries are reported to have come to the bishop, bowed their necks to his knees and kissed his right hand – all unmistakable signs of subservience – then commended themselves to his prayers.[82] As Daniel Sheerin notes, this act must be understood against the backdrop of the 'anti-monastic reaction', about which Wulfstan is otherwise silent: it marks the reconciliation of Æthelwold with those who had troubled his foundations in previous years.[83] It is interesting to note the form that this took: a public ritual of self-abasement, not a plea before a local shire court; this was conciliation not censure.[84] Of course, we are dealing with an idealized account: Wulfstan presents the bishop as the perfect prelate, one of the 'blessed peacemakers' about whom Christ had spoken in his Sermon on the Mount, a man who is able – in Wulfstan's words – to make 'sheep out of wolves' (*oues ex lupis*). Still, there is no reason to doubt the essence of the story: Wulfstan writes as an eye-witness, for an audience which would have included many others who had been present. Indeed, the rededication of the Old Minster, capping off substantial building work in recent years, was itself something of a coup for Æthelwold and his associates: it was a chance

---

[82] Wulfstan Cantor, *Vita S. Æthelwoldi*, ch. 40 (ed. Lapidge and Winterbottom, 60–2). Cf. Wulfstan's verse account of the event, which does not mention these details: *Narratio metrica de S. Swithuno*, 'De dedicatione magne ecclesie', ll. 61–114, ed. M. Lapidge, *The Cult of Saint Swithun* (Oxford, 2003), 376–80.

[83] D.J. Sheerin, 'The Dedication of the Old Minster, Winchester, in 980', *Revue Bénédictine* 88 (1978), 261–73, esp. 262–3.

[84] L. Roach, 'Penance, Submission and *deditio*: Religious Influences on Dispute Settlement in Later Anglo-Saxon England', *ASE* 41 (2012), 343–71, at 355–6.

to show a united front and an opportunity for rapprochement with old foes. It may be for this occasion that the Benedictional of Æthelwold was produced, a richly illuminated manuscript, celebrating the prelate's episcopal status along with those saints venerated within his circles.[85]

Though Dunstan and Oswald may have backed Edward's bid for the kingship in 975, there is every indication that they were now won over. The archbishops appear in the witness-lists of almost all of Æthelred's early diplomas and it is likely that they too had a part to play in the politics of the minority, though we can only speculate as to the precise nature of this. Still, while there is much we should like to know, the general drift is clear enough: Ælfthryth and Æthelwold were once more at the fore, but not to the exclusion of those who had been dominant in the meantime. Above all, the effort was to return to the politics of Edgar's reign: attacks on monasteries were brought to a halt and reform was able to progress further under renewed royal patronage. It was apparently in these years that Tavistock was founded by Ælfthryth's brother, Ordulf (c. 981), and it may also be around this time that the queen-mother founded (or refounded) the female monastic houses at Amesbury and Wherwell (otherwise first attested in 1002).[86] Edgar's preference for promoting monks to episcopal seats was also maintained, with Æscwig of Bath being made Bishop of Dorchester c. 979 and Æthelgar of the New Minster being promoted to Selsey in 980.[87] In other respects too continuity can be traced. Thus, Edgar's original reform issue was initially continued in Æthelred's name and, though this soon gave way to the king's own first type, the *Hand* (c. 979–91, with the *First Hand* variant running c. 979–85), such arrangements were probably in keeping with Edgar's intentions. Whether we can read any deeper message into the iconography of this issue, which bears the Hand of God in place of the cross on the reverse (or 'tails'), is hard to say, but certainly its introduction shows the coinage system operating as it was meant to. Indeed, the years following Edgar's reform were ones of innovation and experimentation where coinage was concerned and as the first major recoinage this issue was to set the tone

---

[85] Hudson, 'Æthelwold's Circle', 92–3. Cf. R. Deshman, *The Benedictional of Æthelwold* (Princeton, NJ, 1995), 140 and 214.

[86] S. Foot, *Veiled Women*, 2 vols. (Aldershot, 2000), II, 21–5 and 215–19. Cf. *ibid.*, I, 161.

[87] Keynes, *Atlas*, tables LX and LXI; with Keynes, *Diplomas*, 175.

for the future: periodic changes of type were gradually becoming an established feature of English coinage. That this should have come at a time
when Æthelwold was once more at the forefront of politics may be no coincidence: as we have seen, his vision for English monasticism placed particular emphasis on unity of worship, and it may be that his hand lies behind
similar developments within the realm's coinage.[88]

Although the evidence regarding the young king becomes somewhat richer
in these years, in other respects our sources are more opaque than ever: we
have no surviving royal decrees, for example, and only a handful of charters. This must in part be a reflection of the tumult of the period: it is
during times of relative stability that we tend to see law-making and regular
charter production. The situation may also reflect the exigencies of the
minority. Successful rule on behalf of a child monarch took the form of
establishing a holding pattern and did not lend itself to more programmatic acts of law-making and land granting. Be that as it may, we should
not be too harsh in our judgements of these years. Just as Sir Frank Stenton
famously saw it as a sign of competence that Edgar's reign was 'singularly
devoid of recorded incident', so too we may see the silence of our sources
for Æthelred's earliest years as a testament to the success of his regency
regime. Certainly, one imagines that these years left their mark on Æthelred:
the experiences of familial and political faction in the mid-970s and the
influence of his mother and her associates thereafter must all have had a
lasting effect. His father's death must initially have brought sadness, then
hope as to his own prospects of rule. These were soon dashed by his elder
half-brother's success, which much have rancoured. Indeed, Æthelred may
well have felt undermined and betrayed – not only by those who had
backed his brother, but also (and perhaps especially) by those who had
promised him the crown in the first place. His own accession a few years
later would have helped soothe such feelings of disappointment, but the

---

[88] R. Naismith, 'The Coinage of Æthelred II: A New Evaluation', *English Studies* 97 (2016),
117–39, at 128. See also [R.H.]M. Dolley, 'An Introduction to the Coinage of Æthelred II',
in *Ethelred the Unready*, ed. D. Hill (London, 1978), 115–33; and M. Blackburn, 'Æthelred's
Coinage and the Payment of Tribute', in *The Battle of Maldon, AD 991*, ed. D. Scragg
(Oxford, 1991), 156–69. Cf. Molyneaux, *Formation*, 189–93.

manner in which this transpired probably tainted any true feelings of jubi-lation; if a victory, this was a decidedly Pyrrhic one. Thereafter, his minority seems to have been calmer, witnessing a return to the politics of earlier years. While this may initially have accorded with Æthelred's desires, by the early 980s he was no longer a child and there are signs that he was keen to strike out on his own: having been promised the kingship, he had been delivered a regency in which his own freedom of action was decidedly restricted. The resulting tensions were to determine the course of politics in future years.

CHAPTER 3

THE PRODIGAL SON
984–93

There are signs of a distinct change of course as we move into the mid-980s. In 983 Ælfhere died and two years later his kinsman and successor, Ælfric Cild, was exiled, bringing an end to the dominance this family had enjoyed in Mercia (and at times also central Wessex) over the previous generation. Perhaps more importantly, on 1 August 984 Bishop Æthelwold died. Æthelred later recalled this as a decisive turning point and the charter record bears this out: between August 984 and Pentecost 993 Ælfthryth, who had hitherto attested over half of her son's acts, disappears entirely. What is more, during this period the king himself undertook a number of acts which he was later to regret. It follows that Æthelred's minority regime was eclipsed at this point and the king started to make his own mark. It was, however, also in these years that the viking raids which were to characterize Æthelred's reign began in earnest, a coincidence which was to have lasting effects for the young monarch.

In order to elucidate these developments we will first consider the evidence of Æthelred's growing independence in the mid-980s, then examine how he used this to turn against the politics of his regents. This naturally leads on to a consideration of the viking raids of the period, culminating in the famed Maldon campaign of 991.

Growing independence: ruling the roost and the realm

One of the key questions during any royal minority was how and when the king would begin to rule independently. This was a delicate question, since those who had been active on his behalf were by no means guaranteed a warm welcome thereafter – it was in their interests to hold on to as much power as possible for as long as possible and conflicts between boy-kings and their regents (*de facto* or otherwise) frequently arose. In Æthelred's case he had come to the throne at somewhere between eight and twelve and would not, therefore, have expected to wait too long before taking over. Whether it was ever envisaged that the king should take over control at a specific moment is a good question. In the early Middle Ages, at least, there was no formal age of majority and opinions seem to have varied as to when a boy became a man. The Old English *Scriftboc* ('Confessor's Book'), the earliest vernacular penitential – that is, a work listing the appropriate penances for various sinful acts – gives fifteen as the age of adulthood of a boy and thirteen or fourteen for a girl, and this may reflect more widely held assumptions (one of the sermons in the *Blickling Homilies*, for example, reports that Martin of Tours reached manhood at fifteen).[1] Still, other ages were also considered significant: Æthelstan famously decreed that thieves over the age of twelve should be treated as adults and, though he later raised this to fifteen, subsequent rulers were to stick with the original figure.[2] There was thus a general sense that adulthood was reached somewhere in one's early to mid-teens and this squares with the evidence elsewhere in Europe, where twelve and fifteen are frequently given as ages of maturity.[3] Still, medieval concepts of youth could stretch well into the twenties – Isidore of Seville placed the end of childhood (*pueritia*) at fourteen, but considered adolescence (*adolescentia*) to go up to twenty-eight,

---

[1] *Scriftboc* (ed. Frantzen, X13.01.00–X.13.02.01); *The Blickling Homilies*, ed. R. Morris, EETS o.s. 58, 63, 73 (Oxford, 1874–80; repr. as 1 vol.: Oxford, 1967), no. XVIII, 213. See further S. Crawford, *Childhood in Anglo-Saxon England* (Stroud, 1999), 52–3.

[2] *II As* 1 (ed. Liebermann, I, 150–1); *VI As* 12 (ed. Liebermann, I, 182–3); *II Cn* 20 (ed. Liebermann, I, 322–3).

[3] Offergeld, *Reges pueri*, 10–21; S. Shahar, *Childhood in the Middle Ages* (London, 1990), 24–31; R. Meens, 'Children and Confession in the Early Middle Ages', *SCH* 31 (1994), 53–65.

while in the central Middle Ages twenty-one was often considered to be the age of majority in England[4] – and in any case one should imagine that in practice things tended to be less clear-cut than in theory.

Though earlier scholarship, working from the more fulsome evidence of the central and later Middle Ages, presumed that royal minorities came to an abrupt end when the monarch achieved one of these key ages, recent work suggests that matters were rarely so simple: even if there was a set age at which manhood was reached, the absence of a formal regency meant that there was no need for power to be handed over at a precise moment. In fact, all indications are that boy-kings took over control gradually as they neared maturity.[5] That this often took place around the age of fifteen is not surprising, but need not indicate the strict adherence to any rules. In Æthelred's own case there are hints that he may have begun to take on a more active role in the months and years leading up to 984: in 983 he starts subscribing charters with the distinctive phrase 'holding the most exalted rank of the (entire) kingdom' (*regni [totius] fastigium tenens*), which may have been intended to signal growing influence (it becomes uncommon after the 980s and was dropped entirely by the mid-990s).[6] In 984, when we then see a more dramatic break, Æthelred was somewhere between fourteen and eighteen. It is a rather pleasant thought that he might have been precisely fifteen and undergone some kind of rite of passage to mark this transition, but there is no concrete evidence to this effect. In any case, more important than his age were other developments – namely, the deaths of Ælfhere (983) and Æthelwold (1 August 984). Æthelwold's passing, in particular, seems to have been the spur for him to strike out on his own; with the influential bishop of Winchester gone, Æthelred was finally free to go it alone.

One of the signs of this new-found independence is his first marriage, struck around this time (*c.* 985). Marriage was an important stage in the medieval life cycle: it was when one set up a household and as such marked

---

[4] Isidore of Seville, *Etymologiae* XI.2 (ed. Linsay [unpaginated]); J. Hudson, *The Oxford History of the Laws of England*, II, *871–1216* (Oxford, 2012), 805–6 (cf. *ibid.*, 241 and 452).

[5] Kölzer, 'Königtum Minderjähriger', 314–15; Offergeld, *Reges pueri*, esp. 10–43.

[6] For the initial flurry: S 844 (KCD 639), S 851 (*Abing* 120), S 853 (*Burt* 24), S 855 (*Abing* 122), S 856 (KCD 648), S 857 (KCD 652), S 858 (*Abing* 123), S 860 (KCD 650). The last attestation is S 883 (*Abing* 125).

the transition to full adulthood – only a married man could have legitimate heirs, which were essential for the future of his family. We know remarkably little about Æthelred's first wife, a fact which is itself noteworthy. Post-Conquest Worcester sources record that her name was Ælfgifu and that she was the daughter of an 'Ealdorman (*comes*) Æthelberht'; however, no ealdorman of this name is known and the report is probably a product of later confusion (if not outright invention).[7] William of Malmesbury, for his part, does not give her name and implies that she was of low birth, but without supporting evidence this assertion must also be treated with caution – it seems most unlikely that a royal consort would be of low stock, though it may be that she paled in comparison with Æthelred's later wife, Emma.[8] More informative is Ailred of Rievaulx, writing in the early 1150s: he does not name the queen, but states that she was the daughter of an 'Earl (*comes*) Thored'. There was indeed an earl of York by this name in the 980s, lending credence to this report.[9] Ailred had served in the household of David I of Scotland (1124–53), who was himself a great-great-grandson of Æthelred with his first wife, so may have had access to privileged information here. How we are to square these contradictory reports is a good question. It is possible that we are dealing with two different women; however, in the absence of corroborating evidence it may be simpler to conclude that the Worcester sources are garbled at this point and that we are dealing with just one person, an Ælfgifu, daughter of Thored.[10] If she was indeed the daughter of the earl of York, the marriage was probably intended to strengthen Æthelred's hand in this region, where southern rulers frequently struggled for support. As noted, Ælfthryth disappears from the witness-lists of diplomas around this time and it has been suggested that there was a connection between this and her son's marriage; there could only be one true queen at a medieval court, and as Ælfgifu assumed this role her mother-in-law may have been pushed into

---

[7] *Florentii Wigornensis Chronicon ex chronicis*, ed. B. Thorpe, 2 vols. (London, 1848–9), I, 275.

[8] William of Malmesbury, *Gesta regum Anglorum* II.179 (ed. Mynors, 312).

[9] Ailred of Rievaulx, *Vita S. Eadwardi*, ch. 2, PL 195, col. 741.

[10] Keynes, *Diplomas*, 187, n. 118; Stafford, *Queen Emma*, 91, n. 116; Williams, *Æthelred*, 24–5.

the background.[11] That there is a connection of sorts is likely: Æthelred's marriage is symptomatic of his growing independence, an independence which perforce involved a reduction in his mother's influence. Nevertheless, it is surprising that the new queen did not leave more of an imprint on the historical record: she does not attest any of Æthelred's charters and there is no sign of her taking on the roles previously filled by Ælfthryth. Indeed, the impression is that for whatever reason Ælfgifu did not cut quite the same figure as her lofty predecessor. Perhaps Ælfthryth's influence still hung over the court; alternatively, it may be that having freed himself from the influence of one powerful female adviser, Æthelred was not keen to replace her with another. In any case, indicative of Ælfgifu's lower standing is the fact that her eldest son – and probably also her other offspring – was not brought up by the queen herself, but by his grandmother Ælfthryth and a foster-mother.[12] Whatever the precise grounds for Ælfgifu's relative quiescence, we know that this match was blessed with offspring: when, in 993, the young princes first subscribe one of their father's charters – and no ordinary charter at that – there were no fewer than four: Æthelstan, Ecgberht, Edmund and Eadred. In 997 these are joined by Eadwig and in 1001 by Edgar. In addition to these six sons, we know of at least two (and possibly three) daughters from these years, and there may have been more. If marriage was a first step towards setting up a household, the birth of a son was an essential further one; Æthelred was now a father and his dynasty's future secured. His sons all bear good West Saxon names and, with the exception of Ecgberht, they mirror the order of succession in the tenth century precisely.[13] The king was clearly proud of his family and the fact that Æthelstan stands atop this list speaks volumes: though later overtaken by Alfred the Great in fame, in the 980s it must have

---

[11] Pratt, 'Voice of the King', 198–9. See also P. Stafford, 'Sons and Mothers: Family Politics in the Early Middle Ages', in *Medieval Women*, ed. D. Baker (Oxford, 1978), 79–100 at 92–3.

[12] In his will the ætheling Æthelstan bequeaths land to his foster-mother (*fostormeder*) Ælfswith and refers to how Ælfthryth had 'brought me up' (*me affede*): S 1503 (*CantCC* 142). The former may have been the prince's wet-nurse, though fosterage generally came at a later age; cf. R.V. Turner, 'Eleanor of Aquitaine and Her Children: An Inquiry into Medieval Family Attachment', *Journal of Medieval History* 14 (1988), 321–35, at 325–6.

[13] As F. Barlow, *Edward the Confessor*, rev. edn (London, 1997), 28, first noted (in 1970).

seemed as if everything had begun with the king's great-uncle (a view with which many modern historians would be inclined to concur).[14] These names suggest a real sense of pride in his progeny: Æthelred was recreating the line of his forebears in miniature, doubtless in the hope that his sons would replicate the deeds of their venerable namesakes.

As Æthelred slowly emerged from the protection of his guardians he will have begun to perform the core functions of a medieval monarch, as spelled out in the coronation oath: defence of the realm, protection of the church and the weak, and promotion of justice. In practice, this meant overseeing an increasingly sophisticated (though by modern standards still decidedly makeshift) bureaucratic apparatus and balancing the various competing interests at court. As noted, the court itself was thought to be a microcosm of the polity. At its heart lay the royal household, whose members were in more or less permanent attendance on the king, being charged with overseeing the smooth operation of affairs. Beyond this it consisted of a rather nebulous group of individuals, ranging from national grandees, to local notables, to occasional hangers-on. The court was, in the words of one later commentator, 'constant only in its inconstancy' (*sola . . . mobilitate stabilis*): it was in a state of continual flux, expanding and contracting over the course of the year, depending upon the season and the region(s) through which the king happened to pass.[15] Yet herein lay its appeal: the court was a live entity, endlessly changing and evolving, reflecting not only the interests of the king, but also the abilities of leading noblemen to dominate discussion and debate there; it was a place of counsel and consideration, but also of secrecy and intrigue. Because it was an embodiment of the wider body politic, the court was also a place of pomp and circumstance: codes of conduct and behaviour were of particular importance and public demonstrations punctuated its progress through

---

[14] Foot, *Æthelstan*, 228.

[15] Walter Map, *De nugis curialium*, Dist. 1, ch. 1 (ed. James, 2). For masterful surveys, see S. Airlie, 'The Palace of Memory: The Carolingian Court as Political Centre', in *Courts and Regions in Medieval Europe*, ed. S.R. Jones, R. Marks and A.J. Minnis (York, 2000), 1–20; and N. Vincent, 'The Court of Henry II', in *Henry II: New Approaches*, ed. C. Harper-Bill and N. Vincent (Woodbridge, 2007), 278–334. See also J. Campbell, 'Anglo-Saxon Courts', in *Court Culture in the Early Middle Ages: The Proceedings of the First Alcuin Conference*, ed. C. Cubitt (Turnhout, 2003), 155–69, assembling some of the pre-Conquest material.

the realm. Indeed, much of the business of government was undertaken on the hoof, as the king moved from estate to estate and town to town throughout his kingdom. Major decisions, however, were held off for large kingdom-wide assemblies, grand occasions on which the monarch could consult a wider cross-section of the realm's ruling elite: it was here that ordinances were discussed and promulgated, diplomas were issued, and much else besides.

However, the court could not be everywhere at once and kings therefore relied heavily on local agents and officers. The core functionaries in this respect were the ealdormen, who oversaw large parts of the realm as royal representatives. Within these regions they acted in the king's name, supervising justice at the local shire and hundred courts and raising military levies in case of external threat. There were normally between three and six of these figures at any given time, drawn from the very highest echelons of the aristocracy.[16] Beneath the ealdormen were many other officers, the most important being the reeve. In origin, the reeve was an individual charged with just about any administrative duties (often the oversight of an estate); however, by the later tenth century reeves had begun taking on more significant responsibilities, both for kings and other lords.[17] The most important of the resulting offices was the shire reeve (or sheriff), who was in charge of a single county, where he took on similar responsibilities to the ealdorman. The two frequently acted in tandem, though when there were vacancies amongst the ranks of the ealdormen (as was not infrequently the case) reeves may have helped fill the gaps. Indeed, the most powerful of these figures enjoyed a status akin to that of an ealdorman and it may be this which lies behind the occasional designation of individuals as 'high-reeves'. There were many other kinds of reeve as well, however, the most important being those charged with the oversight of towns and fortified centres (*burh*-reeves) and ports (port-reeves). Reeves generally belonged to the rather more amorphous group of 'king's thegns',

[16] N. Banton, 'Ealdormen and Earls in England from the Reign of Alfred to the Reign of Æthelred II' (DPhil diss., Univ. of Oxford, 1981); S. Baxter, *The Earls of Mercia: Lordship and Power in Late Anglo-Saxon England* (Oxford, 2007), 61–124.

[17] P. Stafford, 'Reeve', in *The Wiley Blackwell Encyclopedia of Anglo-Saxon England*, ed. M. Lapidge *et al.*, 2nd edn (Chichester, 2013), 397–8.

those men of aristocratic status who had sworn a special oath of fidelity to the monarch. How many of these there were at any given time is hard to say, but they clearly formed the backbone of royal administration and it was from their ranks that reeves and ealdormen were chosen. It was through these figures – ealdormen, reeves and king's thegns – that royal power and authority was articulated in the locality.

Royal rule was not, however, simply a top-down affair. One of the key duties of such officers was to act as a point of contact between court and countryside: they relayed messages back and forth between the monarch and his people. Of particular importance here were the local shire and hundred assemblies: it was at these events that important announcements were made, issues discussed, and problems raised (and if needs be relayed back to the king). One must therefore imagine an entire network of regular – if often somewhat *ad hoc* – gatherings along which messages and information travelled. The best evidence of such communication comes from royal ordinances, which were not only sent out to local assemblies, but also garnered responses there (sometimes in written form).[18] The existence of this network served to mitigate the growing distance between the king and his people, allowing access to royal justice even in the ruler's absence. Nevertheless, they did not entirely replace the need for royal oversight and monarchs of the tenth and eleventh centuries remained very much itinerant, traversing large portions of the realm over the course of the year.[19] These movements served a number of loosely related purposes. They enabled the monarch to check up on his local officers, getting a sense for the lie of the land and ensuring that his will was being implemented. They also helped facilitate meetings with figures below the highest level of ealdormen and thegns, allowing kings to build and maintain firmer bonds of association between court and locality. Finally, and perhaps most importantly, these movements offered an opportunity to present the king to the people of his realm, providing a visible face to royal authority. The royal

---

[18] Pratt, 'Written Law'; L. Roach, 'Law Codes and Legal Norms in Later Anglo-Saxon England', *Historical Research* 86 (2013), 465–86.

[19] Foot, *Æthelstan*, 77–91; Roach, *Kingship and Consent*, 45–76. See also S. MacLean, 'Palaces, Itineraries and Political Order in the Post-Carolingian Kingdoms', in *Diverging Paths? The Shape of Power and Institutions in Medieval Christendom and Islam*, ed. A. Rodriguez and J. Hudson (Leiden, 2014), 291–320.

progress was thus a deeply symbolic affair: a chance for the ruler to be seen dispensing justice, showering gifts and rewards on faithful retainers and punishing those who had broken his peace.[20] However, despite their obvious significance, we know less about the king's movements than we should wish. Unlike on the continent (or, for that matter, in the later Anglo-Norman and Plantagenet realms), Anglo-Saxon monarchs seem to have reserved the production of diplomas and ordinances for large-scale assemblies, meaning that we can rarely locate the court more than four or five times a year (at best). What is more, most charters (and some decrees) do not state their place of production, meaning that it is not uncommon for us to go a year or more without being able to locate the king and court at all. Partial and problematic though the record thus is, it points to a focus of activity around central Wessex (Wiltshire, Hampshire, Somerset and Dorset) with the centre of gravity shifting slightly north- and eastwards in the latter half of the tenth century, when London and the Thames Valley start to appear more prominently, reflecting the growing socio-economic significance of the future metropolis.[21] Beyond these regions and immediate outliers – most notably Sussex, Surrey, east Devon and Gloucestershire – the king was rarely present in person further afield; in other regions he made his influence felt indirectly through ealdormen, reeves and other representatives.

The movements of the king were enabled by the royal household. This was, in effect, a subdivision of the court, charged with seeing to the well-being of the ruler and his entourage. It consisted of everything from cooks and cleaners to the kingdom's most prominent and powerful magnates. At the head of the household stood the seneschals (or stewards) and butlers, who oversaw the provision of food and drink. There could be up to three or four of these officers at any time and it is likely that securing victuals was only one of their many functions; they were the king's right-hand men, available on the spot to assist in any way possible. Though menial in origin, these were much vaunted positions by Æthelred's day. The reason

---

[20] L. Roach, 'Hosting the King: Hospitality and the Royal *iter* in Tenth-Century England', *Journal of Medieval History* 37 (2011), 34–46.

[21] D.[H.] Hill, *An Atlas of Anglo-Saxon England* (Oxford, 1981), 87–91. See also Wormald, *Making of English Law*, 430–8; and Keynes, 'Church Councils', 140–57.

lay in the proximity they brought to the king: those who oversaw the household had direct access to the monarch and thus possessed an ability to curry pardon and favour that few could match. Whether they still served the king at the dining table, as their titles suggest, is hard to say; though waiting on any other lord would have been deemed ignoble, monarchs may have been the exception here.[22] In any case, alongside these 'officers of the mouth' there were other household figures associated with the chamber (the chamberlain) and perhaps also the king's horses (the marshal, though the evidence here is slight). In addition to these secular officers, there were also chaplains attached to the court, who were entrusted with caring for the royal reliquary (which housed the king's personal collection of saints' relics), overseeing religious observations and perhaps also writing documents in the king's name.[23] These posts – particularly those of seneschal and butler – brought with them substantial power and influence: those who can be identified as such are generally sons or brothers of ealdormen and tend to attest amongst the very highest ranks of the thegns. Indeed, since these figures were in almost permanent attendance on the king, they in certain respects wielded more influence than an ealdorman: it was they who formed the inner cadre around the monarch, what in a somewhat different context Steffen Patzold has termed the 'tone-setting circle' (*tonangebender Kreis*),[24] and by tracing their composition we can get a sense of who was calling the shots at any given time.

From regency rule to 'youthful indiscretion'

As noted, there was clearly a significant rupture in the mid-980s, one which led to the temporary disappearance of Ælfthryth from diploma witness-lists and presumably also from court. Whether the queen-mother was

---

[22] L.M. Larson, *The King's Household in England before the Norman Conquest* (Madison, WI, 1904), 117–45; A. Gautier, 'Butlers and Dish-Bearers in Anglo-Saxon Courts: Household Officers at the Royal Table', *Historical Research* (forthcoming). Cf. G. Althoff and C. Witthöft, 'Les services symboliques entre dignité et contrainte', *Annales* 58 (2003), 1293–1318.

[23] Keynes, 'Regenbald', 187–95.

[24] Cf. S. Patzold, 'Konsens und Konkurrenz. Überlegungen zu einem aktuellen Forschungskonzept der Mediävistik', *FMSt* 41 (2007), 75–103.

driven out, or simply chose to keep her distance, her estrangement from her son and the prevailing regime is hard to miss.[25] Gaimar's twelfth-century *Estoire des Engleis* ('History of the English') reports that in her later years Ælfthryth retired to her foundation at Wherwell, and this may well reflect her experiences in these years (she would certainly not be the first dowager queen to enter into monastic retirement). However, the account is late, heavily embellished, and places Ælfthryth's withdrawal improbably early (immediately following Edward's martyrdom in 978), all of which raises serious questions as to its reliability.[26] Whatever the precise circumstances, what followed was a conscious reaction against the politics of Ælfthryth and her associates (and also, in a sense, Edgar): the proportion of diplomas issued in favour of lay recipients increases, while religious houses lost lands and rights, in many cases to the king's new favourites. It is no coincidence that one of the houses to suffer most was Abingdon, Æthelwold's first foundation and one of Ælfthryth's favoured centres. Later charters restoring lands and rights lost in these years – about which we shall have more to say in the following chapter – report that around this time Æthelred sold the office of abbot to a certain Eadwine upon the request of the latter's brother, Ealdorman Ælfric (of Hampshire), and the local diocesan bishop, Wulfgar of Ramsbury. This act contravened the monks' right to elect their own abbot, as enshrined in the Benedictine Rule (and also the *Regularis concordia*), and was thus a direct assault on the reformers' legacy.[27] Eadwine himself apparently went on to abuse his post and we later hear of estates which were 'unjustly' acquired by a local reeve during these years.[28] Similar events transpired at the Old Minster in Winchester, Æthelwold's sometime bishopric, where the king is said to have taken and withheld lands from the monks, granting these on to new associates.[29] An anecdote recorded by William of Malmesbury suggests that Glastonbury may have suffered

[25] Keynes, *Diplomas*, 176–7. Cf. Stafford, *Queen Emma*, 203–4.

[26] Gaimar, *Estoire des Engleis*, ll. 4084–8, ed. I. Short (Oxford, 2009), 222. Cf. S. MacLean, 'Queenship, Nunneries and Royal Widowhood in Carolingian Europe', *P & P* 178 (2003), 3–38.

[27] S 876 (*Abing* 124). See also *ASC* 985 CDE (ed. O'Brien O'Keeffe, 85).

[28] S 918 (*Abing* 135). See also *Historia ecclesie Abbendonensis*, ch. 96, ed. J. Hudson, 2 vols. (Oxford, 2002–7), I, 138–40.

[29] S 891 (KCD 698). Cf. S 861 (KCD 655).

similarly: according to this report a certain Ælfwold joined the community in anticipation of his death, granting it his properties; however, upon recovering from illness, the magnate sought to relinquish religious life and regain his lands. To this end, he enlisted the support of Æthelred and it was only Dunstan's timely intervention which prevented the abbey's spoliation: the prelate cursed Ælfwold, who promptly died, becoming food for the foxes.[30] This is a somewhat fanciful tale and probably tells us more about Dunstan's later reputation than the realities of the 980s. Nevertheless, William was well acquainted with Glastonbury's archive (which has suffered significant subsequent losses) and there are other signs of strain in these years: a letter survives from a certain 'Pope John', probably John XV (985–96), to an 'Ealdorman Ælfric', urging the latter to restore what he had taken from Glastonbury.[31] Though there were two ealdormen by this name in these years, the letter probably refers to Ælfric of Hampshire, the same individual who had been the driving force behind Eadwine's appointment at Abingdon (the other candidate, Ælfric Cild, was an associate of the regency regime and had been exiled in 985, in only his second year in office). Such attacks and expropriations clearly created problems for the houses in question: the papal letter to Ælfric was written in response to appeals from the monks, while the brothers of the Old Minster seem to have resorted to forgery to secure their holdings at this point; evidently they could not count on royal support.[32]

Hardest hit, however, was the see of Rochester. The *Chronicle* reports that Æthelred 'laid waste' (*fordyde*) to this in 986 and post-Conquest sources provide further detail. Osbern of Canterbury reports that the king besieged the town unsuccessfully, then proceeded to ravage the bishopric's estates, stopping only after Dunstan bribed him to cease and desist.[33]

[30] William of Malmesbury, *Vita S. Dunstani* II.25 (ed. Winterbottom and Thomson, 280–2).

[31] *Papsturkunden 896–1046*, ed. H. Zimmermann, 2 vols. (Vienna, 1984–5), no. 282.

[32] See S 540 (BCS 863), a purported grant by Eadred of estates later restored in S 891 (KCD 698), written in imitative script: Wormald, 'Æthelwold', 187; Keynes, 'Church Councils', 117, n. 362. Wormald identifies the same hand in two other forgeries, and one wonders if these estates and rights were also lost or challenged in these years: S 376 (BCS 621), S 443 (BCS 727).

[33] Osbern, *Vita S. Dunstani*, ch. 39 (ed. Stubbs, 117). Cf. William of Malmesbury, *Vita S. Dunstani* II.22 (ed. Winterbottom and Thomson, 274), who largely follows Osbern here.

Sulcard of Westminster, on the other hand, records something of the king's motives: according to him Æthelred had granted an estate belonging to Rochester to one of his soldiers (a *miles*), whom the bishop had ejected. This roused the king's anger and Æthelred went on to devastate the bishopric, for which Dunstan upbraided him.[34] These reports must be treated with caution: they come from a period in which Dunstan's reputation was on the rise and Æthelred's on the wane, and both end with the venerable prelate prophesying future death and destruction on the king. Be that as it may, the fact that these attacks drew the attention of the *Chronicle* says something about their severity. There certainly is reason to believe that the king and bishop of Rochester, Ælfstan, were at loggerheads, since the latter attests no diplomas between 984 and 988 (a further sign, incidentally, that 984 marks a change of course).[35] Local documents also reveal something about these developments. A diploma of 987 records the grant of Bromley to a certain Æthelsige (of whom more anon), an estate to which Rochester had a traditional claim and which had been under dispute for some time.[36] In 998 the king went on to restore these lands in a document which singles out Æthelsige for censure, noting that the magnate had subsequently been declared a 'public enemy' (*publicus hostis*) for his rapacity.[37] These events clearly troubled Ælfstan and the clerics of Rochester cathedral, and at some point in these years the latter seem to have forged a diploma in Edgar's name granting Bromley to St-Andrew's. Though the supposed date of this document (955) is impossible and the script too late for the 950s, it speaks volumes of the problems created by Æthelred's interventions; like the monks of the Old Minster, the local canons felt the need to use forgery to secure their rights. However, if initially an expression of impotence and exasperation, this charter was eventually to have the desired effect: it – and not the earlier diplomas concerning Bromley – was to form the basis of

---

[34] Sulcard, *Prologus de construccione Westmonasterii*, ch. 5, ed. B.W. Scholz; 'Sulcard of Westminster, "Prologus de construccione Westmonasterii"', *Traditio* 20 (1964), 59–91, at 89–90. Cf. *ibid.*, 74–6.

[35] Keynes, *Atlas*, table LXa.

[36] S 864 (*Roch* 30); with S. Keynes, 'King Æthelred the Unready and the Church of Rochester', in *Textus Roffensis: Law, Language, and Libraries in Early Medieval England*, ed. B. O'Brian and B. Bombi (Turnhout, 2015), 315–62, at 334–6.

[37] S 893 (*Roch* 32).

Æthelred's later restitution (both share a variant version of the estate's bounds).[38] But Bromely was not the only loss at this point: a diploma of 995 records a restitution of lands at Wouldham and Littlebrook which also seem to have come into Æthelred's hands in the mid- to later 980s.[39] It may be that one of these three estates is that alluded to by Sulcard – indeed, it is tempting to identify Æthelsige as the soldier of his account and Bromley as the land in question, though the chronology does not quite fit (the attacks mentioned by Sulcard are evidently those described in the *Chronicle* under 986, yet the charter concerning Bromley was issued a year later).[40] These conflicts also find an echo in the numismatic record (that is, coinage): Sideman, a Rochester-based moneyer, used an altered obverse ('heads') die of the *First Hand (c.* 979–85) to strike *Second Hand* coins (*c.* 985–91), suggesting that his normal supply lines failed him at this point. Moreover, while he had been one of three moneyers to produce *First Hand* coins at Rochester, Sideman was the only one to go on to strike the *Second Hand*, perhaps pointing to further disruption at this point.[41] It is evident that Rochester suffered significantly and, unlike elsewhere, there seems to have been open violence between the parties here.

These attacks – and the king's later efforts to amend them – indicate that Æthelred was breaking with past precedent; in the place of Ælfthryth, Ælfhere and Æthelwold, he now sought out new advisers who proposed new policies. The result was a return to a situation something like the 'anti-monastic reaction': lay magnates took the initiative, claiming (or reclaiming) lands and rights from their ecclesiastical neighbours. That this period saw an increase in grants in favour of laymen thus makes perfect sense. Nevertheless, it would be wrong to see these acts as straightforwardly anti-ecclesiastical; as Pauline Stafford notes, the church was not a monolith, and attacks on one or two religious houses do not an outright rejection of the

[38] S 671 (*Roch* 29); with Keynes, 'Church of Rochester', 335 and 345. See also S 280 (*Roch* 19), a purported grant of Snodland to Rochester, forged around this time in imitative script.

[39] S 885 (*Roch* 31).

[40] Scholz, 'Sulcard', 75–6. It is, however, conceivable that the diploma confirmed Æthelsige in possession of lands he had acquired some time earlier.

[41] R.H.M. Dolley, 'Æthelræd's Rochester Ravaging of 986: An Intriguing Numismatic Sidelight', *Spink's Numismatic Circular* 75 (1967), 33–4.

institutional church make.[42] Indeed, churchmen were complicit in Æthelred's actions: the Eadwine appointed abbot of Abingdon in 985 was presumably a professed monk, while Bishop Wulfgar of Ramsbury was also involved in this appointment. If we look at matters on a more personal and less institutional level, however, a clearer picture emerges. The three monastic houses known to have suffered in these years all enjoyed close ties with Æthelwold: Abingdon was the prelate's first foundation, the Old Minster (which by this point was both monastery and cathedral chapter) had been his bishopric, while Glastonbury is where he had learned the tools of the trade under Dunstan. There is, therefore, a distinctly anti-Æthelwoldian bent to these attacks. This is not all: these houses all also enjoyed ties with Ælfthryth and Ælfhere, and it is interesting to note that the latter had been buried at Glastonbury only shortly before these events.[43] Ælfhere's was not the only prominent body interred at Glastonbury: it was also the resting place of Æthelred's father, Edgar.[44] In allowing attacks on the monastery the king was therefore not only breaking with regency politics, but also with paternal precedent. The conflict with Rochester can be viewed in similar terms. It is evident that Ælfstan and the king had a major falling out, perhaps over the latter's use of lands claimed by the bishop to reward his followers. Ælfstan himself was part of the old guard which owed its promotion to Edgar and the reformers and is recorded as a 'brother' of the Old Minster (an associate, perhaps a sometime member of the community), suggesting that he too belonged to the wider Æthelwoldian orbit.[45] Interestingly, Wulfgar of Ramsbury, who acted against the interests of Abingdon at this point, is also recorded as a brother of the Old Minster, raising questions as to his motives. Perhaps his actions reveal divisions within Æthelwoldian circles (infighting was by no means uncommon within reforming movements); alternatively, he may have been acting in

---

[42] Stafford, 'Reign of Æthelred II', 27.

[43] William of Malmesbury, *De antiquitate Glastonie ecclesie*, ch. 31, ed. J. Scott, *The Early History of Glastonbury* (Woodbridge, 1981), 84. Ælfhere's brother Ælfheah was apparently also buried there: John of Worcester, *Chronicon, s.a.* 971 (ed. Darlington and McGurk, 420).

[44] Marafioti, *The King's Body*, 65–77.

[45] BL Stowe 944, fol. 18r. See Keynes, 'Church of Rochester', 322–3 and 331–2.

the interests of his see, whose position was threatened by the growing power and influence of its monastic neighbours at Abingdon.

The reason for these attacks is to be sought in Æthelred's desire to cultivate new contacts. This was perfectly natural: in order to establish themselves, rulers frequently broke with the past, seeking to promote individuals who would owe them direct (if not always exclusive) loyalty. This is what happened in Eadwig's reign, when a number of new figures was advanced at the expense of more established ones. Similar trends can be seen in the early years of Otto I of East Francia (Germany) (936–73), during which the king broke with the more consensual politics of his father, in part in order to establish his own clientele.[46] Nonetheless, it was rare for such shifts to be so abrupt or dramatic as those witnessed in England in the mid- to late 980s; Æthelred did not just favour new men, he actively snubbed the legacy of those who had come before. That these actions met with opposition stands to reason, but with Æthelred now firmly at the helm this seems to have been largely muted (whatever Dunstan's later hagiographers would have us believe). Still, that earlier reformers such as Dunstan and Oswald looked on with dismay is to be presumed; the former's foundation at Glastonbury was amongst the houses to suffer, while Rochester lay only a day's march from Canterbury. That both of these prelates – along with many others who had been prominent at court before 984 – continued attesting royal diplomas should therefore be seen as a sign of acquiescence, not genuine support.[47] It was only when disagreements came to the surface, as in the case of Ælfstan of Rochester (and perhaps also Ælfthryth) that they led to the disappearance of an individual from these lists. Indeed, it is interesting to note that Ælfric Cild, Ælfhere's kinsman and successor, was exiled in 985; one suspects that the ealdorman's fault lay in opposing the king's new politics. Certainly, it is interesting that Ælfric is later said to have been indicted 'by the unanimous legal verdict and just sentence of the bishops, ealdormen and all the leading men of this kingdom' (*episcoporum, ducum omniumque huius regni optimatum unanimo legali consilio aequissimoque iudicio*) – but not, apparently, any abbots.[48]

---

[46] Becher, *Otto I.*, 110–39. A somewhat similar change of factions took place in West Francia upon the accession of Charles the Straightforward (898): Koziol, *Politics of Memory*, 459–79.

[47] Keynes, *Diplomas*, 181–2. Cf. Koziol, *Politics of Memory*, 423–4, for a similar case.

[48] S 896 (*Abing* 128). See also *ASC* 985 DE (ed. Cubbin, 48); and S 937 (*Abing* 129).

If attesting charters alone cannot always be taken as a sign of unalloyed support, we can be confident that those figures who owed their promotion to these years were indeed supporters of Æthelred's actions. Not surprisingly, a number of those individuals who the king was later to blame for his misdemeanours can be identified amongst the witnesses to his charters in these years. Thus, Wulfgar, who is said to have encouraged Æthelred to sell the abbacy of Abingdon, was bishop at Ramsbury between *c.* 981 and *c.* 985/6 and frequently attests in this capacity (if not always very high up the lists). The Eadwine whose career Wulfgar is said to have helped advance first subscribes as abbot in 987 and continues to do so until his death in 990. Ealdorman Ælfric of Hampshire, on the other hand, whose involvement in his brother's promotion was also later criticized by the king, was another leading figure at court; he attests frequently, generally third or fourth amongst the ealdormen.[49] Most of the other bishops and ealdormen owed their positions to Æthelred's predecessors, so we can be less certain as to their allegiances. The senior thegns, meanwhile, were Ælfweard (till 986) and Ælfsige (till 995). These two may have had a hand in developments, but again had achieved their positions earlier, so we cannot be certain. We can be more confident in the case of Ælfgar, however, who first rises to prominence in the later 980s, attesting third or fourth in 985 and then rising to first or second from 987: he is to be identified as the son of Ealdorman Ælfric of Hampshire, who received lands at Ebbesbourne (Wilts.) in 986 which had previously belonged to the Old Minster.[50] A later document in favour of Abingdon reports that a certain 'reeve Ælfgar' had persuaded the king to grant him an estate rightfully belonging to the monastery during Eadwine's abbacy (985–90). Though the charter in question is suspect, there is probably an element of truth to the tale – Abbot Eadwine was Ælfgar's uncle, after all, and the thegn had a track record where ecclesiastical property was concerned.[51] A grant of five hides

---

[49] Keynes, *Diplomas*, tables LX–LXII.

[50] *Ibid.*, table LXIII; S 861 (KCD 655), S 891 (KCD 698). Although Kelly writes of 'the Ælfgar who is mentioned in **124** [S 876]', stating that he was 'one of those who led the king astray after Æthelwold's death' (*Charters of Abingdon*, ed. Kelly, 530), there is, in fact, no mention of the thegn in this document.

[51] S 918 (*Abing* 135). See *Charters of Abingdon*, ed. Kelly, 529–30.

at Wylye, also in Wiltshire, to the king's 'faithful servant' (*fidelis minister*) Ælfgar in 988 is presumably also to the same individual. Interestingly, Edward the Martyr had granted a slightly larger estate at Wylye to a certain Ælfric in 977; though the two estates are distinct, one wonders whether we are seeing similar shifts within secular land-holding towards the king's new favourites (the diploma mentions two other prior occupants, but does not specify how they came into or lost these lands).[52] Indeed, our sources generally favour ecclesiastical landholding and it is possible that the estates of other old hands at court also suffered in these years. In any case, two other thegns also rose to prominence around this time: Wulfsige, who appears in most witness-lists between 980 and 988 and may have had a hand in guiding the king's actions; and Æthelsige, who attests between 984 and 994, generally in one of the top five spots. The latter is almost certainly the same figure who is said to have been involved in Rochester's spoliation (his disappearance in 994 fits this profile, since we know that by 998 this figure had been outlawed).[53] This Æthelsige is probably also the recipient of a grant of twelve hides at *Æsce* in 987; though the location of the estate is uncertain, the most recent suggestion, Ash in Hampshire, would not be inconceivable for a prominent thegn otherwise known to have held land in Kent.[54]

Alongside these new favourites we can also trace the careers of a number of more established individuals. Foremost amongst these are the two most senior ealdormen, Æthelwine of East Anglia, one of the sons of the Half-King, and Byrhtnoth of Essex. One hesitates to ascribe either of these an active role in the ongoing attacks on churches; they owed their promotion to Edgar's patronage and are known supporters of monastic reform, both enjoying ties with houses which suffered in these years (Æthelwine with Glastonbury and Byrhtnoth with Abingdon).[55] Æthelweard, the only other

---

[52] S 868 (KCD 664). See above, Chapter 2, p. 70.

[53] Keynes, *Atlas*, table LXIII. See Keynes, *Diplomas*, 184–5; and *Charters of Rochester*, ed. A. Campbell, Anglo-Saxon Charters 1 (London, 1973), xxvi–xxvii.

[54] S 863 (*Burt* 25). See *Charters of Burton*, ed. P.H. Sawyer, Anglo-Saxon Charters 2 (Oxford, 1979), 42.

[55] *Charters of Glastonbury*, ed. Kelly, 148–51; R. Abels, 'Byrhtnoth (*d.* 991)', *ODNB*, IX, 333–5.

ealdorman in office, probably took a similar stance; he may have received his education under Æthelwold at Winchester and was also sympathetic to the cause of reform. Indeed, Æthelweard is otherwise best known for the Latin chronicle he composed in these years (978 × 988, probably *c*. 985) and it has been suggested that he did not take the narrative into the reigns of Edward and Æthelred – as the chapter headings suggest had been his original intention – precisely because there was little good to be said.[56] The general impression, therefore, is that the consensus regime of the early 980s was beginning to fall apart: a small group of new favourites was making itself heard and other voices were being either silenced or ignored. It is noteworthy that the homilist Ælfric (then of Cerne in Dorset, latterly of Eynsham), who had also received his education under Æthelwold at Winchester, is more ambivalent about royal authority than had been the earlier reformers, perhaps reflecting the experiences of these years; he had seen the darker side of kingship.[57] Similar concerns can be detected behind the Latin *Passion* of SS Æthelberht and Æthelred, written at Ramsey *c*. 991. In this, the inauspiciously named royal adviser Thunor (Thunor being the Old English for the pagan deity Thor) convinces the Kentish ruler Ecgberht (664–73) to execute his young nephews, Æthelberht and Æthelred, to disastrous effect.[58] Royal counsel was evidently a hot topic and it is hard not to see herein a reflex of the rise of a small cadre of new associates in the later 980s.

These events were to leave quite the legacy. They mark the first efforts by Æthelred to go it alone and, though the king later came to regret them, there is every reason to believe that they were carefully considered at the time. As such, they provide some of our first insights into Æthelred's personality: they show the king reacting to the politics of his guardians and doing so in no uncertain terms. If there was a single target of these attacks – not all of which were led by Æthelred himself, but to which the king was

---

[56] Æthelweard, *Chronicon* IV.prol., ed. A. Campbell (London, 1962), 34; with Ashley, 'Æthelweard', 229–30. More generally, see Gretsch, 'Historiography'.

[57] M. Clayton, 'Ælfric and Æthelred', in *Essays on Anglo-Saxon and Related Themes in Memory of Lynne Grundy*, ed. J. Roberts and J.[L.] Nelson (Woodbridge, 2000), 65–88, at 67–9. See also Rabin, 'Holy Bodies'; and Ælfric, *Letter to the Monks at Eynsham*, ed. C.A. Jones (Cambridge, 1998), 47–8.

[58] *Passio SS. Æthelberhti Æthelredique*, ed. T. Arnold, *Symeonis Monachi Opera Omnia*, Rolls Series, 2 vols. (London, 1882–5), II, 3–13; with Denton, 'Hagiography', 102–8.

clearly happy to turn a blind eye – it was the legacy of these figures: Æthelred and his associates moved against institutions and individuals associated with Ælfthryth, Ælfhere and Æthelwold. Rochester may represent a partial exception here: though Ælfstan was a 'brother' of the Old Minster, it is possible that Sulcard of Westminster is right that this was in essence a conflict over church property which spiralled out of control. Still, Ælfstan belonged to the old guard at court and Æthelred's move against him is symptomatic of the drift of politics in these years.

As noted, Æthelred's acts went well beyond the upheaval we might expect to accompany a change of regime. Though it is tempting to dismiss them as a typical 'teenage rebellion', to do so would be to overlook the deeper causes. Æthelred was not the only boy-king to react against the policies of his sometime regents. Upon reaching maturity Otto III of Germany is reported to have dismissed his grandmother and erstwhile guardian Adelheid from court, while Henry IV similarly moved against his earlier regents upon nearing majority in the mid-1060s: he is said to have started favouring the counsel of Adalbert of Hamburg-Bremen, initiating a series of attacks on monastic landholding. Predictably, this inspired jealousy and opposition and eventually Henry was forced to dismiss Adalbert from his counsels.[59] The reign of the next English child monarch, Henry III (1216–72), follows a similar trajectory: during his early years of independent rule Henry came to depend heavily upon the counsel of the powerful bishop of Winchester, Peter des Roches, to the detriment of other advisers, above all Hubert de Burgh and Richard Marshal, both of whom enjoyed ties to the previous regency regime. As in the cases of Æthelred and Henry IV, Henry III was accused of ruling arbitrarily, of depending too heavily upon the advice of an inner cadre of favourites, and in later years the king instituted a kind of moral reform to lift

---

[59] Thietmar of Merseburg, *Chronicon* IV.15, ed. R. Holtzmann, MGH: SS rer. Germ. n.s. 9 (Berlin, 1935), 148–51; with J. Fried, 'Kaiserin Theophanu und das Reich', in *Köln: Stadt und Bistum in Kirche und Reich des Mittelalters. Festschrift für Odilo Engels zum 65. Geburtstag*, ed. H. Vollrath and S. Weinfurter (Cologne, 1993), 139–85, at 184–5 (though cf. Offergeld, *Reges pueri*, 721–2); and Lampert of Hersfeld, *Annales, s.a.* 1063 and 1066, ed. O. Holder-Egger, MGH: SS rer. Germ. 38 (Hannover, 1894), 88–91 and 100–2; with Robinson, *Henry IV*, 58–61; and Althoff, *Heinrich IV.*, 60–6.

this stain.[60] Boys who grew up on the throne thus seem to have found it hard to establish themselves and were inclined to react strongly – indeed, one might well say: overreact – to the policies of their erstwhile caretakers.[61] There were a number of reasons for this. As we have seen, regencies were by their nature compromise regimes: they avoided rocking the boat and often granted substantial freedoms to the kingdom's leading magnates in order to keep them quiet. When the king came of age and tried to reassert traditional monarchical rights, this naturally created tensions. Another bone of contention was the relationship between king and regent(s): while young monarchs often wished to impose their will at the first opportunity, it was in the interest of their guardians to hold on to power as long as possible. There may also have been psychological grounds for these conflicts. Minority regimes were frequently fractious, a fact which seems to have left many child monarchs jaundiced and distrustful; in later years they often showed themselves to be reliant on the counsel of a few chosen favourites and changes of direction (and faction) were not uncommon. Whatever the precise cause, the phenomenon is sufficiently well attested that it need not indicate that Æthelred's regents were particularly overbearing, nor that the young king was particularly defiant. That said, this is exactly how it must have felt to Æthelred; it is clear that he resented the influence of his guardians and sought to escape this at the first opportunity. This is understandable: Ælfthryth was a commanding woman and Æthelwold himself was a man of principle, not compromise – one imagines that they were not the most pliant of regents.

It is, therefore, in these years that Æthelred's personality starts to come to light. He had felt suffocated by the influence of his regents in the 980s and broke with them in the most public manner possible thereafter: he reversed their policies, encouraging attacks on Æthelwold's houses and distancing himself (both physically and politically) from his mother. Ælfthryth herself, still alive and in good health, could only look on with dismay.

---

[60] N. Vincent, *Peter des Roches: An Alien in English Politics, 1205–1238* (Cambridge, 1996), esp. 259–465; B. Weiler, *Kingship, Rebellion and Political Culture: England and Germany, c. 1215–c.1250* (Basingstoke, 2007), 11–21 and 23–5.

[61] This aspect is overlooked in Offergeld's otherwise exemplary study, *Reges pueri*. Cf. C. Hillen, 'Minority Governments of Henry III, Henry (VII) and Louis IX Compared', *Thirteenth Century England* 11 (2007), 46–60, at 57, on Henry (VII) of Germany's efforts to break free from his regency in the late 1220s.

The wages of sin

While Æthelred's new favourites clearly egged him on, others must have felt increasing alarm. Edgar and the reformers had taught that success in this world was achieved through royal and national piety; Æthelred's rejection of this basic principle must have been most troubling. It would not be long before the results became clear.

In 986, the very year Æthelred is said to have ravaged Rochester, the nation was hit by a livestock plague (murrain) – and not for the last time, the chronicler is keen to emphasize.[62] Equally worrying was the growing viking threat. Scandinavian raiders had twice appeared in the years of Æthelred's minority (980 and 982), but thereafter there was something of a lull.[63] When the attacks renewed in earnest in 988, this was only shortly after a number of the king's more prominent moves against church landholding.[64] Yet this was not all. In 991 a larger force – ninety-three ships, if the A-version of the *Chronicle* is to be trusted – ravaged Folkestone and overran Sandwich and Ipswich before defeating Ealdorman Byrhtnoth and the East Saxon levy at Maldon.[65] This event sent shockwaves throughout the realm. Byrhtnoth was the second most senior ealdorman and his loss was a major blow to a nation which had not faced defeat in half a century. As a consequence, the king and his counsellors, led by Archbishop Sigeric of Canterbury, decided to buy off the attackers with a tribute of 10,000 pounds, the first appearance of Æthelred's famed policy of buying time with money. This only won a brief respite, however, and the same force seems to have been active again in the following year. This time the king and his advisers sought to face the raiders at sea, but their efforts met with failure. A raiding army – probably the same force, or a splinter-group thereof – then harried the northern parts of the realm in 993, sacking Bamburgh and ravaging down as far south as Lindsey (roughly speaking modern Lincolnshire) and the Humber. Finally, in 994 Olaf and Swein, who may have led this host since 991, harassed

---

[62] *ASC* 986 CDE (ed. O'Brien O'Keeffe, 85).

[63] *ASC* 980 CDE, 982 CDE (ed. O'Brien O'Keeffe, 84).

[64] *ASC* 988 CDE (ed. O'Brien O'Keeffe, 86).

[65] *ASC* 993 A (= ?991) (ed. Bately, 79), 991 CDE (ed. O'Brien O'Keeffe, 86). On the difficulties posed by the A-version of the *Chronicle*, see below, pp. 120–1.

Essex, Kent, Sussex and Hampshire before being bought off with a new tribute of 16,000 pounds.[66] All this must have been more than a little ominous. But these were not the only blows which the king had to face: his two leading bishops, Dunstan and Oswald, died in 988 and 991 and his most senior ealdorman, Æthelwine, died in early 992, leaving Æthelred bereft of his father's old guard of faithful counsellors.

In the Middle Ages it was something of a commonplace that the well-being of the realm depended on the piety of its ruler and people and, as we have seen, this line of thought had been embraced enthusiastically by the reformers of the tenth century.[67] The Bible, and in particular the Old Testament, provided many examples of pious kings who led their people to greatness (David, Solomon, Josiah) and sinful rulers who brought them to destruction (Saul, Ahab, Rehoboam), and writers such as Bede, whose *Ecclesiastical History* was widely available in these years, were quick to apply such typologies to the rulers of their day.[68] More immediate impetus for such thoughts may have come from the Irish tract known as 'The Twelve Abuses of the Age', mentioned at a number of points already.[69] This work was well known in later Anglo-Saxon England and was especially popular amongst the reformers – Æthelwold had given a copy to his foundation at Peterborough and Ælfric the homilist and Wulfstan of York were both acquainted with it.[70] The 'Twelve Abuses' lists a dozen moral failings, ranging from the 'wise man without (good) works' (*sapiens sine operibus*) to the 'people without law' (*populus sine lege*), and the catastrophes which result from these – it is, in essence, a handbook to the wages of sin. The most famous and frequently cited of these abuses is the ninth, the 'unjust king' (*rex iniquus*), whose reign is said to bring disaster on his nation in the form of foreign invasion, the death of loved ones and children, storms,

---

[66] *ASC* 992–4 CDE (ed. O'Brien O'Keeffe, 86–7).

[67] M. Blattmann, ' "Ein Unglück für sein Volk": der Zusammenhang zwischen Fehlverhalten des Königs und Volkswohl in Quellen des 7.–12. Jahrhunderts', *FMSt* 30 (1996), 80–102.

[68] J. McClure, 'Bede's Old Testament Kings', in *Ideal and Reality in Frankish and Anglo-Saxon Society*, ed. P. Wormald *et al.* (Oxford, 1983), 76–98.

[69] R. Meens, 'Politics, Mirrors of Princes and the Bible: Sins, Kings and the Well-Being of the Realm', *EME* 7 (1998), 345–57.

[70] S 1448 (*Pet* 29). See Clayton, '*De Duodecim*'.

infertile soil and destruction by wild beasts.[71] To an English audience in the early 990s, this must have read like a catalogue of recent events, and it is probably no accident that Ælfric decided to render this work into English around this time (*c.* 995). The homilist abbreviated the text in the process of translation, but chose to keep almost all of the ninth abuse, suggesting a particularly keen interest in this section. It is hard not to read the resulting work as an oblique commentary on the king's actions in the later 980s, especially since – as we have noted – it cites the famous biblical line, 'Woe to thee, oh land, when thy king is a child' (*Vae enium terrae, cuius rex est puer*: Ecclesiastes X.16), in the context of its teachings on the unjust king (a detail which Ælfric notably keeps); in the reign of a child monarch, the implications of this phrase must have been hard to miss.[72] Noteworthy too is the third abuse, 'the young man without obedience' (*adolescens sine obedientia*), a description which might also be felt to apply to Æthelred (though Ælfric seems to have been rather less interested in this section and abbreviates it heavily).[73] The core teachings of the ninth abuse were also distilled in two chapters of the *Collectio canonum Hibernensis*, an Irish collection of church law which was well known in this period: four copies survive and excerpts are found in manuscripts associated with Archbishop Wulfstan.[74]

As setbacks began to mount, the kingdom's ruling elite must have started pointing fingers, and many of these would have been directed towards the king and his closest advisers (interestingly, the sixth abuse, 'the nobleman without virtue' [*dominus sine virtute*], attracted almost as much interest from Ælfric as the 'unjust king').[75] To many, especially within reforming circles, it must have seemed as if their worst nightmares had come true. Still, we must be careful not to exaggerate the gravity of these events. As we have seen, the

[71] Pseudo-Cyprian, *De XII abusivis saeculi*, abusio 9, ed. S. Hellmann (Leipzig, 1910), 51–3.

[72] Ælfric, *De duodecim abusivis*, abusio 9, ed. M. Clayton, *Two Ælfric Texts: 'The Twelve Abuses' and 'The Vices and Virtues'* (Woodbridge, 2013), 128–30.

[73] Pseudo-Cyprian, *De XII abusivis saeculi*, abusio 3 (ed. Hellmann, 36–8). Cf. Ælfric, *De duodecim abusivis*, abusio 3 (ed. Clayton, 116).

[74] *Collectio canonum Hibernensis* XXV.3–4, ed. H. Wasserschleben, *Die irische Kanonensammlung*, 2nd edn (Leipzig, 1885), 77. Cf. S. Ambrose, 'The *Collectio canonum Hibernensis* and the Literature of the Anglo-Saxon Benedictine Reform', *Viator* 36 (2005), 107–18.

[75] Ælfric, *De duodecim abusivis*, abusio 6 (ed. Clayton, 122–4).

main *Chronicle*-account of these years was written some time after Æthelred's death with the benefit of hindsight; to those on the ground, such early raids must have been a cause for concern, but were probably not yet a pressing matter.[76] Indeed, Æthelred's coinage suggests that his regime was not significantly affected by these events, at least from an institutional standpoint: at some point soon after the death of Æthelwold the *First Hand* gave way to the *Second Hand* (apparently a variant version of the same issue, *c.* 985) and, after a brief experimentation with another closely related type, the *Benediction Hand* (*c.* 991), these were replaced by the *Crux*, bearing a cross and the Latin inscription 'CRVX' (that is, 'cross') on the reverse (*c.* 991) (Plate 2). Traditionally, these have been seen as two (or three) distinct *Hand* types, but given the close iconographic similarity between them and the relative absence of coins of the *Second Hand* from the north of the kingdom (where it would seem that the *First Hand* remained in production and circulation throughout the later 980s), it is probably best to see the latter two as variations on the existing *Hand* issue; they are evidence of significant tinkering with the coinage, but not a complete overhaul. The system of regular recoinages was still very much in its infancy, and such variation and experimentation were to be expected. In fact, the *Second* and *Benediction Hand* variants seem to constitute something between what would later be considered a full (or 'substantive') issue and the adjustment of an existing type; they were stepping-stones towards the more major overhaul seen later.[77] All of this suggests 'business as usual': the Hand of Providence, depicted on the first two of these types (and also in modified form on the third) and the cross are both common motifs and little in the production of these coins calls for explanation. The dies of the *Second Hand*, in particular, show great consistency in comparison with the *First Hand* and later *Reform* type coins, suggesting close (and possibly tightening) royal control.[78] Rather less typical is the *Benediction Hand*, which was produced briefly between the *Second Hand* and *Crux*. Its sudden

---

[76] See above, Introduction, pp. 4–5.

[77] Stewart, 'Coinage and Recoinage', 471–4; Naismith, 'Coinage of Æthelred', 127–8; M. Allen, *Mints and Money in Medieval England* (Cambridge, 2012), 35–8. Cf. K. Bornholdt Collins and E. Screen, 'New Moneyers in Æthelred II's Benediction Hand Type', *BNJ* 77 (2007), 270–6.

[78] Dolley, 'Introduction', 120–4.

abandonment has traditionally been explained by iconographic similarity with the preceding *First* and *Second Hand* types (i.e. it proved too hard to distinguish the new coins from the old ones, so the type was abandoned); however, since the *Second Hand* itself does not appear to have been a distinct issue, it is unclear whether such reasoning suffices. Indeed, if Dolley's traditional dating of the *Bendiction Hand* to *c*. 991 is correct – and this remains the most likely date, even if not on the grounds cited by Dolley[79] – then one wonders whether the choice to present the Hand of God in the posture of blessing was inspired by recent events, perhaps the attacks leading up to the Maldon campaign. It might thus have constituted an effort to obtain God's blessing on the English; if so, its rapid abandonment can probably be associated with the catastrophic end of this venture.

In any case, the raids of 980, 982 and 988 were clearly quite small-scale affairs, which probably would not have warranted recording were it not for the fact that they were followed by larger forays in the 990s.[80] Indeed, though these attacks look like a bolt from the blue, the impression is somewhat misleading. In his will King Eadred (d. 955) had left the tidy sum of 1,600 pounds (the largest single bequest) to his people 'that they may redeem themselves from famine and from a heathen force' (*ðæt hi mege magan hungor 7 hæþenne here him fram aceapian*), suggesting that low-level raiding and tribute-taking was conceivable at this point.[81] Other events also only took on their full significance in the light of the subsequent developments. Thus, the chronicler pointedly remarks in 986 that this was when murrain 'first came' (*com ærest*) to England; clearly, it was later events – perhaps the famine of 1005 – which made this occurrence so noteworthy. The association he implicitly draws between this event and the ravaging of Rochester, which immediately precedes it in his narrative, may also be a

[79] R. Naismith, *Medieval European Coinage*, VIII, *Britain and Ireland c.400–1066* (Cambridge, forthcoming), ch. 10. See also D.M. Metcalf and W. Lean, 'The Battle of Maldon and the Minting of Crux Pennies in Essex: *Post hoc propter hoc?*', in *The Battle of Maldon: Fiction and Fact*, ed. J. Cooper (London, 1993), 205–24.

[80] S. Keynes, 'The Historical Context of the Battle of Maldon', in *The Battle of Maldon, AD 991*, ed. D. Scragg (Oxford, 1991), 81–113, at 84–5. See also Stafford, 'Royal Government', 402–3.

[81] S 1515 (*WinchNM* 17).

product of such hindsight.[82] Be that as it may, one cannot help but think that similar connections were already being made in the 980s and 990s. Though initial raids may have done little lasting damage, the arrival of a larger fleet in 991 must have been more worrying. In any case, such attacks were probably more important in symbolic than material terms: they raised serious questions about the wisdom of Æthelred's policies. Such raiding activity provides the backdrop to the tensions visible between Æthelred and Richard of Normandy (942–996) in these years. A letter from Pope John XV of March 991 announces the terms of a peace between Æthelred and Richard – a pact arranged by John's envoy, Bishop Leo of Trevi – amongst which Richard is required not to receive any 'of the king's men or his enemies' (*de hominibus regis vel de inimicis suis*). While this may be a generic reference to political adversaries – one thinks of someone like Ælfric Cild, exiled in 985 – it is tempting to suggest that the duke had been offering safe haven to the viking raiders; the Normans were, after all, of Scandinavian descent and were later to play host to Æthelred's foes.[83]

Given the importance of the Maldon campaign, it is worth examining these events more closely. As we have seen, the impression created by the *Chronicle* is one of steadily mounting raids. Though it would be dangerous to attach too much novelty to these attacks, it is easy to understand why this period should have seen an intensification of such activity. The second half of the tenth century was a decisive time in Danish history: under Harald Bluetooth (*c.* 958–86) and his son Swein Forkbeard (*c.* 986/7–1014) a unified kingdom was forged, an accomplishment which finds expression on the famous rune-stone raised by Harald at the dynastic centre at Jelling (Plate 3), in which he proudly proclaims that he 'won for himself all Denmark and Norway and made the Danes Christian' (*soR · uan*

---

[82] *ASC* 986 CDE (ed. O'Brien O'Keeffe, 85); with Keynes, 'Declining Reputation', 159–60; and Cubitt, 'Prophet in Politics', 151–2.

[83] *Papsturkunden*, ed. Zimmermann, no. 307; with E. John, 'War and Society in the Tenth Century: The Maldon Campaign', *TRHS* 5th ser. 27 (1977), 173–95, at 188–9; and P. Bauduin, 'La papauté, les Vikings et les relations anglo-normandes: autour du traité de 991', in *Échanges, communications et réseaux dans le Haut Moyen Âge. Études offertes à Stéphane Lebecq*, ed. A. Gautier and C. Martin (Turnhout, 2011), 197–210.

· *tanmaurk (·) ala · auk · nuruiak · auk t(a)ni (k)(a)(r)(þ)(i) kristno*).[84] It is in these years that the impressive bridge at Ravning Enge was built and large round fortifications were constructed at Fyrkat, Aggersborg, Nonnebakken, Trelleborg (Sjælland) and Borgeby, and possibly also at Helsingborg, Trelleborg (Skåne) and Borrering (Køge).[85] Such centralization benefited the king's associates, but also created a pool of dissatisfied local leaders and petty-kings who had lost out in the process. Though not all the raiders of the later tenth century were recruited from amongst the ranks of the disgruntled Danish aristocrats, some certainly were, and in any case the development of firmer state structures had a knock-on effect on the size of the forces which both the kings and others could command. As the attacks on England began to build up steam in the 990s, these became as much a cause as consequence of political centralization in Scandinavia: success raiding was often the basis of a political career back at home and no fewer than two kings of Norway, Olaf Tryggvasson (995–9) and Olaf Haraldsson (1015–28), cut their teeth raiding in England (and elsewhere). The Danish ruler Swein was also active in this capacity, eventually conquering England in 1014. Striking material evidence of the wealth won by such means is provided by the large number of English coins which survive in Scandinavia from these years (*c.* 990–1025).[86] England had not witnessed sustained viking activity for some time and the force encountered at Maldon was clearly something new. Indeed, while Eadred had envisaged that 1,600 pounds might suffice to pay off such foreign

---

[84] DR 42, ed. L. Jacobsen and E. Moltke, *Danmarks Runeindskrifter*, 3 pts (Copenhagen, 1941–2), 65–81. See P. Gazzoli, 'Denemearc, Tanmaurk ala, and *Confinia nordmannorum*: The *Annales regni francorum* and the Origins of Denmark', *Viking and Medieval Scandinavia* 7 (2011), 29–43.

[85] M. Weidhagen-Hallerdt, 'A Possible Ring Fort from the Late Viking Period in Helsingborg', *Current Swedish Archaeology* 17 (2009), 187–204, esp. 187–90 and 199–203; E. Roesdahl, S.M. Sindbæk, A. Pedersen and D.M. Wilson, *Aggersborg: The Viking-Age Settlement and Fortress* (Moesgaard, 2014), 184–208 and 383–414. On Borrering (Køge) the best guide is the press release of Denmarks Borgcenter ('The Danish Castle Centre'): 'Enigmatic Viking Fortress Discovered in Denmark' (http://www.danmarksborgcenter.dk/sites/default/files/mediearkiv/pdf/pm_eng_csi_3_9_2014_hg.pdf, accessed 16 Sept. 2015).

[86] M.A.S. Blackburn and K. Jonsson, 'The Anglo-Saxon and Anglo-Norman Element of North European Coin Finds', in *Viking-Age Coinage in the Northern Lands*, ed. M.A.S. Blackburn and D.M. Metcalf, 2 pts (Oxford, 1981), 147–255. See further below, Chapter 5, p. 224.

invaders, the army which fought in this campaign was eventually offered 10,000.

Despite its obvious importance, our knowledge about the Maldon campaign is much scantier than we should like.[87] Our most important sources are the entries in two versions of the *Anglo-Saxon Chronicle*. The standard account is that preserved within C, D and E texts. Its reads simply:

> AD 991. Here Ipswich was ravaged and very shortly thereafter Byrhtnoth the ealdorman was slain at Maldon. And in that year it was first decided that tribute should be paid to the Danes on account of the great terror they had wrought along the coast. That was first 10,000 pounds. Archbishop Sigeric first advised this.[88]

While the proliferation of 'firsts' make the chronicler's hindsight clear, the basic details of the account accord well with our other evidence: it would seem that a large force arrived in Essex, harried Ipswich and then met with the local levy at Maldon where it inflicted a major defeat upon the English. That Æthelred's counsellors, bereft of one of their most experienced colleagues, chose to sue for peace was only natural, though the naming and shaming of Sigeric for proposing this policy is symptomatic of the author's later misgivings. The other report, preserved in the A-version of the *Chronicle*, reads as follows:

> AD 993 [for 991?]. Here in this year Olaf came with ninety-three ships to Folkestone (*Stane*) and they ravaged around there, and then from there he went to Sandwich and so thence to Ipswich and overran it entirely, and so on to Maldon. And Byrhtnoth the ealdorman came against him [or 'them'] there with his army and fought with him [or 'them']; and they slew the ealdorman there, and held the field of

---

[87] See I. Howard, *Swein Forkbeard's Invasions and the Danish Conquest of England, 991–1017* (Woodbridge, 2003), 31–53; and D. Scragg, *The Return of the Vikings: The Battle of Maldon 991* (Stroud, 2006).

[88] *ASC* CDE 991 (ed. O'Brien O'Keeffe, 86): 'AN. Dccccxci. Her wæs Gypeswic gehergod, 7 æfter þon swiðe raðe wæs Brihtnoð ealdorman ofslegen æt Mældune. 7 on þam geare man gerædde þæt man geald ærest gafol Denescum mannum for ðam miclan brogan þe hi worhton be ðam særiman, þæt wæs ærest .x. ðusend punda. Þæne ræd gerædde ærest Syric arcebisceop.'

slaughter. And afterwards peace was made with him [or 'them'] and the king stood sponsor to him afterwards at his confirmation.[89]

The scribe who copied this entry was working during Æthelred's lifetime, perhaps in or shortly after 1001, so the account should by all rights take precedence. However, the entry poses a number of problems. For a start, it is dated to 993, rather than 991, despite clearly describing Byrhtnoth's defeat at Maldon. Moreover, some of the details mentioned, particularly the number of ships and the sponsorship of Olaf, accord better with the events of 993–4, when the main CDE *Chronicle*-account records a peace treaty leading to Olaf's departure from England. It is conceivable that the entry was meant for 991 but entered under 993 because the scribe ran out of space (he had already copied material on the same page, including the annal for 994, before he set to work on this account).[90] However, the most likely explanation is that a textual error has crept into the manuscript (or its exemplar) at this point. As Janet Bately notes, if both the original 991 and 993 (or 994) entries mentioned Maldon (Old English: *Mældune*), then it is possible that the scribe jumped from the first reference to the second while copying out the annals (what is known as eye-skip, or *saut du même au même*), then entered all of this under 993, conflating materials from the two years.[91] This is an intriguing proposition, but it runs up against the difficulty that the mention of Maldon is followed by a description of events clearly relating to 991; it therefore seems more likely that one of the many turns of phrase starting 'and [with] them' (*7 him*) led to a similar error later on in this entry. This would explain the rather awkward syntax of the second half, which moves abruptly from Byrhtnoth being at the centre of attention to Olaf's sponsorship (an

[89] *ASC* 993 A (=991?) (ed. Bately, 79): 'AN. Dccccxciii. Her on ðissum geare com Unlaf mid þrim 7 hund nigontigon scipum to Stane 7 forhergedon þæt onytan 7 for ða ðanon to Sandwic 7 swa ðanon to Gipeswic 7 þæt eall ofereode 7 swa to Mældune; 7 him ðær com togeanes Byrhtnoð ealdorman mid his fyrde 7 him wið gefeaht, 7 hy þone ealdorman þær ofslogon, 7 wælstowe geweald ahtan. 7 him man nam syððan frið wið, 7 hine nam se cing syððan to bisceopes handa.'

[90] Keynes, 'Historical Context', 88–9.

[91] J. Bately, 'The *Anglo-Saxon Chronicle*', in *The Battle of Maldon, AD 991*, ed. D. Scragg (Oxford, 1991), 37–50, esp. 47–9.

event we otherwise know to date to 993–4).[92] Though it has been suggested that the ninety-three ships mentioned at the start should also refer to the force of 994 (which is given a strength of ninety-four ships in the C, D and E texts), there is no particular reason why this must be so: the opening part of the entry clearly relates to the events of 991, and in any case this annal was written before the main *Chronicle*-account of these years. It may simply be that the force remained stable in numbers in the intervening years, during which it seems to have been based in England. Certainly, the other unique details in this entry – the attacks on Folkestone and Sandwich – make good strategic sense in the context of 991 and speak in its favour.

These accounts are thus independent and complementary. Given this, it would seem to follow that Olaf, the future Norwegian king, was indeed one of the commanders of the viking fleet at Maldon (the CDE-version otherwise first mentions him in 994). It is possible that the other figures who are recorded as making peace with the English in 994, Jósteinn and Guthmund, were also present from the start. Less certainty surrounds the presence of Swein Forkbeard. A document datable to the latter half of the 990s (995 × 999) recounts how 'many years earlier' (*manegon earon ær*) the English king had been informed that one of his men, Æthelric Bocking, had betrayed him by agreeing that he 'would receive Swein in Essex when he first came thither with a fleet' (*sceolde on Eastsexon Swegen underfon ða he ærest þyder mid flotan com*).[93] Since these events transpired before Æthelric's death, which itself predates the production of this document, and the latter's disloyalty is said to have taken place 'many years before' during Swein's 'first' attack on Essex, when the Danish king is otherwise only recorded in the region in 994, it has been suggested he must also have been amongst the force present at Maldon in 991.[94] Though this comes

---

[92] See R. Lavelle, 'Law, Death and Peacemaking in the "Second Viking Age": An Ealdorman, his King, and Some "Danes" in Wessex', in *Danes in Wessex: The Scandinavian Impact on Southern England, c. 800–c. 1100*, ed. R. Lavelle and S. Roffey (Oxford, 2015), 122–43, at 126–31.

[93] S 939 (*CantCC* 137).

[94] Whitelock, *EHD*, 579. See also P.[H.] Sawyer, 'Ethelred II, Olaf Tryggvason, and the Conversion of Norway', *Scandinavian Studies* 59 (1987), 299–307, at 300–1; and *Charters of Christ Church Canterbury*, ed. N. Brooks and S.E. Kelly, 2 pts, Anglo-Saxon Charters 17–18 (Oxford, 2013), 1006.

far short of proof, the balance of probability seems to favour the proposition.

Our other sources for the Maldon campaign are more literary, revealing less about the events, but more about how contemporaries reacted to them. The first is preserved in book five of Byrhtferth of Ramsey's *Life* of Oswald. Here the author describes Æthelred's coronation (979), then notes that shortly after the king had achieved puberty Scandinavian attacks began to haunt his kingdom leading to a 'most savage battle' (*durissimum bellum*) in the west (perhaps the ravaging of Watchet in 988) and then not long after another 'most vigorous battle' (*fortissimum bellum*) in the east at which Byrhtnoth and his retinue fell.[95] This account adds little by way of factual detail to our other narratives: the depiction of the battle is fairly conventional, though the description of the ealdorman's stature and flowing white hair finds partial confirmation in the vernacular poem on the event. Unlike the *Maldon* poet, however, Byrhtferth reports that the English broke ranks as soon as Byrhtnoth died. This need not represent fundamental disagreement, however. As we shall see, the poem also has the lion's share of the English force flee at this point; moreover, it is questionable whether either author had factual accuracy foremost in mind – for Byrhtferth the battle is one of many signs of diabolical machination at this point, while for the *Maldon* poet it is a glorious (if misled) act of heroism. The twelfth-century *Liber Eliensis* ('Book of Ely') contains a further prose account of the event. This is largely legendary, reflecting the later growth of tales surrounding the engagement: here Byrhtnoth has inexplicably become ealdorman of Northumbria; there are two battles (not one), and the latter engagement is said to last some fourteen days; and though the death of Byrhtnoth is acknowledged, the English are presented as having won the field. There is, therefore, little factual material to be gleaned from this; nevertheless, it bears eloquent testimony to the enduring interest in Byrhtnoth at his final resting place.[96]

---

[95] Byrhtferth, *Vita S. Oswaldi* V.4–5 (ed. Lapidge, 154–8). See further M. Lapidge, 'The Life of St Oswald', in *The Battle of Maldon, AD 991*, ed. D. Scragg (Oxford, 1991), 51–8.

[96] *Liber Eliensis* II.62 (ed. Blake, 133–5). See T.D. Hill, 'The *Liber Eliensis* "Historical Selections" and the Old English *Battle of Maldon*', *JEGP* 96 (1997), 1–12; and cf. John, 'War and Society', 185–7.

Maldon: the poem and the battle

We now come to the most famous source for the campaign, the poem known as *The Battle of Maldon*. Much has been written about this work, so we may limit ourselves to its historical significance. The poem only survives in an early modern copy, since the original manuscript, Cotton Otho A. xii (now of the British Library), was amongst those largely destroyed in the Cottonian Fire of 1731.[97] The text is fragmentary, lacking an opening and ending, though it is unlikely that much material has been lost. Traditionally, the poem was thought to be an early work, produced in the immediate aftermath of the battle; however, more recently it has been suggested on linguistic and literary grounds that it may have been written some time later, perhaps in the reigns of Cnut (1016–35) or his sons (1035–42).[98] Most attempts to date the poem rely upon content and style, the difficulty being that much depends upon individual interpretation. Thus, for example, some scholars prefer a date from Æthelred's later years on the basis of the poet's perceived criticism of the king, while others favour an early date precisely because they do not detect such signs of censure.[99] In the face of such divergent opinions there is a perennial danger of not seeing the wood for the trees. Common sense would seem to dictate an early date: it was in the aftermath of the battle that the need would have been greatest to memorialize those who had laid down their lives (many of whom are mentioned by name in the poem), and it was in this context that an interested audience was most

[97] H.L. Rogers, '*The Battle of Maldon*: David Casley's Transcript', *Notes and Queries* n.s. 23 (1985), 147–55.

[98] J. McKinnell, 'On the Date of *The Battle of Maldon*', *Medium Ævum* 44 (1975), 121–36; N.F. Blake, 'The Genesis of *The Battle of Maldon*', *ASE* 7 (1978), 119–29; E.R. Anderson, '*The Battle of Maldon*: A Reappraisal of Possible Sources, Date, and Theme', in *Modes of Interpretation in Old English Literature: Essays in Honour of Stanley B. Greenfield*, ed. P.R. Brown, G.R. Crampton and F.C. Robinson (Toronto, 1986), 247–72. However, see *The Battle of Maldon*, ed. D. Scragg (Manchester, 1981), 26–7; C. Clark, 'On Dating *The Battle of Maldon*: Certain Evidence Reviewed' (1983), repr. in and cited from her *Words, Names, and History: Selected Writings of Cecily Clark* (Cambridge, 1995), 20–36; and S.M. Pons-Sanz, 'Norse-Derived Terms and Structures in *The Battle of Maldon*', *JEGP* 107 (2008), 421–44, at 426–7, casting serious doubts on such arguments.

[99] J.E. Cross, 'Mainly on Philology and the Interpretive Criticism of *Maldon*', in *Old English Studies in Honour of John C. Pope*, ed. R.B. Burlin and E.B. Irving, Jr, (Toronto, 1974), 235–53, at 247–8; Clark, 'Dating', 36; J.D. Niles, '*Maldon* and Mythopoesis' (1994), repr. with two addenda in his *Old English Heroic Poems and the Social Life of Texts* (Turnhout, 2007), 203–52, at 206–8.

likely to be found. Memorial verses had a venerable tradition and *The Battle of Maldon* bears comparison with the Old High German *Ludwigslied*, celebrating the Frankish victory over the vikings at Saucourt (881), and the *Chronicle*-poems on the Battle of *Brunanburh* (937), coronation of Edgar (973) and death of Edgar (975), all of which seem to have been written shortly after the events they describe (in the case of the *Ludwigslied* within a year of the battle itself).[100] What is more, the linguistic evidence adduced in favour of a late date is at best questionable, while certain considerations continue to speak for an earlier one – the spelling of Byrhtnoth's name, for example, takes a form which we would not generally expect to see later than the 990s ('Brihtnoth' was the preferred form thereafter).[101] Other features also point towards an earlier date: the descriptions of arms and armour accord with the death dues (or heriots) recorded in Æthelred's early years, while the fact that many of the warriors named in the poem can be identified with historical figures suggests composition within living memory.[102]

There is a certain elegant simplicity to the poem. Since the opening lines do not survive, we pick up the action after the Scandinavians have already made their appearance, with Byrhtnoth marshalling his forces. There follows a famous exchange between a viking messenger and the ealdorman. The former calls across the water which divides the raiding force – apparently on Northey Island off the Essex coast, which is connected to the mainland by a narrow tidal ford (the Blackwater) – from the English, offering terms:

> Bold seafarers sent me to you,
> ordered me to tell you that you must quickly send
> gold rings in exchange for protection. And it is better for you

---

[100] See P. Fouracre, 'The Context of the OHG *Ludwigslied*' (1985), repr. in and cited from his *Frankish History: Studies in the Construction of Power* (Aldershot, 2012), no. IX; and J. Schneider, *Auf der Suche nach dem verlorenen Reich. Lotharingien im 9. und 10. Jahrhundert* (Cologne, 2010), 343–423, on the former work; and Foot, *Æthelstan*, 170–2; Scott, 'Edgar Poems'; and Salvador-Bello, 'Edgar Panegyrics', on the latter works.

[101] D. Scragg, '*The Battle of Maldon*: Fact or Fiction?', in *The Battle of Maldon: Fiction and Fact*, ed. J. Cooper (London, 1993), 19–31, at 27–8. See also *Battle of Maldon*, ed. Scragg, 23–8.

[102] N. Brooks, 'Weapons and Armour in the *Battle of Maldon*' (1991), repr. in and cited from his *Communities and Warfare, 700–1400* (London, 2000), 162–74, at 172–4; M.A.L. Locherbie-Cameron, 'The Men Named in the Poem', in *The Battle of Maldon, AD 991*, ed. D. Scragg (Oxford, 1991), 238–49.

that you should buy off this storm of spears with tribute
than that we should join battle so grievously.
We need not destroy each other if you are wealthy enough:
we wish to establish a truce in exchange for gold.[103]

The messenger continues in this vein for some time before Byrhtnoth responds
that he and his men wish to offer the vikings 'spears as tribute' (*to gafole garas*)
and to defend their country valiantly.[104] The purpose of these speeches is to
build suspense and they play upon the audience's foreknowledge; we know, of
course, that tribute is eventually paid, for all Byrhtnoth's brave words.

It is after this exchange that battle is joined. Initially three of Byrhtnoth's
men hold the causeway, preventing their enemies from engaging the main
English force with their full numbers. Seeing that they can make little
headway, the vikings appeal to the ealdorman that he should let them pass
over to the mainland. The following lines are amongst the most hotly
debated in the poem, so it is worth quoting them in full:

When they realized this and saw clearly
that they had come up against fierce guardians of the causeway there,
then the hateful visitors started to use guile (*lytegian*):
they requested that they be allowed to have passage
to cross over the ford, to advance their troops.
Then, because of his pride (*ofermod*), the leader [Byrhtnoth] began
to allow the hateful people too much land.[105]

Much hinges on how we translate *ofermod* here. Though some have sought
to salvage Byrhtnoth's reputation by suggesting that the term means 'great

---

[103] *Battle of Maldon*, ll. 29–35 (ed. Scragg, 58): 'Me sendon to þe sæmen snelle,/heton ðe
secgan þæt þu most sendan raðe/beagas wið gebeorge. And eow betere is/þæt ge þisne garræs
mid gafole forgyldon,/þo[ne] we swa hearde [hi]lde dælon./Ne þurfe we us spillangif ge
spendaþ to þam;/we willað wið þam goldegrið gæstian.'

[104] *Battle of Maldon*, ll. 45–61 (ed. Scragg, 58–9).

[105] *Battle of Maldon*, ll. 84–90 (ed. Scragg, 59–60): 'Þa hi þæt ongeaton and georne gesawon/
þæt hi þær bricgweardas bitere fundon,/ongunnon lytegian þa laðe gystas;/bædon þæt hi
upgang agan moston,/ofer þone ford faran, feþan lædan./Ða se eorl ongan for his ofermode/
alyfan landes to fela laþere ðeode.'

boldness' or 'great bravery',[106] it is clear in context that it is intended as criticism: it is on account of this that the ealdorman gives the vikings 'too much land' (*landes to fela*), a decision the poet's audience knows leads to his demise.[107] What is more, the preceding lines clearly state that the vikings resorted to deceit, a further indication that Byrhtnoth's actions do not meet with full approbation – he has fallen victim to a trap.[108] Indeed, as we have noted, the listeners know that, despite their heroism, Byrhtnoth and his companions fail; the vanity of their efforts must have been hard to miss.[109] This is why the ealdorman's decision is so important: once the Scandinavian force has crossed the Blackwater the die is cast. The rest of the poem need not detain us long. Once the vikings cross the ford they join battle with the English. Although Byrhtnoth and his men initially make a good impression, the decisive moment comes when the ealdorman is brought down. Thereafter, confusion ensues and a large portion of the English force departs; however, a young warrior named Ælfwine makes a rousing speech reminding the men of their debt to their lord. Similar speeches follow from Offa, Leofsunu and Dunnere, all of whom pledge to fight on. The key theme is loyalty: those who keep their oaths to Byrhtnoth stand firm. The tide of the battle has, however, already turned and the remaining lines are a roll-call of the fallen, describing how they fought on against overwhelming odds.

This is rousing stuff, and it is not difficult to see why *The Battle of Maldon* has become a favourite amongst students and scholars alike. Though once treated as an accurate, almost journalistic report of the battle, few would do so now. Indeed, for all that the poem may provide 'most of

---

[106] See, e.g., G. Clark, 'The Hero of *Maldon*: Vir Pius et Strenuus', *Speculum* 54 (1979), 257–82; J.W. Earle, '"The Battle of Maldon", line 86: OE *lytegian* = Lat. *litigare*', in *Old English and New: Studies in Language and Linguistics in Honour of Frederic G. Cassidy*, ed. J.H. Hall, N. Doane and D. Ringler (New York, 1992), 77–82; and J. Halbrooks, 'Byrhtnoth's Great-Hearted Mirth, or Praise and Blame in *The Battle of Maldon*', *Philological Quarterly* 82 (2003), 235–55.

[107] H. Gneuss, '*The Battle of Maldon* 89: Byrhtnoð's *ofermod* Once Again' (1976), repr. in and cited from his *Language and History in Early England* (Aldershot, 1996), no. X.

[108] Cross, 'Mainly on Philology', 236–43; P. Pulsiano '"Danish Men's Words Are Worse than Murder": Viking Guile and *The Battle of Maldon*', *JEGP* 96 (1997), 13–25.

[109] Niles, '*Maldon* and Mythopoesis'. See also J.D. Niles, 'Byrhtnoth's Laughter and the Poetics of Gesture' (2000), repr. with an addendum in his *Old English Heroic Poems and the Social Lives of Texts* (Turnhout, 2007), 253–78, esp. 272–3.

our information on the event',[110] this information is not terribly detailed (at least in factual terms) and might be summarized as follows: the battle took place by a ford (probably that between Northey Island and the mainland); the English initially held this causeway, but then retreated so that full battle could be joined; and once Byrhtnoth fell, a portion of the East Saxon army fought on to the bitter end. However, even these details cannot be blindly trusted. Fighting to the last man is something of a cliché, which we should hesitate to take as a reflection of the realities of battle.[111] Likewise, though historians have been able to identify the probable site of battle on the basis of the poem (Plate 4), it is by no means certain that we can take the poet's description of the early phases of the conflict at face value. As Ann Williams notes, there is a somewhat legendary air to the description of three men holding the ford; it smacks of the ancient Roman tale of Horatius Cocles and his two companions, who heroically held the *Pons Sublicius* (the only bridge over the Tiber) against the Etruscan king Lars Porsena, and also bears comparison with the later story of the lone viking who held the bridge against the English at the Battle of Stamford Bridge (1066).[112] Moreover, Byrhtnoth's decision to abandon this causeway introduces a key element of pathos into the narrative: the audience must look on hopelessly as the inevitable transpires. Thus, though it is likely that the vikings were indeed based on Northey Island, and it may be that the tides played a role in the course of the battle, we should hesitate before giving the poem's account too much credence; the poet is spinning a good yarn, not simply telling it like it was. Indeed, as with any good yarn, *The Battle of Maldon* is a better source for ideals and mentalities than factual detail. As James Campbell notes, the poet presupposes a strong sense of 'national' identity (for lack of a better word): Byrhtnoth's men constitute a

---

[110] Scragg, 'Fact or Fiction?', 19.

[111] R. Frank, 'The Ideal of Men Dying with their Lord in *The Battle of Maldon*: Anachronism or *nouvelle vague*', in *People and Places in Northern Europe 500–1600: Essays in Honour of Peter Hayes Sawyer*, ed. I.N. Wood and N. Lund (Woodbridge, 1991), 95–106.

[112] A. Williams, 'The Battle of Maldon and *The Battle of Maldon*: History, Poetry and Propaganda', *Medieval History* 2.ii (1992), 35–44, at 35–6; *ASC* 1066 C (ed. O'Brien O'Keeffe, 121–2) (note that the relevant section is a later addition, perhaps of the twelfth century). Cf. M.B. Roller, 'Exemplarity in Roman Culture: The Cases of Horatius Cocles and Cloelia', *Classical Philology* 99 (2004), 1–56.

single people, defending 'Æthelred's land' (*Æþelredes eard*).[113] The combatants are presented as a veritable cross-section of society: the 'simple peasant' (*unorne ceorl*) Dunnere fights alongside thegns and the sons of ealdormen, while Northumbrians and Mercians rub shoulders with their East Saxon counterparts. The poem reads as an expression of unity in the face of external threat. There is a particular emphasis on oaths of fidelity and the poet has been seen as calling for greater loyalty against a common enemy.[114] Nicholas Brooks has even gone so far as to suggest that the poem was intended as a kind of state propaganda 'to encourage its troops to resist the invading enemy without giving them the equipment to make such resistance effective'.[115] This perhaps goes too far, but there can be no doubt that in turning defeat into glory the poet goes some way towards coping with this calamity.

What the poet's views on the politics of his day were is a good question. It has often been presumed that he is critical of Æthelred's regime and it is easy to see why: in an era in which the king's main strategy seems to have been to buy off foreign invaders, here we have a poem celebrating an ealdorman who refused to do so.[116] However, a careful examination of the text suggests a more subtle reading. For all that the audience may admire Byrhtnoth's bravery and sense of duty – not to mention his knack for finding the *mot juste* – it is aware of his failure. What is more, it knows that tribute was indeed paid in the aftermath of the battle; Byrhtnoth's valiance was for naught, and his promise to offer 'spears as tribute' does not ring entirely true. If the poet had an opinion regarding Æthelred's politics of appeasement – and it seems likely that he did – it therefore stands to reason

[113] J. Campbell, 'England, *c.* 991' (1993), repr. in and cited from his *The Anglo-Saxon State* (London, 2000), 157–78, at 176–7. See also N.F. Blake, 'The Battle of Maldon', *Neophilologus* 49 (1965), 332–45, at 337–8.

[114] Williams, 'Battle of Maldon', 39–44.

[115] Brooks, 'Weapons and Armour', 174.

[116] Clark, 'Hero of *Maldon*', 281–2; J. Scattergood, '*The Battle of Maldon* and History', in *Literature and Learning in Medieval and Renaissance England: Studies Presented to Fitzroy Pyle*, ed. J. Scattergood (Dublin, 1984), 11–24; R. Abels, 'Paying the Danegeld: Anglo-Saxon Peacemaking with the Vikings', in *War and Peace in Ancient and Medieval History*, ed. P. de Souza and J. France (Cambridge, 2008), 173–92, at 174–5.

that it was positive, not negative.[117] While it may seem surprising that the payment of tribute, for which medieval chroniclers and modern scholars alike have excoriated Æthelred, should find approval from a contemporary observer, our poet probably did not enjoy the benefit of hindsight. From the perspective of the mid- to later 990s it might well have seemed like this approach had borne fruit: in 991 Byrhtnoth had gambled and got it wrong and since then the English had learned to avoid a repeat. Certainly, there was nothing inherently cowardly in the payment of tribute: caution was often the better part of valour and even militant rulers such as Alfred the Great are known to have resorted to the tactic.[118]

It is perhaps the existence of the poem itself which tells us most, however. Although the corpus of Old English poetry is small and we must reckon with substantial losses, it is striking that this event should have inspired such an ambitious piece of verse. Indeed, *The Battle of Maldon* represents an anomaly amongst the 'historical' poems of the period, most of which were composed to celebrate victories (not defeats) and none of which comes anywhere close to *Maldon* in length and scope. The English losses left deep scars and the poem is clearly an attempt to heal these; it turns a disastrous defeat into a courageous stand, whose very heroism derives in part from its futility. As Donald Scragg notes, the poem reads like a medieval 'Charge of the Light Brigade': a moving (though not strictly factual) account of bravery against all odds.[119] The poet's perspective on the stand of Byrhtnoth's hearth-troop might thus be compared with Bosquet's famous quip at the Battle of Balaclava (1854), which inspired Tennyson's verses: *C'est magnifique, mais ce n'est pas la guerre*. We must, of course, be wary of ascribing too much importance to this engagement; the simple existence of *The Battle of Maldon* has ensured the encounter a scholarly interest out of all proportion to its contemporary significance.[120] That being

---

[117] Niles, '*Maldon* and Mythopoesis'. See similarly L. Neidorf, '*II Æthelred* and the Politics of *The Battle of Maldon*', *JEGP* 111 (2012), 451–73.

[118] S. Keynes, 'A Tale of Two Kings: Alfred the Great and Æthelred the Unready', *TRHS* 5th ser. 36 (1986), 195–217, at 198–200; Abels, 'Paying the Danegeld', esp. 181–3. Cf. S. Coupland, 'Frankish Tribute Payments to the Vikings and their Consequences', *Francia* 26.i (1999), 57–75.

[119] Scragg, 'Fact or Fiction?', 29–31.

[120] Stafford, 'Royal Government', 359–61.

said, this was more than just another clash with the vikings in an era in which these were no rarity: it was the first major English defeat within living memory. To make matters worse, it saw the death of a senior ealdorman. It is, therefore, not surprising that Archbishop Sigeric, who was a key player in the early 990s, should counsel offering tribute, nor is it surprising that this counsel found acceptance. The defeat seems to have come as a rude surprise to Æthelred and his senior advisers and may well have conditioned their approach in future years: they had learned the hard way that refusing tribute was not all that it was made out to be.

The defeat at Maldon stands at the start of more active efforts to combat the viking threat. The reverberations caused by this defeat are reflected in the wide range of sources which record it: not only the main *Chronicle*-account, but also the sparser A-version of this work, not to mention Byrhtferth of Ramsey's *Life* of Oswald. Seen in this light, the poem does not so much exaggerate the battle's significance as bear witness to it: it reveals the great difficulty the English encountered in trying to rationalize this event. It was apparently not the only effort to do so and the twelfth-century *Liber Eliensis* mentions the existence of a tapestry, commemorating the battle, at Ely, where the ealdorman's body lay.[121] The severity of this defeat is also revealed by the events of the following years: in 992 a ship levy was undertaken and the force placed under the leadership of Ealdorman Ælfric, who went on to betray the English by leaving the ships from East Anglia and London to face defeat, while in the following year a large army was brought together to face an attack on Lindsey and Northumbria, though again this came to naught when the generals took flight.[122] The apparent hopelessness of these endeavours should not deceive us – here we are captive to the later perspective of the chronicler. Such events do, however, speak of real urgency. The complete absence of royal diplomas from 991 and 992 also points in this direction: the regular business of rulership seems to have been put on hold. Moreover, when the stream of charters resumes, it is in dramatic fashion – the defeat at Maldon and other setbacks had evidently led to something of a crisis, and by 993 at the latest the king had decided

---

[121] *Liber Eliensis* II.63 (ed. Blake, 136). See M. Budny, 'Byrhtferth's Tapestry or Embroidery', in *The Battle of Maldon, AD 991*, ed. D. Scragg (Oxford, 1991), 263–78.

[122] *ASC* 992–3 CDE (ed. O'Brien O'Keeffe, 86–7).

that a different tack was needed. As with his change of direction in 984, this was a very personal affair: having struck out on his own, rejecting the advice of wiser heads at court (including his mother), he had now come to see the error of his ways. The *Battle of Maldon* and other sources thus point to a crisis of confidence at and beyond court. As noted, this was not only a political but also a personal matter: the battle of Maldon and its aftermath seem to have finally convinced Æthelred of the wisdom of his mother's ways. His response to this defeat was therefore very much like that of his people: to ask searching questions about its underlying causes. While the *Maldon* poet found the answer in Byrhtnoth's pride, Æthelred did not need to look any further than his own recent actions.

The period between 984 and 993 is of great importance for understanding Æthelred's reign. The source-base for these years is not particularly rich and at a number of points we are forced to infer details from later documents and accounts. Nevertheless, taken together the sources create a remarkably coherent picture. Following the death of Bishop Æthelwold of Winchester, Æthelred struck out on his own, actively distancing himself from the politics of his erstwhile mentors. Removed from their protective oversight, the king showered favour on new figures, many (though not all) of whom were laymen. At their encouragement he plundered a number of the kingdom's leading religious establishments. This was in part a reaction against the reforming agenda of his regents, but above all it was a strike against Æthelwold and his legacy. It therefore comes as little surprise that the king's mother ceases to appear in the witness-lists of his diplomas at this point; she had been the bishop's closest ally in previous years and this was thus as much a rejection of her politics as it was of Æthelwold's. It was, however, also in these years that events took a turn for the worse for Æthelred. The Scandinavian raids, which had been gradually picking up pace for some time, started to reach critical levels and the Maldon campaign, in particular, ushered in a new phase of activity. Yet foreign invasion was not the only cause for concern; every bit as worrying must have been the livestock plague of 986, which seems to have followed swiftly on from the king's attacks on Abingdon, Winchester and Rochester. It would not have taken much to put two and two together: Æthelred had abandoned the reform-minded policies of his father, mother and sometime mentor Æthelwold, and the results had been predictably disastrous. In this respect, the Maldon campaign seems to have been the tipping point: as we have seen, a range of sources attest to the scars left by this defeat on the national psyche and it would not be too much to see herein the immediate impetus behind the new politics of the 990s. Æthelred was clearly shaken: divine disfavour did not come much clearer than this, and while the later 980s had been characterized by efforts to break free from the politics of his regents, the following decade was to witness a systematic attempt to resurrect these. Æthelred had learned his lesson the hard way: he had ignored his mother's advice – and possibly even driven her from court – only to find out that she had been right all along.

CHAPTER 4

REPENTANCE AND REFORM
993–1002

It was Maundy Thursday in the year of Our Lord 998. Æthelred stood in a sackcloth before the doors of Rochester cathedral, awaiting re-entry into the Christian community. The king was filled with concern – concern for his kingdom, which had suffered repeated setbacks in recent years; concern for the church and its reform, which he had undermined; and above all concern for his own salvation, which he had placed in peril through his youthful recklessness. For Æthelred had sinned most grievously: he had turned his back on the advice of his mother and his tutor Æthelwold, despoiling churches and overturning ecclesiastical liberties. Recent misfortunes were signs of divine wrath, the wages of sin. All that remained was to amend what he could in the hope that it was not too late. It was in this hope that he had restored church lands and rights over the last half decade; and it was in this hope too that, when these acts failed to have the desired effect, he had decided to go further and perform penance for his misdeeds. On Ash Wednesday he had donned the penitent's sackcloth and been ritually driven from the church; now, having spent the Lenten period in fasting and prayer, Æthelred was ready to be absolved of his sins and re-enter the Christian community. It was only appropriate that this should take place at Rochester, which had felt the brunt of his ire in previous years; by coming here he hoped to placate St Andrew, the see's patron. The king had, in a sense, come full circle: having abandoned the ways of his father and mother, he had come to embrace them; having ravaged Rochester, he had come to support it.

When the appointed time came, Æthelred entered into the church. Stepping forward, he offered a silent prayer that his efforts would meet with divine approval. As he walked up the nave towards the altar he was surprised to note the number of people in attendance; it was not every day that an anointed king performed penance. He could just make out his sons near the front of the crowd. He felt humbled; sin weighed heavily upon him, and all those present knew it. Yet that was the point: only by humiliating himself could he hope to regain God's favour. Æthelred approached the altar and prostrated himself, listening as the ecclesiastics in attendance sang Psalm 50, 'Have mercy on me, O God, according to thy great mercy', the song David had sung upon being chastised by Nathan for the killing of Uriah, the husband of his beloved Bathsheba. Æthelred could identify with the Israelite king: he had been a most pious ruler, yet he too was struck down by sin. The example of David offered solace – after all, he had proven his greatness by admitting his wronging; perhaps Æthelred would achieve the same. It was as if the words of the psalm were tailor-made for Æthelred's situation:

> Turn away thy face from my sins, and blot out all my iniquities.
> Create a clean heart in me, O God: and renew a right spirit within my
> bowels.
> Cast me not away from thy face; and take not thy holy spirit from me.
> Restore unto me the joy of thy salvation, and strengthen me with a
> perfect spirit.
> I will teach the unjust thy ways: and the wicked shall be converted to
> thee.

When the psalm was finished the bishop recited a prayer of absolution: 'We absolve you in the place of blessed Peter, prince of the apostles, to whom the Lord gave the power to bind and loose.' This was followed by further prayers entreating mercy and forgiveness for the sinner, emphasizing his sorrow and contrition. At the highpoint of the ceremony the king was led by hand to the bishop, before whom he bowed, before finally being reconciled to the Christian community. Æthelred was once more within the church. He felt both hope and anxiety; hope that this act of satisfaction would be deemed fitting in the eyes of the Almighty, and concern lest it not. Only time would tell.

The preceding details will not be found in any of the standard accounts of this period, and rightly so: they are strictly speaking fictional. We know little for certain of Æthelred's actions during Eastertide 998 and it is but a surmise – though a plausible one – that he undertook penance at this juncture.[1] That this took place at Rochester is more speculative. A strikingly worded charter was issued to Godwine, bishop of Rochester, at this point, and it is tempting to suggest that this took place at St Andrew's cathedral itself. Nevertheless, there are many other places this could have transpired. The details of the ceremony are similarly speculative: they are taken from the *ordo* for the reconciliation of penitents preserved in a number of contemporary manuscripts, a text which describes how penitents ought to be absolved, not necessarily how they were in practice.[2]

Nonetheless, for all its embellishment this account is not entirely invented. The legacy of Edgar, Æthelwold and Ælfthryth was of crucial importance in these years, as we shall see, as was the memory of Rochester's ravaging, and there is reason to believe that these weighed heavily upon the ruler. Indeed, imaginative though such a reconstruction may be, it arguably takes us closer to the essence of Æthelred's politics in the 990s than any sober source-critical analysis will.[3] The personal tone of the diplomas issued in his name at this point indicates that the king was deeply troubled by recent events: he could see that something was very rotten in the state of England and he had reason to believe that he was himself to blame (at least in part). It is only when we appreciate this that we can begin to understand the direction of politics in these years. In order to do so, we

---

[1] See below, pp. 146–9.

[2] S. Hamilton, 'Rites for Public Penance in Late Anglo-Saxon England', in *The Liturgy of the Late Anglo-Saxon Church*, ed. H. Gittos and M.B. Bedingfield (Woodbridge, 2005), 65–103, esp. 79–82 and 93–103.

[3] See similarly Koziol, *Politics of Memory*, 401–7; and cf. Fried, 'Wissenschaft und Phantasie'.

shall first examine the charters of restitution issued in Æthelred's name at this point, which provide the context for his other activities in these years: the cultivation of reform in all its many guises, and the support of the fledgling cult of his elder half-brother. Yet Æthelred was not only active on the religious front and the latter sections of the chapter examine the many military undertakings of this period. What emerges is above all the king's determination to put things right, whatever the cost.

The politics of penance

Although the viking attacks of the later 980s and early 990s may not have posed a great material threat, they raised questions about Æthelred's suitability for rule which could not be brushed aside easily. One suspects that accusations were made against the monarch (though perhaps not to his face) and, as we have seen, anyone acquainted with the 'Twelve Abuses' would have found it hard not to think of its teachings regarding the 'unjust king' within this context. There are signs that Æthelred himself began to doubt his actions; the rash youth of the mid-980s was perhaps happy to ignore the advice of his elder counsellors, but in the aftermath of the murrain of 986 and the defeat at Maldon five years later it must have been harder to do so. By 993 at the latest Æthelred had become convinced that he had indeed done wrong and the diplomas issued from this point on speak of a pressing need to amend past misdeeds. The king clearly saw recent misfortunes as divine justice and in doing so he tacitly accepted the teachings of the reformers.[4] It must have seemed as if the most dire warnings of his tutors had come to pass; they had taught him of the wages of sin, but he had not listened and now was paying the price.

It is in this light that we should understand both the lull in charter production in 991 and 992 and the dramatic fashion in which it was resumed in 993. The reverse at Maldon and death of Byrhtnoth had brought matters to a head, and the king's failure to defeat the viking force in the following year must only have exacerbated matters. It is within this context

---

[4] L. Roach, 'Apocalypse and Atonement in the Politics of Later Æthelredian England', *English Studies* 95 (2014), 733–57, at 735–6. See also above, Chapter 1, p. 41.

that Æthelred came to the conclusion that his previous actions were responsible for recent misfortunes and set about remedying these. The first sign of rapprochement between the king and his mother comes in these years, when Ælfthryth is recorded intervening with Æthelred on behalf of Wynflæd in a dispute (990 × 993).[5] Likewise, it is around this time that Sigeric began to play a major part in royal counsels: in 990 he had been translated to Canterbury as Dunstan's successor and he is likely to have been instrumental in obtaining papal support for the peace treaty with Normandy in this year. A year later he was at the heart of discussions which led to the first payment of tribute to the vikings. Sigeric enjoyed close contacts with the reform movement: he had been educated at Glastonbury and was abbot of St Augustine's in Canterbury before his promotion to Ramsbury, whence he was transferred to Canterbury; and it was to him that Ælfric dedicated the First and Second Series of his Catholic Homilies, completed in these years (990 × 994). Sigeric's rise is a sign of things to come and he deserves to be considered one of the architects of the new politics of the 990s.[6]

It would be 993, however, before the king was ready to take more drastic measures. At Pentecost of this year he called together a council at Winchester at which he admitted to wrongdoing and committed to mend his youthful indiscretions, starting by restoring liberty to Abingdon. This is recorded in a diploma issued six weeks later at Gillingham (probably in Dorset). It would seem that the restitution was promised and enacted on the first occasion, but that it was deemed preferable to hold off production of the written documentation for a few weeks, presumably on account of the complexity of the transaction (the resulting charter runs to some 1,300 words). It may also be that the king was waiting for the monks of Abingdon to complete the religious undertakings they had promised him in return for his generosity (the celebration of 1,500 masses and singing of 1,200 psalters). Everything about this act was carefully choreographed: the original council took place at Pentecost, a time of moral and spiritual purification,

---

[5] S 1454 (*CantCC* 133). See Rabin, 'Queen Ælfthryth', 274–5; and P. Wormald, 'Giving God and King their Due: Conflict and its Regulation in the Early English State' (1997), repr. in and cited from his *Legal Culture in the Early Medieval West: Law as Text, Image and Experience* (London, 1999), 333–57, at 343–51.

[6] Cf. the suggestive remarks of Keynes, 'Church Councils', 110 and 122.

celebrating the moment when the Holy Spirit had descended upon Christ's followers and prepared them for the mission; it was held at Winchester, Æthelwold's old see; and it witnessed the restitution of liberty to Abingdon, Æthelwold's first foundation. The core message is hard to miss: Æthelred is turning his back on his youthful errors and embracing the legacy of his father, mother and sometime regents (above all Æthelwold). The charter recording this act makes its programmatic nature clear: it is the first diploma attested by Ælfthryth since Æthelwold's death and its text is unusually long and detailed (it is the second longest authentic document in the king's name).[7] It opens with a preamble meditating upon original sin and the Fall of Man, poignant themes in the light of Æthelred's recent actions. Yet there is still cause for hope, as the draftsman goes on to note: the virgin birth of Christ through Mary has paved the way for humankind to atone for its sinful nature. After these initial thoughts, the diploma moves on to a long narrative section (or *narratio*) detailing how the king and his nation had suffered various afflictions ever since Æthelwold's death. These, so the king explains, had inspired him to reflect upon his actions, coming to the conclusion that recent misfortunes (*infortunia*) had come to pass partly as a result of his youth and partly as a result of the detestable love of money (*philargiria*) of others (i.e. his counsellors), who ought to have advised him better. Æthelred singles out Bishop Wulfgar of Ramsbury and Ealdorman Ælfric of Hampshire for particular censure, since it was they who had offered him money to infringe upon Abingdon's liberty, appointing the latter's brother Eadwine as abbot. However, wishing now to be freed from the 'terrible anathema' (*exhorrendo anathemate*) he had thus incurred, the king notes that he called together a council at Winchester at Pentecost, at which he publicly admitted to wrongdoing, promising to undo his previous misdeeds and restore Abingdon's liberty in the hope of receiving God's mercy. The king then explains that he confirmed this act at Gillingham on 17 July with the assent of Abbot Ælfsige (of the New Minster) and the two noblemen Æthelmær and Ordulf, not in exchange for money (as he had previously), but in gratitude for the masses and psalms freely undertaken

---

[7] S 876 (*Abing* 124). See Keynes, 'Church Councils', 107–16; Cubitt, 'Politics of Remorse'; and L. Roach, 'Penitential Discourse in the Diplomas of King Æthelred "the Unready"', *Journal of Ecclesiastical History* 64 (2013), 258–76, esp. 260–1.

by the monks for the redemption of his soul. There follows a lengthy historical account of the abbey's liberty, which is followed by a sanction threatening eternal damnation on any who for love of money (*philargiria*: mentioned here for a second time) seek to infringe on its terms. The publicity of this act is reflected in the unusually long witness-list which follows, incorporating not only a large cross-section of the kingdom's great and good (especially churchmen), but also the king's four sons – their first appearance in a royal charter. Given the context, one cannot help but feel that Æthelred was trying to make a point, hoping that his offspring would learn from the errors of their father.

The tenor of the document suggests a heightened degree of royal interest: it speaks of the king's innermost thoughts and concerns and singles out individual magnates – including Ealdorman Ælfric, who was still alive and in office – for censure. What is more, the manner in which these thoughts are expressed suggests that the king was motivated by church teachings about sin and repentance: he (or more accurately: his draftsman, acting in his name) presents recent misfortunes as a consequence of youthful error and expresses the sincere hope that by making amends he will be able to restore order to the realm. The language employed confirms the repentant nature of this act. The Fall of Man, with which the charter opens, is a penitential commonplace, often alluded to in continental rites for penance (and also mentioned in Wulfstan of York's later sermons on Ash Wednesday and Maundy Thursday); it was the act which had first brought sin into the world.[8] The manner in which the king's reflections are described is similarly suggestive: he is said to be 'pricked by conscience through the grace of the Lord' (*Domini conpunctus gratia*), a phrase carrying distinctly penitential undertones, since *compunctio*, not *contritio*, was used to designate penitential contrition in this period.[9] The

---

[8] S. Hamilton, *The Practice of Penance, 900–1050* (Woodbridge, 2001), 18, 34, 36 and 114; M. Mansfield, *The Humiliation of Sinners: Public Penance in Thirteenth-Century France* (Ithaca, NY, 1995), 173; Wulfstan, *Sermo in XL*, and *Sermo in Cena Domini*, ed. D. Bethurum, *The Homilies of Wulfstan* (Oxford, 1957), 233–8 (the latter of which, however, draws heavily on Abbo of St-Germain's sermon on the same theme).

[9] B. Poschmann, *Buße und letzte Ölung* (Freiburg, 1951), 87–8. See also H. Foxhall Forbes, 'The Development of the Notions of Penance, Purgatory and the Afterlife in Anglo-Saxon England' (PhD diss., Univ. of Cambridge, 2008), 103–7.

issuing of this diploma was clearly an important gesture: it not only restored Abingdon's liberty, but in doing so laid the foundations for the king's future actions. The prominence given to Mary in the preamble is particularly appropriate: Abingdon was dedicated to the Blessed Virgin and her cult was popular within reforming circles.[10] The focus on avarice (*philargiria*) is also striking and finds echoes in other contemporary works; the increasing availability of movable wealth seems to have been a cause for concern amongst churchmen, as Malcolm Godden notes, and the king's own simony would only have served to heighten this.[11] As noted, the overall message would have been unmistakable: the depredations of the 980s were over, as was the dominance of those who had been behind them; Æthelred was turning his back on one group of favourites and opening the way for a new one to emerge. In this respect, it is significant that Ealdorman Ælfric's son, Ælfgar, was blinded in this year.[12] Why he and not his father should be punished is not entirely clear, but it may be that Ælfgar was more directly implicated in despoiling the church (as we have seen, he – and not his father – was remembered as a predator at both the Old Minster and Abingdon). Whatever the reason, it is clear that the faction to which he and his father belonged was no longer calling the shots.

This message is reinforced by two sets of textual allusions to the *Regularis concordia* within this document.[13] The first comes in the description of Æthelred's youthful errors, in which the king mentions how 'this misfortune came to pass, in part on account of my youth, which is accustomed to engage in various pursuits (*diversis solet uti moribus*), and in part on account of the detestable love of money of those who ought to have counselled for my benefit'. The first half of this phrase is clearly a calque

[10] M. Clayton, *The Cult of the Virgin Mary in Anglo-Saxon England* (Cambridge, 1990), 122–38 and 158–67.

[11] M. Godden, 'Money, Power and Morality in Late Anglo-Saxon England', *ASE* 19 (1990), 41–65. Cf. Murray, *Reason and Society*, 59–80.

[12] *ASC* 993 CDE (ed. O'Brien O'Keeffe, 86–7).

[13] H. Vollrath, *Die Synoden Englands bis 1066* (Paderborn, 1986), 309–10, esp. 309, n. 70; S. Keynes, 'Re-Reading King Æthelred the Unready', in *Writing Medieval Biography, 750–1250: Essays in Honour of Professor Frank Barlow*, ed. D. Bates, J. Crick and S. Hamilton (Woodbridge, 2006), 77–97, at 91, n. 70. See also Roach, 'Penitential Discourse', 266–7; and Keynes, 'Church Councils', 110–11.

on the preface to the *Regularis concordia*, where it is said of Edgar that 'from the start of his boyhood, as is customary of that age (*uti ipsa solet aetas*), he engaged in various pursuits (*diversis uteretur moribus*), but was also touched by divine regard; diligently admonished and shown the royal way of orthodox faith by a certain abbot, he began to fear, love and venerate God greatly.'[14] A subtle but unmistakable contrast is drawn here: while despite the natural distractions of youth Edgar listened to the advice of 'a certain abbot' (almost certainly Æthelwold), Æthelred fell prey to them.[15] As we have seen, the *Concordia* was a programmatic statement of the reform, drafted by Æthelwold and issued under Edgar's aegis (and probably also in his presence – though this is not stated explicitly) at the Council at Winchester (*c.* 970).[16] Æthelred's reconciliation with the bishop of Winchester thus even takes on a textual guise: he frames his regret and renewed commitment to reform in Æthelwold's own words. That the charter was indeed meant to represent a return to the kind of politics seen under Edgar, Ælfthryth and Æthelwold is confirmed by a second, lengthier set of borrowings from this work: the entire first dating clause is an extended calque on that of the *Regularis concordia,* and the 'synodal council of Winchester' (*synodale concilium Wintoniae*) of Pentecost 993 is thus presented as a direct equivalent to the original 'synodal council of Winchester' which had witnessed the production of the *Concordia*. The choice of Winchester for this event would have further underlined the parallel: Æthelred chose to announce his change of tack at a site with close associations with Æthelwold, Edgar and the reform.

This charter is, therefore, in many respects extraordinary: its length, its allusions to contemporary events, its criticism of named royal advisers and its textual links with the *Regularis concordia* all make it stand apart from

---

[14] S 876 (*Abing* 124): 'ad memoriam reduxi . partim hec infortunia pro meae iuuentutis ignorantia *que diuersis solet uti moribus* . partim etiam pro quorundam illorum detestand[a] philargiria qui meae utilitati consulere debebant accid[isse].'; *Regularis concordia*, ch. 1 (ed. Symons and Spath, 69): '. . . ab ineunte suae pueritiae aetate, *licet uti ipsa solet aetas diuersis uteretur moribus,* attamen respectu diuino attactus abate quodam assiduo monente ac regiam catholicae fidei uiam demonstrante cepit magnopere deum timere, diligere ac uernarari.' (Italics added.)

[15] Cf. the similar remarks in 'Edgar's Establishment of Monasteries' (ed. Whitelock, 147–8).

[16] See above, Chapter 1, p. 39.

other documents of the era. It can be read as something of a political manifesto, laying out the new direction of the 990s. Its appearance is commensurate with its political importance: it is one of the grandest charters to survive in its original format from the Anglo-Saxon period (Plate 5). Written throughout in a clear Anglo-Caroline hand, even its script sends a message: Caroline writing had been popularized by the reformers, as we have seen, and had only made sporadic appearances in diplomas before this point.[17] What is more, the specific form of script used (Style I Anglo-Caroline) is that associated with Æthelwold's circles: it is written in the prelate's own preferred style, perhaps by a former student.[18] One further anomaly deserves comment: the charter's witness-list. Since diplomas were first introduced to England in the seventh century, it had been customary for them to bear lists of those present at the time of their enactment. Though modelled on continental documents in which the interested parties would actually sign their own names (or make autograph crosses next to them), in England it was the scribe of the main text who generally added these details (presumably in the earliest cases because the illiterate English were incapable of doing so themselves).[19] The only certain exception to this rule is the Abingdon privilege in question. As the most cursory glance at its witness-list reveals, the crosses next to the names of the attestors are different in shape and aspect, strongly suggesting that they are autograph (Plate 6).[20] It would seem that the document was produced in the following manner: first, at the council of Winchester the king promised to restore Abingdon's liberty; then at a second, smaller gathering at the oratory of the royal estate at Gillingham a diploma was drawn up recording the act; finally, those present at this latter event added crosses next to their

---

[17] D.N. Dumville, 'English Square Minuscule Script: The Mid-Century Phases', *ASE* 23 (1994), 133–64, at 161–3; S.D. Thompson, *Royal Anglo-Saxon Diplomas: A Palaeography* (Woodbridge, 2006), 56–63.

[18] T.A.M. Bishop, *English Caroline Minuscule* (Oxford, 1971), xxi–xxii and 11; Rushforth, 'Caroline Minuscule', 200. Though some doubts have been raised about this hand, these are not sufficient to discard the charter as a later copy. See Keynes, 'Church Councils', 112–16; and cf. D.N. Dumville, *English Caroline Script and Monastic History: Studies in Benedictinism, A.D. 950–1030* (Woodbridge, 1993), 135, n. 110.

[19] Chaplais, 'Origin and Authenticity', 33; Keynes, 'Church Councils', 70, 73, 75 and 94–5.

[20] BL Cotton Augustus ii.38. A facsimile can be found in E.A. Bond *et al.*, ed., *Facsimiles of Ancient Charters in the British Museum*, 4 vols. (London, 1873–8), iii, no. 36.

names (perhaps in two distinct stages).[21] This final act was clearly anticipated by the draftsman, since he left spaces for the crosses. What is more,
he also left space for further names to be added to the witness-list. In two
cases names were indeed inserted – those of Bishop Wulfsige of Sherborne
and Abbot Ælfwig of Westminster. These figures were presumably
promoted to their posts between the two gatherings. In fact, in Wulfsige's
case the bishop's original subscription as abbot of Westminster (reflecting
his role at the time of the Winchester assembly) has also made its way into
the final charter. It would thus seem that the list represents attendance of
the original Winchester council, updated (or at least partially updated!) at
the Gillingham gathering. The signing of this document would certainly
have been a ceremonial act, much like the signing and sealing of documents elsewhere in Europe; the difference, however, is that whereas on the
continent such acts were the norm, in England this was a novelty and must
have been all the more striking for this fact.[22] What we are dealing with is
a promise to rule better, personally signed by the kingdom's leading
magnates.

The formulation of this diploma is very close to that of a series of documents known as the *Orthodoxorum* charters (after a distinctive turn of
phrase in their shared preamble). The other examples of this charter type
claim to record grants or confirmations of liberty to Abingdon and related
houses: one is in Eadwig's name (for Abingdon) and four are in Edgar's (for
Abingdon, Pershore, Worcester and Romsey). This is not the place to go
into detail, but suffice to say all pre-Æthelredian diplomas of this type
contain features which throw serious doubt on their authenticity.[23] As

---

[21] Keynes, 'Church Councils', 112–16; L. Roach, 'A Tale of Two Charters: Diploma
Production and Political Performance in Æthelredian England', in *Writing Kingship and
Power in Anglo-Saxon England: Studies in Honour of Simon Keynes*, ed. R. Naismith and
D.A. Woodman (Cambridge, forthcoming). Cf. *Charters of Abingdon*, ed. Kelly, cxiv, for
the alternative proposition that the crosses were added in many different stages after the
Gillingham gathering.

[22] Cf. B.-M. Tock, 'La mise en scène des actes en France au Haut Moyen Âge', *FMSt* 38
(2004), 287–96; H. Keller and S. Ast, '*Ostensio cartae*. Italienische Gerichtsurkunden des
10. Jahrhunderts zwischen Schriftlichkeit und Performanz', *Archiv für Diplomatik* 53 (2007),
99–121, esp. 120.

[23] Keynes, *Diplomas*, 98–102; Cubitt, 'Politics of Remorse', 181, n. 12; Pratt, 'Voice of the
King', 186, n. 221. Cf. *Charters of Abingdon*, ed. Kelly, lxxxiv–cxv.

confirmations of ecclesiastical liberty, the earliest of these stick out like a sore thumb in the 950s; they are the type of grant we might expect to see – and indeed do see – from the reform at its height, when it sought to consolidate its gains, but not before it had yet to build up steam. What is more, the two earliest of these documents, both in favour of Abingdon, look tailor-made to protect the centre's interests in the early 990s: not only do they state that the monks have the right to elect their abbot freely, but they emphasize that this should take effect after Æthelwold's death, the very event which later precipitated Æthelred's simoniacal intervention at the centre.[24] Indeed, the rhetoric of these diplomas, which bemoan prior usurpations of monastic land, finds its closest echoes in authentic documents of the 990s, and the statement in most of them to the effect that any 'new hereditary charters' for estates belonging to the house should be repudiated makes best sense against the backdrop of the usurpations of the 980s, when the king had indeed granted monastic lands by charter to new favourites.[25] All indications, therefore, are that the earliest of these are forgeries, produced under the oversight of Abbot Wulfgar (990–1016). They were clearly modelled on the authentic Abingdon privilege of 993, whose assertion that Eadwig and Edgar had previously secured the centre's liberty may have given rise to the fabrication of documents in their names; the intention would have been to fill in the gaps in the documentary record. Though it may seem rather brazen for the monks to claim the moral high ground on the basis of such false privileges, such behaviour was by no means uncommon and can also be seen in France and Germany.[26] Wulfgar himself may have seen these as 'forgeries in the service of the truth' (to use Horst Fuhrmann's felicitous turn of phrase): documents which

---

[24] S 658 (*Abing* 83), S 673 (*Abing* 84).

[25] S 673 (*Abing* 84), S 786 (BCS 1282), S 788 (BCS 1284), with Keynes, *Diplomas*, 99. Kelly argues that such clauses could refer to any of the 'many other periods in which church lands passed into secular hands' (*Charters of Abingdon*, ed. Kelly, cii), but the examples she cites are not known to have led to the production of such documents. See further L. Roach, 'The Privilege of Liberty in Later Anglo-Saxon England', in *Magna Carta: New Interpretations*, ed. S. Ambler and N. Vincent (forthcoming).

[26] See, e.g., Koziol, *Politics of Memory*, 315–99; and W. Huschner, *Transalpine Kommunikation im Mittelalter. Diplomatische, kulturelle und politische Wechselwirkungen zwischen Italien und dem nordalpinen Reich (9.–11. Jahrhundert)*, MGH: Schriften 52, 3 pts (Hannover, 2003), 169–72 and 756–94.

though strictly speaking false were felt to speak a deeper truth – after all, Edgar had certainly wanted the monks of Abingdon to remain free under the stipulations Rule, even if he had not issued a diploma to this effect.[27]

There is, therefore, every reason to believe that the Abingdon privilege of 993, with its lengthy meditation on sin and redemption, is an original statement of 993, not simply a variation on an existing theme; it is a key witness to Æthelred's concerns at this point. That such thoughts are to be ascribed to the king and his closest advisers should not be doubted: it would not have been in the interests of a local Abingdon scribe to explain the reasons behind Æthelred's change of heart in detail, nor does one imagine that he would have dared put such words in the king's mouth – these sentiments can only have served a royal agenda.[28] The charter claims to have been dictated by Abbot Wulfgar, and this is by no means inconceivable; but whoever drafted it, there must have been a great deal of royal input. In this respect, one imagines that other figures at court, such as Archbishop Sigeric, Abbot Ælfsige of the New Minster and the thegns Æthelmær and Ordulf (the last three of whom are named as playing an active role at the Gillingham gathering) also had a say. The resulting charter was the first of a series of restitutions issued in the 990s, all of which frame Æthelred's actions in remarkably similar terms. The next, in favour of St Andrew's, Rochester, was issued in 995, two years after the council of Winchester, restoring estates at Wouldham and Littlebrook in Kent.[29] This document does not go into the same degree of detail as the Abingdon privilege, but it similarly refers to the neglect of Æthelred's youth and the ignorance that the king then showed, an ignorance which he has been able to rectify since achieving maturity. As before, the king's personal interest in restoring these lands is evident: he has done wrong, and now that he has attained a sufficient age feels the need to correct his youthful error. Beyond thematic similarities, there is a textual link between the charters: the reference to Æthelred's youth and its 'various pursuits' in this diploma is taken almost verbatim from the Abingdon privilege, right down to

---

[27] Cf. H. Fuhrmann, 'Fälschungen im Dienste der Wahrheit', in his *Überall ist Mittelalter. Von der Gegenwart einer vergangenen Zeit* (Munich, 1996), 48–62 and 277–8.

[28] Roach, 'Penitential Discourse', esp. 265–72.

[29] S 885 (*Roch* 31).

the allusion to the preface of the *Regularis concordia*.[30] The two documents were evidently part of the same programme and the draftsman is advertising this fact. At Wantage two years later (Easter 997), Æthelred then restored lands to the Old Minster, Winchester, expressing remarkably similar sentiments. Here he admits to having earlier taken estates amounting to a massive hundred hides at Downton and Ebbesborne (Wilts.) – a portion of which we know to have gone to Ælfgar in 986 – on account of his immoderate youth; now, however, admonished by his advisers and fearing apostolic wrath, the king promises to restore the lands which he has unjustly possessed.[31] Again Æthelred's guilt and fear are clear, as is their cause: the intemperate actions of his youth.

These themes are returned to at greater length in the next document in this series, a second restitution in favour of Rochester, issued at Easter 998.[32] Here Æthelred revisits his wrongdoing in a level of detail not seen since the Abingdon privilege: the king again mentions his youth and the role of bad counsellors, in this case singling out Æthelsige, who had taken advantage of him and obtained permission to despoil St Andrew's. Nevertheless, the king maintains that his actions were performed 'not so much cruelly as ignorantly' (*non tam crudeliter quam ignoranter*) and goes on to explain that he has since deprived Æthelsige of office, promising now to restore the relevant estate (Bromley) to Rochester. The diploma reaches a crescendo with the following details:

> Now, however, because I have reached a mature age thanks to merciful heavenly kindness, I have decided to amend my childhood deeds. Therefore, encouraged by the grace of the Lord, I am reconsidering whatever I have unjustly done, encouraged then with wicked instigation against the sacred apostle of God; now, fully before God, with tearful contrition of my heart, I repent (*peniteo*) and restore freely that

---

[30] Keynes, 'Re-Reading', 91, n. 70; Roach, 'Penitential Discourse', 266–7.
[31] S 891 (KCD 698).
[32] S 893 (*Roch* 32).

which rightly belongs to this place, hoping to receive the tears of my repentance and to be loosened from the fetters of my earlier ignorance by Him, Who does not desire the death of a sinner, but rather that he convert and live.[33]

What is significant here is the use of the Latin verb *peniteo*, 'I repent, I do penance'. That specifically penitential contrition is intended is suggested by the wording of the rest of the passage: Æthelred's conscience is pricked (he is *compunctus*) and he wishes to receive the 'tears of repentance' (*lacrimas penitentiae*); *compunctio*, as we have seen, was associated with penitential regret and the tears of repentance were another important sign of contrition, an indication that penance was not undertaken cynically.[34] The final phrase of this passage, taken from Ezekiel XXXIII.11, is a classic penitential motif, probably drawn from contemporary rites for the reconciliation of penitents.[35] This is not the only liturgical allusion in this document: its preamble borrows elements of its formulation from the mass text for Maundy Thursday (the Thursday before Good Friday).[36] Since the diploma was issued on Easter Sunday, only three days after those present would have witnessed these rites (possibly including the reconciliation of penitents), these allusions can hardly have fallen on deaf ears. Indeed, the textual links between this charter and the liturgy of penance raises the

---

[33] S 893 (*Roch* 32): 'Nunc autem quia superna michi parcente clementia ad intelligibilem etatem perueni . et que pueriliter gessi in melius emendare decreui ; iccirco domini compunctus gratia quicquid tunc instigante maligno contra sanctum dei apostolum me inique egisse recogito . totum nunc coram deo cum flebili cordis contritione peniteo . et queque opportuna ad eundem locum pertinentia libenter restauro . sperans penitentie mee lacrimas suscipi . et prioris ignorantie uincula solui ab eo qui non uult mortem peccatoris . sed ut magis conuertatur et uiuat .' On which, see also S. Thompson Smith, *Land and Book: Literature and Land Tenure in Anglo-Saxon England* (Toronto, 2012), 56–60.

[34] Foxhall Forbes, 'Notions of Penance', 103–7; T.-A. Cooper, 'The Shedding of Tears in Late Anglo-Saxon England', in *Crying in the Middle Ages: Tears of History*, ed. E. Gertisman (London, 2011), 175–92.

[35] Roach, 'Penitential Discourse', 262–3.

[36] S 893 (*Roch* 32): 'pro redemptione generis humani in ara sancte crucis semetipsum *patienter* in odorem suauitatis *immolari permisit* .'; *The Leofric Missal*, ed. N. Orchard, 2 vols., HBS 113–14 (Woodbridge, 2002), II, 166: 'Sed filius tuus dominus noster, tanquam pia hostia, et *immolari* se tibi pro nobis *pacienter permisit*, et peccatum quod mundus commiserate relaxauit' (italics added). See further Keynes, 'Church of Rochester', 345, n. 102, who notes the influence of the liturgy, but does not specify the nature of the allusions.

distinct possibility that Æthelred underwent these rites three days earlier; such remarks are unlikely to have been a mere literary fiction.[37]

'Public' or 'solemn' penance, as it is often termed, had a venerable tradition. Based upon Late Antique church regulations, it represented a more serious form of repentance than normal confession: public penitents were formally expelled from the church at the start of Lent on Ash Wednesday and remained outside the Christian community until Maundy Thursday, when they were reconciled and absolved of sin.[38] In the interim they were effectively in a state of temporary excommunication; they were to refrain from sexual activity, arms-bearing and the other trappings of secular life. What in principle distinguished 'public' from 'normal' (or 'private') penance was the nature of the sin: public sins, those that were thought to cause 'scandal' (*scandalum*), were meant to be atoned for by public means.[39] The distinction between these two forms was not always clear, and mixed rites combining features of both were not uncommon. Nevertheless, ideas about public penance were circulating in later Anglo-Saxon England and the fact that the draftsman of this charter was able to quote from the relevant rites suggests that he knew these well.[40] Might Æthelred have actually undergone them? It is a tantalizing proposition, which would fit well with both the wording and timing of the grant (coming, as it does, hot on the heels of Maundy Thursday). Whether the king would have followed all the strictures which were meant to pertain to this practice is, of course, hard to say – as Timothy Reuter noted, kings and notables often bent the rules when it came to penance.[41] Still, it is

---

[37] Cf. C. Insley, 'Charters, Ritual and Late Tenth-Century Kingship', in *Gender and Historiography: Studies in the Earlier Middle Ages in Honour of Pauline Stafford*, ed. J.L. Nelson, S. Reynolds and S.M. Johns (London, 2012), 75–89, at 79–80, for a somewhat different perspective.

[38] Hamilton, *Practice of Penance*, esp. 1–24 and 173–206; R. Meens, *Penance in Medieval Europe: 600–1200* (Cambridge, 2014), 15–25, 118–30 and 158–64.

[39] M. de Jong, 'What was Public about Public Penance? *Paenitentia publica* and Justice in the Carolingian World', *Settimane* 44 (1997), 863–904, at 896–8.

[40] Hamilton, 'Rites'; B. Bedingfield, 'Public Penance in Anglo-Saxon England', *ASE* 31 (2002), 223–55.

[41] T. Reuter, 'Contextualising Canossa: Excommunication, Penance, Surrender, Reconciliation', in his *Medieval Polities and Modern Mentalities,* ed. J.L. Nelson (Cambridge, 2006), 147–66, at 159–60. See also S. MacLean, 'Ritual, Misunderstanding and the Contest for Meaning: Representations of the Disrupted Royal Assembly at Frankfurt (873)', in *Representations of Power in Medieval Germany, c .800–1500*, ed. S. MacLean and B. Weiler (Turnhout, 2006), 97–120, at 105–6.

not so much the details of the penance as the fact of its performance which matters: the king seems to have sought the most extreme means of absolution available. As previously, this was a very personal affair: the diploma draws attention to Æthelred's contrition and his sons appear prominently in the witness-list, with the young Eadwig now making his first appearance. It is conceivable that earlier restitutions had been accompanied by similar gestures; however, in the absence of explicitly penitential language it seems more likely that we are witnessing the intensification of an existing programme: repentance and regret have now given way to fully fledged penance. Why this should be so is hard to say. It may be that the return of the Scandinavian raiders spurred Æthelred into action: after two years of silence, the vikings had come back with a vengeance in 997 and 998. As important, however, must have been the longer history of relations with Rochester. St Andrew's had suffered more than any other house in the 980s and the king's actions weighed particularly heavily here (murrain had apparently struck in the very year Æthelred ravaged the diocese). The king himself was clearly concerned about what he had done 'against the sacred apostle of God' (*contra sanctum dei apostolum*),[42] as he puts it, and the logic would seem to have been that the punishment should fit the crime: because Æthelred had treated St Andrew's most harshly, it was St Andrew who most needed to be propitiated.

Æthelred's final act of repentance, in favour of Abingdon, returns to the established format.[43] This charter (datable 990 × 1006, probably *c.* 999) is rather more complex than the previous ones. It is not a straightforward restitution, and though a degree of royal guilt is acknowledged, it is less apologetic in tone. The king explains that he had been granted estates at Hurstbourne, Bedwyn and Burbage (Hants. and Wilts.) during the reign of his half-brother, which his father had previously donated to Abingdon. The reason for confiscating these lands and passing them on to Æthelred was that they were traditionally allocated to the king's sons.[44] As such, Æthelred's guilt lay less in receiving these estates – which, incidentally, he

---

[42] Similar sentiments are found in S 891 (KCD 698).

[43] S 937 (*Abing* 129).

[44] See above, Chapter 2, pp. 70–1; and cf. R. Lavelle, *Royal Estates in Anglo-Saxon Wessex: Land, Politics and Family Strategies* (Oxford, 2007), 1 and 90.

does not restore to the abbey and would remain in the hands of the fisc – than in not compensating Abingdon for its loss. Still, he clearly regrets the transaction and notes that since he has obtained a sufficient age to understand his mistake, he has seen fit to donate a series of other estates in compensation, hoping thereby to be freed from the malediction he incurred by receiving these lands.

These documents are in many respects extraordinary. Their texts return to the same themes time and again: Æthelred expresses regret, blames his previous advisers and hopes to be freed from what he refers to as the 'nets' or 'snares' of sin. Since the charters survive in the archives of three different religious houses, the common denominator is to be sought at court. Indeed, these documents all touch upon matters of great personal interest to Æthelred: the well-being of the realm and the fate of his eternal soul. It is hardly credible that anyone but the king would have been so concerned about such matters, and one does not imagine that he would have left the formulation of such thoughts to anyone but a member of his inner circle. Æthelred would not be the only ruler of this period to express himself in charter form: Geoffrey Koziol argues that the only diploma in the name of Robert I of West Francia (France) (922–3) can be read as a statement of the rebel king's feelings at a decisive moment in his reign, while Hartmut Hoffmann has made a similar case for treating a number of diplomas in the name of Otto III (983–1002) and Henry II (1002–24) as products of these rulers' 'personal dictation' (*Eigendiktat*).[45] It emerges from these documents that two events particularly hung over Æthelred's regime: the death of Æthelwold and the ravaging of Rochester – the former precipitated the king's 'youthful indiscretions', while the latter saw these reach their peak. It is for this reason that Æthelwold and Rochester bulk so large in the restitutions of the 990s: Abingdon received two of these, including the first and longest, and the Old Minster one; meanwhile Rochester received two, including the most penitentially worded. Of similar importance was

---

[45] G. Koziol, 'Is Robert I in Hell? The Diploma for Saint-Denis and the Mind of a Rebel King (Jan. 25, 923)', *EME* 14 (2006), 233–67; H. Hoffmann, 'Eigendiktat in den Urkunden Ottos III. und Heinrichs II.', *DA* 44 (1988), 390–423. Cf. Koziol, *Politics of Memory*, 447–58 and 524–9; and A. Scharer, 'Herrscherurkunden als Selbstzeugnisse?', *Mitteilungen des Instituts für Österreichische Geschichtsforschung* 119 (2011), 1–13.

Æthelred's mother, Ælfthryth: her disappearance from court had coincided with the start of the king's youthful errors and it is now on the tide of these restitutions that she returns, attesting a number of them prominently. The manner in which Æthelred's youth is described conforms to medieval teachings about childhood, which presented it as an unstable and intemperate age; like the Prodigal Son, after a wayward youth the king has now come to accept the teachings of his parents and guardians.[46] Such rhetoric also helped justify the change of course taken in these years: by presenting his earlier actions as a product of youthful folly, Æthelred not only explained these acts (and placed part of the blame on the shoulders of others), but also underlined the necessity of a new direction. Interestingly, he was not the only child monarch to avail himself of this line of thought: in 1073 Henry IV of Germany sent the newly elected Pope Gregory VII (1073–85) an extraordinary letter bemoaning the misdeeds he had previously perpetrated at the prompting of bad counsellors – above all, acts of simony and keeping counsel with excommunicates – and promising now to make amends. Around the same time Henry started subscribing some of his diplomas as 'most humble' (*humillimus*) rather than 'most invincible' (*invictissimus*), as was conventional, further underlining his humility and regret.[47] However, while in this case one might doubt the ruler's sincerity – within two years Henry would be demanding Gregory's dismissal – Æthelred seems to have embraced such ideals more thoroughly. Indeed, though there may have been pressure on the king to undertake these acts, it would be wrong to imagine him doing so unwillingly; not only does the tone of these documents speak of genuine concern, but the consistency with which Æthelred pursued his politics of atonement in subsequent years belies such a cynical reading.[48] A major concern of these documents is good counsel, as Pauline Stafford notes: Æthelred had been led astray in the 980s and now seeks to return to the correct path with the guidance of a new group of advisers, led by the likes of Abbot Wulfgar of Abingdon,

---

[46] Cf. Le Goff, 'Le roi enfant', 231–7.

[47] *Die Briefe Heinrichs IV.*, ed. C. Erdmann, MGH: Deutsches Mittelalter 1 (Leipzig, 1937), no. 5, 8–9; C. Schneider, *Prophetisches Sacerdotium und heilsgeschichtliches Regnum im Dialog, 1073–1077. Zur Geschichte Gregors VII. und Heinrichs IV.* (Munich, 1972), 48–78.

[48] See Cubitt, 'Politics of Remorse', 190–1; and Roach, 'Penitential Discourse', 267–8.

Abbot Ælfsige of the New Minster and the thegns Ordulf and Æthelmær (all named in the text of the first Abingdon privilege).[49]

These charters bear witness to the anxiety which had taken root within Æthelred's regime. The king and his advisers were not in danger of losing control of the realm – it would be some time before the viking raids reached such intensity – but the ideological foundations of their rule had been shaken: good governance was meant to bring prosperity and so long as the kingdom suffered there would be questions about Æthelred's suitability as monarch (and also, for that matter, the suitability of his senior advisers). If the primary aim of the king's restitutions was spiritual, to redeem his sins, then a secondary concern was certainly to present himself as a just and God-fearing ruler. We can be confident that he and his counsellors were versed in the lessons of the 'Twelve Abuses' and the implicit message of these documents is that Æthelred was not an 'unjust king', but a repentant sinner – he was David, not Ahab; he had erred but made amends. While we might think of penance as a sign of weakness, it was not necessarily so in the Middle Ages: David provided a powerful model for the repentant ruler and the reformers of the ninth and tenth centuries taught that he who exalted himself would be humbled, while he who humbled himself would be exalted (cf. Matthew XXIII.12; Luke XIV.11).[50] Penance could thus be an assertive act: it had the power to transform weakness into strength, making prior mistakes into signs of humility, a cardinal virtue for rulers. Æthelred was acting in a venerable tradition: the Carolingian emperor Louis the Pious had performed penance twice (once under duress, admittedly), while Emperor Theodosius I (379–95), whose rule was synonymous with peace and justice in the Middle Ages, had also done so.[51] Still, emotions were running high and the very fact that the king had to fall on his sword in this manner says something: Æthelred was deeply troubled by recent events and desperate to find a way to make amends.

[49] See further Stafford, 'Political Ideas', 74–5.

[50] L. Bornscheuer, *Miseriae regum. Untersuchungen zum Krisen- und Todesgedanken in den herrschaftstheologischen Vorstellungen der ottonisch-salischen Zeit*, Arbeiten zur Frühmittelalterforschung 4 (Berlin, 1968). See also Koziol, *Begging Pardon*, 98–103 and 166–73.

[51] R. Schieffer, 'Von Mailand nach Canossa. Ein Beitrag zur Geschichte der christlichen Herrscherbuße von Theodosius d. Gr. bis zu Heinrich IV.', DA 28 (1972), 333–70.

Repentance and reform

Though Æthelred's charters of restitution give us the clearest insights into royal thought in the 990s, much can also be gleaned from other documents of these years.[52] Of particular importance here is the close nexus between repentance and reform, first established in the Abingdon privilege of 993: an essential part of Æthelred's *volte-face* was a return of royal support to reform. Since the reformers of Edgar's reign had taught that political success and national piety went hand in hand, it stood to reason that by returning to the politics of his father and erstwhile regents Æthelred could usher in a new 'Golden Age'. Reform here was to the institutional church what penance was to the individual sinner: a means of rectifying past wrongs. Indeed, the monastic vocation itself carried distinctly penitential undertones: the Rule describes life in a monastery as 'an eternal Lent', a never-ending period of prayer and penitence.[53]

The large number of charters issued in favour of religious houses (and in particular reformed monastic centres) in these years must be viewed in this light; like the restitutions discussed above, these were designed to court divine favour. Thus, when Æthelred granted liberty to the bishopric of Cornwall in 994, the document in question opens with a dramatic preamble considering the Fall of Man and closes with a sanction threatening eternal damnation on any who, seduced by love of money (*philargiria*), infringes upon its terms.[54] It is hard not to see herein echoes of the Abingdon privilege of the previous year, which also opens with a lapsarian proem and places particular blame on the 'detestable love of money' (*detestanda philargiria*) displayed by Æthelred's advisers in the 980s. The connections between these documents are not only thematic: the latter

---

[52] Keynes, 'Re-Reading', 91–3; Cubitt, 'Politics of Remorse', 188.

[53] *Regula Benedicti*, ch. 49.1 (ed. Neufville, 604). See Hamilton, *Practice of Penance*, 77–103; and cf. C. Cubitt, 'Bishops, Priests and Penance in Late Saxon England', *EME* 14 (2006), 41–63.

[54] S 880 (KCD 686); with Insley, 'Episcopal Scriptoria', 188–9. The background is provided by earlier conflicts with the bishopric of Crediton: *Councils*, ed. Whitelock, no. 35, 165–73, esp. 165–7.

also draws elements of its formulation from the Abingdon diploma.[55] The reference to how 'this charter was written by the venerable Archbishop Sigeric of the church of Canterbury' (*scripta est hec cartula ab uenerabili archiepiscopo Sigerico Dorobernensis aecclesie*) suggests that the kingdom's senior metropolitan had an active hand in its drafting; if so, such similarities can hardly be coincidental, since Sigeric had been a prominent presence at the previous year's council of Winchester. These reminiscences advertise the connection between this document and the programme unveiled at that event; it was clearly born of the same spirit.[56] This may explain why this privilege claims to be issued not only for the redemption of Æthelred's soul – something of a commonplace in such documents – but also for the absolution of his sins (*pro absolutione criminum meorum*), a rather less common turn of phrase, possibly alluding to the misdeeds of the 980s. The importance of this diploma is further indicated by the use of gold script to highlight initials and the names of key individuals within the text – it was designed to impress (Plate 7).

The wording of many other charters suggests a connection with this programme of repentance and reform. A diploma issued in favour of Wilton in 994 draws the reader's attention to the strict Benedictine observance of the nuns there, and a privilege in favour of Muchelney a year later likewise notes the monks' rigorous application of the Rule; in both cases, a distinctly reformist agenda is evident.[57] More telling, perhaps, is a document of 996 granting the Old Minster a bequest which had hitherto been blocked, which is said to have been issued 'for the expiation of my sins and the state of my realm' (*pro meorum expiatione piaculorum, meique statu imperii*).[58] That such documents were indeed issued with an eye to courting divine favour is shown by a charter issued to St Albans in 996, in which the king requests that the monks celebrate masses and sing psalms to assist him and

---

[55] Roach, 'Apocalypse and Atonement', 738, n. 28 (reading 'bishopric of Cornwall' for 'bishopric of Crediton'). See also C. Insley, 'Where did All the Charters Go? Anglo-Saxon Charters and the New Politics of the Eleventh Century', *ANS* 24 (2002), 109–27, at 117.

[56] See Keynes, 'Church Councils', 122.

[57] S 881 (KCD 687); S 884 (ed. E.H. Bates, *Two Cartularies of the Benedictine Abbeys of Muchelney and Athelney in the County of Somerset* [London, 1899], no. 4).

[58] S 889 (KCD 1291).

the Christian nation, that they might merit victory 'against both visible and invisible enemies' (*contra uisibiles et inuisibiles hostes*); clearly, the king was trying to marshal the spiritual weapons available, hoping that masses and psalms would succeed where hard steel had failed.[59] The phrase used here is of particular interest. To speak of the 'visible and invisible' was common enough in the Middle Ages (the Nicene Creed, which since 325 had been the cornerstone of Christian orthodoxy, opens by referring to 'all things visible and invisible'); nevertheless, the specific line employed here was probably lifted from the royal coronation *ordo*, in which it forms part of the prayer said over the king immediately before his consecration.[60] We thus seem to be witnessing further reflections upon the nature and duties of royal office. What is more, the connection between Æthelred's undertakings and present ills is made clear by the king's hope that by virtue of the monks' masses and psalms – 'spiritual arms' (*arma spiritualia*), as the draftsman puts it – not to mention the intercession of the blessed martyr Alban, he and his people will yet merit victory over their adversaries. The message of this document, like that of the restitutions of these years, is that Æthelred does indeed measure up to the expectations placed upon him; he invokes the help of the saints and the religious communities of his realm and rules in accordance with the instructions received at the time of his consecration. That the coronation *ordo* should be a source for such reflections is perfectly natural and this document's draftsman was not alone here: a short vernacular text composed at some point in Æthelred's reign (perhaps in his later years) uses the coronation oath as a springboard to consider broader themes of kingship and justice.[61] That these thoughts stemmed from the king or

---

[59] S 888 (*StAlb* 9). This charter may be interpolated, but the section in question is probably authentic: *Charters of St Albans*, ed. J. Crick, Anglo-Saxon Charters 12 (Oxford, 2007), 171–3.

[60] Conn, 'Pontificals', 116: 'contraque omnes visibiles et invisibiles hostes idem potenter regaliterque tuae virtutis regimine regat et defendat' (cf. the later benediction hoping that God will free the king 'from all assaults of visible and invisible foes' [*ab omnibus uisibilium et inuisibilium inimicorum insidiis*] and grant him victory 'over visible and invisible enemies' [*de inuisibilibus atque uisibilibus hostibus*]: ibid., 121–2). I am grateful to Sarah Hamilton for discussion on this point. On the visible and invisible, see also Foxhall Forbes, *Heaven and Earth*, 63–128.

[61] Clayton, '*Promissio regis*'. Though Clayton prefers a date later in Æthelred's reign (*c.* 1014), it is conceivable that the text was written as early as the mid- to later 990s: by 996 Wulfstan, the leading candidate for author, was bishop of London and he even attests the diploma in question.

one of his closest advisers should be presumed; in the wake of recent misfortunes, just rule was on the mind. This was, in any case, not the only charter to request masses and psalms for the king and nation: the Abingdon privilege of 993 had been issued in return for such services, as we have seen, and in 1002 an estate was granted to Westminster not only in exchange for a hundred mancuses (the mancus being one eighth of a pound, or thirty pence) but also on the condition that the monks celebrate masses and sing psalms for the king.[62]

Similarly revealing is a charter of 998, which grants Bishop Wulfsige permission to reform the cathedral chapter at Sherborne, confirming the centre's holdings and liberty in the process. This opens by explaining how Archbishop Ælfric (of Canterbury) and the rest of the king's leading men had taken part in deliberations leading to the chapter's reform, then launches into a series of instructions for Wulfsige's successors, who are to be pastors, not tyrants, looking to the best interests of the brothers. This, so the diploma continues, is necessary because the king and his countrymen are those 'upon whom the ends of the world are come' (*nos sumus in quos fines seculorum deuenerunt*: I Corinthians X.11); the human race is multiplied, there is a shortage of land, and everywhere the love of money (*philargiria*) is on the rise.[63] Again, we see echoes of the kinds of thoughts and concerns expressed in the Abingdon charter of 993; again, the tone is distinctly reformist. Wulfsige himself is one of a number of reform-minded individuals who rose to senior positions within the English church in these years, and other sources help shed further light on his pontificate. Pride of place goes to an anonymous letter to Wulfsige from his metropolitan (perhaps Archbishop Ælfric, given the emphasis placed on his involvement in Sherborne's reform). Most of the epistle is lifted from an earlier letter to Eanbald, archbishop of York, written by the eighth-century scholar Alcuin, who hailed from York but had made his career on the continent, eventually

---

[62] S 903 (ed. J.A. Robinson, *Gilbert Crispin, Abbot of Westminster* [Cambridge, 1911], 167–8).

[63] S 895 (*Sher* 11). See *Charters of Sherborne*, ed. M.A. O'Donovan, Anglo-Saxon Charters 3 (Oxford, 1988), xvii–xx and 41–4; and S. Keynes, 'Wulfsige, Monk of Glastonbury, Abbot of Westminster (*c* 990–3), and Bishop of Sherborne (*c* 993–1002)', in *St Wulfsige and Sherborne: Essays to Celebrate the Millennium of the Benedictine Abbey 998–1998*, ed. K. Barker, D.A. Hinton and A. Hunt (Oxford, 2005), 53–94, at 69–72.

retiring to St-Martin's, Tours: it comprises a general guide on how bishops ought to behave. The opening address to Wulfsige, however, is not taken from this exemplar and presumably reflects contemporary concerns: it gives thanks to God that the author has been set up to govern the church 'in such dangerous and most difficult times' (*in tam periculosis et laboriosissimis temporibus*: see II Timothy III.1), praying for divine assistance in all good works.[64] That Wulfsige was keen to receive advice on his new duties is further indicated by another letter written to him, this time by Ælfric the homilist (then of Cerne in Dorset, within Wulfsige's diocese). This offers some guidance to the secular clergy, but is unmistakably monastic in focus, expressing concern for the lax standards amongst clerics and affirming the superiority of the monastic vocation.[65] Clearly, there is a connection here between current events and the need for reform: the letter from Wulfsige's metropolitan speaks of the 'dangerous times' in which they live, an allusion to the dangerous times which according to II Timothy will precede the end of time, while later versions of Ælfric's pastoral letter splice this together with the homilist's tract 'On the Prayer of Moses' (*De oratione Moysi*, *c.* 995), an eschatologically charged work which presents recent misfortunes as punishment for the neglect of monastic life and divine services.[66] Hints of such concerns can also be detected in the 'earlier' version of Ælfric's letter, which contains a set of later pronouncements inserted into the main text. These clearly stem from a church council and were presumably added by Wulfsige himself. Amongst the stipulations is an instruction that the mass *contra paganos* ('against the pagans') should be sung in larger religious houses of the kingdom every Wednesday; as the viking incursions ramped up, the kingdom's bishops evidently thought it wise to entreat divine support for the nation.[67] The lucky circumstance – if it is to be ascribed to

---

[64] *Councils*, ed. Whitelock, no. 40, 196–226. Cf. Alcuin of York, *Epistola* 124, ed. E. Dümmler, *Epistolae Karolingi aevi* II, MGH: Epp. 4 (Berlin, 1895), 166–70, at 167–8. Interestingly, this letter was included within Archbishop Wulfstan's collection of Alcuin's letters. See below, Chapter 6, p. 283, with n. 91.

[65] *Councils*, ed. Whitelock, no. 40, 196–226.

[66] M. Godden, 'Apocalypse and Invasion in Late Anglo-Saxon England', in *From Anglo-Saxon to Early Middle English: Studies Presented to E.G. Stanley*, ed. M. Godden, D. Gray and T.F. Hoad (Oxford, 1994), 130–62, at 133–7.

[67] *Councils*, ed. Whitelock, no. 40, 226.

luck alone – that so many sources shed light upon Wulfsige's actions at this point allows us to say with confidence here what we can often only infer: that reform and other pious endeavours were intimately associated with the growing viking threat.[68]

The stipulations of individual charters only tell part of the tale, however, and much can also be learned from the witness-lists accompanying these documents.[69] We have already noted that Sigeric's activities during his episcopate in Canterbury (990–4) seem to have paved the way for Æthelred's actions in subsequent years, and much the same can be said for other figures. Thus, Wulfsige was appointed abbot of Westminster *c.* 990 (whether under royal fiat or not is unclear) and makes his first appearance as bishop of Sherborne in the witness-list of the Abingdon charter of 993; he would appear to have been one of the new wave of advisers who ushered in the penitential politics of the 990s. Other individuals of a distinctly reformist bent also owed their promotion to these years: Ælfric, who may have received his education at Abingdon and had hitherto been abbot of St Albans (*c.* 970–*c.* 995), succeeded Sigeric as bishop of Ramsbury in the early 990s and then again as archbishop of Canterbury in 994 or 995, holding the see in plurality with (i.e. alongside) Ramsbury; Ealdulf, who had been a monk at the Old Minster, became Oswald's successor at Worcester in 992 and within three years had also been appointed to York (in plurality with Worcester, as was then customary); Wulfstan, whose background is unclear, but may have received his early training at the Æthewoldian foundation at Peterborough (and was later buried at Ely), was elected to the strategically important see of London in 996; and finally Wulfgar, a local Abingdon monk, was elected successor to the simoniacally appointed Eadwine in 990 and went on to oversee a remarkable revival at the centre. There are also signs that others, whose voices were not heard – or at least not heeded – in the later 980s were now beginning to take on greater prominence in royal counsels. Bishop Ælfheah of Winchester (984–1006), the sometime abbot of Bath (?963–84) and future archbishop of Canterbury (1006–12), should be counted amongst these. Others

---

[68] See Keynes, 'Wulfsige', 59–72.

[69] For the following, see Keynes, *Atlas*, tables LX–LXIV; with discussion in Keynes, *Diplomas*, 189–93; and Williams, *Æthelred*, 29–42.

include Ælfweard of Glastonbury (c. 975–1009), an associate of Archbishop Sigeric whose centre had suffered in the 980s, but may also have enjoyed a revival of sorts at this juncture, and Ælfsige of the New Minster (988–1007), whose neighbours at the Old Minster had felt the king's ire in previous years and whose involvement at the Gillingham gathering in 993 is highlighted in the surviving charter. In general, it seems that abbots were starting to play a greater role at court: during the mid- to late 980s it was rare for more than three of four to attest Æthelred's diplomas, but from 990 on it is not uncommon to find ten or more – more, that is, than had been seen since the heyday of reform in Edgar's later years.[70]

Yet it is not only bishops and abbots who are prominent at this point. In addition to Abbot Ælfsige, laymen by the name of Æthelmær and Ordulf are singled out as playing an active role in overseeing the restitution of Abingdon's liberty in 993. These can be identified as the thegns of these names who regularly attest royal charters, generally in the first and second positions. They are also said to have advised the king to compensate Abingdon for its loss of lands (c. 999) previously donated by Edgar and therefore deserve to be seen as another driving force behind the restitutions of these years.[71] The first of these figures was the son of Ealdorman Æthelweard 'of the western provinces' and thus a relative of Ælfhere of Mercia (himself a relation of the queen-mother Ælfthryth). Though Æthelweard owed his promotion to Edward the Martyr, thanks to these connections he may also have been an associate of Ælfthryth during the regency years, when his son was the beneficiary of a grant at Thames Ditton. Certainly, he and Æthelmær were important patrons of reform, founding Cerne (c. 987) and Eynsham (1005), and the latter's prominence is further reflected in the fact that he is recorded as one of the king's seneschals (Old English: discðegn).[72] As we have seen, this was an honourable post, reserved for the most influential magnates. The second of these figures, Ordulf, was the king's maternal uncle, who also shared a passion for monastic life. He had been responsible for founding Tavistock

---

[70] Keynes, *Atlas*, table LXI. Cf. *ibid.*, table LV.

[71] S 876 (*Abing* 124), S 937 (*Abing* 129).

[72] S 914 (*CantCC* 140); with *Charters of Christ Church*, ed. Brooks and Kelly, 1026–31.

(*c.* 981) – dedicated appropriately enough to the Blessed Virgin – and may have retired to the house in later years.[73] In fact, Tavistock itself may have been amongst the centres to suffer in the 980s: the only early charter to survive from the abbey, a purported grant of privileges from 981, declares that it was issued after a period in which, as a consequence of his youth, the king had been unable and unwilling to prevent attacks on the house. This is a problematic document, since in 981 Æthelred can have been no more than fifteen (and was perhaps only twelve); it is hard to imagine how he would have been in a position to express regret for the errors of his youth at this point. However, while unconvincing as a document of 981, this diploma fits well into the politics of the 990s, when Ordulf's fortunes – like those of his sister – were on the rise, and when the king was issuing similar charters of restitution to other monastic houses. Indeed, much of the document concerns the right of free election, which was a hot topic in the wake of Æthelred's simoniacal intervention at Abingdon. One suspects, therefore, that the charter was concocted shortly after the sack of Tavistock in 997, perhaps on the basis of local memories of earlier struggles.[74] Like Æthelweard and Æthelmær, who were patrons of the homilist Ælfric, Ordulf seems to have been a learned layman, since he was left a copy of one of Hrabanus Maurus's works and a martyrology by the local bishop of Crediton, Ælfwold (1008 × 1012).[75] Although Ordulf is not recorded as occupying a household office, his prominence in diploma witness-lists suggests that he too was accorded such a dignity. Other important figures amongst the ranks of the thegns at this point include Wulfgeat, who is named alongside Æthelmær and Ordulf as those who advised the king to compensate Abingdon for its loses *c.* 999 and is to be identified with the man of this name whom John of Worcester calls the king's particular

---

[73] C. Holdsworth, 'Tavistock Abbey in its Late Tenth Century Context', *Report and Transactions of the Devonshire Association for the Advancement of Science* 135 (2003), 31–58.

[74] S 838 (KCD 629). See Roach, 'Privilege of Liberty'; and cf. *Charters of Abingdon*, ed. Kelly, xci–xciii; and Holdsworth, 'Tavistock Abbey', who believe the document to be substantially authentic. What Kelly and Holdsworth fail to explain is how Æthelred could have responded to the 'helplessness' and 'unwillingness' of his youth in 981. See also Stafford, 'Royal Government', 44–5; and Keynes, *Diplomas*, 180, n. 101.

[75] S 1492 (ed. Whitelock, *Councils*, no. 51).

favourite; and Wulfric Spot, who founded Burton Abbey and endowed the centre with a substantial part of his patrimony in the early eleventh century.[76] It was also around this time that Wulfric's brother, Ælfhelm, was appointed ealdorman of Northumbria. He and his two sons, Wulfheah and Ufegeat (the former of whom often attests alongside Æthelmær, Ordulf and Wulfric amongst the ranks of the thegns), were also a significant presence at court. We do not know what happened to Ælfhelm's predecessor, Thored; it may be that he died around this time (after a career of over a decade, this would be no surprise), but it has been suggested that he was removed to make way for Ælfhelm following his failure to face down viking forces in 992 and 993.[77] If so, this would be a further sign of Æthelred's change of direction. In any case, it was also at this point that Leofsige and Leofwine were appointed to the ealdordoms of Essex and the Hwicce (a west-Midlands people); though their role in the resulting regime is somewhat less clear, we can be confident that they too were supportive of the new politics of the 990s.

Many of these new favourites were recipients of and participants in royal diplomas: Wulfric received a grant in 995 and another two in 996, and the king confirmed lands donated by Æthelmær to Muchelney in 995.[78] Æthelweard himself attests as senior ealdorman from 993 onwards and one suspects that he played an especially important part in developments at this point; as a literate layman, who may have received his education at Winchester, his sympathy for reform is clear. Finally, it should not be forgotten that Ælfthryth herself returned to the scene in 993, and though she never quite regains the position she had enjoyed during her son's minority, there are signs that she was once again exerting significant influence at (and beyond) court: she appears periodically in the witness-lists of diplomas (including two of Æthelred's four key restitutions); she

---

[76] John of Worcester, *Chronicon, s.a.* 1006 (ed. Darlington and McGurk, 456); C. Insley, 'The Family of Wulfric Spott: An Anglo-Saxon Marcher Dynasty?', in *The English and their Legacy, 900–1200: Essays in Honour of Ann Williams*, ed. D. Roffe (Woodbridge, 2012), 115–28, esp. 122–7.

[77] Whitelock, 'Dealings', 80; Stafford, 'Reign of Æthelred II', 29; Williams, *Æthelred*, 28.

[78] S 878 (*Burt* 27), S 879 (*Burt* 26), S 886 (*Abing* 126), S 884 (ed. Bates, *Muchelney Cartulary*, no. 4).

seems to have been charged with raising the king's sons (a job with which she may have been entrusted upon her return); and in the early 990s she was involved in an important exchange of estates which paved the way for the foundation of Cholsey Abbey (to which we shall return).[79] It is, therefore, clear that she and her son had put the 980s behind them. Her involvement in the upbringing of her grandsons, alongside whom she frequently attests, is especially striking; if Æthelred's actions in previous years had been a rejection of her (and Æthelwold's) teachings, this decision reveals just how far the king had back-tracked: he was now entrusting her with imparting these same lessons to his sons and heirs. It has been suggested that Ælfthryth's return to political life occasioned the side-lining of Æthelred's first wife and possibly also the removal of the latter's father, Thored.[80] This may be true, insofar as these years saw a general shift away from the politics of the 980s; however, even then Ælfgifu had not attested Æthelred's diplomas, so it is by no means clear that we can read so much into her invisibility at this point. The fact that she continued to bear Æthelred children throughout the 990s certainly indicates that she was accommodated within the new regime. Indeed, though it is probably no more than a coincidence, it is fitting that it should be during these years of reforming zeal that Ælfgifu gave birth to sons bearing the evocative names Eadwig and Edgar.[81]

Viewed in this light, it comes as little surprise that, despite viking ravages, the 990s were a period of substantial literary and intellectual activity. It was in the early years of the decade that Ælfric completed the First and Second Series of Catholic Homilies (990 × 994), which he dedicated to Archbishop Sigeric (though Ealdorman Æthelweard also received a special version of at least the first of these).[82] These were followed shortly by his *Lives of Saints* (994 × 998), which are a supplement of sorts to the Catholic Homilies, written with a keener eye to political developments and

---

[79] Keynes, *Atlas*, table LIX; S 877 (*WinchNM* 31). See also above, Chapter 3, p. 95, with n. 12.

[80] Williams, *Æthelred*, 28. See also Stafford, 'Sons and Mothers', 92.

[81] Eadwig first attests in 997 and Edgar in 1001: Keynes, *Atlas*, table LIX.

[82] Ælfric, *CH: FS*, prol. (ed. Clemoes, 177, n.); with M. Godden, *Ælfric's Catholic Homilies: Introduction, Commentary and Glossary*, EETS s.s. 18 (Oxford, 2000), 7.

appropriately enough dedicated to Æthelweard.[83] Alongside these major collections many shorter works can be ascribed to this most productive of English homilists.[84] Yet if Ælfric was the most prolific writer of these years, he was certainly not alone. It was in the 990s, perhaps soon after his appointment to the see of London (996), that Wulfstan began writing sermons. Many of his early works address the coming of Antichrist and end of time, events which he anticipated coming to pass in the near future. These were soon followed by writings on pastoral themes, including the correct conduct of religious life, provision of sacraments and payment of church dues.[85] The works of these two figures can be placed alongside the rich Latin literary production of these years. Wulfstan Cantor (also known as Wulfstan of Winchester) is known to have produced a veritable slew of texts: a poem on the ceremonial transfer (translation) and miracles of the relics of St Swithun (*Narratio metrica de S. Swithuno*; 992 × 994, updated in or soon after 996); a *Life* of Bishop Æthelwold (996 × 1002, probably late 996 or early 997); a work on musical theory (no longer extant); and various shorter poems and hymns, which cannot be securely dated, but are probably to be assigned to the 990s.[86] Rather more idiosyncratic, but no less interesting, are the writings of Byrhtferth of Ramsey, a sometime student of the continental reformer Abbo of Fleury, who had taught briefly at Ramsey (985–7). Byrhtferth composed *Lives* of Ramsey's founder, Bishop Oswald (995 × 1005, probably 997 × 1002) and the obscure eighth-century Mercian bishop Ecgwine; a work of history which later formed the basis for the earlier sections of Symeon of Durham's *Historia regum*; a selection of extracts from earlier writers (the so-called *Glossae in Bedam*); and a bilingual handbook or *Enchiridion* (1004 × 1016), designed to accompany

---

[83] Ælfric, *LS*, prol. (ed. Skeat, I, 2–4). See M. Godden, 'Ælfric's Saints' Lives and the Problem of Miracles', *Leeds Studies in English* n.s. 16 (1985), 83–100, at 94–7; and C. Cubitt, 'Ælfric's Lay Patrons', in *A Companion to Ælfric*, ed. H. Magennis and M. Swan (Leiden, 2009), 165–92.

[84] P.A.M. Clemoes, 'The Chronology of Ælfric's Works', in *The Anglo-Saxons: Studies in Some Aspects of their History and Culture Presented to Bruce Dickens*, ed. P.A.M. Clemoes (London, 1959), 212–47.

[85] J.T. Lionarons, *The Homiletic Writings of Archbishop Wulfstan: A Critical Study* (Woodbridge, 2010).

[86] L. Roach, 'Wulfstan Cantor', in *The Wiley Blackwell Encyclopedia of Medieval British Literature*, ed. S. Echard and R. Rouse (Chichester, forthcoming).

a now-lost work of *computus* (that is, a guide to the reckoning of dates, especially those of movable church feasts such as Easter).[87] Taken together this constitutes a very substantial literary output, a fact which is all the more impressive when one considers that other works are likely to have been lost in transmission. Alongside such new works, this was also a period in which many existing texts were copied and circulated: it was around the turn of the millennium that the Blickling Homilies (a selection of anonymous sermons) were transcribed, as were two of the four great manuscripts of Old English verse, the Junius and *Beowulf* codices (the other two, the Exeter Book and the Vercelli Codex, were probably produced slightly earlier).[88] Such manuscripts may reveal something about the concerns of those copying them and it has been suggested that the *Beowulf* manuscript, in particular, with its pronounced interest in foreign invasion and the monstrous, reflects the problems faced by the English at this point: its readers were meant to meditate on men and monsters.[89]

There is, therefore, reason to speak of a 'second generation' of reform in these years, typified by Ælfric of Eynsham, Wulfstan of York and Wulfstan Cantor. That these figures were not satisfied with maintaining the *status quo* is clear: the pastoral letters of Ælfric and sermons of Wulfstan reveal a firm belief that there is much work to be done. This generation was more concerned with consolidating previous gains than spreading them to new centres, as we might expect, and pastoral matters bulk particularly large. Still, reform was also taken forward in important manners. A number of centres were founded anew or reformed, including Cerne (*c.* 987), Cholsey (993 × 997), Sherborne (998), Burton (1003) and Eynsham (1005), which join the foundations of the early 980s (Tavistock and perhaps also Amesbury and Wherwell). Existing centres also did well in the 990s: the monks of Abingdon were to recall the abbacy of Wulfgar (990–1016) as a second 'Golden Age' and in Winchester the dedication of a new tower (993 × 994) and the translation of Æthelwold (10 September 996) speak

---

[87] *Byrhtferth of Ramsey*, ed. Lapidge, xxx–xliv.

[88] D. Scragg, 'Old English Homiliaries and Poetic Manuscripts', in *The Cambridge History of the Book in Britain*, I, *c.400–1100*, ed. R. Gameson (Cambridge, 2012), 553–61, at 553–7.

[89] K. Powell, 'Meditating on Men and Monsters: A Reconsideration of the Thematic Unity of the *Beowulf* Manuscript', *Review of English Studies* 57 (2006), 1–15.

of new-found confidence.[90] It is against the backdrop of renewed royal patronage that such activity is to be understood.

That the works of these years should reflect contemporary concerns is not surprising and the viking raids naturally take pride of place here. Indeed, though the literary flourishing of the period is not simply a reflex of the Scandinavian attacks, there is no mistaking the urgency of many of these works, an urgency which becomes more pronounced as we move through the 990s. Already in the preface to his Second Series of Catholic Homilies (c. 992 × 994) Ælfric complained of the 'many injuries of hostile pirates' (multae iniuriae infestium piratarum) he had suffered since completing the First Series (c. 990 × 992) and in later writings the homilist shows signs of growing concern.[91] It was only shortly after finishing the Second Series that he rendered the 'Twelve Abuses' into the vernacular (c. 995), a text which, as we have seen, carried clear contemporary resonances. His 'On the Prayer of Moses' (De oratione Moysi), written around the same time (c. 995), can be read in a similar vein: here the homilist asserts that present invasions are divine punishment for earlier attacks on monastic life (apparently those of the 980s). Ælfric also includes an account of God's punishment of David, the archetypal penitent ruler who may have been the model for Æthelred's own actions at this point.[92] This work was composed for inclusion in Ælfric's Lives of Saints, and other texts within this collection betray a similar interest in current events: the account of the deeds of the Maccabees, who had resisted foreign dominion of Judea in the Hellenistic period, and the rendering into English of the Passion of Edmund, who had died at the hands of the viking 'Great Army' in 869, may have been intended as models for the English in their hour of need; meanwhile, the assurance at the end of the account of the martyrdom of the Forty Soldiers that 'heathens' – heathen being a common synonym for viking – who oppress Christians will receive their just deserts from the Almighty must have come as welcome

---

[90] Historia ecclesie Abbendonensis, ch. 97 (ed. Hudson, I, 140); Wulfstan, Narratio metrica de S. Swithuno, 'Epistola specialis ad Ælfegum episcopum', ll. 213–50 (ed. Lapidge, 390–2), and Vita S. Æthelwoldi, ch. 43 (ed. Lapidge and Winterbottom, 66).

[91] Ælfric, CH: SS, prol.13–15 (ed. Godden, 1). For much of what follows, see Godden, 'Apocalypse', 131–42; and Clayton, 'Ælfric and Æthelred'.

[92] Ælfric, LS XIII.147–77, 240–72 (ed. Skeat, I, 294–6, 300–2); with Cubitt, 'Politics of Remorse', 188–9. Interestingly, Ælfric briefly summarizes the 'Twelve Abuses' in this work.

news to many.[93] Similar interest attaches to the unusual tract known as *Wyrdwriteras* (998 × 1002), in which Ælfric undertakes a learned discussion on how kings of old had delegated military command to 'ealdormen' and generals so that they might concentrate on other business, such as prayer; clearly, military manoeuvres and royal piety were matters of interest.[94] Further evidence of such thoughts comes from Ælfric's translation of the Book of Kings (992 × 1002), which frequently expands on or adjusts the original, giving particular attention to the role of royal counsel; as Stacy Klein notes, it is tempting to see herein a commentary on Æthelred's recent indiscretions.[95] Whether such references should be read as ruler criticism, however, is a good question. There can be no doubt as to Ælfric's disapproval of recent attacks on monasteries, but it must be borne in mind that by the time he wrote these works Æthelred himself had expressed similar sentiments. Indeed, much of what the homilist has to say sits comfortably alongside the king's own actions in these years: he urges prayer and piety, but also military support when necessary. Ælfric was critical of the boy who had brought his nation to the brink of disaster in the 980s, not the man seeking to redress this in the 990s. That the homilist should be broadly in agreement with Æthelred's regime makes perfect sense: his chief patrons, Æthelweard and Æthelmær, were a dominant force at court in these years, while Archbishop Sigeric, to whom he dedicated the Catholic Homilies, also played an important part in developments.[96]

Ælfric was not alone in reflecting upon the present state of England. Though the *Lives* of Æthelwold, Oswald and Dunstan, produced in quick succession around the turn of the first millennium, were probably inspired in the first instance by the need to support the cults of these recently deceased figures, they too represent a wistful evocation of a past 'Golden Age'. For an increasingly beleaguered nation, it must have been reassuring

---

[93] Ælfric, *LS* XI.353–5, XXV, XXXII (ed. Skeat, I, 258–60, II, 66–120, 314–34).

[94] Ælfric, *Supplementary Homilies* XXII (ed. Pope, 725–33); W. Braekman, 'Wyrdwriteras: An Unpublished Ælfrician Text in Manuscript Hatton 115', *Revue belge de philologie et d'histoire* 44 (1966), 959–70.

[95] Ælfric, *LS* XVIII (ed. Skeat, I, 384–412); with Klein, *Ruling Women*, 144–61.

[96] S. Keynes, 'An Abbot, an Archbishop, and the Viking Raids of 1006–7 and 1009–12', *ASE* 36 (2007), 151–220, at 162; Gretsch, 'Æthelweard', 247. Cf. Clayton, 'Ælfric and Æthelred'.

to think back upon the successes of a previous generation, successes which might in turn provide a framework for future action. Alone amongst these, Byrhtferth's *Life* of Oswald speaks of contemporary attacks, while Adelard of Ghent's slightly later *Lections* on Dunstan (1006 × 1011) assert that the venerable saint had foreseen the 'attack of the barbarians' (*barbarorum . . . impugnationem*) which followed his death, expressing the hope that God will yet free the English through the intercessions of his prophet.[97] The literary output of Wulfstan of York (then bishop of London) is even more clearly influenced by such developments. Though he rarely refers directly to the viking ravages, these clearly inform the bishop's eschatological outlook, an outlook which in turn influences his more pastoral writings.[98] Thus, while such literary production is not simply a reaction to the Scandinavian raids, these certainly helped concentrate the mind and many of these works can be read as part of an effort to restore or evoke the *status quo ante*. They provide a backdrop to the king's own state of mind in these years: clearly, Æthelred was not the only one who sought to invoke the legacy of Edgar and the reformers and, as we have seen, leading royal advisers are amongst the patrons and recipients of these texts.

The cult of King Edward

While Æthelred was willing to take some of the blame for recent events, he makes it clear that this is not his to bear alone: he repeatedly points to the role of bad advisers, who ought to have counselled him better. The king was not alone in thinking thus: Ælfric's rendering of the 'Twelve Abuses' shows almost as much interest in the 'nobleman without virtue' (*dominus sine virtute*) as the 'unjust king', and elsewhere the homilist stresses that every counsellor (*wita*) should speak his mind and that the king should not be taken in by 'secret advice' (*runung*), but rather act in consultation with all.[99]

---

[97] Adelard of Ghent, *Lectiones in depositione S. Dunstani*, ch. 12 (ed. Winterbottom and Lapidge, 142).

[98] Lionarons, *Homiletic Writings*, 75–146. See further below, Chapter 5, pp. 241–51.

[99] Ælfric, *De duodecim abusivis*, abusio 6 (ed. Clayton, 122–4), and *Supplementary Homilies* IX.31–47 (ed. Pope, 380). See *Two Ælfric Texts*, ed. Clayton, 57 and 66–8; and *Homilies of Ælfric*, ed. Pope, 372–7 and 389–90.

Wulfstan likewise emphasizes that the counsellors of the nation (*ðeodwitan*) bear responsibility for its affairs alongside the king, noting the key role of bishops within this context.[100] A sense of collective responsibility could not, therefore, be denied. What is more, it was not only the king and his 'bad' counsellors who had erred in previous years: the murder of the young Edward in 978 cast a shadow over the entire nation. While the translation and reburial of the king's body may have temporarily lifted this, the viking attacks of the later 980s and early 990s must have served as a timely reminder of this earlier sin. Æthelred himself was not responsible for this – at worst, he was guilty by association – and all indications are that the blame was felt to fall upon the nation at large: Edward's 'own people' (*propria gens*), as the Latin poem preserved in a Canterbury manuscript of *c.* 1000 puts it.[101] If some saw the misfortunes of the early 990s as divine retribution for Æthelred's misdeeds, others seem to have seen them as a consequence of the disgraceful treatment of Edward in 978.[102]

It is against this backdrop that we must view the efforts to establish Edward's cult in these years. The veneration of saints had first developed in the late Roman Empire and was well established by the tenth century. The appeal lay above all in the ability of saints to make the divine tangible; their remains were where heaven and earth met, points of contact between the human and divine.[103] Within the circles of Gerard of Brogne (d. 959) on the continent the veneration of saints played a key role and similar developments can be seen amongst the English reformers, who accorded great interest not only to so-called 'universal' saints such as Benedict of Nursia and the Blessed Virgin, but also to more local (and often half-forgotten) figures such as Swithun of Winchester and Æthelthryth of Ely.[104] By the

---

[100] Wulfstan, *Institutes of Polity*, chs. 41–2, ed. K. Jost (Bern, 1959), 62.

[101] *Omnibus est recolenda*, l. 3 (ed. Dumville, 'Death', 281).

[102] Keynes, 'Alfred the Great and Shaftesbury', 48–55.

[103] P. Brown, *The Cult of Saints: Its Rise and Function in Latin Christianity*, rev. edn (Chicago, IL, 2014), 1–22.

[104] D.W. Rollason, *Saints and Relics in Anglo-Saxon England* (Oxford, 1989), 164–95; Clayton, *Cult of the Virgin Mary*, 122–38 and 158–67; Denton, 'Hagiography'; Hudson, 'Æthelwold's Circle'; A. Thacker, 'Cults at Canterbury: Relics and Reform under Dunstan and his Successors', in *St Dunstan: His Life, Time and Cult*, ed. N. Ramsay, M. Sparks and T. Tatton-Brown (Woodbridge, 1992), 221–44. Cf. D. Misonne, 'Gérard de Brogne et sa dévotion aux reliques' (1982), repr. in and cited from *Revue Bénédictine* 111 (2001), 90–110.

990s these were joined by the reformers Æthelwold, Dunstan and Oswald, as well as newly sainted members of the royal family (Edward, Edith). In the case of Edward, there is little evidence of a cult before the 990s and, though it is possible that popular opinion was already laying the foundations for his later sainthood, by the time we can trace his veneration in any detail it clearly enjoyed royal support.[105] Byrhtferth of Ramsey is a key witness here: he reports that miracles began to be seen at Edward's grave eleven years after his death (*c.* 990), information he says he owes to Archbishop Ælfric, who was the local diocesan bishop at Ramsbury at the time.[106] That the cult should take off as the viking attacks intensified is no accident; as noted, such signs of divine displeasure must have made Edward's death appear in a new light. We can see evidence of his changing reputation in Byrhtferth's account: here Edward is a saint almost despite himself, a petulant young man whose death alone has earned him sanctity. He conforms to the type of the 'holy innocent', one who like the children executed by Herod (Matthew II.16–18) has earned sainthood not through piety or good deeds, but as a result of his blameless demise.[107] Further evidence for the early development of the cult comes from the foundation of Cholsey Abbey, the first religious house dedicated to the royal martyr. The history of this centre is obscured by the fact that it did not last long; it may have been sacked in 1006, when the vikings are reported to have passed through the area, and after Æthelred's reign it retreated into obscurity (by the time of the Conquest it had disappeared entirely).[108] Yet Cholsey's later fate should not mislead us as to the house's contemporary significance; it is clear that as originally conceived this was a very important centre indeed. Though we know little of its endowment, Germanus was its first abbot. Educated at Fleury and Winchester, he had previously been abbot of Westbury, Ramsey and

---

[105] Keynes, 'Cult'. Cf. C. Cubitt, 'Sites and Sanctity: Revisiting the Cult of Murdered and Martyred Anglo-Saxon Royal Saints', *EME* 9 (2000), 53–83, at 72–4 and 83.

[106] Byrhtferth, *Vita S. Oswaldi* IV.21 (ed. Winterbottom and Lapidge, 144).

[107] P.A. Hayward, 'The Idea of Innocent Martyrdom in Late Tenth- and Eleventh-Century English Hagiology', *SCH* 30 (1993), 81–92.

[108] P. Stafford, '*Cherchez la femme*. Queens, Queens' Lands and Nunneries: Missing Links in the Foundation of Reading Abbey' (2000), repr. in and cited from her *Gender, Family and the Legitimation of Power: England from the Ninth to the Early Twelfth Century* (Aldershot, 2006), no. XII, 7–8 and 20–1.

Winchcombe and numbered amongst the leading reformers of the era.[109] The window for Cholsey's foundation is provided by Germanus's last attestation as abbot of Ramsey (993) and his first as abbot of Cholsey (997). If Goscelin of St-Bertin's late eleventh-century *Life* of St Ivo (which draws on local Ramsey traditions) is to be trusted, this window can be narrowed further, since he reports that Sigeric of Canterbury (d. 994) had encouraged the king to found the centre.[110] Sigeric is certainly likely to have had a hand in the development of the cult. Not only was he an important player in these years, but as bishop of Ramsbury (985–90), in whose diocese Edward's tomb lay, he would have had the chance to develop an early interest in the saint's remains. Another important figure was Ælfric, Sigeric's successor at both Ramsbury and Canterbury: according to Byrhtferth, it was he who first witnessed miracles at Edward's tomb during his tenure of the former see and his will (1002 × 1005) includes a bequest to Cholsey.[111] That one of the earliest narratives celebrating Edward's death and translation should come from a Canterbury manuscript is therefore entirely appropriate. A further piece of the puzzle is provided by a charter of 996 in which Æthelred grants a series of estates forfeited by Wulfbald to his mother in return for Cholsey, 'which she had previously given to me' (*illa michi prius donauerat*). Much of this document concerns the so-called 'Crimes of Wulfbald', which are of great interest in their own right; what matters from our present perspective, however, is that Ælfthryth had owned the estate on which the monastery was founded and had granted this to the king at some point before 996, presumably in connection with the centre's foundation (though this is not stated explicitly).[112] While it is conceivable that Ælfthryth's hand was forced, all indications are that she was an active and

---

[109] M. Lapidge, 'Abbot Germanus, Winchcombe, Ramsey and the Cambridge Psalter' (1992), repr. in and cited from his *Anglo-Latin Literature 900–1066* (London, 1993), 387–417, at 405–14. Immediately before the foundation of Cholsey, Germanus was apparently abbot of Ramsey (and not Winchcombe, as Lapidge maintains), since he attests S 876 (*Abing* 120) as *Ram' abbas*.

[110] Goscelin of St-Bertin, *Vita S. Yvonis*, ch. 3, PL 155, cols. 87–8. See Keynes, 'Cult', 119.

[111] Byrhtferth, *Vita S. Oswaldi* IV.21 (ed. Winterbottom and Lapidge, 144); S 1488 (*Abing* 133). See further Dumville, *Caroline Script*, 82–4.

[112] S 877 (*WinchNM* 31). See *Charters of the New Minster*, ed. Miller, 152–3; and cf. Stafford, 'Cherchez la femme', 20–1. The estate had belonged to Æthelflæd of Damerham, the second wife of King Edmund, and may have been one of the queen's *ex officio* holdings: Stafford, *Queen Emma*, 129–30.

willing participant; there is, therefore, every reason to believe that she was involved in the growth of Edward's cult from the start (rather than opposing it, as is often supposed).

An early sign of the cult's growth is provided by the Latin poem relating to Edward's translation added to a Canterbury manuscript around the turn of the millennium; by this point the saint's fame had clearly reached the metropolitan see. It is also from these years that Byrhtferth's reports of Edward's miracles stem (997 × 1002), reports which the author may have received not only from Ælfric (whose authority he mentions), but also Germanus, who as former abbot of Ramsey is likely to have remained in contact with the centre after his move to Cholsey. Indeed, Ramsey itself boasted the remains of two other holy innocents, Æthelberht and Æthelred (d. *c.* 669), whose remains had been translated shortly before this (*c.* 991), and Germanus may thus have been gazetted to Cholsey as an expert on the phenomenon.[113] A Latin poem commemorating an altar dedicated to Edward, Eustace and Kenelm added to an Abingdon manuscript in the early eleventh century attests to his veneration there and soon his name also found its way into the 'litanies of saints' (prayers invoking the intercession of Christ and his saints).[114] The clearest evidence for the burgeoning cult, however, comes from the translation of Edward's remains on 20 June 1001. This act is only recorded in the post-Conquest *Passion* of the saint, but there is little reason to doubt its historicity: the text draws on local Shaftesbury traditions and, while allowances must be made for the portrayal of Ælfthryth, the report of the translation itself is perfectly acceptable – indeed, the initiative ascribed to Æthelred speaks in its favour, since there would have been little reason to invent such details in the late eleventh century, when the king's reputation was otherwise entering terminal decline.[115] According to this account the king encouraged the translation, which was overseen by Wulfsige of Sherborne and an *Ælfsinus praesul*, probably Abbot Ælfsige of the New

---

[113] Denton, 'Hagiography', 114.

[114] M. Lapidge, 'Æthelwold and the *Vita S. Eustachii*' (1988), repr. in and cited from his *Anglo-Latin Literature 900–1066* (London, 1993), 213–23, at 218; *Anglo-Saxon Litanies of the Saints*, ed. M. Lapidge, HBS 106 (London, 1991), 101, 102, 116, 133, 143, 158, 175, 183, 188, 236, 245, 251, 297.

[115] *Passio S. Eadwardi* (ed. Fell, 11–12). See Denton, 'Hagiography', 35–62; and cf. Hayward, 'Translation-Narratives', 85–9, whose doubts about the account of the translation are perhaps overstated.

Minster.[116] This was thus a decidedly local event, but one overseen by leading royal advisers. It was also undertaken at an important moment, since 1001 saw a series of serious attacks on the south-west – if Edward's cult was indeed promoted in the hope of aiding the English in their ongoing efforts against the vikings, this would have been the ideal moment to do so. Further light is shed by a charter issued in favour of Shaftesbury a few months later. The document grants the centre the community (*cenobium*) of Bradford-on-Avon in order to offer a safe place of retreat in the face of the ongoing attacks. It opens with a preamble alluding to the dire straits in which the realm finds itself, then goes on to explain that the privilege has been issued to the resting place of Æthelred's brother 'so that the same religious community, with the relics of the blessed martyr [Edward] and other saints may obtain there a refuge against the snares of the barbarians and serve God undisturbed'.[117] Questions have been raised as to the authenticity of this document and it has been suggested that the refer-ences to Edward the Martyr, in particular, represent a later addition (or interpolation).[118] However, there is nothing else suspicious about the diploma and, as we have seen, there are other signs that Æthelred was involved in the promotion of his half-brother's cult. Indeed, the fact that the charter was issued so soon after Edward's second translation speaks in its favour; though it does not refer to this event, it reveals an active royal interest in the safety of the saint's relics at a moment we know him to have been engaged on Shaftesbury's behalf. Further evidence is provided by the remains of a late Anglo-Saxon church at Bradford (Plate 8). This was built in these years, probably to house Edward's remains. The fact that work was left unfinished suggests that construction was abandoned at some point, perhaps after 1016, when Cnut's conquest might have rendered the chapel's original purpose redundant.[119]

---

[116] Cf. Denton, 'Hagiography', 52.

[117] S 899 (*Shaft* 29): 'quatenus aduersus barbarorum insidias ipsa religiosa congregacio cum beati martiris ceterorumque sanctorum reliquiis ibidem Deo seruiendi impenetrabile optineat confugium'.

[118] P. Wormald, Review of Ridyard, *Royal Saints, Journal of Ecclesiastical History* 42 (1991), 101–2, at 102, and *Making of English Law*, 343–4, n. 373. See also Hayward, 'Translation-Narratives', 87, n. 94.

[119] J. Haslam, 'The Unfinished Chapel at Bradford on Avon, Wiltshire, and Ecclesiastical Politics in the Early Eleventh Century', *Archaeological Journal* 170 (2013), 272–301, with further references.

Æthelred's own interest in these developments is indicated in his sons' attestations to the Shaftesbury charter: the king evidently wanted to involve the young princes in the promotion of their uncle's cult. He seems to have been successful in this regard, since his eldest son, Æthelstan (d. 1014), later left a bequest to Shaftesbury, noting the presence of Edward's remains there.[120] There was certainly a personal tone to this. Though there is no reason to believe that Æthelred was involved in his half-brother's death, he had been its beneficiary and may well have considered himself tainted by association. It was, after all, the fraternal rivalries of the 970s which lay behind Edward's demise. It may be that Ælfthryth felt similarly: the earliest signs of Edward's cult come from those years in which she was once again making her influence felt at court and, as we have seen, it was her willingness to exchange lands at Cholsey which enabled the foundation of the first church dedicated to the martyr.

Edward's translation parallels those of many other saints in these years: during the first half of Æthelred's reign (perhaps *c.* 991) the Kentish princes Æthelberht and Æthelred had been translated to Ramsey (whose abbot, Germanus, was later to be placed in charge of Cholsey); according to later tradition Cuthbert was translated from Chester-le-Street to Durham in 995; Æthelwold's remains were translated at the Old Minster, Winchester, on 10 September 996; Æthelred's half-sister, Edith, whose cult closely mirrors that of her half-brother Edward, was translated (apparently also at the king's orders) at Wilton in early 997; and Oswald was translated at St Mary's, Worcester, on 15 April 1002.[121] Clearly, Æthelred and the English were seeking the support of the saints at every turn. There is, therefore, ample evidence to suggest that Æthelred supported the cult of his half-brother from at least the mid-990s, and it is perfectly understandable that when in 1008 he and his leading advisers, led by Archbishop Wulfstan, came to designate those feast days which were to be celebrated throughout the nation, they included Edward's alongside those of Mary

---

[120] S 1503 (*CantCC* 142). See further below, Chapter 6, pp. 298–300.

[121] Keynes, 'Alfred the Great and Shaftesbury', 50–1; Thacker, 'Saint-Making', 248–51; *Byrhtferth*, ed. Lapidge, xli; Ridyard, *Cults*, 152–5; Yorke, 'Legitimacy of St Edith', 111. However, on Cuthbert, see now N. McGuigan, 'Neither Scotland nor England: Middle Britain, *c.*850–1150' (PhD diss., Univ. of St Andrews, 2015), 74–81 (to which Alex Woolf kindly drew my attention).

and the apostles.[122] The development of this cult also accords with the general trajectory of developments in Æthelred's reign: we see hesitant moves in this direction during the king's minority, then hear nothing till the 990s. When we do hear more, it is at a time when the king was actively throwing his support behind reform. In his restitutions Æthelred often expresses concern about offences he may have caused the saints and it was presumably similar thoughts – in this case on the part of the nation – that inspired his support for Edward's veneration.[123] The fact that so many of these cults were centred on reformed monastic houses is no accident; as we have seen, the cult of saints was channelled above all by the reformers and these acts bear comparison with Æthelwold's own efforts to foster the veneration of Swithun during Edgar's reign.[124] Here as elsewhere, Æthelred was following the example of his father and the reformers.

Defending the realm

We have hitherto focused almost exclusively on religious and ideological responses to the viking attacks. This in part reflects the nature of the surviving evidence: charters, our most eloquent sources for Æthelred's thoughts and feelings at this point, tend to focus on the king's relations with specific recipients (above all individual religious houses). It would be wrong, however, to suggest that Æthelred pursued only one solution to the 'viking problem'. Just as we can see a variety of religious responses, from restoring misappropriated monastic lands to fostering the cult of St Edward, so too many more strictly political and military measures were undertaken. It would, of

---

[122] *V Atr* 16 (ed. Liebermann, I, 240–1); with Keynes, 'An Abbot', 178–9.

[123] S 891 (KCD 698): 'cognoui me hanc iniuste possidere . . . furoremque apostolicum incurrere . . .'; S 893 (*Roch* 32): 'iccirco domini compunctus gratia quicquid tunc instigante maligno contra sanctum dei apostolum me inique egisse recogito'. There may have been similar anxieties where the legacy of Æthelwold was concerned, since it was in these years that the latter's cult was established (a process which would have begun some time before his formal translation in 996): *Wulfstan*, ed. Lapidge and Winterbottom, xcix–ci and cxii–cxliii.

[124] Thacker, 'Cults at Canterbury', 230–5; Denton, 'Anglo-Saxon Hagiography', 110–15 and 216–22; C. Cubitt, 'Reading Tenth- and Eleventh-Century Latin Hagiography in the Context of the Reign of Æthelred II "the Unready"', in *Hagiography in Anglo-Saxon England: Adopting and Adapting Saints' Lives into Old English Prose (c. 950–1150)*, ed. L. Lazzari, P. Lendinara, C. Di Sciacca (Turnhout, 2014), 345–64.

1 Frontispiece of the New Minster Refoundation Charter: King Edgar, stationed between the Virgin Mary and St Peter, presents the charter (in his left hand) to Christ.

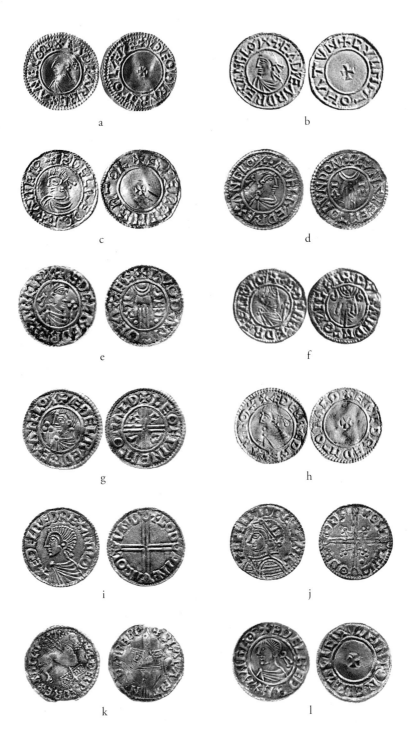

2 Post-reform coinage of Edgar, Edward the Martyr and Æthelred: a) Edgar, *Reform Small Cross*; b) Edward, *Small Cross*; c) Æthelred, *First Small Cross*; d) Æthelred, *First Hand*; e) Æthelred, *Second Hand*; f) Æthelred, *Benediction Hand*; g) Æthelred, *Crux*; h) Æthelred, *Intermediate Small Cross*; i) Æthelred, *Long Cross*; j) Æthelred, *Helmet*; k) Æthelred, *Agnus Dei*; l) Æthelred, *Last Small Cross*.

3 The Jelling Stone, erected by Harald
Bluetooth at the dynastic centre at Jelling in
Jutland. The inscription reads: 'King Harald
ordered this monument made in memory of
Gorm, his father, and in memory of Thyre, his
mother; that Harald who won for himself all
Denmark and Norway and made the Danes
Christian' (*haraltr : kunukR : baþ : kaurua :
kubl : þausi : aft : kurm faþur sin : auk aft :
þourui : muþur : sina : sa : haraltr (:) ias : soR ·
uan · tanmaurk ala · auk · nuruiak (·) auk t(a)
ni (k)(a)(r)(þ)(i) kristno*).

4 The tidal causeway between Maldon and Northey Island, Essex, where the Battle of Maldon was reputedly fought.

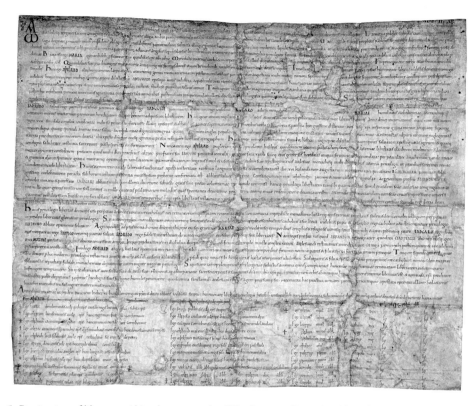

5 Restitution of liberty to Abingdon, enacted at Winchester at Pentecost (4 June) 993 and completed at Gilligham (? Dorset) on 17 July.

6 Witness-list to the restitution of liberty to Abingdon in 993: note the different shape and aspect of many of the crosses, suggesting that these were added by the attestors themselves, probably at the Gillingham gathering (17 July).

7 Confirmation of liberty to the bishopric of Cornwall in 994, written partly in gold script, perhaps drafted by Archbishop Sigeric of Canterbury.

8 The unfinished chapel at Bradford-on-Avon, maybe constructed to house the relics of Edward's half-brother, Edward the Martyr.

9 Execution burial at Ridgeway Hill, Dorset. The victims were all male and probably of Scandinavian origin. It is likely that they met their demise during Æthelred's reign, possibly as a consequence of the Massacre of St Brice's Day (1002).

10 Execution burial at St John's College, Oxford. As at Ridgeway Hill, the victims were all male and of apparent Scandinavian origin. It is possible that they, too, died during Æthelred's reign.

11 Cuckhamsley Barrow (Scutchamer Knob), Berkshire: the local meeting place of the shire, which the viking 'Great Fleet' symbolically occupied in 1006. Legend had it that, if the invaders ever reached this site, they would not make it back to their ships.

12 The defences at South Cadbury (Somerset): refurbished under Æthelred, probably in connection with the relocation of the local mint from Ilchester.

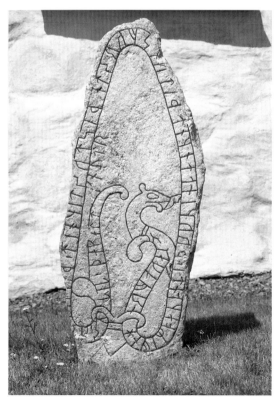

13 Yttergärde rune-stone (Vallentuna, Uppland, Sweden). The inscription reads: 'And Ulf has taken three payments (*kialt*) in England; that was first the one paid by Tosti, then Thorkell paid; then Cnut paid' (*in ulfr hafiR o| |onklati ' þru kialt| |takat þit uas fursta þis tusti ka-t ' þ(a) ---- (þ)urktil ' þa kalt knutr*).

14 Rubrics to the medium version of the *Sermo Lupi ad Anglos*. These read: 'The sermon of the wolf [i.e. Wulfstan] to the English at the time when the Danes persecuted them most greatly, which was the ninth year of the millennium since the incarnation of our Lord Jesus Christ [i.e. 1009]' (*Sermo Lupi ad Anglos quando Dani maxime persecuti sunt eos, quid fuit anno millesimo. VIIII. ab incarnatione domini nostri Iesu Cristi*).

15 Rubrics to the long version of the *Sermo Lupi ad Anglos*. These are identical to those of the medium version, except that *VIIII* has been replaced with *XIIII*, making the last phrase read 'the fourteenth year of the millennium [i.e. 1014]'. Note, however, the lighter link of *XIIII*, which is apparently a later correction.

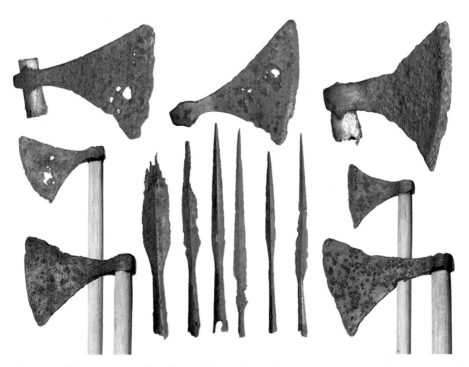

16 An assemblage of weapons found at London Bridge in the 1920s. It was presumably such items that Swein Forkbeard and his men brought in tow when they attacked London in 1013.

course, be dangerous to draw too firm a line here between 'religion' and 'politics'; in an era of reform, religion was always a political matter, while politics were rarely devoid of religious undertones. Still, the sound and fury generated by Æthelred's religious undertakings should not deafen our ears to other efforts. Indeed, despite his later reputation for inactivity, Æthelred was more than willing to apply himself when called for and it is above all variety which characterizes his response to the Scandinavian threat.

Where the defence of the realm is concerned, the 990s might be termed a period of experimentation. From 993 onwards the king sought to entreat divine favour through reform and repentance and this was combined with more proactive efforts to defend the realm and redirect the violence of its erstwhile attackers. As we have seen, the force which had been paid tribute in 991 seems to have reappeared in the following year. After abortive defensive undertakings in 992 and 993 and further attacks on Essex, Kent, Sussex and Hampshire in 994, attempts were made to come up with a more permanent solution: at this point the king and his advisers promised provisions for the winter and a larger tribute of 16,000 pounds on the condition that the vikings desist from their harrying.[125] This led to a treaty, which superseded the local agreements forged earlier in the year by Archbishop Sigeric (for Kent), Ealdorman Æthelweard (for the south-west) and Ealdorman Ælfric (for Hampshire).[126] This was intended to establish a lasting peace, bringing at least a portion of the raiding force into English service. One of the opening clauses stipulates that 'if any fleet harries in England, we are to have the help of them all [i.e. the vikings]; and we [the English] must supply them with provisions as long as they are with us' (*gif ænig sciphere on Englaland hergie, þæt we habban heora ealra fultum; 7 we him sculon mete findon, ða hwile ðe hy mid us beoð*: 1.1); the English were setting a thief to catch a thief and were evidently more than happy to cover the costs. This is followed by a clause to the effect that any land which offers protection to those who attack England shall be regarded as an enemy 'by us and by the

---

[125] *ASC* 992–4 CDE (ed. O'Brien O'Keeffe, 86–7).

[126] *II Atr* (ed. Liebermann, I, 220–4). On which: Keynes, 'Historical Context', 103–7; N. Lund, 'Peace and Non-Peace in the Viking Age – Ottar in Biarmaland, the Rus in Byzantium, and Danes and Norwegians in England', in *Proceedings of the Tenth Viking Conference*, ed. J.E. Knirk (Oslo, 1987), 255–69, at 264–8; J. Benham, 'Law or Treaty? Defining the Edge of Legal Studies in the Early and High Medieval Periods', *Historical Research* 86 (2013), 487–97, at 490–1.

whole [viking] army' (*wið us 7 wið ealne here*: 1.2), a measure which seems
to have been directed against Normandy, which as we have noted may have
been acting as a base for the raiders. The remaining clauses deal with
arrangements for keeping the peace, including an armistice on previous
crimes, and end with a note to the effect that 22,000 pounds have been paid
for the truce. This figure is higher than that recorded in the *Chronicle*, but
the two can be reconciled by presuming that the treaty's total includes earlier
local payments by Sigeric, Æthelweard and Ælfric (mentioned in the
treaty).[127] In any case, the intention is clear enough: if the English could not
defeat the vikings by force, they were better off with them in their employ.
There was a venerable tradition of turning poachers into gamekeepers in
this fashion: in Late Antiquity barbarian forces from beyond the frontier
were often taken into imperial service as 'federates' (*foederati*), while more
recently the Frankish rulers of the ninth and early tenth centuries had
resorted to similar tactics against the vikings (the most famous case being
the grant of what was to become Normandy to Rollo in 911).[128]

Shortly after peace had been made, one of the three viking leaders
mentioned in the treaty, Olaf, was sponsored by Æthelred at his confirmation at Andover (he had apparently been baptized some years earlier).
Ritual sponsorship was part of the repertoire commonly used to forge alliances, particularly between Christian kings and their pagan neighbours.[129]
In this case, the act may have been necessitated by Olaf's desire to return
to Scandinavia; it served to create a firm bond of commitment. Initially
these efforts seem to have borne fruit: as the *Chronicle* notes – with more
than a hint of relief – Olaf kept his promise: in 995 he returned to Norway,
where he set himself up as king in opposition to Earl Hákon of Hláðir
(Lade), who had hitherto governed the region under the loose overlordship
of the Danish ruler Swein. It has been suggested that this was part of a

---

[127] Keynes, 'Historical Context', 100.

[128] P.J. Heather, '*Foedera* and *foederati* of the Fourth Century', in *Kingdoms of the Empire: The Integration of Barbarians in Late Antiquity*, ed. W. Pohl (Leiden, 1997), 57–74; S. Coupland, 'From Poachers to Gamekeepers: Scandinavian Warlords and Carolingian Kings', *EME* 7 (1998), 85–114.

[129] A. Angenendt, *Kaiserherrschaft und Königstaufe. Kaiser, Könige und Päpste als geistliche Patrone in der abendländischen Missionsgeschichte*, Arbeiten zur Frühmittelalterforschung 15 (Berlin, 1984), 106–9 and 215–23. See also Lynch, *Christianizing Kinship*, 205–28.

long-term strategy to divide England's enemies and it may thus be significant that Swein is not mentioned in the treaty of 994; though he had been with the army earlier in the year, he was apparently not party to this agreement.[130] It is certainly conceivable that Æthelred had a sense for the lie of the land in Scandinavia: Norwegian traders such as Ohthere had been known at the court of Alfred the Great, while King Hákon góði ('the Good') of Norway (d. c. 961) had been fostered at the court of Æthelred's great-uncle, Æthelstan.[131] York's own contacts with its North Sea neighbours were not immediately severed upon its incorporation into the English realm in the second half of the tenth century and Æthelred may thus have had access to specific information regarding the situation in Scandinavia through his father-in-law, Earl Thored, or the latter's successor, Ealdorman Ælfhelm. In later years English missionaries were also to play a significant part in the Christianization of Norway, reflecting the ties forged by Hákon, Æthelred, Olaf and others in these years.[132]

Whether part of a grand strategy or simply a last-ditch attempt to bring an intractable foe to heel, Æthelred's undertaking seems to have been successful in the short term. It was only when raids resumed in 997 that matters took a turn for the worse: in this year a major force ravaged Devon and Cornwall, sacking Ordulf's foundation at Tavistock; and in the following one it struck at Dorset before settling down to overwinter on the Isle of Wight.[133] In 999 the raiders continued their steady eastward progress, travelling up the Medway to Rochester, where local Kentish levies were defeated and subsequent attempts to counter their progress foundered on

---

[130] T.M. Andersson, 'The Viking Policy of Ethelred the Unready', *Scandinavian Studies* 53 (1987), 284–95. See also Sawyer, 'Ethelred II'.

[131] J.M. Bately and A. Englert, ed., *Ohthere's Voyages: A Late 9th-Century Account of Voyages along the Coasts of Norway and Denmark and its Cultural Context* (Roskilde, 2007); A. Englert and A. Trakadas, ed., *Wulfstan's Voyage: The Baltic Sea Region in the Early Viking Age as Seen from Shipboard* (Roskilde, 2008); G. Williams, 'Hákon Aðalsteins fóstri: Aspects of Anglo-Saxon Kingship in Tenth-Century Norway', in *The North Sea World in the Middle Ages: Studies in the Cultural History of North-Western Europe*, ed. T.R. Liszka and E.M. Walker (Dublin, 2001), 108–26.

[132] L. Abrams, 'The Anglo-Saxons and the Christianization of Scandinavia', *ASE* 24 (1995), 213–49.

[133] *ASC* 997–8 CDE (ed. O'Brien O'Keeffe, 88). Cf. M.K. Lawson, '"Those stories look true": Levels of Taxation in the Reigns of Aethelred II and Cnut', *EHR* 104 (1989), 385–406, at 393, n. 1.

delays. It was only in 1000 that the vikings finally departed, apparently of their own volition. The following year saw further strikes, however: a major force under the command of Pallig came to Sussex, where it defeated a levy from nearby Hampshire before travelling west to Devon, sacking Pinhoe and routing those who had assembled to defend the region. Finally, in 1002 a tribute of 24,000 pounds was paid.[134] There is reason to believe that elements of the army active in the later 990s were drawn from the mercenaries who had entered Æthelred's employ in 994: John of Worcester refers to this force as having 'remained amongst the English' (*remanserit in Angliis*) between then and 997, returning to its old ways at this point; meanwhile Pallig is presented as a pledge-breaker in the entry in the A-version of the *Chronicle* for 1001.[135] That there were indeed Scandinavians present at Æthelred's court is shown by the survival of a fragmentary Old Norse praise-poem in the king's honour, Gunnlaugr ormstunga's *Aðalráðsdrápa* (traditionally dated *c.* 1002, though conceivably composed earlier).[136] If much of the raiding army was recruited in this fashion, this would explain why we do not hear of any opposition being offered by the king's Scandinavian mercenaries, as we might have expected under the terms of the treaty of 994.

In any case, it is in these years that our main narrative, the CDE-version of the *Anglo-Saxon Chronicle*, begins to take on its characteristic 'doom and gloom' tone: in 999 the chronicler states emphatically that 'and always, as things ought to have been advanced, they were delayed from one hour to the next, and ever they let their enemy's force grow, and ever the English retreated from the sea and the Danes continually followed after', while under 1001 he observes that 'and each successive attack was worse than the one before it' – the exasperation is tangible.[137] We are, therefore, fortunate

[134] *ASC* 999–1002 CDE (ed. O'Brien O'Keeffe, 88–9).

[135] John of Worcester, *Chronicon, s.a.* 997 (ed. Darlington and McGurk, 446); *ASC* 1001 A (ed. Bately, 79–80); with Keynes, 'Historical Context', 92–3.

[136] See M. Townend, 'Norse Poets and English Kings: Skaldic Performance in Anglo-Saxon England', *Offa* 58 (2001), 269–75, esp. 269–71.

[137] *ASC* 999 CDE (ed. O'Brien O'Keeffe, 88): '7 a swa hit forðwerdre beon sceolde, swa wæs hit lætre fram anre tide to oþre, 7 a hi leton heora feonda werod wexan, 7 a man rymde fram þære sæ, 7 hi foron æfre forð æfter'; *ASC* 1001 CDE (ed. O'Brien O'Keeffe, 89): '7 wæs æfre heora æftra siþ wyrsa þonne se æra'.

to possess an alternative account of one of these years, preserved in the near-contemporary A-version of the *Chronicle* (probably composed before 1006). This reports many of the same events under 1001 and what is striking is not so much the occasional difference in emphasis – the A-version notes a first English defeat, which is omitted in the CDE-version, while the CDE-account reports an abortive attempt on Exeter – as the contrast in tone: while the author of the main *Chronicle*-account sees these events as part of a crescendo building up to the Danish conquests of 1014 and 1016, the A-version is more matter of fact.[138] The chance survival of this alternative voice is a reminder of how beholden we otherwise are to the narrative of the main *Chronicle*-account. Indeed, if we read between the lines we can reconstruct a less defeatist account of the events of the preceding years. Thus, in 997 we are informed that the Scandinavian force travelled inland 'until they came to Lydford' (*oð hi comon to Hlydanforda*).[139] What transpired at this point is not stated, but it would seem that the attackers were forced to retreat: Lydford boasted substantial earthworks – it has been identified as one of the fortified sites of the *Burghal Hidage* (a list of the main forts of Wessex and southern Mercia, drawn up in the early tenth century) – and faced with these the vikings presumably decided that prudence was the better part of valour.[140] The account of the following year, which reports a string of English defeats in Dorset, might likewise be read less as the rear-guard actions of a nation on the verge of collapse than as an example of valiant defence in the face of superior numbers. Certainly, the report for 999 shows that the English resolve was far from broken: first a Kentish levy met the viking force and thereafter plans were made for a more substantial offensive. That this came to naught may be due to delays and incompetence, as the chronicler claims; however, no further attacks

---

[138] *ASC* 1001 A (ed. Bately, 79–80), 1001 CDE (ed. O'Brien O'Keeffe, 89); with Keynes, 'Tale of Two Kings', 201–3, and 'Re-Reading', 78–9. See also Bately, 'The *Anglo-Saxon Chronicle*', 46.

[139] *ASC* 997 CDE (ed. O'Brien O'Keeffe, 88).

[140] R. Lavelle, *Alfred's Wars: Sources and Interpretations of Anglo-Saxon Warfare in the Viking Age* (Woodbridge, 2010), 249–50; D. Gore, *The Vikings in the West Country* (Exeter, 2015), 56–7. Cf. D.[H.] Hill, 'Gazetteer of Burghal Hidages Sites', in *The Defence of Wessex: The Burghal Hidage and Anglo-Saxon Fortifications*, ed. D.[H.] Hill and A.R. Rumble (Manchester, 1996), 189–231, at 209.

are recorded and it may be that Æthelred's force actually cordoned off the raiders successfully. Indeed, the fact that the vikings departed in the following year, when Æthelred himself went on the offensive in the Isle of Man and Cumbria, may suggest that these efforts had more effect than the *Chronicle* implies; there must have been good reason to break off what was otherwise proving to be a most profitable venture.

At least two things emerge from these undertakings. The first is that, notwithstanding his later reputation, Æthelred was actually quite reserved about offering tribute; it was only after a major defeat at Maldon in 991 and further raiding in 992, 993 and 994 that he first resorted to this measure, and it was not until 1002 that he would do so again (as previously, hot on the heels of a series of major defeats). It is, therefore, unfair to assert that Æthelred expected 'gold to do the work of steel';[141] both were part of the broad arsenal of measures which the king brought to bear. The second is that, despite the recorded defeats, the defences of the English realm were in relatively good working order. As we have seen, in 997 the raiding force was turned back at Lydford, one of the fortified sites (or *burhs*) which Alfred the Great had incorporated into a sophisticated system of civil defence. Likewise, in 1001 the CDE-version of the *Chronicle* reports that the vikings first travelled up the Exe to the *burh* (i.e. Exeter) but were stoutly resisted there; the outcome is not reported, but there can be little doubt that the English prevailed.[142] Other evidence also points in this direction. Thus, while the English struggled to defeat their opponents in open battle, their ability to bring them to the field is itself worthy of note. One of the main strategic problems posed by the vikings was their mobility: as a naval force which used horses for inland raiding, they could often strike and retreat before resistance could be organized. To counter this, the English employed networks of beacons in conjunction with fortified sites to provide early warning.[143] The repeated ability of English forces to locate

---

[141] Freeman, *History of the Norman Conquest*, 277.

[142] Though Keynes, 'Re-Reading', 79, casts doubt on the historicity of this attack, I remain more optimistic about the chronicler's sources and accuracy (cf. Brooks, '*Anglo-Saxon Chronicle*', 51–2).

[143] J. Baker and S. Brookes, *Beyond the Burghal Hidage: Anglo-Saxon Civil Defence in the Viking Ages* (Leiden 2013), 179–99.

and engage their foes, often before too much damage had been done, speaks of the effectiveness of these measures (even if the result was frequently still a defeat). The English also had naval forces at their disposal, as we can see in 992, and the chance survival in a post-Conquest manuscript of a memorandum from St Paul's detailing how ships were to be manned reveals how the local bishop – probably Wulfstan (996–1002), the later metropolitan of York – responded to the financial demands of military support in these years.[144] The difficulties that such burdens posed is also revealed by a later letter from Bishop Æthelric of Sherborne to Æthelmær (the son of Æthelweard) requesting the restitution of lands which had traditionally contributed to the cost of manning ships.[145]

It is, therefore, clear that Æthelred was anything but a 'do nothing' king. He and his advisers undertook a number of efforts to see off the vikings: they raised naval forces and engaged them at sea; they ordered local levies to confront them on land; and only when this failed did they offer tribute. In this respect, their efforts look little different from those of Æthelred's more illustrious forebear, Alfred the Great.[146] Yet one difference does emerge: whereas Alfred is often recorded taking the military initiative, Æthelred rarely is. It is not that Æthelred was unwilling to take the fight to his adversaries when circumstances allowed. In 1000 we are informed that he ravaged Cumbria and the Isle of Man, actions which were presumably a response to the attacks of previous years, some of which may have been launched from (or found support within) the so-called 'Irish Sea zone' (Dublin, it should be recalled, was ruled by a Scandinavian dynasty with traditional ties to York).[147] Æthelred's apparent inactivity in other cases is in part a reflection of the difficulties posed by a kingdom much enlarged since Alfred's days: Alfredian Wessex, even at its largest

---

[144] *Charters of St Paul's, London*, ed. S.E. Kelly, Anglo-Saxon Charters 10 (Oxford, 2004), 97–100 and 192–201 (no. 25).

[145] S 1383 (*Sherb* 13). The document is datable 1001 × 1012.

[146] See below, Conclusion, pp. 312–14.

[147] *ASC* 1000 CDE (ed. O'Brien O'Keeffe, 88). Typically, the chronicler focuses on the failures of this venture. See C. Downham, 'England and the Irish Sea Zone in the Eleventh Century', *ANS* 26 (2003), 55–73, esp. 59–63; and M. Blackburn, 'Currency under the Vikings, Part 4: The Dublin Coinage *c.* 995–1050', *BNJ* 78 (2008), 111–37, esp. 123–7, on 'Insular' dimensions.

extent, constituted little more than a quarter of Æthelred's sprawling realm and it was therefore inevitable that the latter would be further from the frontline – by the time he had raised an army and brought it into position, one imagines that any self-respecting viking would long since have taken to his heels (or keels, as it were). It was natural, therefore, that local office-holders leading smaller, more flexible forces should bear the brunt of the kingdom's defence. In some cases it was ealdormen who took up this mantle: Byrhtnoth famously led the local East Saxon levy to defeat in 991, while Ealdorman Ælfric of Hampshire was involved in the abortive attempts to face down the vikings at sea in 992. In many others, however, it was reeves who performed this task: it may have been a reeve who organized the defence of Lydford in 997, while in 1001 we are informed that two 'royal high-reeves' (*cinges heahgerefa*) were amongst those who fell defending Hampshire against Pallig.[148] Indeed, reeves of various descriptions begin to make regular appearances in our sources around this time, perhaps reflecting increased responsibilities.[149] This was by no means an ill-conceived response to these challenges and Ælfric's allusive *Wyrdwriteras* seems to advocate just such a policy, describing how kings of old had devolved military command on to ealdormen and other generals so that they could dedicate themselves to prayer.[150]

There are other signs that Æthelred remained firmly in control of the realm. His ability to restore church lands and redress past wrongs speaks of a ruler at the height of his powers, not one struggling to bring his influence to bear. His apparent hesitance to appoint new ealdormen, which has attracted much comment, points in the same direction: this was presumably an attempt to reduce the influence of figures such as Ælfric of Hampshire, who had proven unreliable in previous years, concentrating power in the hands of more trustworthy individuals, particularly reeves.[151] Similarly informative is the evidence of coinage: Æthelred's *Crux* and *Long*

---

[148] *ASC* 1001 A (ed. Bately, 79–80).

[149] Williams, *Æthelred*, 63–6; Cubitt, 'Reeves', 1034–44. See further below, Chapter 5, pp. 190–1 and 239.

[150] Ælfric, *Supplementary Homilies* XXII (ed. Pope, 725–33); with Keynes, *Diplomas*, 206–8; and Sheppard, *Families of the King*, 83–4. Cf. Clayton, 'Ælfric and Æthelred', 82–6.

[151] Stafford, 'Reign of Æthelred II', 29; Keynes, *Diplomas*, 197–8, n. 163.

Cross issues, which span these years (*c.* 991–*c.* 1003), are amongst the most uniform since Edgar's reform.[152] That the first of these, bearing the inscription 'CRVX' ('cross') on the reverse, should be introduced in the early 990s, when we have other indications of a change of course, is entirely appropriate: the message sent was one of unity through piety. Of particular interest is the *Intermediate Small Cross* coinage of the mid- to later 990s (perhaps *c.* 997), which was only briefly minted, mostly in the west of the kingdom, towards the end of the *Crux* issue. It would seem that a new type was introduced, then withdrawn for reasons which are not entirely apparent. Whatever the grounds, the iconography of the *Intermediate Small Cross*, which harks back to the coinage of Edgar and Edward the Martyr (and also Æthelred's own earliest years), sits well alongside other efforts to evoke the age of Edgar and Æthelwold. The very act of changing type was itself significant: the maintenance of correct weights and measures was a core duty of a Christian monarch and in showing such concern Æthelred was living up to these expectations.[153]

This period also witnessed the king's first legislative endeavours, which likewise constitute an effort to present an image of just and God-fearing rulership. In 997 Æthelred held assemblies at Woodstock in Oxfordshire and Wantage in Berkshire, leading to the production of two closely related sets of ordinances (*I* and *III Æthelred*). The former are addressed to those regions which follow 'English law', while the use of Scandinavian vocabulary and reference to wapentakes in the latter suggests that they were intended for circulation in more northerly climes.[154] Both texts are relatively short and focus on similar issues: sureties, ordeals, land purchases and men of 'ill repute'. At certain points the Wantage ordinances provide greater detail (not least on the subject of coin forgery), suggesting that they were the second to be issued; but in essence the two are complementary, as revealed by related clauses and common allusions to an earlier gathering at *Bromdun* (location unknown). Neither set of decrees is terribly

---

[152] Naismith, 'Coinage of Æthelred', 129–30. See also Dolley, 'Introduction', 121–3.

[153] E. Screen, 'Anglo-Saxon Law and Numismatics: A Reassessment in the Light of Patrick Wormald's *The Making of English Law*', *BNJ* 77 (2007), 150–72.

[154] *I Atr* (ed. Liebermann, I, 216–20), *III Atr* (ed. Liebermann, I, 228–32); with Keynes, *Diplomas*, 196–7; and Wormald, *English Law*, 328–9.

novel, but novelty may not have been the intention; rulers struggled to stamp out crime throughout the tenth century and it was often necessary to repeat and expand earlier initiatives.[155] Indeed, the issuing of decrees was itself a powerful gesture, as Patrick Wormald has shown: it presented the king in a uniquely royal fashion, showing him to be living up to the expectations placed upon him.[156] In the aftermath of the indiscretions and misdemeanours of the 980s, this must have been especially important. In this respect, it is surely no accident that the Wantage assembly also witnessed one of the king's more prominent acts of repentance: the restitution of a hundred hides to the Old Minster. The charter and ordinances send complementary messages here: the former looks to the past, atoning for prior misdeeds, while the latter look to the future, seeking to prevent further misdemeanours.[157] Æthelred was thus doing everything within his power to cultivate the image of a good and God-fearing king: he was restoring church lands; he was promoting reform and the cult of saints (including that of his recently martyred half-brother); he was requesting masses and psalms for the well-being of his nation; he was reforming the coinage and maintaining correct weights and measures; and he was issuing new ordinances to curb a wide variety of lawless behaviour.

The 990s were thus a dynamic period. Spurred into action by the viking raids and other misfortunes, the king undertook a comprehensive programme of repentance and reform. This was a deeply personal matter: it involved turning his back on one group of associates; it involved admitting to wrongdoing; and it involved rehabilitating the legacy of his father, mother and earlier regents. Yet the king was not alone in his guilt; the nation too bore a stain, that of having killed its anointed ruler. In the eyes of Æthelred and his leading advisers it was these moral concerns which loomed largest. Though the viking attacks were cause for concern, their

---

[155] S. Keynes, 'Crime and Punishment in the Reign of King Æthelred the Unready', in *People and Places in Northern Europe 500–1600: Essays in Honour of Peter Hayes Sawyer*, ed. I.N. Wood and N. Lund (Woodbridge, 1991), 67–81, at 68–73.

[156] Wormald, '*Lex scripta* and *verbum regis*'.

[157] Keynes, *Diplomas*, 102, n. 56; Williams, *Æthelred*, 56. More generally, see M.R. Rambaran-Olm, 'Trial by History's Jury: Examining Æthelred II's Legislative and Literary Legacy, AD 993–1006', *English Studies* 95 (2014), 777–802, at 787.

root was felt to lie within English society: they were the wages of sin, and only once this had been lifted could lasting peace be achieved. Nevertheless, this does not mean that military measures were shunned. Quite the opposite: we see feverish defensive activity, and though by 1001 this had yet to achieve any lasting success, it was not so hopeless as the *Chronicle* would have us believe. This was, therefore, a period in which searching questions were asked of Æthelred's regime and tentative answers were formulated; only time would tell whether these would prove to be the right ones.

CHAPTER 5

APOCALYPSE AND INVASION
1002–9

A s we have seen, in the 990s signs of anxiety can be discerned within Æthelred's regime. Concerns seem to have stemmed less from the physical damage done by the viking attacks – though this should not be underestimated – than from their symbolism: they were, in keeping with prevailing teachings about divine favour, understood to be signs of moral failings on the part of the king and nation. As the turn of the millennium approached, it must have become increasingly clear that initial efforts to remedy these had not borne fruit; barring a brief hiatus between 994 and 997, the 990s had witnessed almost constant raiding. The following decade saw further, more frantic efforts to find a solution to the 'viking problem'; if the 990s were characterized by concern, the 1000s saw this become desperation. Nevertheless, the increasingly feverish atmosphere at court should not blind us to deeper-seated continuities; while Æthelred and his advisers may have found themselves forced to take ever more drastic measures, their goals remained much the same.

In what follows we shall first examine the two most dramatic events of these years – the Massacre of St Brice's Day (1002) and the 'palace revolution' of 1005–6 – contextualizing these in the light of other developments. Both show tendencies which can then be traced through the later years of the decade, which saw further viking attacks and further attempts at moral and military reform. Toward the end of the chapter, dedicated sub-sections then consider two other themes in these years: law and order, and concerns about the apocalypse and end of time.

The Massacre of St Brice's Day

The period from 997 onwards had seen sustained viking activity within England. The only year in which no raids are recorded is 1000, when the fleet is said to 'have gone to Richard's kingdom [i.e. Normandy]' (*wæs . . . gewend to Ricardes rice*). The reasons for this are not entirely clear; it may be that recent losses had made a period of rest and recuperation advisable, but it may simply be that the force wished to take some time off to enjoy its winnings. Whatever the grounds, this sojourn rekindled hostilities between the English and Normans. The latter were of Scandinavian descent and the Norman court was probably still bilingual, so it is not surprising that they should be sympathetic to the viking raiders.[1] In the 980s the Normans may already have been offering safe harbour to vikings, as we have seen, and a condition of the peace agreement overseen by Pope John XV and his legate Leo in 991 was that Richard would not receive Æthelred's enemies.[2] The Norman actions in 1000 clearly broke these terms. The reasons for this breach of faith are not entirely clear, but probably lie in recent developments in Normandy: in 996 Richard I was succeeded by his son, Richard II (996–1026), who may not have felt bound by his father's agreements. Writing in the 1050s, William of Jumièges records an English attack on the Cotentin in Normandy around this time (*c.* 1002), which may have been a response to these actions (though William's chronology is unreliable and his account must be treated with caution).[3]

---

[1] L. Abrams, 'Early Normandy', *ANS* 35 (2013), 45–64; F. McNair, 'The Politics of Being Norman in the Reign of Richard the Fearless, Duke of Normandy (r. 942–996)', *EME* 23 (2015), 308–28.

[2] *Papsturkunden* ed. Zimmerman, no. 307; with discussion above, Chapter 3, p. 117.

[3] William of Jumièges, *Gesta Normannorum ducum* V.4, ed. E.M.C. van Houts, 2 vols. (Oxford, 1992–5), II, 10–14; with Keynes, 'Historical Context', 94–5; and E.[M.C.] van Houts, 'Normandy's View of the Anglo-Saxon Past in the Twelfth Century', in *The Long Twelfth-Century View of the Anglo-Saxon Past*, ed. M. Brett and D.A. Woodman (Farnham, 2015), 123–40, at 125–6.

In any case, Richard's welcoming of Æthelred's enemies, coupled with the desertion of one of the king's Scandinavian mercenaries (Pallig) in the following year, must have served to highlight the deficiencies of Æthelred's defensive strategy. In response, negotiations were initiated with the Norman duke, which culminated in the marriage of the latter's younger sister Emma to the English king in 1002. The new queen was immediately given an Old English name, Ælfgifu, though she continued to go by Emma in certain contexts (and, for reasons of clarity, continues to be referred to as such by modern scholars). What happened to Æthelred's first wife (also an Ælfgifu) is unknown: perhaps she was ousted to make way for this new match, but it seems more likely that she passed away at some point in the later 990s (her youngest son makes his first appearance in 1001). The fuss made over this marriage befits Emma's status as a foreign princess: this is the first marriage mentioned in the *Chronicle* since that of Ælfthryth and Edgar, and Emma may have been the first royal consort to be consecrated since this time.[4] Indeed, the parallels between these unions do not stop here: in both cases the king had male offspring from a previous marriage and in both the new spouse was destined to play a more prominent political role than had her immediate predecessor. There may even be a connection: Emma was in certain respects heir to her mother-in-law's position at court, and it has been suggested that the latter's death first paved the way for the match.[5] This is certainly conceivable, though we must be wary of treating correlation as causation: Æthelred's marriage to Emma was made desirable and expedient by recent political developments, so it is by no means certain that Ælfthryth's death was decisive; indeed, it is possible that the dowager queen had even been involved in the marriage negotiations (she may still have been alive in autumn 1001).[6] The marriage was certainly intended to cement a new alliance between the English and Normans and the position conceded to Emma at court reflects the importance of this pact. The union also broke with established practice: though many royal daughters and sisters had been married off to foreign rulers in

---

[4] *ASC* 1002 CDE (ed. O'Brien O'Keeffe, 89); Stafford, 'Queen's Wife', 18.

[5] Stafford, *Queen Emma*, 216–17. See also Stafford, 'Sons and Mothers', 92–3.

[6] On the date of Ælfthryth's death (17 November 999 × 1001), see Keynes, *Diplomas*, 210, n. 203.

the tenth century, no English monarch had taken a foreign bride since the mid-ninth. This could be seen as a sign of desperation, but is perhaps better understood as part of a broader process whereby a common European elite emerged in the course of the eleventh and twelfth centuries: across the Latin-speaking west inter-dynastic marriage blossomed and a more self-consciously 'international' brand of politics developed.[7] In any case, the marriage opened up new avenues for Æthelred and must have changed dynamics within the royal family considerably. As we have seen, the remarriage of a reigning monarch, particularly one (like Æthelred) who was not especially old, often created tensions. The new queen tended to bring new favourites with her, upsetting the balance at court. If she produced male heirs, as Emma soon did, this compounded the situation: there were now two branches of the royal family, each of which might attract backers hoping to play the role of king-maker.

Not surprisingly, it is around this time that we see efforts to secure Ælfthryth's legacy: in 1002, perhaps shortly after Æthelred's remarriage, the king confirmed the endowment of his mother's foundation at Wherwell as well as the nuns' right to elect their own abbess (subject to the approval of the local diocesan bishop), and it is likely that a similar privilege was issued to Amesbury.[8] This document's preamble opens with a consideration of the Fall of Man – a popular theme within reforming circles, as we have seen – and ends by quoting the biblical injunction to 'honour thy father and thy mother, that thou mayest be long-lived upon the land [Exodus XX.12]' (*Honora patrem tuum et matrem tuam, ut sis longaeuus super terram*). It is clear that Æthelred was trying to live up to this commandment by protecting his mother's most prized foundation. Indeed, the phrase suggests that the king was moved by his mother's loss: she had been the dominant force in his life up to this point and had played an important part in the politics of the 990s. Interestingly, in addition to confirming the endowment of the centre, this document also grants Wherwell a large sixty-hide estate at *Æthelingadene*, which up to this point had belonged to the queen-mother. The name of this estate suggests an

---

[7] R. Bartlett, *The Making of Europe: Conquest, Colonization and Cultural Change, 950–1350* (London, 1993), esp. 5–59.

[8] Foot, *Veiled Women* II, 23 and 215.

association with royal offspring and, as we have seen, it may be that Æthelred himself had spent part of his childhood there; he was potentially granting the centre an old haunt, one with a strong emotional bond to his mother. There is also a hint of criticism here, however, as Ælfthryth is said to have 'seized' this estate 'for her own use' (*in usus usurpauit proprios*) in earlier years; it would seem that Æthelred was also trying to make good his mother's failings. Still, the overall tone remains positive and the document reads as a strong endorsement of his mother's reforming efforts. That this was a particularly personal donation is suggested by the witness-list, which contains the attestations of the young princes, those grandchildren who Ælfthryth is said to have raised (perhaps at this self-same estate).[9]

However, if on the one hand Æthelred and his advisers sought rapprochement with their enemies' allies, they also took more proactive measures. It is probably around this time that a gathering of bishops ordained, *inter alia*, that the entire nation should fast before the feasts of Mary and the apostles and that the mass *contra paganos* ('against the pagans') should be sung each Wednesday at larger (or 'minster') churches.[10] In early 1002 Æthelred and his counsellors also agreed to give the viking force a record tribute of 24,000 pounds on the condition that it cease its 'evil-doing' (*yfele*). Leofsige of Essex, who had been appointed Byrhtnoth's successor as ealdorman in 994, was entrusted with the arrangements. Though these went smoothly enough, soon thereafter the ealdorman became embroiled in a dispute with the high-reeve Æfic, whom he and his associates were found guilty of killing.[11] The root cause of this conflict is not stated, but it reveals something of the fault-lines within Æthelred's kingdom. As we have noted, the king was remarkably restrained when it came to appointing ealdormen, often leaving long vacancies and using reeves and thegns in their stead (and perhaps to their detriment).[12] One imagines that this created tensions between ealdormen

---

[9] S 904 (KCD 707); with Stafford, *Queen Emma*, 79. See also Stafford, 'Queens', 26–8, who places greater emphasis on the criticism of Ælfthryth; and above, Chapter 1, p. 58, on *Æthelingadene*.

[10] *Councils*, ed. Whitelock, no. 40, 226. See *Councils*, ed. Whitelock, 193–5; and Keynes, 'An Abbot', 170–1.

[11] *ASC* CDE 1002 (ed. O'Brien O'Keeffe, 89).

[12] In addition to the works cited above, Chapter 4, p. 182, n. 149, see Stafford, 'Royal Government', 304–10 and 322–30; and Banton, 'Ealdormen and Earls', 176–82.

and such other functionaries and it is interesting to note that this was not Leofsige's first clash with a reeve: seven years earlier he had come into conflict with Æthelwig of Oxford and Wynsige of Buckingham over the burial (on consecrated land) of two men who had been slain defending a thief (who by all rights should have been denied a church burial).[13] Interestingly, in both cases the king backed his reeves: in 995 the decision of the two reeves to allow the men's burial was upheld and in 1002 the lands of Leofsige and his associates were declared forfeit and the ealdorman was banished from the realm. Thereafter, his estates were sold off, perhaps in an attempt to recoup some of the recent costs of tribute.[14] What happened to the Scandinavian forces thereafter is unclear; some probably returned home, but others may have tarried in England, perhaps even resuming their careers as mercenaries.[15]

While the truce established at this point may look like a continuation of earlier efforts to buy off the Scandinavian raiders, it was, in fact, the prelude to a rather more dramatic act. At the end of the main *Chronicle*-account for this year is included the following notice:

> And in this year the king ordered all the Danish men who were in England to be slain; this was done on St Brice's feast day, because it was made known to the king that they wanted treacherously to deprive (*besyrwan*) him and then all his counsellors of life and to possess this kingdom thereafter.[16]

This event, known as the Massacre of St Brice's Day, has attracted much comment. Edward Augustus Freeman famously called it 'not only a crime but a blunder', while Sir Frank Stenton clearly had this in mind (along with the events of 1006) when he wrote of the king's 'acts of spasmodic

---

[13] S 883 (*Abing* 125).

[14] S 916 (*StAlb* 12). See further below, p. 221.

[15] S. Keynes, 'The Massacre of St Brice's Day (13 November 1002)', in *Beretning fra seksogtyvende tværfaglige vikingessymposium*, ed. N. Lund (Aarhus, 2007), 32–67, at 38.

[16] *ASC* 1002 CDE (ed. O'Brien O'Keeffe, 89): '7 on þam geare se cyng het ofslean ealle þa Deniscan men þe on Angelcynne wæron; ðis wæs gedon on Britius mæssedæig, forðam þam cyninge wæs gecyd þæt hi woldan hine besyrwan æt his life 7 siððan ealle his witan 7 habban siþþan þis rice.'

violence'.[17] Recent assessments have been more measured. It was already clear to Freeman that the massacre was directed not at the entire Scandinavian population of eastern England, but rather more recent settlers, perhaps the remnants of the mercenaries recruited in 994.[18] Certainly, it is hard to imagine that those Scandinavians who had settled in the Danelaw over a century earlier could have been distinguished from their 'English' counterparts.[19] All indications are therefore of a dramatic event, but something short of ethnic cleansing in the modern sense. That the massacre was not meant to target all those of Danish descent – and perhaps not even all Danes – is suggested by the fact that a few years later a 'Dane' called Toti is recorded receiving land at Beckley and Horton, not far from Oxford, where we know the massacre to have been implemented.[20] However, regardless of whether we wish to see this event as a triumph of late Anglo-Saxon administrative efficiency (as some have been inclined),[21] it is certainly a sign of growing desperation; more measured solutions had failed, so extreme ones were now being trialled. The *Chronicle*'s allusion to accusations of treachery smacks of intrigue and the impression is that Æthelred's court was becoming a place of rumour and secrecy. Indeed, that the king and his counsellors were willing to listen to such whispers may say something about their state of mind: after almost a decade of concerned effort they had failed to stem the flow of invaders, and it is understandable that they now started seeing enemies in their midst.

It is not hard to understand historians' distaste for the St Brice's Day Massacre, which raises ghosts of Europe's more recent experiences of genocide and ethnic cleansing. Still, we do not have to approve of Æthelred's actions in order to comprehend them. Indeed, for all that modern parallels may inform, it is important to bear in mind that this act was not on the same scale, nor was it probably intended to be. Æthelred's regime did not

---

[17] Freeman, *Norman Conquest*, 317; Stenton, *Anglo-Saxon England*, 374.

[18] Freeman, *Norman Conquest*, 315–16. See also Lavelle, *Aethelred II*, 104–9.

[19] D.W. Hadley, '"Cockle amongst the Wheat": The Scandinavian Settlement of England', in *Social Identity in Early Medieval Britain*, ed. W.O. Frazer and A. Tyrell (London, 2000), 111–35, at 117–20.

[20] S 943 (ed. Hart, *Early Charters*, 190–1).

[21] Cf. Campbell, 'England, France, Flanders and Germany', 200.

in any case possess the systems of coercion now widely available and any such undertaking would have been unthinkable without the willing support of a large proportion of the population. In fact, disturbing though the thought may be, this was probably one of the king's more popular policies: by this point the English had faced some twenty years of unprovoked attack, and to many it must have seemed as if the Danes were simply receiving their just deserts.[22] That the most recent attacks had been perpetrated by sometime allies would have been especially galling: in 997 a first group of mercenaries had apparently defected and in 1001 they were joined by Pallig, who, as the author of the entry in the A-version of the *Chronicle* notes (with more than a hint of frustration), deserted the king 'in spite of all the pledges he had given to him' (*ofer ealle ða getrywða ðe he him geseald hæfde*) and without regard to the gifts 'in estates, and in gold and silver' (*on hamon, 7 on golde 7 seolfre*) he had received.[23] The rumours of a conspiracy reported in the *Chronicle* under 1002 were therefore not entirely unfounded and it may have seemed but a matter of time before the remaining mercenaries – their numbers perhaps swelled by those who had made peace earlier in the year – turned on the king.

However, important as such concerns doubtless were, it would be wrong to view this event purely in terms of *Realpolitik*. It appears in a rather different light in a notice preserved in the charter of renewal issued to St Frideswide's, Oxford, in 1004. Although the diploma does not survive in its original form, there is no reason to doubt its authenticity; the formulation is perfectly acceptable for the period and there is nothing suspicious about the transaction.[24] The diploma renews the charters of St Frideswide's, which had been destroyed in the course of the massacre. It is worth quoting the relevant section in its entirety:

> In the year of the incarnation of Our Lord 1004, the second indiction, in the 25th year of my reign, by the ordering of God's providence, I, Æthelred, governing the monarchy of all Albion [i.e. Britain], have

---

[22] Keynes, 'Tale of Two Kings', 212.
[23] *ASC* 1001 A (ed. Bately, 80).
[24] Keynes, *Diplomas*, 127. See further Keynes, 'Massacre', 33–4.

made secure with the liberty of a privilege by royal authority a certain
monastery situated in the town which is called Oxford, where the body
of the blessed Frideswide rests, for the love of the all-accomplishing
God; and I have recouped the territories which belong to the monastery of Christ by the restoration of a new title-deed; and I will relate in
a few words to all who look upon this document for what reason it was
done. For it is certain that all dwelling in this country will be well aware
that a decree was sent out by me with the counsel of my leading men
and magnates, to the effect that all the Danes who had sprung up in
this island, sprouting like cockle amongst the wheat, were to be slain
(*necarentur*) by a most just extermination (*iustissima exterminacione*),
and this decree was to be put into effect even as far as death. Those
Danes who dwelt in the aforementioned town, striving to escape death,
entered this sanctuary of Christ, having broken by force the doors and
bolts, and resolved to make a refuge and a defence for themselves
therein against the people of the town and the suburbs; but when all
the people in pursuit strove, compelled by necessity, to drive them out,
and could not, they set fire to the planks and burnt, as it seems, this
church with its ornaments and its books.[25]

There is much of interest here. For a start, it is significant that the diploma
concerns a foundation in Oxford, since Oxford does not lie within the
Danelaw. The Danes living in the city – for which there is archaeological

---

[25] S 909 (ed. S.R.Wigram, *The Cartulary of the Monastery of St Frideswide at Oxford*, I [Oxford,
1895], 2–7): 'Anno dominicae incarnationis millesimo quarto, indictione secunda, anno
uero imperii mei uicesimo quinto, dei disponente prouidentia, ego Æðelred, totius Albionis
monarchiam gubernans, monasterium quoddam in urbe situm quae Oxoneforde appellatur,
ubi beata requiescit Frideswide libertate priuilegii auctoritate regali pro cunctipatrantis
amore stabiliui, et territoria quae ipsi adiacent Christi archisterio noui restauratione libelli
recuperaui, cunctisque hanc paginam intuentibus qua ratione id actum sit paucis uerborum
signis retexam. Omnibus enim in hac patria degentibus sat constat fore notissimum, quoddam
a me decretum cum consilio optimatum satrapumque meorum exiuit, ut cuncti Dani qui
in hac insula uelut lolium inter triticum pullulando emerserant, iustissima ex[ter]minacione
necarentur, hocque decretum morte tenus ad effectum perduceretur, ipsi quique in praefata
urbe morabantur Dani mortem euadere nitentes, hoc Christi sacrarium fractis per uim ualuis
et pessulis, intrantes asylum sibi propugnaculumque contra urbanos suburbanosque inibi fieri
decreuerunt; sed cum populus omnis insequens, necessitate compulsus, eos eiicere niteretur
nec ualeret, igne tabulis iniecto, hanc aecclesiam, ut liquet, cum munimentis ac libris,
combusserunt.' Translation adapted from Whitelock, *EHD*, no. 127, 590–1.

evidence[26] – must therefore have been recent settlers, either elements of the mercenary forces recruited in 994 and (possibly) 1002, or urban-dwelling merchants (perhaps both).[27] Still, the core details of this account accord well with that of the *Chronicle*: both claim that the attacks were directed at 'all Danes', but in both cases there are reasons to suspect a restricted application of the term. Though the charter does not mention the date of the attacks, it notes that this decision was taken not only by the king, but also his counsellors. Though it was normal for rulers to consult their leading advisers on important matters of state, this report serves as a salutary reminder that this was anything but a rash and impulsive decision. Indeed, it likely that figures such as Ælfric of Canterbury, Wulfstan of York (who had just been promoted to this new dignity) and Æthelmær of the western shires, not to mention the new queen (all of whom attest a diploma in favour of Abingdon around this time), had a hand in the decision.[28]

Of particular interest is the manner in which the Danish settlement is described here. The draftsman alludes to the parable of the cockles (or tares) and the wheat (Matthew XIII.24–30), which likens the kingdom of heaven to the field of a man who has sown good seeds of wheat, only to discover that his enemies have planted cockles (a form of weed) amongst them. In order to prevent the cockles damaging the wheat, the man lets them grow unfettered, explaining that come harvest time he will separate the two, burning the cockles and storing the wheat. At the heart of this tale lies the problem of evil; the cockles represent sin, which shall be eliminated come the Last Judgement. Though the parable can be interpreted as a call for toleration, for letting sinners be, in the Middle Ages it was more often read as a cry to action, a stern warning about the danger posed by false belief (it is in this vein that Ælfric refers to it in his Catholic

---

[26] J. Blair, *Anglo-Saxon Oxfordshire* (Stroud, 1997), 167–70.

[27] S. Reynolds, 'What Do We Mean by "Anglo-Saxon" and "Anglo-Saxons"?', *Journal of British Studies* 24 (1985), 395–414, at 412; Stafford, *Unification*, 66; Keynes, 'Massacre', 39–40.

[28] Keynes, *Atlas*, table LIX. It is possible that S 902 (*Abing* 131) stems from the meeting at which this decision was made, in which case its witness-list may provide a guide to those involved: J. Wilcox, 'The St. Brice's Day Massacre and Archbishop Wulfstan', in *Peace and Negotiation: Strategies for Co-Existence in the Middle Ages and the Renaissance*, ed. D. Wolfthal (Turnhout, 2000), 79–91, esp. 85–6.

Homilies).[29] Such religiously charged language suggests a view of the Danes as not so much a political and military threat as a moral one – they are the polluting (foreign) cockles amongst the pure (English) wheat. This religious zeal explains the manner in which the act is described: it is called a 'most just extermination' (*iustissima exterminacio*) and the draftsman shows little sympathy for the Danes who sought sanctuary within the Church of St Frideswide.[30] Indeed, there is no sign of censure for those who violated this sanctuary – on the contrary, they are said to have been 'compelled by necessity' (*necessitate compulsus*) to fulfil this command. In the end the Danes, like the cockles of the biblical parable, go up in smoke; the only pity would seem to be that so too did the church's ornaments and archive. It is not surprising that this act should carry such religious undertones: disloyalty – the crime of which the Scandinavian mercenaries were apparently accused – involved a breach of faith (Latin: *fides*) and was thus both a sin and a crime.[31] Given that this account was drawn up soon after the events, probably by someone with close ties to the court (perhaps a royal chaplain), such details may well take us into the thought world of the king himself. Indeed, if, as the *Chronicle*-report suggests, he and his advisers had begun to see enemies in their midst, then it is likely that such teachings about purity and pollution lay behind this.

Perhaps the most intriguing feature of the St Brice's Day Massacre is that it may have left a mark in the archaeological record. Two important recent discoveries are of note here. The first is the mass burial of around fifty skeletons discovered at Ridgeway Hill, Dorset, by Oxford Archaeology in 2009 (Plate 9). The individuals, who are all male and almost all in their late teens to mid-twenties, were found piled carelessly in an Iron Age pit. Stable isotope analysis has established that at least thirty-one of them are likely to have come from Scandinavia and had lived there until shortly before they met their demise. This, along with the fact that the bones can

---

[29] Ælfric, *CH: FS* XXXV.122–32 (ed. Clemoes, 480). See Wilcox, 'Massacre', 84.

[30] Though Keynes, 'Massacre', 36, suggests that the Danes may not have consciously sought sanctuary, the language employed by the draftsman suggests otherwise.

[31] Cf. J.L. Nelson, 'Religion and Politics in the Reign of Charlemagne', in *Religion und Politik im Mittelalter. Deutschland und England im Vergleich*, ed. L. Körntgen and D. Waßenhoven (Berlin, 2013), 17–29.

be dated with relative certainty to between 970 and 1025 (and in all likelihood to 980 × 1020), has led scholars to associate them with Æthelred's reign.[32] This period saw a great deal of viking activity and Dorset was hit a number of times (982, 998 and possibly 1001), providing the obvious context for the burial. That the individuals are male and for the most part quite young fits well with the presumption that they came to England as raiders. The signs of trauma around the head and neck of most of the bones and the absence of characteristic signs of defensive wounds suggest that they met their death by execution. This would explain why the bodies were discarded carelessly on unconsecrated ground, as was common for criminals and non-Christians.[33] How they came to be executed is, of course, the million-pound question. It is conceivable that they were simply part of a raiding party which fell into enemy hands, as the site excavators suggest. Nonetheless, it is tempting to associate the find with the St Brice's Day Massacre. Indeed, though the all-male composition of the group discouraged the excavators from drawing this conclusion, it might actually speak in its favour: as we have seen, there is reason to believe that the massacre targeted Danish mercenaries, some of whom may have first entered Æthelred's employ in 1002.[34] Associating the burial with the massacre would also explain why the individuals, who were young men in good physical condition, did not put up much of a fight: if, as the *Chronicle* and the St Frideswide's charter suggest, the Danes were taken off guard, then there might not have been much opportunity to put up a defence. The location of the burial also makes good sense within this context: the vikings had been most active around the south coast in previous years and this is probably where Æthelred's mercenaries were stationed.[35] Ridgeway

---

[32] L. Loe *et al.*, *'Given to the Ground': A Viking Age Mass Grave on Ridgeway Hill, Weymouth* (Oxford, 2014). See also A. Boyle, 'Death on the Dorset Ridgeway: A Viking Murder Mystery', *HSJ* 25 (2013), 19–33.

[33] See A. Reynolds, *Anglo-Saxon Deviant Burial Customs* (Oxford, 2009), 151–79, 219–27 and 247–50.

[34] Cf. Boyle, 'Death on the Dorset Ridgeway', 32, asserting that 'the Danes who were slaughtered on St Brice's Day were not an invading army but a settled civilian population'. See also Loe *et al.*, *'Given to the Ground'*, 211, now leaving the question more open.

[35] Cf. Keynes, 'Massacre', 38, suggesting that much of the mercenary force was based on the Isle of Wight.

Hill itself occupies a strategic position above the coast, not far from the royal vill at Corfe (later a favoured castle of King John) and within sight of Portland to the south, the latter of which had seen viking activity in 982; either of these could conceivably have been a mercenary base.[36]

Equally intriguing, though no less elusive, is the evidence of a mass grave of at least thirty-four bodies discovered at St John's College, Oxford, in 2008 and excavated by Thames Valley Archaeological Services (Plate 10).[37] There are a number of similarities between this find and the Ridgeway Hill burial: the individuals were all male and mostly aged between sixteen and twenty-five, and the bodies were found carelessly discarded in the ditch of a Neolithic henge monument just outside the boundaries of the early medieval town. All of the skeletons show signs of injuries inflicted around the time of death, most commonly multiple blade wounds to the back, and several show evidence of charring, indicating that they had been burned before deposition. No personal items were found with the bodies, apart from an iron belt buckle, suggesting that the victims were stripped of such objects before burial. There can be little doubt that we are dealing with another mass execution. Though the radiocarbon dates of many of the bones tested are too early for Æthelred's reign, some match this period and there can be little doubt that all were deposited at the same time; a date in Æthelred's reign is thus still conceivable, though an earlier one may be preferable. Stable isotope analysis suggests a coastal (possibly Scandinavian) origin for the men and a marine diet is known to have a distorting effect on carbon dates, making finds appear older than they are; it may be that this is what we are observing here (though such major variation would be rare indeed).[38] In short, these finds perhaps belong in an Æthelredian context, as the site excavators propose, though further investigation is needed. If a product of these years, a case can certainly be made for associating this burial too with the events of

[36] *ASC* 982 C (ed. O'Brien O'Keeffe, 85). Cf. Æthelweard, *Chronicon* III.4 (ed. Campbell, 30). See further Lavelle, 'Law, Death and Peacemaking', 131–4.

[37] S. Wallis *et al.*, *The Oxford Henge and Late Saxon Massacre with Medieval and Later Occupation at St John's College, Oxford* (Reading, 2014). See also A.M. Polland *et al.*, '"Sprouting like Cockle Amongst the Wheat": The St. Brice's Day Massacre and the Isotopic Analysis of Human Bones from St. John's College, Oxford', *Oxford Journal of Archaeology* 31 (2012), 83–102.

[38] *Ibid.*, 92–3. See further Wallis *et al.*, *Oxford Henge*, 137–9 and 151–7.

St Brice's Day 1002. As at Ridgeway Hill, this would explain why a group of robust young men was executed without characteristic signs of self-defence. It would also explain why some of the bodies had been burnt before deposition: if these are indeed the remains of the Oxford-based Danes who sought refuge in St Frideswide's, then we know from the charter of 1004 that they were driven out by fire. The fact that the victims seem to have been cut down in flight, rather than beheaded on the spot (as at Ridgeway Hill), fits this scenario: as the Scandinavians emerged from the church, they were apparently hacked down by those awaiting them.[39] Whether in these cases we are dealing with mercenary (or raiding) forces is hard to be certain: there are few signs of prior injury on the bones at either the Oxford Henge or Ridgeway Hill sites, which might indicate that we are dealing with merchants; however, it may simply be that the individuals were at the start of their military career and yet to acquire such distinctive signs of their vocation. Whatever the case, the excavators' verdict that this is indeed a product of the Massacre of St Brice's Day should not be dismissed out of hand.[40]

It is almost *too* tempting to associate these finds with St Brice's Day 1002 and it is salutary to recall that many other events could have led to such executions; these were years in which conflict was not rare and emotions frequently ran high. Nevertheless, the similarities between the two sites (if they are indeed coeval) are sufficient that a global explanation is to be preferred. And in this respect they reveal precisely the sort of signature we might anticipate of the St Brice's Day Massacre: mass graves of males of probable Scandinavian origin, whose remains have been consciously mishandled. In a sense, it does not matter whether these were products of 1002, or of similar tensions in the preceding or following years: they demonstrate what the Massacre of St Brice's Day must have looked like on the ground. Indeed, what our understanding of this event may have lost in romanticism in recent interpretations, it has gained in the physicality of the remains unearthed in Oxford and Dorset. These serve as a reminder that, though this act may have been justified in the eyes of many, its victims were very real. As one of the excavators of the Ridgeway Hill site notes, it is likely that

---

[39] On the injuries, see also Loe et al., 'Given to the Ground', 231.
[40] Wallis et al., Oxford Henge, 233–5. Cf. Pollard et al., 'St Brice's Day Massacre', 98.

the execution was a matter of public spectacle: locals will have looked on (and perhaps even participated) and most of those killed would have had to witness their friends and associates being butchered before them.[41] The scene at Oxford is if anything more brutal: men fleeing into a church, then being forced out by fire, only to be slaughtered by those lying in wait, egged on and assisted by the local townsfolk. Thus, even if restricted in scope, these attacks speak unmistakably of desperation and paranoia, both of which were to be very much in evidence in Æthelred's later years. They show that the king was starting to chase shadows, and he was unlikely to stop there.

The 'Palace Revolution', 1005–6

If the Massacre of St Brice's Day was meant to alleviate the kingdom's problems, it seems to have had if anything the reverse effect. In 1003–4 Swein Forkbeard returned, apparently for the first time in almost ten years, devastating the eastern coast of the kingdom. William of Malmesbury was later to connect the Danish king's reappearance with the events of the previous year: he reports that amongst the victims of the massacre had been Swein's sister, Gunhild, and her husband the powerful 'jarl (*comes*) Palling'.[42] Though historians have often taken William at face value, there are reasons for caution. He was heavily influenced here by the account of William of Jumièges, which itself was written from a very particular Norman perspective in the 1050s.[43] There is, moreover, no earlier evidence for the existence of a sister of Swein called Gunhild. With Palling we can make better headway: he could conceivably be the turncoat mentioned in the A-version of the *Chronicle* under 1001, though this would require us to presume that he had been allowed to rejoin the king's forces after accepting tribute in 1002. All indications are that William of Malmesbury was struggling to make sense of difficult and disparate materials here and one should note that he also reports that this Palling was executed by Eadric Streona, who only seems to have risen to prominence some years later.[44]

---

[41] Boyle, 'Death on the Dorset Ridgeway', 31. See also Loe *et al.*, 'Given to the Ground', 224–35.

[42] William of Malmesbury, *Gesta regum Anglorum* II.177 (ed. Mynors, 300).

[43] William of Jumièges, *Gesta Normannorum ducum* V.6 (ed. van Houts, II, 14–16).

[44] Keynes, 'Massacre', 48–50.

Although William's testimony is problematic, the association he draws between the massacre and Swein's reappearance is harder to dismiss. If the massacre was indeed directed at elements of the Danish force settled in 994, then one imagines that Swein would have been acquainted with many of the victims. Still, it is unlikely that revenge was the Danish king's primary motive; more important were probably recent developments in Scandinavia. As we have seen, Swein's dominance over Norway had been challenged by Olaf Tryggvason in 995 and he spent much of the following years seeking to reassert his claims over the region, efforts which were crowned with success in 999 when Olaf was finally defeated and killed.[45] Allowing a year or two to re-establish control, it may well have been 1003 before Swein was in a position to return to his raiding ways. He was clearly picking up where he had left off. However, while in the 990s Swein was only one of many viking leaders, now he was alone; buoyed by recent successes, his prestige and power had apparently reached a point at which he could embark on such undertakings independently. The Danish king certainly returned with a vengeance, storming Exeter (whose reeve, Hugh, an appointee of the new queen, is singled out for blame) before heading inland. This may have been designed as a strike against Æthelred's Norman alliance: by sacking a centre associated with the new queen, he might hope to weaken her position at court. In any case, local forces from Wiltshire and Hampshire came out to meet him as he proceeded inland, but were apparently undermined (as before) by Ealdorman Ælfric, allowing Swein to take and burn Wilton, then move on to Salisbury before returning to his ships on the coast.[46] It is around this time that Æthelred seems to have introduced the *Helmet* coinage (*c.* 1003/5–9). Given the iconographic similarity between this and the preceding *Long Cross* type (the main distinction being that the royal portrait now bears a helmet and a few ornaments have been added to the reverse), it has been suggested that this was not a full type, but a variant on the existing one (much like the *Second* and *Benediction Hand*). Other considerations also point in this direction, including the low weight standard (new types were normally introduced

[45] P.[H.] Sawyer, 'Cnut's Scandinavian Empire', in *The Reign of Cnut: King of England, Denmark and Norway*, ed. A.R. Rumble (London, 1994), 10–22, at 16–17.
[46] *ASC* 1003 CDE (ed. O'Brien O'Keeffe, 89–90).

at a higher weight than the previous ones, then reduced over the course of the issue) and the relatively small number of surviving specimens.[47] Interestingly, *Helmet* coins were not struck at Wilton, but many of the moneyers who had previously been active there now appear at Salisbury, suggesting that the town's sack in 1003 encouraged them to take refuge within the superior defences of nearby Old Sarum (which the vikings are only said to have passed through).[48] In any case, it is certainly significant that the obverse ('heads') of these coins presents the king in helmet and armour, rather than bareheaded or wearing a crown or diadem, as was by now customary (Plate 2). Helmed figures had appeared on English coinage of the seventh and eighth centuries and the ultimate iconographic inspiration lay in late Roman coins, in which the helm was a common symbol of authority.[49] The return to such imagery is an unmistakably militant gesture; whether intended to signal the king's own willingness to resist, or to inculcate such feelings amongst his people, the martial resonances are hard to miss.

In the following year Swein directed his attention towards East Anglia, landing at Norwich, which he put to the torch before heading inland to Thetford. After sacking the town, he was confronted by a substantial force led by Ulfcytel, the local leader (probably reeve or high-reeve) and *de facto* ealdorman.[50] A fierce battle ensued in which the vikings emerged the victors, though not without sustaining substantial losses; the chronicler reports that they were later known to say 'that they never met worse fighting amongst the English than that which Ulfcytel dealt them' (*þæt hi næfre wyrsan handplegan on Angelcynne ne gemitton þonne Ulfcytel him to brohte*). In the following year Swein returned to Denmark, but this brought little respite, as famine struck the realm (it is this which

---

[47] Naismith, *Medieval European Coinage*, ch. 10, and 'Coinage of Æthelred', 130–1.

[48] R.H.M. Dolley, 'The Sack of Wilton in 1003 and the Chronology of the "Long Cross" and "Helmet" Types of Æthelræd II', *Nordisk Numismatisk Unions Medlemsblad* 5 (May 1954), 152–6; C.E. Blunt and C.S.S. Lyon, 'Some Notes on the Mints of Wilton and Salisbury', in *Studies in Late Anglo-Saxon Coinage in Memory of Bror Emil Hildebrand*, ed. K. Jonsson (Stockholm, 1990), 25–34.

[49] A. Gannon, *The Iconography of Early Anglo-Saxon Coinage: Sixth to Eighth Centuries* (Oxford, 2003), 51–4.

[50] Marten, 'Shiring of East Anglia', 14–17.

presumably occasioned Swein's departure).[51] To the beleaguered English it must have seemed as if they had jumped out of the frying pan and into the fire. This famine, which hit much of western Europe, was especially severe. Raoul Glaber, writing within Cluniac circles in Burgundy some thirty years later, reports that people were forced to eat not only the flesh of 'unclean animals and reptiles' (*immdous animalius et reptilius*) but also men, women and children, bearing eloquent witness to the scars left by this event.[52]

Given the failure of previous attempts to assuage God's wrath, it must have been clear that a new direction was needed. It is in this light that developments in the following years are to be understood, and at this point that the 'palace revolution' took place (1005–6), a wide-ranging changing of the guard at court: Æthelmær retired to his foundation at Eynsham and Ordulf may have similarly withdrawn to Tavistock; Ealdorman Ælfhelm was executed and his sons, Wulfheah and Ufegeat, were blinded; and their associate Wulfgeat had his lands confiscated.[53] These were all major political players: Ælfhelm was the second most senior ealdorman (of only three); Æthelmær, Ordulf and Wulfgeat had been the most prominent thegns at court since the 990s; and Ælfhelm's elder son, Wulfheah, was also a thegn of some note.[54] The main force behind these changes has been identified in Eadric Streona ('the Grasper'), who owed his meteoric rise to this clearing of the decks.[55] However, while the consequences of this event are well known, little is known of the motives behind it. As the second great sea change of Æthelred's reign, this act bears comparison with the earlier change of direction in 993: in both cases

---

[51] *ASC* 1004–5 CDE (ed. O'Brien O'Keeffe, 90–1).

[52] Raoul Glaber, *Historiarum libri quinque* II.17, ed. J. France, *Rodulfus Glaber Opera* (Oxford, 1989), 80–2; with P. Bonassie, 'Consommation d'aliments immondes et cannibalisme de survie dans l'Occident du haut Moyen Âge' (1989), repr. in and cited from his *Les sociétés de l'an mil. Un monde entre deux âges* (Brussels, 2001), 143–68, at 163–5. See further F. Curschmann, *Hungersnöte im Mittelalter. Ein Beitrag zur deutschen Wirtschaftsgeschichte des 8. bis 13. Jahrhunderts* (Leipzig, 1900), 108–10.

[53] *ASC* 1006 CDE (ed. O'Brien O'Keeffe, 91); S 918 (*Abing* 135); with Keynes, *Diplomas*, 209–14. See also E. Boyle, 'A Welsh Record of an Anglo-Saxon Political Mutilation', *ASE* 35 (2006), 245–9.

[54] Keynes, *Atlas*, tables LXII–LXIII.

[55] Keynes, 'Tale of Two Kings', 211–17; Williams *Æthelred*, 69–75.

certain figures fell from grace, while others rose to take their place; and in both an unusually lengthy royal charter was issued to inaugurate these changes. Thus, as twelve years earlier, in 1005 Æthelred issued a particularly impressive diploma, the Eynsham foundation charter. This is a worthy successor to the Abingdon privilege of 993: it is the longest authentic charter in the king's name and, though it does not survive in its original format, it must have been of a similar size, if not somewhat larger.[56]

What the size of this document already suggests is confirmed by its wording: like its Abingdon predecessor, it is in a number of respects extraordinary, bearing witness to the politically charged atmosphere at court in the mid-1000s. It opens with a meditation on the ills which the English are enduring and the decisions taken by the king and his counsellors to avert them. Æthelred explains that he has decreed that God's wrath, which has come upon the nation 'more than is usual' (*plus solito*), should now be assuaged 'by the continuous display of good works' (*continua bonorum operum exhibitione*). He notes that this has become necessary because 'in our times we suffer the fires of wars and the pillaging of our wealth, and also from the cruellest plundering of the ravaging barbarian host, the manifold tribulation of pagan peoples, and of those reducing us almost to destruction', from which 'we discern that we live in dangerous times'.[57] It is rare for charters to refer to contemporary events directly, even in these fateful years, and thus, as with the restitutions of the 990s, we have a privileged view into the king's thought world.[58] The last line of this passage – explaining that the viking attacks are signs that the English are living in the 'dangerous times' (*tempora periculosa*) which according to the Bible will precede the end of time (II Timothy III.1) – introduces an

---

[56] S 911 (KCD 714); with S. Keynes, 'King Æthelred's Charter for Eynsham Abbey (1005)', in *Early Medieval Studies in Memory of Patrick Wormald*, ed. S. Baxter *et al.* (Farnham, 2009), 451–73, at 459. For much of what follows, see Roach, 'Tale of Two Charters'.

[57] S 911 (KCD 714): 'Et quia in nostris temporibus bellorum incendia direptionesque opum nostrarum patimur, necnon ex uastantium crudelissima depraedatione hostium barbarorum, paganarumque gentium multiplici tribulatione, affligentiumque nos usque ad internecionem tempora cernimus incumbere periculosa'. On the relationship between this passage and the proem of the 'First Decimation' charters of 844 (which were almost certainly forged on this basis), see Keynes, 'Æthelred's Charter', 464–8; and cf. *Charters of Malmesbury Abbey*, ed. S.E. Kelly, Anglo-Saxon Charters 11 (Oxford, 2005), 80–7.

[58] Cf. F.M. Stenton, *The Latin Charters of the Anglo-Saxon Period* (Oxford, 1955), 27–8.

apocalyptic tone which is then maintained as the charter continues. Æthelred (or the draftsman, acting in his name) goes on to state that it is most fitting that those 'upon whom the ends of the world are come' (*in quos fines seculorum deuenerunt*: I Corinthians X.11) should now examine themselves, thinking about how their souls are destined to live not only in this world but also the next. The same biblical line had been used in the charter issued upon the reform of Sherborne in 998, suggesting an association between this act and Æthelred's earlier reforming efforts.[59] However, it is not just the proximity of the end which is emphasized here; the second half of this phrase goes on to offer the English guidance as to how they should respond to earthly transience: since they are come unto the ends of the ages, they must consider the fate of their souls. The rest of the preamble develops this line of thought, noting the fleeting nature of earthly riches before going on to cite Boethius's *Consolation of Philosophy* to the effect that all human action is dependent on two factors, the will and the power, in the absence of which it is impossible to perform any task. Written by the late Roman senator Boethius (d. 524) while awaiting execution, the *Consolation of Philosophy* was one of the most influential philosophical works of the Middle Ages, which was often turned to for comfort by those in adversity. This work was well known in later Anglo-Saxon England and had been translated into the vernacular in the late ninth or early tenth century, perhaps by Alfred the Great.[60] Though the line in question had been cited in earlier diplomas,[61] the quotation here is considerably longer than those seen previously and it is tempting to conclude that Æthelred and his advisers had direct recourse to Boethius's wisdom in their hour of need; certainly, someone with close connections to the court did.

This phrase sets the tone for the main dispositive section of the charter, which covers the core legal details of the foundation. This maintains the

---

[59] S 895 (*Sher* 11). See above, Chapter 4, pp. 156–8.

[60] *The Old English Boethius: An Edition of the Old English Versions of Boethius's* De Consolatione Philosophiae, ed. M. Godden and S. Irvine, 2 vols. (Oxford, 2009). See further *ibid.*, I, 140–151; and Bately, 'Alfredian Canon'; and cf. R. Love, 'Latin Commentaries on Boethius's *Consolation of Philosophy*', in *The Brill Companion to Alfred the Great*, ed. P. Szarmach and N.G. Discenza (Leiden, 2015), 83–110.

[61] S 429 (*Shaft* 9), S 438 (BCS 714), S 470 (*WinchNM* 12). See Keynes, *Diplomas*, 114, n. 103.

Boethian theme, stating that since Æthelred has both the will and the power (implied: to do good), he has seen fit to have the following transaction recorded for future generations. He then explains that, at Æthelmær's request, he has conceded the following privilege to Eynsham. The endowment is described as comprising an estate of thirty hides which Æthelmær had received from his son-in-law (*gener*) in exchange for lands elsewhere.[62] Stipulations are then set for the future of the foundation: the king announces that the monks are to conduct their lives in accordance with the Rule of St Benedict and that Æthelmær himself is to live amongst them 'in the guise of a father' (*patris uice*). Æthelred further notes that Æthelmær has appointed an abbot (unnamed, but Ælfric the homilist is intended) after whom successors are to be chosen from amongst the monks by free election in consultation with the king. Finally, Æthelred charges himself with overseeing the abbey to the exclusion of any other secular authority. These stipulations are, for the most part, what one would expect for a reformed monastic house, and it is not surprising that the final lines about abbatial election and preventing secular domination echo the Benedictine Rule and the *Regularis concordia*.[63] The rest of the dispositive section then gives a potted history of the abbey's estates, ending with a statement to the effect that Eynsham will be free from all secular burdens save those required of all the land (military service, bridgework and fortress-work). There follows a blessing on those who support the foundation and a curse on any who undermine it, after which the bounds of the endowment are given.

It is at this point, immediately after the boundary clauses and before the dating clause and witness-list, that the most singular feature of the diploma is to be found: a first-person statement in the vernacular by Æthelmær to Æthelred and his counsellors (*witan*). In this the nobleman announces that he has given Eynsham to God and St Mary, and also to all the saints and St Benedict, so that those who observe the Rule there might enjoy

---

[62] On the process of endowment, see S. Wood, *The Proprietary Church in the Medieval West* (Oxford, 2006), 408–12; and B. Yorke, 'Aethelmaer: The Foundation of the Abbey at Cerne and the Politics of the Tenth Century', in *The Cerne Abbey Millennium Lectures*, ed. K. Barker (Cerne Abbas, 1988), 15–25, at 19–20.

[63] *Regula Benedicti*, ch. 64.1–2 (ed. Neufville, 648); *Regularis concordia*, chs. 9–10 (ed. Symons and Spath, 74–6). See further below, p. 215.

it for all time. He notes that he intends to remain leader (*ealdor*) of the community during his lifetime, but thereafter the monks are to choose a successor in accordance with the stipulations of the Rule. This is followed by a blessing on those who obey these injunctions and a curse on those who breach them, after which Æthelmær declares his intention to live at the centre for the rest of his days. Quite what we are to make of all this is far from clear. Æthlemær is clearly trying to reserve a degree of control over his foundation and this section adds further detail to the rather allusive statement earlier on to the effect that the thegn would continue to oversee affairs there 'in the guise of a father'.[64] Such a first-person address to the king and his counsellors is unique amongst Anglo-Saxon royal diplomas and finds its closest parallels in contemporary wills, which sometimes include a statement to the effect that they are to be read before the king and his advisers (dying men not always having a chance to gain royal approval for their bequests, as was customary); it also echoes the epistolary conventions found in the vernacular writ, a type of sealed royal communiqué which may have been in use in these years.[65] The wording of this section suggests that it is the record of an address made by Æthelmær before a royal assembly, presumably that which witnessed the foundation of the monastery.[66] Indeed, it is possible that the text of the declaration itself was incorporated into this act, rather like the oath which the king laid on the altar at his consecration. Thus, like the autograph crosses appended to the Abingdon privilege of 993, this statement takes us into the ritualized world of the assembly: on the occasion of Eynsham's foundation not only was an unusually lengthy diploma presented, but the centre's founder made a public declaration confirming the endowment (and conditions on it). That this is the only proclamation of this nature to survive may not be coincidental; this charter was intimately associated with political developments at this point, as we shall see.

To appreciate the significance of this document we must return to its context. As noted, it was issued at a moment of crisis: after years spent

---

[64] Wood, *Proprietary Church*, 408–12. Cf. *ibid.*, 312–408, for the bigger picture.
[65] L. Tollerton, *Wills and Will-Making in Anglo-Saxon England* (Woodbridge, 2011), 67–70; *Anglo-Saxon Writs*, ed. F.E. Harmer (Manchester, 1952), 1–38.
[66] Keynes, 'Æthelred's Charter', 462.

seeking a solution to the viking problem, by 1005 those in power were starting to lose faith in previous policies. If the Massacre of St Brice's Day is a first sign of desperation, the 'palace revolution' reveals how far the situation had now deteriorated. This act bears comparison with Æthelred's earlier *volte-face* of 993: as then, in 1005–6 he decided that a change of course was required, and this decision was advertised by issuing an unusually long diploma; moreover, as at the council of Winchester, this change went hand in hand with a change in court factions. However, for all the similarities, there are important differences. While the years after 993 witnessed a relatively gentle change of course, in which few figures fell dramatically (only Ælfgar is known to have suffered directly), the 'palace revolution' saw a spate of violent reprisals: Ælfhelm was slain, his sons Wulfheah and Ufegeat blinded and Wulfgeat – conceivably the husband of Ælfgar's widow[67] – had his lands confiscated. Only shortly before this Ordulf and Æthelmær had left the scene: the former's attestations stop in 1005 and, since he receives bequests in the will of Bishop Ælfwold of Crediton (1008 × 1012), it has been suggested that he retired to his foundation at Tavistock; the latter, on the other hand, departed at the very moment of Eynsham's foundation in 1005 (which also marks the last appearance of Ordulf).[68] The importance of the Eynsham charter lies in the fact that it was an essential part of this process: it is the document which paved the way for Æthelmær's (and possibly also Ordulf's) disappearance from political life. It was thus the opening act of the 'palace revolution', marking the retirement of these two figures and preparing the ground for the more dramatic acts of the following year. As such, the diploma provides a unique insight into the king's thoughts at this point. Like the Abingdon privilege of 993, it casts recent viking activity as divine punishment and presents itself as an attempt to assuage this: by assisting in the foundation of a reformed monastic house – exactly the kind of centre which Æthelred had been promoting since the early 990s – the king clearly hoped that he might secure divine favour. However, given these clear

---

[67] S 918 (*Abing* 135); with Keynes, *Diplomas*, 210–11; and *Charters of Abingdon*, ed. Kelly, 530.

[68] S 1492 (ed. Whitelock, *Councils*, no. 51); S 911 (KCD 714); with Keynes, *Diplomas*, 209; and Williams, *Æthelred*, 69.

similarities with the programme initiated in 993, the question must be why Æthelred now turned his back on so many of those who had risen to prominence since.

The answer lies at least in part in the very ideals of repentance and reform which had been promoted at court in the intervening years. As we have seen, at the heart of the efforts undertaken by Æthelred and his advisers since 993 had been the eradication of sin. Hints of such a perspective can be detected not only in the restitutions of the 990s and the fostering of Edward the Martyr's cult, but also in the St Frideswide's charter of 1004, which presents the Massacre of St Brice's Day as an act of cleansing. As the situation got worse, it would seem that Æthelred and his counsellors decided to scale up this programme of penitence and purification. The line of logic would seem to have run something like this: if the king himself was not to blame, then the rot must have gone deeper, right down to his own most trusted advisers. The fact that Ordulf and Æthelmær retired to monasteries supports this interpretation: monastic retirement was a well-established practice elsewhere in Europe, where it carried distinctly penitential connotations; it implied a degree of guilt on the part of the retiring party, and the time spent in a monastery might be considered analogous to a period of penance.[69] Yet this was also a compromise measure: it allowed the individual to withdraw from public life peacefully and left open the possibility of future reconciliation; just as a penitent might be absolved of his sins, so too the monastic exile might be allowed to return to political life. The punishment of blinding, meted out on Ælfhelm's sons, might also be understood in such terms: blinding and mutilation were seen as acts of kindness, which allowed the offender time to atone for his wrongdoing before death.[70]

It would thus seem that the 'palace revolution' was a further effort to purify English society; desperate times called for desperate measures, and

[69] de Jong, 'Paenitentia publica', 877–87. See also M. de Jong, 'Monastic Prisoners or Opting Out? Political Coercion and Honour in the Frankish Kingdoms', in Topographies of Power in the Early Middle Ages, ed. M. de Jong and F. Theuws (Leiden, 2001), 291–328; and Cubitt, 'Lay Patrons', 175–6.

[70] Keynes, 'Tale of Two Kings', 212–13; N. Marafioti, 'Punishing Bodies and Saving Souls: Capital and Corporal Punishment in Late Anglo-Saxon England', HSJ 20 (2008), 39–57. Cf. G. Bührer-Thierry, '"Just Anger" or "Vengeful Anger"? The Punishment of Blinding in the Early Medieval West', in Anger's Past: The Social Uses of an Emotion in the Middle Ages, ed. B.H. Rosenwein (Ithaca, NY, 1998), 75–91.

Æthelred was not one to shirk his duty. That the very ideas about sin and society developed and supported by figures such as Ordulf and Æthelmær in the 990s should now be used against them is ironic, but by no means surprising. As Mayke de Jong and Courtney Booker have shown, penitential ideals were a double-edged sword in medieval politics. Equating worldly success with religious purity might inspire reforming zeal when the going was good, but had a tendency to backfire (often quite spectacularly) when things took a turn for the worse, forcing rulers into ever more drastic efforts to purge court and society before it was too late. The situation faced by Æthelred in the first decade of the new millennium thus bears comparison with that of Louis the Pious in the later 820s and early 830s, as discussed by de Jong and Booker: having bought into a penitential reading of contemporary events, the only option available when matters did not improve was to up the proverbial ante. The punishments of 1006 are therefore signs that, to borrow de Jong's turn of phrase, 'the penitential state was spinning . . . out of control'; what had once been constructive efforts to improve society through repentance and reform threatened to become a vicious cycle of mutual recrimination.[71] As we have seen, such ideas about purity and pollution lay at the heart of the reform, which presented itself as an attempt to cleanse church and society of the sinful practices of a previous age. The 'palace revolution' was thus an extension of the efforts initiated in 993; it was the same programme, writ large. In this respect, it may be more than a coincidence that Wulfstan, who had attested Æthelred's later charters of restitution and went on to write a number of reforming decrees in his name, subscribes the Eynsham charter second, above the archbishop of Canterbury and all other lay and ecclesiastical magnates; one suspects that he played a prominent role behind the scenes here.

It is important to emphasize these religious undertones, because this act has hitherto been interpreted in political terms, as a product of the machinations of Eadric Streona. This is not to say that Eadric was not involved. According to John of Worcester, the Mercian magnate was responsible for

---

[71] de Jong, *Penitential State*, 213. See also C. Booker, *Past Convictions: The Penance of Louis the Pious and the Decline of the Carolingians* (Philadelphia, PA, 2009).

Ælfhelm's death, and though this report has a whiff of the legendary to it (John has the ealdorman killed while out hunting, a common literary and folkloric motif), Eadric's involvement can be inferred on other grounds.[72] Thus, in the first diploma issued after this event Eadric moves to first place amongst the thegns, leapfrogging many more senior figures in the process. One year later he was appointed ealdorman and attests his first charter in this role in second place (above Leofwine, who was considerably his senior). In subsequent years his star rose further: he married one of the king's daughters, Eadgyth (Edith), and in 1012 he moves to first amongst the ealdormen, a position he would enjoy till Æthelred's death.[73] Eadric's relatives also benefited from his rise. John of Worcester lists six of his brothers by name, many of whom can be identified amongst the upper echelons of the thegns in these years, including Æthelweard, Æthelwine, Brihtric and Æthelmær.[74] There can, in short, be little doubt that Eadric and his associates were the main beneficiaries of these developments, and further light is shed on them by the regional power constellations at play. As Charles Insley notes, Eadric's power base lay in the north-west Midlands, not far from that of the family of Ælfhelm, which was eclipsed at this point; we are, therefore, not simply witnessing a change in court factions, but also a struggle for dominance in the northern Midlands.[75] Indeed, Ælfhelm's brother, Wulfric Spot, died only a few years before these events (1002 × 1004), around the same time that Eadric first appears as thegn (1002); one wonders if the latter's death helped pave the way for Eadric's initial rise.[76]

Much has been made of Eadric's union with a royal daughter, as previously the preference seems to have been to avoid such alliances with the aristocracy, reserving royal blood to a select few by marrying princesses off to foreign rulers or placing them in dynastic nunneries such as Wilton and

---

[72] John of Worcester, *Chronicon, s.a.* 1006 (ed. Darlington and McGurk, 456–8 [with *errata* slip]).

[73] Keynes, *Atlas*, tables LXII–LXIII.

[74] John of Worcester, *Chronicon, s.a.* 1007 (ed. Darlington and McGurk, 460); Keynes, *Atlas*, table LXIII ('Group Three').

[75] C. Insley, 'Politics, Conflict and Kinship in Early Eleventh-Century Mercia', *Midland History* 26 (2001), 28–42, esp. 30–5. See also Banton, 'Earls and Ealdormen', 185–6.

[76] Wulfric disappears from diploma witness-lists in 1002 and his will was confirmed in 1004: Keynes, *Atlas*, table LXIII; S 1536 (*Burt* 29), S 906 (*Burt* 28).

Shaftesbury; like Æthelred's marriage to Emma, this would seem to break all the rules. However, if this was indeed a special honour (and in some sense it surely was), Eadric was not alone in enjoying it: Uhtred of Northumbria married another royal daughter, Ælfgifu, during these years, and one of the leaders who fell at Ringmere in 1010 is reported to have been the king's son-in-law (or brother-in-law) and thus also a royal relative by marriage.[77] One might see these matches as a sign of weakness, an indication that whereas previous rulers had been able to command respect, Æthelred now had to buy it, but it is doubtful whether matters were so simple. Medieval rulers always had to work with their leading aristocrats and concessions such as marriage into the royal family could be as much a sign of successful politicking as decaying authority. The Ottonian rulers of Germany frequently married daughters off to leading local magnates, apparently without any ill effects; perhaps Æthelred was taking a leaf out of their book. In any case, it would be dangerous to make too much of the novelty of this: with the exception of Æthelstan's sisters in the 920s and 930s and Edgar's sainted daughter Edith in the 960s, we are not informed about the marriage patterns of any royal daughters before this point. It is, therefore, possible that such practices had long been the norm. Indeed, we know that most ealdormen of the tenth century were related to the king in some way or another and it is hard to imagine all of these connections being achieved through collateral branches of the royal family.[78]

We know little about Eadric's background. He apparently hailed from the north-west Midlands (perhaps around Shrewsbury) and can first be identified as the witness to a royal charter in 1002.[79] There is circumstantial evidence to suggest that he may have owed his promotion to the patronage of Queen Emma, who was crowned in this year; if so, the 'palace revolution' might be seen as a move against a group loosely associated with Ælfthryth, whose position at court Emma had taken. Certainly, it is striking that

[77] Stafford, *Queen Emma*, 92, n. 118. Stafford notes that *Jomsviking Saga* mentions a further daughter of Æthelred as the wife of a certain Ulfkell (Ulfcytel of East Anglia?); however, these details are only found in the 'supplement' to this work in the late-fourteenth-century *Flateyjarbók* and find no confirmation in contemporary sources: *Encomium Emmae reginae*, ed. A. Campbell, Camden Classics Reprints 4 (Cambridge, 1998), 87–91.

[78] Cf. R. Fleming, *Kings and Lords in Conquest England* (Cambridge, 1991), 21–39.

[79] S. Keynes, 'Eadric Streona (*d.* 1017)', in *ODNB*, XVII, 538–9.

Ordulf, the former's brother, retired from political life at this juncture, and later opposition to Eadric seems to have centred on the king's eldest sons, Æthelstan and Edmund, whom Ælfthryth had apparently raised. It may even be that Eadric was sympathetic to the claims of Emma's children. The queen's first son with Æthelred, Edward, begins attesting diplomas around this time (1005), appearing not least in the Eynsham privilege itself; had Emma wished to prepare the ground for his succession, now would have been the time to start. Edward's name certainly suggests that he was seen as a throne-worthy candidate: it brought with it associations not only with his great-great-grandfather, Edward the Elder, but also more immediately with his martyred uncle, whose cult was being actively promoted at court.[80] By this point Æthelred's own eldest son, Æthelstan, was probably about twenty, and it may be that pressure was starting to be exerted from this angle: royal progeny were rarely patient when it came to waiting for their accession and, as we shall see, long-lived monarchs frequently fell afoul of their sons. Still, concrete evidence for tensions is hard to find and there is a danger of exaggerating the degree of intrigue in these years; it may simply be that as Emma's star rose, so too did that of Eadric.[81]

Harder to explain than Eadric's motives are Æthelred's – why was the king so easily persuaded to act in favour of this relatively new appearance on the political scene? Part of the explanation must lie in personal affinity: for whatever reason Æthelred seems to have genuinely liked Eadric. Still, whatever his personal hold on the monarch, we must presume that Eadric and his associates presented a persuasive rationale for the purge of 1005–6. Indeed, though a number of magnates left the scene at this point, many others remained: the ranks of the senior thegns (who probably constituted the core of the royal household) were hit hard, but Ealdormen Ælfric and Leofwine remained a regular presence at assemblies and the episcopate was left untouched – in fact, Wulfstan of York seems if anything to have grown in the king's confidence in these years. We must presume that many of these figures gave their

---

[80] S. Keynes, 'Edward the Ætheling (c. 1005–16)', in *Edward the Confessor: The Man and the Legend*, ed. R. Mortimer (Woodbridge, 2009), 41–62, at 43–4; Barlow, *Edward the Confessor*, 30. See also P.H. Sawyer, *From Roman Britain to Norman England*, 2nd edn (London, 1998), 128; and Stafford, *Queen Emma*, 222.

[81] See below, Chapter 6, pp. 303–4.

endorsement (tacit or otherwise) to these measures and some may actively have advocated them. It is here that the religious ideas about sin and purity mentioned earlier must have come into play. If Eadric was indeed whispering into the king's ear, one imagines that the message went something like this: that previous efforts at atonement had failed not because they were wrong-headed, but because they had stopped too short; that something was very rotten in the state of England and that only a fresh start could ensure a return to the victorious ways of Æthelred's forebears. The charged atmosphere at court would certainly have helped his case; the failure of previous efforts must have been painfully evident and it probably did not take much to persuade the king that some of his old advisers were culpable. Accusations of negligence and conspiracy thus seem to have been part of the process and it is telling that those who fell from grace were treated as traitors and outlaws: they were executed, blinded or deprived of their lands.

We can only guess as to the perspective of someone like Æthelmær at this point. On the face of it, the Eynsham foundation charter was a ringing endorsement of the thegn's efforts: Æthelred gave royal support to his new monastery and protected it in the strongest possible terms. Still, in the context of the blindings and executions of the following year, it is hard not to see something more sinister afoot. Indeed, those who disappeared were a veritable who's who of Æthelmær's associates, a fact which cannot have escaped his notice.[82] It may be that Æthelmær (and Ordulf, who also disappears at this juncture) saw the direction of developments and chose to make an exit while they still could. Alternatively, they may have been forced out. Whatever the case, monastic retirement was probably in the best interests of all concerned: it spared the thegns the danger and humili-ation of a trial, while giving the king a free hand to move against their friends and allies. (A modern analogy is perhaps offered by the process whereby company CEOs or government ministers choose to resign rather than being fired, resignation being a convenient face-saving conceit for all.) Moreover, since retirement to a monastery could be understood in penitential terms, it left open the possibility of reconciliation at a later

---

[82] Keynes, *Atlas*, table LXIII (note the almost complete disappearance of 'Group Two' at this point); with Keynes, *Diplomas*, 187–93 and 209–13.

date.[83] In this respect, royal acknowledgement of Eynsham's liberty and holdings was probably part of the bargain: Æthelmær would retreat from public life, but only if he could be confident that his legacy was secure.

While we can only speculate as to the West Country thegn's feelings, we can trace those of his new foundation's abbot, Ælfric, in some detail. Already at Cerne Æthelmær had been one of Ælfric's most important patrons and one imagines that living together at Eynsham would only have strengthened this bond. It is, therefore, interesting to note that the tone of Ælfric's writings becomes distinctly darker during his Eynsham years. This is already clear in his 'Letter to the Monks at Eynsham' (*c.* 1005), designed to set the tone for monastic life at the centre. Much of this is an adaptation of the *Regularis concordia*; however, while the latter had allowed the king substantial powers of oversight over monastic foundations, in the 'Letter' these are significantly curtailed. What is more, Ælfric specifies that the king should exercise what powers he possesses 'for the protection of the place, not the exercise of tyranny' (*ad munimen loci, non ad tirannidem*), a line which finds no equivalent in the *Concordia* and seems to anticipate a strained relationship between monarch and religious house. Interestingly, this distinctive phrase appears not only in the 'Letter', but also in the Eynsham foundation charter (whence it is apparently drawn); one wonders whether the long arm of Ælfric was at work here.[84] In any case, this is not the only sign of the homilist's darkening mood. In his Second Homily on the Feast of a Confessor (*c.* 1006 × 1012), Ælfric goes off on something of a tangent, providing a striking list of biblical figures who suffered divine vengeance for their ills, an aside which may betray deeper concerns on the part of the author.[85] The prolific homilist similarly ends his work 'On the Old and New Testaments' (*c.* 1005 × 1012) by recounting the punishments meted out on the Jews for

---

[83] In addition to the literature cited above, n. 69, see K. Sprigade, 'Die Einweisung ins Kloster und in den geistlichen Stand als politische Maßnahme im frühen Mittelalter' (PhD diss., Univ. of Heidelberg, 1964).

[84] Ælfric, *Letter to the Monks at Eynsham*, ch. 63 (ed. Jones, 140); S 911 (KCD 714). See further *Letter*, ed. Jones, 44–5; and Roach, 'Tale of Two Charters'.

[85] *Angelsächsische Homilien und Heiligenleben*, ed. B. Assmann with a supplementary introduction by P. Clemoes (Darmstadt, 1964), no. 4, 49–64; with M. Clayton, 'Of Mice and Men: Ælfric's Second Homily for the Feast of a Confessor', *Leeds Studies in English* n.s. 24 (1993), 1–26, at 14–21.

their treatment of Christ: the siege of Jerusalem, the ensuing famine and the fate of the children taken into captivity thereafter – all events with potential contemporary resonances.[86] It is also during these years that Ælfric under-took a number of significant revisions to his Catholic Homilies, including the addition of a lengthy passage to the homily on the Second Sunday after Easter, in which he inveighs against wicked counsellors who lead others astray, noting the internecine conflict which results. Robert Upchurch suggests that this was intended to be preached before the king and his senior advisers and, whatever the precise purpose, it is hard not to see herein dark allusions to the circumstances surrounding Eadric's rise.[87] Ælfric also added a section to his homily for the Twelfth Sunday after Pentecost (c. 1005) telling the tale of Theodosius I's penance for the massacre of Thessalonica. This may represent an oblique critique of the St Brice's Day Massacre, as Mary Clayton suggests; however, it may simply be a meditation on the peni-tential brand of rulership which Æthelred had embraced so energetically since the 990s (certainly, it is hard to see Theodosius, who was celebrated as one of the great Christian rulers of antiquity, as a bad role model).[88] Indeed, while Ælfric clearly cared more about contemporary politics than scholars once thought, there is no mistaking the detached and at times downright ambiguous nature of his allusions to contemporary events. Given the context in which he was writing, one wonders if this reflects the feelings of his patron Æthelmær (or at least elements thereof): increasing concern, but expressed in restrained terms, suggestive of a residual attachment to the king and his regime. If so, this ambivalence may go some way towards explaining why in his later years Æthelred reconciled himself with Æthelmær, promoting him to his father's office of ealdorman in the south-west.[89]

---

[86] *Old English Version of the Heptateuch*, ed. S. Crawford, EETS o.s. 160 (London, 1922), 72–4.

[87] Ælfric, *CH: FS* XVIIb (ed. Clemoes, 535–42); with R.K. Upchurch, 'A Big Dog Barks: Ælfric of Eynsham's Indictment of the English Pastorate and *Witan*', *Speculum* 85 (2010), 505–33. Note that Upchurch's dating of the revision to 1002 × 1006 depends (indirectly) on Fehr's dating of Ælfric's homily on the Nativity of the Virgin (1005 × 1006), which itself is not above question: *Councils*, ed. Whitelock, 259–60. It is conceivable that this revision was made later, though probably still in Ælfric's early years as abbot: Godden, *Introduction*, 136. See also Treharne, *Living Through Conquest*, 71–8.

[88] Ælfric, *Supplementary Homilies* XXVI (ed. Pope, 762–69); with Clayton, 'Of Mice and Men', 21–2; and Cubitt, 'Politics of Remorse', 189–90.

[89] See below, Chapter 6, p. 287.

Sin and society, 1006–9

The years between 1006 and 1009 can be seen as ones of rising crisis, a period in which Æthelred tried to develop the programme presented in the Eynsham charter, but struggled in the face of mounting external opposition. Already 1006 saw the resumption of Scandinavian activity with the arrival in midsummer – hot on the heels of the famine, it must have seemed – of what the chronicler calls 'the great fleet' (*se micel flota*).[90] This force was probably composed for the most part of bands previously active in the British Isles, but it clearly posed a new kind of threat. The army ravaged Sandwich and in response the 'entire nation of Wessex and Mercia' (*ealne peodscipe of Wesseaxum 7 of Myrcnum*) was called up, the first reference to a response on a national scale. Despite the large call-out, the English were able to make little headway, however, and the chronicler laments the damage suffered by the countryside not only from the foreign invader, but also from its notional defenders. As always, such rhetoric must be taken with a pinch of salt; nevertheless, we should not doubt that supporting such a large force was indeed a real strain on resources.[91] As winter began to approach the English army disbanded and the Scandinavians withdrew to the Isle of Wight, a site which the chronicler sardonically refers to as a *friðstol* ('a place of sanctuary'), thus likening the security enjoyed by the raiders there to that offered to the Christian faithful by consecrated churches. As Christmas approached they made a further foray, however, riding out through Hampshire to Reading in Berkshire, then proceeding to raze Wallingford before overnighting at Cholsey (the fate of the monastery is unknown). The chronicler underlines the bitter irony of these events, speaking of these ravages in terms of the lighting of beacons; the fires of the towns put to the torch are thus compared to the defence mechanisms which were meant to provide succour and early warning to the English. The next day the force travelled west to Cuckhamsley Barrow (Scutchamer Knob) in Berkshire (now Oxfordshire) where it stopped and waited. This was a taunting gesture, since it had been said that if the vikings

[90] *ASC* 1006 CDE (ed. O'Brien O'Keeffe, 91–2). See further Keynes, 'An Abbot', 155–6.
[91] Cf. G. Halsall, *Warfare and Society in the Barbarian West, 450–900* (London, 2003), 125–30.

(or perhaps any foreign invader – it is not entirely clear in context) made it to this site, they would not make it back to the sea again.[92] Cuckhamsley itself was a place of some importance: the barrow remains a prominent local landmark and it seems to have served as the meeting place of the local shire (Plate 11). There was also a deeper significance to this site: its name, literally 'the barrow of Cwichelm' (Old English: *Cwicelmeshlaew*), indicates that it was thought to house the earlier West Saxon king of this name (d. 636).[93] This was, therefore, a location of great symbolic significance to the English polity and its West Saxon rulers; by occupying it the vikings underlined their dominance over them. On their return, the raiders met with the main English army, which they put to flight at the River Kennet (near Reading) before marching back out to sea past the gates of Winchester, the traditional centre of West Saxon royal authority (and the resting place of many of Æthelred's ancestors).[94]

These attacks sent shockwaves throughout the realm and it may be significant that no royal charters survive from this year. Winter campaigns were a favoured viking tactic: they caught opponents unawares and frequently led to the capture of valuable stores stockpiled for the season.[95] In this case the king himself is said to have retreated to the safety of Shropshire for Christmas – far from the Scandinavian ravages, but also far from the West Saxon heartlands where he was normally to be found. (It may be no coincidence that Eadric, who had just risen to prominence, also hailed from this region.) At the advice of his counsellors, Æthelred made contact with the viking army, promising tribute and provisions in exchange for a truce. In the following year a record sum of 36,000 pounds was then raised to buy them off.[96] It is easy in retrospect to see these events as the

[92] *ASC* 1006 CDE (ed. O'Brien O'Keeffe, 91–2). See G. Halsall, 'Anthropology and the Study of pre-Conquest Warfare and Society: The Ritual War in Anglo-Saxon England', in *Weapons and Warfare in Anglo-Saxon England*, ed. S.C. Hawkes (Oxford, 1989), 155–77, at 166–7. (Though note that the *Chronicle* does not state that the viking force remained encamped there for two weeks, as Halsall states.)

[93] A. Sanmark and S. Semple, 'Places of Assembly: New Discoveries in Sweden and England', *Fornvännen* 103 (2008), 245–59, at 252–5.

[94] T.J.T. Williams, 'Landscape and Warfare in Anglo-Saxon England and the Viking Campaign of 1006', *EME* 23 (2015), 329–59, esp. 339–58.

[95] Halsall, *Warfare and Society*, 146 and 154–6.

[96] *ASC* 1006–7 CDE (ed. O'Brien O'Keeffe, 91–2).

beginning of the end for Æthelred and England: for the first time the vikings seem to have been able to penetrate into the kingdom's heartlands and to many it must have seemed as if the king was incapable of stemming the onslaught. Nevertheless, it is important not to fall victim to teleology, be it of the chronicler's or our own making. It is clear that Æthelred was still able to raise substantial forces, and that alone says something. What is more, it is clear that his policy was not to pay tribute at all costs: as previously, his hand was forced by the defeat of his main army. In fact, this strategy was not a complete failure (even if one hesitates to call it a true success): the raiders departed and we hear of no further Scandinavian activity till the arrival of Thorkell's 'great raiding army' two years later. In the interim Æthelred used the time he had won well. Eadric Streona was appointed ealdorman of Mercia (1007), presumably in an attempt to shore up administration in the region. In the following year, the king ordered that a warship be built for every 310 (or possibly 300) hides (an extension of existing arrangements) and that a helm and mail coat be provided for every eight hides.[97] One of the difficulties the English had experienced in previous years was the superior mobility of their enemies, who could strike and depart almost at will; the new warships were intended to rectify this situation, allowing them to take the fight to the vikings on their own turf (or surf, as it were).[98] Nicholas Brooks suggested that a further problem was that Æthelred's forces were less heavily armoured than their Scandinavian counterparts; if so, then the provision of additional helms and mail shirts would have helped further close the gap between the military capabilities of the English and their foes.[99] These measures presume a high degree of logistical and administrative sophistication and have understandably been seen as a sign of the precocity of late Anglo-Saxon royal authority.[100] Be that as it may, they were by no means unprecedented and bear comparison with the military undertakings of Charles the Bald of

[97] Keynes, *Atlas*, table LXII; *ASC* 1008 CDE (ed. O'Brien O'Keeffe, 92).

[98] As elsewhere, there are clear Alfredian precedents: Lavelle, *Alfred's Wars*, 141–76.

[99] Brooks, 'Weapons and Armour', 172–4. See also Lavelle, *Alfred's Wars*, 111–29.

[100] R. Abels, 'English Logistics and Military Administration 871–1066: The Impact of the Viking Wars', in *Military Aspects of Scandinavian Society in a European Perspective, AD 1–1300*, ed. A.N. Jørgensen and B.L. Clausen (Copenhagen, 1997), 257–65, esp. 262–3.

West Francia (France) against the vikings in the mid-ninth century and Henry I of East Francia (Germany) against the Magyars in the 920s and 930s: in both cases fortifications were built and attention was given to arms and armament.[101]

That such measures were deemed necessary speaks volumes about the scale of the viking threat; that they were conceivable shows that the king remained firmly in control of the situation. It is perhaps not surprising that in these years we start to have a clearer idea of the impact of the Scandinavian raids on English society. In a charter in favour of St Albans in 1005 we are informed that the king had recently given the abbot three estates in exchange for 200 pounds of gold and silver, used to pay off the Danes (though the largest of these estates was subsequently redeemed). Such arrangements were probably common: tribute payments had been growing steadily for some time and it must often have been difficult to raise the requisite funds.[102] In this case, it would seem that Æthelred resorted to selling off lands and rights in exchange for quick cash. Such a policy might work well as a short-term expedient, but risked undermining royal landholding in the long run, a fact which may explain the later reversion of the lion's share of these lands to the king: as the charter makes clear, these were intended as a surety or pledge, a guarantee on a loan, which the king might later redeem. It is likely that other charters issued in return for movable wealth were inspired by similar considerations, even though this is not always stated. Thus, Simon Keynes notes that five diplomas of 1002 mention that a sum has been given in return for the grant (the first of Æthelred's charters to do so), a development which he plausibly associates with the payment of 24,000 pounds' tribute in this year.[103] Similar trends

---

[101] J.L. Nelson, 'The Frankish Empire', in *The Oxford Illustrated History of the Vikings*, ed. P.[H.] Sawyer (Oxford, 1997), 19–47; K.-U. Jäschke, *Burgenbau und Landesverteidigung um 900. Überlegungen zu Beispielen aus Deutschland, Frankreich und England*, Vorträge und Forschungen: Sonderband 16 (Sigmaringen, 1975); E.J. Schoenfeld, 'Anglo-Saxon *Burhs* and Continental *Burgen*: Early Medieval Fortifications in Constitutional Perspective', *HSJ* 6 (1994), 49–66; B.S. Bachrach and D.[S.] Bachrach, 'Saxon Military Revolution, 912–973?: Myth and Reality', *EME* 15 (2007), 186–222; D.S. Bachrach, *Warfare in Tenth-Century Germany* (Woodbridge, 2012), 15–38.

[102] S 912 (*StAlb* 11); with *Charters of St Albans*, ed. Crick, 183–4 and 186.

[103] Keynes, *Diplomas*, 108, n. 73. See further R. Naismith, 'Payments for Land and Privilege in Anglo-Saxon England', *ASE* 41 (2012), 277–342, at 293–4.

can be observed following the tribute of 1007. In this year Æthelred granted his reeve Ælfgar an estate at Waltham St Lawrence (Berks.) in exchange for 300 mancuses of gold and silver, while in another document of 1007 he confirmed an earlier grant to St Albans of lands forfeited by Ealdorman Leofsige of Essex in return for an unspecified sum (though it is unclear precisely when this was paid).[104] A year later the king is reported as having donated nineteen hides to Ely in return for nine pounds of purest gold 'according to the great measure of the Northmen' (*iuxta magnum pondus Normannorum*), a rather allusive reference which may indicate that the sums were intended for use as tribute.[105] It is also around this time (1006 × 1011) that we hear of the king granting six hides of land to a Dane (!) called Toti in exchange for 'a payment of one pound of silver in purest gold' (*unius libre argenti appensionem de auro purissimo*).[106] Though it had long been customary to give sums in exchange for privileges,[107] it is hard to escape the impression that many of these transactions were made with an eye to filling royal coffers in the face of demands for tribute. The burden of raising these funds did not fall on the king alone, however, and there are indications that similar measures were taken by other leading magnates. Already in 994 we hear of Archbishop Sigeric of Canterbury selling an estate to his colleague Æscwig of Dorchester in order to raise money to pay off the vikings (a policy which Sigeric had been instrumental in introducing, it should be recalled), while in his will Ælfric of Canterbury (1002 × 1005) forgives the people of Middlesex and Surrey the money which he had paid on their behalf, presumably in the form of tribute levies.[108] We can be sure that such cases represent but the tip of the metaphorical iceberg.

These documents raise broader questions regarding the collection of taxation and tribute. There has been much debate as to whether the figures given for these in the *Chronicle* can be trusted and, if so, how such sums

---

[104] S 915 (*Abing* 134), S 916 (*StAlb* 12). See above, pp. 190–1, on the Leofsige case.

[105] S 919 (KCD 725). Cf. Naismith, 'Payments for Land', 311–12.

[106] S 943 (ed. Hart, *Charters of Eastern England*, 190–1).

[107] Naismith, 'Payments for Land'; Roach, *Kingship and Consent*, 94–5 and 98–9.

[108] S 882 (*CantCC* 134), S 1488 (*Abing* 133). Ælfric's will also refers to a debt owed by the men of Kent to the archbishop; this too could refer to tribute payments on their behalf.

were raised. Neither of these questions is easily answered. We have noted the tendentiousness of the *Chronicle*-account at a number of points, and it has been suggested that the tribute figures given are a further means by which its anonymous author sought to paint his picture of catastrophe and collapse.[109] He would not be the first medieval chronicler to exaggerate numbers for dramatic effect and there is, it must be acknowledged, a certain suspicious symmetry to the incremental increase in payments from year to year. Nevertheless, there are numerous reasons for thinking that these figures are at least broadly reliable. For a start, the chronicler does not place particular emphasis on these numbers, as we might expect had they been part of his literary ploy. More to the point, in at least one case we have a degree of external confirmation in the form of Æthelred's treaty with Olaf, Jósteinn and Guthmund; though, as we have seen, the treaty gives a higher figure of tribute than that recorded in the *Chronicle* (22,000 rather than 16,000 pounds), the two can be easily reconciled by presuming that the former takes into account the earlier local payments mentioned in the treaty.[110] Indeed, the fact that the *Chronicle* records the smaller of these sums suggests that its author was hardly prone to wild exaggeration. It would seem to follow that payments of up to 22,000 pounds were conceivable. While questions might still be raised about the larger sums mentioned in Æthelred's later years, it is clear that matters had reached a more critical point by then; commensurately larger payments were thus to be expected.

It would seem, therefore, that the tribute figures given in the *Chronicle* are broadly reliable. Raising such sums must have required much effort and not a little ingenuity and, as we have seen, there are signs of strain on royal and episcopal purse-strings in these years. That the tributes were collected at all certainly speaks of the organizational capabilities of Æthelred's regime; that they were necessary reveals the dire straits in which

[109] J. Gillingham, ' "The Most Precious Jewel in the English Crown": Levels of Danegeld and Heregeld in the Early Eleventh Century', *EHR* 104 (1989), 373–84, and 'Chronicles and Coins as Evidence for Levels of Tribute and Taxation in Late Tenth- and Early Eleventh-Century England', *EHR* 105 (1990), 939–50. Cf. Lawson, 'Levels of Taxation', and 'Danegeld and Heregeld Once More', *EHR* 105 (1990), 951–61.

[110] See above, Chapter 4, p. 176.

the English found themselves.[111] As elsewhere, however, it is important not to press the evidence too far: the tributes raised were very much *ad hoc* measures and there is no reason to believe that such sums could be collected in the normal run of things. Indeed, to speak of Æthelredian England as a 'tax state', like those which were to emerge in the early modern period, would go too far: the collection of tribute was only ever a periodic expedient, and even the annual 'army tax' (*heregeld*) instituted in Æthelred's final years need not have exceeded the profits on fiscal lands (profits which, incidentally, may also have contributed to these payments).[112] Moreover, such measures were by no means an exclusively English phenomenon; while the recorded payments are larger than the sums used to buy off Scandinavian raiders in ninth-century Francia, the principle was much the same, and it is conceivable that the tribute raised by Henry I in the face of the Magyar threat was of a similar order of magnitude (though our sources fail us as to the details here). In any case, the *Chronicle* consistently refers to these payments as 'tribute' (*gafol*) not 'tax' (*geld*), emphasizing their informal nature. Though some of the sums may have been raised in a similar manner to the later *heregeld*, by means of a levy on each hide, one suspects that other measures were also employed: lands were sold or given in pledge, those with greater wealth stumped up money for those with fewer available funds and existing stores of gold and silver were liberally raided.[113] This is what we see in the charter record and there are signs of similar practices elsewhere. Around this time (perhaps *c.* 1009) Wulfstan of York complained that churches had been 'entirely despoiled within and without' (*inne 7 ute clæne berypte*) and 'stripped within of all that is fitting'

[111] M.K. Lawson, 'The Collection of Danegeld and Heregeld in the Reigns of Aethelred II and Cnut', *EHR* 99 (1984), 721–38. See also D.M. Metcalf, 'Large Danegelds in Relation to War and Kingship: Their Implications for Monetary History, and Some Numismatic Evidence', in *Weapons and Warfare in Anglo-Saxon England*, ed. S.C. Hawkes (Oxford, 1989), 179–89.

[112] A. Wareham, 'Fiscal Policies and the Institution of a Tax State in Anglo-Saxon England within a Comparative Context', *Economic History Review* 65 (2012), 910–31. Though we do not know the revenue on royal lands at this point, recent assessments place those of Edward the Confessor at just under 8,100 pounds *per annum*, and a figure in this order of magnitude seems likely: Baxter, *Earls of Mercia*, 125–51. Cf. R. Naismith, *Money and Power in Anglo-Saxon England: The Southern English Kingdoms, 757–865* (Cambridge, 2012), 43–6, on minting profits, which were probably much lower than Wareham presumes.

[113] Keynes, 'Historical Context', 100–1. A similar distinction is made between *tributum* and *locarium* by continental chroniclers: Coupland, 'Poachers to Gamekeepers', 101–2.

(*innan bestrypte ælcra gerisena*) and the monks of Worcester – who were under Wulfstan's oversight in these years – were later to claim that they had been forced to melt down many treasures to meet such payments.[114] Plundering churches was a common expedient in times of need and Henry I may have resorted to similar measures in order to raise the Magyar tribute.[115] In any case, it is clear that the sums were not paid in coin alone, a fact which goes some way towards explaining why finds of Anglo-Saxon coins from Scandinavia, though plentiful, do not map neatly on to known payments of tribute: coins of the *Last Small Cross* type (*c.* 1009–18) are not especially common, whereas there is a heavy concentration of *Long Cross* coins (*c.* 997–1003/5), which were issued in a period in which only one payment of tribute is reported, and finds of English coins remain high well after such payments end. Moreover, there are even larger quantities of German coins, without any evidence for substantial payments of tribute from these regions.[116]

As noted, such a diverse approach to raising funds is suggested by the cases in which lands were sold or exchanged for movable wealth. Here we hear of 'one pound of silver in purest gold' (*unius libre argenti . . . de auro purissimo*) and 'a weight of red gold and also a gift of purest silver' (*auri quoque pondus rubicundi argentique munus purissimi*) amounting to 300 mancuses; clearly, pounds and mancuses were measures of value, not references to coinage *per se*.[117] This is also clear from the treaty of 994, where

---

[114] Wulfstan, *Sermo Lupi ad Anglos*, (EI) ll. 32–3 and 40–2 (ed. Bethurum, 268); *Hemingi chartularium ecclesiæ Wigorniensis*, ed. T. Hearne, 2 vols. (Oxford, 1723), I, 248–9.

[115] M. Lintzel, 'Die Schlacht von Riade und die Anfänge des deutschen Staates', *Sachsen und Anhalt* 9 (1933), 27–51, at 43–4. Cf. Bachrach and Bachrach, 'Saxon Military Revolution', 220–2, whose argument that Widukind of Corvey only refers to 'gifts' (*munera*) not 'tribute' (*tributum*) in connection with the Magyars takes insufficient account of his reference to how, after victory, Henry ordered the *tributum*, which would have been paid to maintain the peace, be allocated to the church and poor: Widukind of Corvey, *Res gestae Saxonicae* I.39, ed. H.-E. Lohmann and P. Hirsch, MGH: SS rer. Germ. 60 (Hannover, 1935), 57–8.

[116] Blackburn and Jonsson, 'Anglo-Saxon and Anglo-Norman Element'; Blackburn, 'Æthelred's Coinage', 165–6. See also D.M. Metcalf, 'Inflows of Anglo-Saxon and German Coins into the Northern Lands *c.* 997–1024: Discerning the Patterns', in *Coinage and History in the North Sea World, c. AD 500–1250: Essays in Honour of Marion Archibald*, ed. B. Cook and G. Williams (Leiden, 2006), 349–88.

[117] S 943 (ed. Hart, *Charters of Eastern England*, 190–1), S 915 (*Abing* 134); with Naismith, 'Payments for Land', 311–12. Cf. Murray, *Reason and Society*, 30–5.

the payment is said to constitute 22,000 pounds 'of gold and silver' (*goldes 7 seolfres*), gold coinage not being in usage in this period.[118] The tributes raised do not, therefore, represent the maximum 'tax capacity' of the realm, but rather what could be found when no other options were available. The complaints of Wulfstan and the monks of Worcester give us a sense of the burden these payments represented and it may be these which inspired Ælfric's famous assertion that God approves that kindness be shown to those suffering afflictions from 'various taxes' (*mislicum geldum*).[119] Similarly informative, though less well known, are the remarks of the anonymous Latin tract 'On Tribulations' (*De tribulationibus*), which survives in a manuscript associated with Archbishop Wulfstan and was apparently composed in these years, perhaps within the prelate's circles.[120] The text laments the ills that have come upon the nation on account of sin, asserting that recent misfortunes represent the greatest trials faced by the English since their arrival in Britain. Amongst these travails the author complains specifically about the 'vast amount of money' (*infinitam pecuniam*) which has been expended in ensuring the liberty of the English, a sum which he believes they may never recoup.[121] However, here as elsewhere tribute is but one of many causes for concern and the author's main message is that his people must mend their ways. We have seen that in the Eynsham charter Æthelred expresses his commitment to good works and rooting out sin, and the author of *De tribulationibus* clearly felt similarly; only a return to pious ways could save the English.

There are, in fact, many indications that the royal programme of reform and renewal introduced in 993 was maintained in the years following the 'palace revolution'. In the charter confirming a portion of the lands originally given to St Albans in order to help raise tribute, Æthelred underlines his pious motives for doing so. This may seem like special pleading, since the king took back the lion's share of these estates at this point. However,

---

[118] *II Atr* 7.2 (ed. Liebermann, I, 224).

[119] Ælfric, *Supplementary Homilies* XIII.67–71 (ed. Pope, 500). Cf. *Homilies of Ælfric*, ed. Pope, 508.

[120] *Sermo Lupi ad Anglos*, ed. D. Whitelock, 3rd edn (London, 1963), 35, n. 2; Keynes, 'An Abbot', 172–7.

[121] *De tribulationibus*, ed. and trans. Keynes, 'An Abbot', 174–5.

these lands (or most thereof) had been intended as a surety or pledge, as we have seen, which was now being redeemed (in exchange for an appropriate payment, it should be noted); a degree of generosity was thus still involved.[122] This is not the only privilege the monks of St Albans received in these years: they were also the recipients (for a price) of the forfeited estates of Ealdorman Leofsige, who fell from grace in 1002 and whose lands were confirmed in their possession in 1007.[123] Both this and the preceding diploma are framed as restitutions of lands once granted to the centre by Offa of Mercia (757–96) and in issuing these documents Æthelred was acknowledging the traditional (and doubtless largely legendary) claims of the monks. In fact, the second of these diplomas states that the king was acting 'so that I might restore to God what is God's' (*ut Deo quae Dei erant restituerem*), an allusion to the oft-quoted biblical dictum that the faithful are to render to Caesar the things that are Caesar's and to God those that are God's (Mark XII.17, Matthew XX.21, Luke XX.25) – his pious intentions are hard to miss. St Albans itself had been reformed by Ælfric, the later bishop of Ramsbury (990–5) and archbishop of Canterbury (995–1005, probably in plurality with Ramsbury), and thus belonged to the same circles the king had favoured since 993.[124] The centre clearly benefited from these and other transactions and Matthew Paris, writing in the mid-thirteenth century, was to speak of Æthelred as a particularly generous benefactor.[125] Other monastic houses also enjoyed royal favour in these years: Æthelwold's foundation at Ely was also involved in buying lands from the king, as we have seen; Wulgeat, abbot of Wulfric Spot's foundation at Burton, exchanged lands with the monarch in 1008; and Athelney received a small grant of land at Hamp in Somerset in 1009.[126] In all of these documents Æthelred emphasizes his pious intentions and, though such statements may come across as rather clichéd, there can be little doubt as to the king's sincerity. Indeed, in the last of these documents, in favour

---

[122] S 912 (*StAlb* 11). See *Charters of St Albans*, ed. Crick, 186–7.

[123] S 916 (*StAlb* 12).

[124] *Charters of St Albans*, ed. Crick, 18, 20–2 and 186–7.

[125] Matthew Paris, *Chronica majora: additamenta*, ed. H.R. Luard, Rolls Series (London, 1882), 387.

[126] S 919 (KCD 725), S 920 (*Burt* 31), S 921 (KCD 1306).

of Alfred the Great's foundation at Athelney, Æthelred states that the grant has been made so that the monks might intercede with frequent prayers 'for our frailty' (*pro nostra fragilitate*), a poignant expression of piety in an hour of particular need; it does not take much of a leap of faith to conclude that Æthelred himself was feeling decidedly frail at this point.[127] Thus, despite – or indeed perhaps because of – the strains on royal finances, the king continued to support religious houses where and when he could.

However, the clearest sign of Æthelred's reforming zeal at this point comes not from his diplomas, but from the decrees enacted at Enham in 1008. These are the first of a series of ordinances whose composition Æthelred and his successor Cnut entrusted to Wulfstan of York. We have already had occasion to note Wulfstan's role behind the scenes at a number of points, but this is when he finally steps out from behind the shadows. Charging the archbishop with drafting ordinances in the king's name was a remarkable sign of trust; it may also reflect the mood at court. Wulfstan had made a name for himself in the 990s and early 1000s by preaching the apocalypse and, though he started to show a greater interest in pastoral themes following his promotion to York (1002), the archbishop remained firmly convinced of the proximity of the end.[128] In the years immediately preceding 1008 he had turned his hand to themes of law and order, writing the so-called *Laws of Edward and Guthrum*. These claim to represent the terms on which the English and Danes had established peace in the early tenth century, but in reality offer a conspectus of Wulfstan's views on local law and custom. Around the same time he also wrote the *Canons of Edgar*, a compendium of ecclesiastical regulations purportedly issued under Edgar's oversight, but clearly composed by Wulfstan and designed to complement *Edward and Guthrum*.[129] Both of these texts are strictly speaking 'forgeries', though it is unclear whether the archbishop ever expected them to be taken

---

[127] S 921 (KCD 1306).

[128] Lionarons, *Homiletic Writings*. See also M.McC. Gatch, *Preaching and Theology in Anglo-Saxon England: Ælfric and Wulfstan* (Toronto, 1977), 18–22 and 105–28.

[129] *EGu* (ed. Liebermann, I, 128–35); *Canons of Edgar* (ed. Whitelock, *Councils*, no. 48, 313–38); with K. Jost, 'Einige Wulfstantexte und ihre Quellen', *Anglia* 56 (1932), 265–315, at 288–301; and D. Whitelock, 'Wulfstan and the So-Called Laws of Edward and Guthrum' (1941), repr. in and cited from her *History, Law and Literature in 10th–11th Century England* (London, 1981), no. IX.

seriously as statements of traditional law and custom; rather, they represent his first efforts to address pressing issues of social order: clearly, Wulfstan felt that all was not well in England and was starting to formulate his own responses. In entrusting law-making to the archbishop, Æthelred was thus choosing an eloquent and outspoken critic of contemporary society; we should do well to presume that he shared the prelate's fears. Indeed, as the English gathered at Enham at Pentecost 1008, it must have been clear that there was much to be done. Though the 'great fleet' had not shown any signs of reappearing, the English can have been under no illusion as to the severity of their situation: money had bought time, but the vikings would be back sooner or later. It is for this reason that Æthelred and his counsellors ordained the building of ships and provision of wargear, as noted in the *Chronicle* (decisions probably made at this gathering); it is for this reason too that the king had persevered in his support of reform in all its guises. Both of these strategies find expression in the Enham decrees, which combine administrative and military undertakings with moral exhortation. The ordinances survive in three distinct (but related) forms: the vernacular text known as *V Æthelred*, dated to 1008; a Latin version, known as *VI Æthelred* (Lat) or the *Relatio*, which provides greater detail on the context of the code's production and seems to represent a later stage in the text's evolution; and *VI Æthelred*, a second Old English version which is close to the Latin *Relatio*, but includes some unique material.[130] Only the *Relatio* states that Wulfstan composed the decrees, but there is no reason to doubt the assertion: all three versions survive in manuscripts associated with the archbishop – and in the latter two cases were subject to his annotations – and all also show signs of his characteristic prose style.[131] There has been much discussion of the precise relationship between these texts, but all indications are that *V Æthelred* should take priority: the other versions draw on this text

---

[130] *V Atr* (ed. Liebermann, I, 236–47; ed. Whitelock, *Councils*, no. 49.i, 344–62), *VI Atr* (Lat) (ed. Liebermann, I, 247–59; ed. Whitelock, *Councils*, no. 49.ii, 362–73); *VI Atr* (ed. Liebermann, I, 246–58) (Liebermann's edition offers the Latin and Old English of *VI Atr* on facing pages).

[131] P. Wormald, 'Æthelred the Lawmaker', in *Ethelred the Unready*, ed. D.[H.] Hill (London, 1978), 47–80, at 49–52. Cf. N.R. Ker, 'The Handwriting of Archbishop Wulfstan', in *England Before the Conquest: Studies in Primary Sources Presented to Dorothy Whitelock*, ed. P. Clemoes and K. Hughes (Cambridge, 1971), 315–31.

and it stands to reason that it most closely represents the ordinances originally agreed upon at Enham.[132] Nevertheless, the many variations between
these texts serve as a reminder that royal decrees were flexible instruments,
and it would be misleading to imagine that there was ever meant to be a
single, authorized text of the enactments; though later versions show signs
of revision and adjustment, they were in a sense just as 'authentic' as the
earlier ones.[133] Despite this flexibility, it would be dangerous to treat any of
these texts simply as products of Wulfstan's imagination (as some have been
inclined to do): they are framed as royal ordinances and if the archbishop
exerted an unusually strong influence on their formulation, this is presumably because Æthelred wished it so.[134]

More important than the specific relationship between these texts is the
general impression they make. They lay out a broad programme of reform,
starting by enjoining that 'all love and honour one God, and zealously
observe one faith' (*ealle ænne God lufian 7 wurðian 7 ænne Cristendom
georne healdan*: prologue 1) – one of Wulfstan's favoured turns of phrase
– and that 'justice be promoted and any injustice zealously suppressed'
(*rihte lage up arære 7 ælce unlage georne afille*: prologue 1.1). Here we see
the kinds of ideas previously expressed in diplomas starting to find their
way into royal decrees: the aim is to reform church and society. In keeping
with this, many of the ordinances reveal a decidedly ecclesiastical outlook:
men of all estates, but especially 'servants of God' (*Godes þeowas*), are to
fulfil their duties (chapter 5), all monks are to remain in their monasteries
and keep their vows (chapter 6), ordained clerics are to maintain celibacy
(chapters 7, 9) and all Christian men are enjoined to avoid illicit unions
and observe church laws (chapter 10). Further decrees address the payment
of church dues (chapters 11–12), the observance of the Sabbath and
church feasts, including Edward the Martyr's (chapters 13–17, 19), and

---

[132] K. Jost, *Wulfstanstudien*, Schweizer anglistische Arbeiten 23 (Bern, 1950), 35–43;
K. Sisam, 'The Relationship of Æthelred's Codes V and VI', in his *Studies in the History of
Old English Literature* (Oxford, 1953), 278–87; Wormald, 'Æthelred the Lawmaker', 50–8;
Keynes, 'An Abbot', 177–8.

[133] Stafford, 'Royal Government', 215–70. Cf. Roach, 'Law-Codes'.

[134] Cf. M.K. Lawson, 'Archbishop Wulfstan and the Homiletic Element in the Laws of
Æthelred II and Cnut', *EHR* 107 (1992), 565–86, esp. 572–9. For a more judicious
assessment, see Hudson, *Oxford History*, 19.

the necessity of penance for 'every Christian' (*æghwilc Cristen man*) (chapter 22).[135] There are, however, also ordinances of a more secular nature: Christians are not to be sold (into slavery) in foreign lands, especially to pagans (chapter 2); men are not to be condemned to death for trivial offences (chapter 3); widows are to lead respectable lives and enjoy royal protection (chapter 21); injustices and crimes of various natures are to be avoided (chapters 24–5); those who oppose the law shall pay their wergild or a fine (chapter 31); and arrangements for the transferring of property are to be regularized (chapter 32). As these lists show, the distinction between 'secular' and 'ecclesiastical' matters is often a fine one: the primary concern is for the ordering of Christian society. Here Wulfstan's legislation builds on the ideals set out by the reformers of Edgar's day: society is understood in Christian terms, with the very distinction between 'secular' and 'ecclesiastical' blurring.[136] As elsewhere, there is a distinctly homiletic element to the archbishop's laws: some clauses are legal injunctions, but others are largely rhetorical commands to the effect that 'all love one God' (*ealle ænne God lufian*: prologue) or 'every injustice is to be zealously cast out' (*æghwilc unriht awurpe man georne*: chapter 23). Cumulatively, the message is clear enough: divine favour is to be courted in all manners imaginable. What is new is the scope of these ordinances: whereas previously the focus had been on the king and court – Æthelred sought to amend his youthful indiscretions, then to support individual religious centres within his realm – now piety and reform are being enjoined upon the nation at large. There has thus been a subtle but unmistakable shift of focus, one already heralded by the more general terms in which the Eynsham charter is couched: now all the English are to do 'good works'. That this shift should coincide with a change in medium is only appropriate: whereas Æthelred's earlier acts of repentance and reform had been communicated primarily through diplomas, documents best suited to

---

[135] It has been suggested that the mention of Edward's feast day is a later interpolation, since it is not found in either *VI Atr* or the Latin *Relatio*. However, Edward's cult was well established by this point, so there is no reason to doubt that the reference is original. See Keynes, 'An Abbot', 178–9; and cf. Wormald, 'Æthelred the Lawmaker', 53–4, and *Making of English Law*, 343–4; and Williams, *Æthelred*, 15.

[136] P. Wormald, 'Archbishop Wulfstan: Eleventh-Century State Builder', in *Wulfstan, Archbishop of York*, ed. M. Townend (Turnhout, 2004), 9–27.

communicating with specific individuals and groups (above all individual religious houses), henceforth it was royal ordinances that would be preferred – the entire nation was being called to action.[137]

Reforming in tone though the Enham decrees are, they also touch on a number of more pragmatic matters of defence and administration. One of the more famous clauses declares that military service (*fyrdunga*) and the repairing of fortresses and bridges (*burhbot* and *bricbot*) – traditional public duties, it should be noted – are to be attended to diligently throughout the realm (chapter 26.1).[138] This is followed by further clauses on military matters: ships are to be fitted out so that they might be ready soon after Easter every year (chapter 27) and anyone who deserts an army led by the king is to forfeit his life or wergild, while those abandoning any other army are to pay a fine of 120 shillings (chapter 28). These clauses clearly relate to the efforts mentioned in the *Chronicle* under this year. However, the emphasis is different: while the chronicler focuses on what seem to have been a set of new royal demands (for ships, helms and armour), the Enham ordinances enjoin the correct fulfil- ment of existing duties. Indeed, the reference to repairing ships suggests that this was (or was meant to become) an annual affair. Perhaps most interesting are the injunctions regarding desertion, which imply that morale was starting to flag; evidently loyalty could no longer be presumed. The main *Chronicle*- account records many examples of treacherous behaviour and, while some of these are probably exaggerated for dramatic effect, there may be a kernel of truth to the tales, at least where Æthelred's later years are concerned (indeed, it has been suggested that the author transposes the problems of this period on to earlier parts of Æthelred's reign).[139]

While it is difficult to know the extent to which these ordinances were followed, they reveal something of the resolve at Æthelred's court. There are other indications that the kingdom's defences were strengthened around this

---

[137] Roach, 'Tale of Two Charters'.

[138] Although bridgework is only mentioned in one of the surviving witnesses to *V Atr*, there is reason to believe that it is original: Wormald, 'Æthelred the Lawmaker', 50 (and cf. *ibid.*, 52–3). See further N. Brooks, 'The Development of Military Obligations in Eighth- and Ninth-Century England' (1971), repr. in and cited from his *Communities and Warfare, 700–1400* (London, 2000), 32–47.

[139] Keynes, *Diplomas*, 204–6; R. Abels, 'Cowardice and Duty in Anglo-Saxon England', *Journal of Medieval Military History* 6 (2006), 29–48, at 47–8.

time. A number of fortified sites came into use as minting centres and their defences may have been refurbished as part of this process (we have evidence for this at South Cadbury: see Plate 12).[140] On this basis it has been suggested that secondary fortification with stone revetments at various 'burghal' sites, such as Cricklade, Hereford, Lydford, Wallingford and Wareham, also took place in these years.[141] Similar evidence can be found beyond the classic 'burghal' centres: the defences on top of Silbury Hill (Wilts.) can be associated with Æthelred's later years on the basis of a *Last Small Cross* (*c.* 1009–17) cut farthing found there, and it may be that nearby Avebury underwent a degree of replanning in these years;[142] the second phase of fortification at Daws Castle (Som.) has been dated to Æthelred's reign (perhaps the 990s, though conceivably the 1000s);[143] Oldaport (south Devon) has produced evidence of refortification in the later Anglo-Saxon period (873 × 1020), which has been plausibly associated with Æthelred's efforts;[144] there are indications that the defences at Dover and the nearby coast were reorganized around this time, a process which involved establishing look-outs and beacons at sites such as St-Mary-in-Castro and using existing settlements such as Hythe, Romney and Sandwich (a favoured viking landing-place);[145] the second phase of pre-Norman fortification at Carisbrooke Castle, located on a strategic hill-top on the Isle of Wight (another favoured Scandinavian base), can probably also be placed in these years;[146] and finally, it was in the late tenth or early eleventh century that fortified bridges of the continental type

---

[140] D.[H.] Hill, 'Trends in the Development of Towns in the Reign of Ethelred II', in *Ethelred the Unready*, ed. D.[H.] Hill (London, 1978), 213–26; L. Alcock, *Cadbury Castle: The Early Medieval Archaeology* (Cardiff, 1995), 165–9.

[141] Baker and Brookes, *Beyond the Burghal Hidage*, 80–3 and 85. However, see J. Haslam, 'Daws Castle, Somerset, and Civil Defence Measures in Southern and Midland England in the Ninth to Eleventh Centuries', *Archaeological Journal* 168 (2011), 195–227, at 210–17, for caveats.

[142] R.J.C. Atkinson, 'Silbury Hill, 1969–70', *Antiquity* 44 (1970), 313–14; J. Pollard and A. Reynolds, *Avebury: The Biography of a Landscape* (Stroud, 2002), 226–7.

[143] Haslam, 'Daws Castle', 204–6.

[144] P. Rainbird and D. Druce, 'A Late Saxon Date from Oldaport', *Proceedings of the Devon Archaeological Society* 62 (2004), 177–80. See also Gore, *Vikings*, 64–5.

[145] Baker and Brookes, *Beyond the Burghal Hidage*, 355–8.

[146] *Ibid.*, 398–9.

were built at London and Bristol.[147] While we cannot be sure precisely when most of these locations were (re)fortified and reorganized, they provide a tangible sense of the efforts undertaken; far from being a period of terminal decline for Alfredian (and post-Alfredian) fortified sites, the reign of Æthelred saw a renewed interest in civil defence, one which went well beyond (though certainly also included) the old 'burghal' network. It may be that this was a case of 'too little, too late', as some have suggested, but archaeological dating is not a precise science and it may be that much of this work had begun in the 990s or even earlier. Indeed, the unusually expressive form in which the 'three common burdens' (bridgework, fortress-work and military service) are stipulated in two diplomas of Æthelred's early years suggests that these were already a matter of interest in the late 980s.[148]

It is above all the stalwart determination of Æthelred and his counsellors to do whatever is necessary for the well-being of the kingdom which emerges from the Enham decrees. If Karl Jost is correct, then the short text known as Napier 51 may take us to the very heart of the deliberations. A hortatory speech, written in Wulfstan's distinctive style, it may have been delivered by the archbishop to the king and his assembled counsellors at Enham. The text opens by enjoining the archbishop's listeners to remain steadfast in their faith 'so that the security of all the people will be greater than it is at present' (*þæt ealles folces frið wyrðe betere, þonne hit git sig*). What follows is a number of instructions, many of which find close parallels in the Enham decrees: all are to love God and reject other deities; justice is to be promoted and injustice abolished; murderers, traitors and 'those that abandon their lord at his hour of greatest need' (*þa, þa heora forlætað, þær him mæst neod byð*) are to be hated by God, as are perjurers and oath-breakers; penance is to be performed diligently by all; and sanctuary is not to be violated. Finally, the archbishop invokes divine mercy on

---

[147] B. Watson, T. Brigham and T. Dyson, *London Bridge: 2000 Years of a River Crossing* (London, 2001), 53–7; R.H. Leech, 'Arthur's Acre: A Saxon Bridgehead at Bristol', *Trans. of the Bristol and Gloucestershire Archaeological Soc.* 127 (2009), 11–20, at 16–17. Cf. S. Coupland, 'The Fortified Bridges of Charles the Bald', *Journal of Medieval History* 17 (1991), 1–12.

[148] S 869 (*WinchNM* 30) (from 988), S 874 (KCD 673) (from 990); with Keynes, *Diplomas*, 93–4.

his people.[149] What emerges is a mix of hope and concern: hope that the present situation might be righted, but concern lest it not be. Moreover, here as in the Enham ordinances secular and ecclesiastical concerns are closely related – the entire social order depends upon the English following the laws of God and man. This association is especially clear in Wulfstan's treatment of traitors: by breaking their oaths of loyalty, these men have contravened both divine and human law and are rightly hated by God.

This is all stirring stuff, but the question arises as to whether we are simply hearing Wulfstan's voice. Indeed, since first identified as products of the archbishop in the first half of the twentieth century, it has been common to view the Enham decrees through the lens of Wulfstan's other writings, treating them as an expression of the archbishop's own thoughts and concerns. This is perfectly natural, but there is a danger of forgetting that they were issued in Æthelred's name and proceed from discussions with the king and his other leading advisers. In fact, many of the ideas expressed find close parallels in earlier documents: to present current ills as the wages of sin and to prescribe piety, penitence and reform in response was nothing new, and Wulfstan must have known it. The real change is not of substance but of tone – whereas Æthelred's earlier diplomas declare and declaim, Wulfstan's decrees exhort and exclaim. In part this reflects the prelate's own stylistic preferences: as an experienced preacher, he naturally slipped into hortative mode. It may also reflect growing concern at court: matters had gone from bad to worse in recent years, and if Æthelred chose a man known for his vocal criticism of contemporary society to compose his decrees, it is presumably because this was the tone he wanted to strike. The strains of the viking attacks were thus starting to reach critical levels and Æthelred's response was to redouble existing efforts to build a Christian society. The overarching aim remained a return to the 'Golden Age' of reform. The choice of site is particularly poignant in this regard. As M.K. Lawson notes, Enham (*Eanham*) literally means the 'the place where lambs are bred' and it may be that this location was chosen with the symbolism of the Lamb of God in

---

[149] *Wulfstan. Sammlung der ihm zugeschriebenen Homilien nebst Untersuchungen über ihre Echtheit*, I, *Text und Varianten*, ed. A.S. Napier (Berlin, 1883), no. 51, 274–5; with Jost, *Wulfstanstudien*, 104–9. See also Wormald, *Making of English Law*, 337, n. 344; and A. Rabin, *The Political Writings of Archbishop Wulfstan* (Manchester, 2015), 14 and 127.

mind, the biblical figure who was to take away the sins of the world.[150] More to the point, Enham lies only two and a half miles north of Andover, where Edgar had issued an important set of decrees on the payment of church dues and the celebration of religious festivals, whose stipulations provide the immediate model for a number of the Enham ordinances; Æthelred was quite literally following in the footsteps of his father.[151]

Crime and punishment

A further sign of strain in these years has sometimes been identified in the high number of recorded cases of litigation, which have been seen as amounting to a veritable crime wave. However, as Patrick Wormald observed, close inspection reveals this to be something of a chimera: forfeiture for crime was common throughout the tenth century and Æthelred's reign saw no notable rise in this regard (at least in statistical terms).[152] Indeed, what is new is not so much the cases themselves as the detail in which they are recorded. As Sir Frank Stenton first noted, there is an 'air of retrospection' in Æthelred's diplomas, which often record individual estate histories (including prior cases of litigation) in greater detail than had hitherto been customary; our records thus become more expressive. Simon Keynes has therefore argued that the 'crime wave' of these years was more apparent than real, a product of richer sources rather than rising lawlessness.[153]

Certainly, it would be dangerous to associate these records with a crisis in law and order. The tendency for charter draftsmen to provide greater narrative detail regarding estate histories is visible in Æthelred's earliest years and thus pre-dates what might be considered the true 'crisis years' of

---

[150] Lawson, 'Archbishop Wulfstan', 575–6.

[151] *V Atr* 11.1, 12.3, 17 (ed. Liebermann, I, 240–1). Cf. *II Eg* 2.3, 3, 5 (ed. Liebermann, I, 196–200). Note also the possible verbal parallel at *V Atr* 15 (ed. Liebermann, I, 240–1), 'swa swa þe heoldon þa ðe betst heoldon'; and *II Eg* 5.3 (ed. Liebermann I, 200), 'swa swa hit betst stod'.

[152] P. Wormald, 'A Handlist of Anglo-Saxon Lawsuits' (1986), repr. in and cited from his *Legal Culture in the Early Medieval West: Law as Text, Image and Experience* (London, 1999), 253–87, esp. 286.

[153] Stenton, *Latin Charters*, 74–82; Keynes, *Diplomas*, 200–2. See also Stafford, 'Royal Government', 62–70; and Keynes, 'Crime and Punishment', 76–7.

his reign: it is best seen as a symptom of growing literate mentalities, not of sudden and widespread criminality. Indeed, the most infamous case of this period, the so-called 'Crimes of Wulfbald', took place in the mid- to later 980s and many others are found dotted through the early to mid-990s. Another factor may have been the disruptions to ecclesiastical landholding in the later 970s and 980s, which seem to have made churchmen more circumspect about the legal basis of their propertied rights. In any case, a careful reading of these accounts reveals Æthelred's reign to have been anything but lawless. The 'Crimes of Wulfbald' are a case in point. Preserved in a diploma of 996 in which Æthelred grants his mother lands in Kent in exchange for Cholsey, the Old English account of Wulfbald's activities runs roughly as follows. After the death of his father, Wulfbald took the lands and goods of his stepmother by force and when commanded by the king to return these, he refused and his wergild was assigned to the king (in other words, he was ordered to pay a fine of 1,200 shillings). A second royal command to cease and desist met with no greater success and Wulfbald's wergild was assigned to the king once more. This only provoked Wulfbald, who then overran the land of another kinsman, Byrhtmær. There followed a third and a fourth command to vacate these lands, which – predictably – fell on deaf ears. A 'great meeting' (*micel gemote*) of the king and his counsellors at London then proceeded to assign Wulfbald's possessions as well as the offender's life to Æthelred. The king apparently took mercy, though, since we are informed that Wulfbald died some time later unrepentant. After this his widow took up where her husband left off, occupying an estate which had belonged to Wulfbald and killing its present occupant, Eadmær, who was a king's thegn (and also Wulfbald's cousin). This second case was then considered at a 'great synod' (*miclan sinoþ*) – perhaps another royal assembly, though the king is not listed amongst the witnesses – in London *c.* 990 and the estates in question were assigned to the king once more, apparently successfully this time.[154] At a glance, it is easy to understand why an earlier generation of scholars was inclined to see signs of 'extraordinary feebleness' in this document;

[154] S 877 (*WinchNM* 31). See R. Abels, '"The Crimes by which Wulfbald Ruined Himself with His Lord": The Limits of State Action in Late Anglo-Saxon England', *Reading Medieval Studies* 40 (2014), 42–53.

Æthelred and his court seem to have been almost powerless to bring Wulfbald and his widow to justice.[155] Nevertheless, it is important to bear in mind the constraints under which Æthelred was operating: in an era before standing armies, police forces and other means of coercion, ruler-ship depended heavily upon the consent of the kingdom's great and good.[156] Rulers were always vulnerable to opposition from within the aristocracy and earlier English kings had complained repeatedly about how powerful and well-connected individuals were wont to evade justice (*plus ça change*, one might think).[157] Thus, if Wulfbald was apparently impervious to royal demands, he was not alone. In any case, there are numerous signs that Æthelred's control over justice was not as weak as has often been presumed. The fact that the case was brought to the king on numerous occasions suggests that he kept abreast of criminal activity and possessed both the means and inclination to relay messages back and forth to the local shire court (where Wulfbald's wergild was repeatedly assigned to him). What is more, it is not certain that Æthelred's demands were ignored. It has been suggested that Wulfbald actually paid his wergild on each of these occasions in a bid to maintain his hold on the estate; though this is not perhaps the most natural reading of the account, it raises the possibility that we are actually witnessing royal government at its most assertive.[158] Furthermore, though initial efforts to evict Wulfbald failed, Æthelred ulti-mately succeeded in bringing him to justice at a royal assembly, at which the felon was dispossessed of his lands (as was his wife at a later 'synod'). Janet Nelson is therefore right to note that by tenth-century standards this case was actually something of a success; despite difficulties, royal justice ultimately prevailed.[159]

---

[155] The phrase is that of Whitelock, *EHD*, 47.

[156] S. Reynolds, *Kingdoms and Communities in Western Europe 900–1300*, 2nd edn (Oxford, 1997), is now the classic statement. See also B. Schneidmüller, 'Rule by Consensus: Forms and Concepts of Political Order in the European Middle Ages', *Medieval History Journal* 16 (2013), 449–71.

[157] *III As* 6 (Liebermann, I, 170), *IV As* 3 (Liebermann, I, 171), *VI As* 8.2 (Liebermann, I, 178).

[158] *Charters of the New Minster*, ed. Miller, 151–2. Cf. Abels, 'Limits', 49.

[159] J.L. Nelson, 'Rulers and Government', in *The New Cambridge Medieval History*, III, *c. 900–1024*, ed. T. Reuter (Cambridge, 1999), 95–129, at 123.

If we look to the types of crimes mentioned in other records of forfeiture, it is striking how similar these are to those of previous years: theft looms large,[160] as do fighting and killing (sometimes in conjunction with theft),[161] and there is at least one case of sheltering a fugitive.[162] This is not, however, to say that no new developments can be seen. In particular, Æthelred's reign witnesses some of the first recorded cases of forfeiture for sexual offences, reflecting the growing importance of church regulations on matrimony.[163] More noteworthy, perhaps, is the growing number of cases of treachery: in the previous century we have only one of these, while three are recorded for Æthelred's reign. That such offences should be more common in periods of foreign invasion speaks for itself and it is striking that the one earlier case comes from Alfred's reign, when similar threats were encountered.[164] It is probably also no accident that these cases cluster around Æthelred's later years: the first is from the early to mid-990s, while the other two are from his last half-decade on the throne.[165] These thus represent something new and it is against this backdrop that the Enham ordinances regarding treachery and flight from battle should be understood. Some of the other cases of criminality may be related indirectly to the strains of having to defend the realm, but it would be dangerous to presume too strong a connection; as we have noted, lawlessness itself was nothing new. Likewise, though it has been suggested that the non-payment of tax and tribute frequently led to forfeiture, there is little evidence of this from these years (which is not, of course, to say that this did not happen).[166]

A perusal of the dispute records of these years also reveals how active hundred and shire courts were and how well connected these were with

[160] S 877 (*WinchNM* 31), S 886 (*Abing* 126), S 893 (*Roch* 32), S 927 (*Abing* 136).

[161] S 892 (ed. A.S. Napier and W.H. Stevenson, *The Crawford Collection of Early Chapters and Documents* [Oxford, 1895], no. 8), S 893 (*Roch* 32), S 916 (*StAlb* 12).

[162] S 926 (*Roch* 33).

[163] S 901 (*Abing* 132) (forfeiture for adultery), S 927 (*Abing* 136) (Leofric's crimes included adultery). Cf. S 911 (KCD 714) (forfeiture of the *matrona* Leoftæt 'on account of her improper behaviour').

[164] S 362 (BCS 595). See Pratt, *Political Thought*, 33–4, 235–6 and 239.

[165] S 939 (*CantCC* 137), S 927 (*Abing* 136), S 934 (*Abing* 137).

[166] Lawson, 'Collection', 723–6 (who is aware of the limitations of his evidence, especially where Æthelred's reign is concerned). Cf. *ibid.*, 732–4.

the royal court. Indeed, though our sources may at times exaggerate the formality of legal proceedings, there is no mistaking the drift towards greater judicial formality. As we have seen, it is only from the reign of Edgar that we begin to see the workings of local shire and hundred courts in any detail and the evidence becomes much richer here as we move into Æthelred's reign. This is not the only sign of administrative developments: it is also in Æthelred's reign that many shires are first attested and that shire reeves start to make a real impression on the written record.[167] That new kinds of offences, such as adultery, start finding their way into the dispute record points in the same direction: as the judicial system became more centralized and institutionalized, kings and their agents were in a position to bring a wider range of regulations to bear more effectively. One should not, of course, exaggerate the efficacy of the resulting arrangements; as the case of Wulfbald illustrates, there remained much room for manoeuvre. Still, far from being a period of decline or stagnation, Æthelred's reign seems to mark a decisive moment in the development of what James Campbell has termed the 'late Anglo-Saxon state'; it was a time in which royal control over justice and administration was strengthened and developed.[168]

It has become almost axiomatic that later Anglo-Saxon England was governed more intensively than its continental counterparts, and the evidence of dispute records can here be placed alongside other indications that despite – or indeed perhaps on account of – the viking onslaught royal authority remained vital throughout Æthelred's reign: shires and shire reeves make prominent appearances; recoinages become a regular feature of the monetary system; tribute and tax were raised on an unprecedented scale; fortifications were strengthened and renovated, ships built and arms and armour produced; and the king was able to appoint and dismiss senior officers seemingly at will (as in 1005–6 and 1015). However, while there can be little doubt that England was ruled more intensively than all but its most centralized

---

[167] Williams, *Æthelred*, 64–6; Molyneaux, *Formation*, 157–72 and 179–82. Cf. C.S. Taylor, 'The Origin of the Mercian Shires', in *Gloucestershire Studies*, ed. H.P.R. Finberg (Leicester, 1957), 17–45.

[168] J. Campbell, 'The Late Anglo-Saxon State: A Maximum View' (1994), repr. in and cited from his *The Anglo-Saxon State* (London, 2000), 1–30. See also P. Wormald, 'Germanic Power Structures: The Early English Experience', in *Power and the Nation in European History*, ed. L. Scales and O. Zimmer (Cambridge, 2005), 105–24.

continental counterparts – generally duchies or principalities (such as Anjou or Bavaria), which were closer in size to southern England – there is a danger of exaggerating the differences. Royal authority never disappeared entirely in Capetian France, as recent studies have shown, while in Henry II's Germany (1002–24) it may have enjoyed something of a renaissance.[169] Moreover, none of the measures undertaken by Æthelred is unique to England: as we have seen, Henry I had resorted to fortress-building, rearmament and tribute-raising in the face of the Magyar threat and similar approaches had been taken against the vikings in West Francia half a century earlier. More to the point, many of the developments of these years – large-scale collection of tribute and taxation; growing reliance on shire reeves; harsh treatment of political opponents and suspected traitors – are best seen as emergency measures which only later became an established feature of royal rule. The coincidence that Edgar's initial moves towards institutionalization and centralization were followed by an extended 'crisis period' under Æthelred might thus be said to have given birth to the assertive brand of royal authority so evocatively described by James Campbell and Patrick Wormald; it was out of the crucible of these years that the 'late Anglo-Saxon state' emerged. Such developments were neither inevitable, nor were they welcomed by all of Æthelred's subjects; more invasive systems of rule tend to benefit those closest to central authority and to many these changes must have been unwelcome. Lantfred of Winchester, writing in the 970s or early 980s, already expressed hostility towards the local reeve at Calne (Wilts.) and such sentiments may have been shared by Ealdorman Leofsige, who, as we have seen, clashed repeatedly with Æthelred's reeves.[170] There were other implications of these developments. As George Molyneaux notes, greater demands also seem to have been made on the ruler in these years; as kingship became more intensive and invasive, expectations of the king grew commensurately.[171]

---

[169] F. Mazel, *Féodalités, 888–1180* (Paris, 2010), 17–97; S. Weinfurter, 'Die Zentralisierung der Herrschaftsgewalt im Reich durch Kaiser Heinrich II.' (1986), repr. in and cited from his *Gelebte Ordnung, gedachte Ordnung. Ausgewählte Beiträge zu König, Kirche und Reich* (Sigmaringen, 2005), 213–64.

[170] Lantfred of Winchester, *Translatio et miracula S. Swithuni*, ch. 25, ed. M. Lapidge, *The Cult of Saint Swithun* (Oxford, 2003), 308–10. On the dating, see Hudson, 'Æthelwold's Circle', 97, n. 40.

[171] Molyneaux, *Formation*, 216–30. Cf. Reuter, 'Ottonian Ruler Representation', 133.

However, while the evidence for an Æthelredian 'crime wave' has proven illusory, it should be borne in mind that personal safety is a matter of individual perception, not objective reality; as other evidence of English sinfulness mounted, figures such as Wulfstan would doubtless have been quick to fasten on to such ongoing problems as signs of growing lawlessness (and indeed godlessness). And if Wulfstan was troubled, we can be sure that Æthelred was too – after all, it was to combat such criminality that the king had charged the archbishop with law-making duties in these years.

Apocalypse and atonement

Though, as we have seen, a strong tradition associated the viking raids with sinfulness, this was only one element of contemporary understandings of these events. Another tradition, already alluded to at a number of points, held that they heralded the end of time. According to this line of thought, the viking ravages and other calamities of the 990s and 1000s signalled the proximity of the Last Judgement; rather than being signs of remediable errors, they presaged the end of the ages. This view is neatly exemplified by the writings of Wulfstan. We know little of Wulfstan's life before his elevation to the strategically important (if relatively poor) bishopric of London in 996, but it is likely that he received his education amongst reformed circles, perhaps in the fenlands (Peterborough is the most recent suggestion).[172] Already in his London years Wulfstan appears prominently amongst the witness-lists of royal diplomas, attesting at least one of Æthelred's restitutions of the 990s and appearing frequently in the latter years of the decade.[173] It is in this period that he seems to have begun preaching the apocalypse, which was to become a favourite theme. His first efforts are short, but full of rhetorical vim: he deplores the excesses of the age and urges his listeners to prepare themselves for the worst. Central to Wulfstan's understanding of developments is the figure of Antichrist,

---

[172] C. Cubitt, 'Personal Names, Identity and Family in Benedictine Reform England', in *Verwandschaft, Name und soziale Ordnung (300–1000)*, ed. S. Patzold and K. Ubl (Berlin, 2014), 223–42, at 230–7.

[173] A. Rabin, 'Wulfstan at London: Episcopal Politics in the Reign of Æthelred', *English Studies* 97 (2016), 186–206.

with whom he was acquainted through Adso's 'Letter on the Place and Time of Antichrist' (*Epistola de ortu et tempore Antichristi*), a work produced within the circles of monastic reform in West Francia (France) in the mid-tenth century. Yet whereas Adso had been primarily interested in the course of Antichrist's life, Wulfstan was more concerned with the moral implications of this figure; for him Antichrist is as much a symbolic embodiment of hypocrisy as a literal being. Indeed, though the prelate clearly saw the proximity of the end reflected in the events of his day, he rarely goes into detail, preferring to allude generally to how his people anger God more than they ought to and how deceit and false belief are rife. The closest he comes to mentioning the vikings in these early years is thus a passing remark about how 'foreigners and strangers greatly oppress us' (*ælþeodige men 7 utancumene swyðe us swencað*).[174] The reason why Wulfstan is not more interested in the details of these attacks – which clearly inform his outlook – is because to him they are but signs of a deeper problem: the growth of iniquity, which is itself an indication of the proximity of the end.

Wulfstan was certainly not alone. An anonymous figure translated Adso's letter on Antichrist at some point in Æthelred's reign and his adjustments to the original reveal similar concerns: he is less interested in the details of Antichrist's life than in the moral threat posed by this figure, whose advent he sees as imminent.[175] Other individuals were also interested in eschatology. Æthelweard, the son-in-law and later successor to Æthelmær in the south-west, owned a manuscript containing Bede's commentary on Revelation, which he later donated to a 'monastery of St Mary' in the region (perhaps Buckfast or Crediton).[176] Ælfric the homilist, who owed his position in no small part to Æthelmær's patronage, was himself acquainted with Adso's work and clearly also entertained the

---

[174] Wulfstan, *Secundum Lucam*, ll. 14–22 (ed. Bethurum, 123–4). See also *De temporibus Antichristi*, ll. 74–9 (ed. Bethurum, 132), and *Secundum Marcum* ll. 23–7 and 36–52 (ed. Bethurum, 135, 136–7).

[175] *Wulfstan*, ed. Napier, no. 42, 191–205; with R.K. Emerson, 'From *epistola* to *sermo*: The Old English Version of Adso's *Libellus de Antichristo*', *JEGP* 83 (1983), 1–10, esp. 5–10.

[176] R. Gameson, 'The Origin of the Exeter Book of Old English Poetry', *ASE* 25 (1996), 135–85, at 170–2.

possibility that the end of time was at hand. As mentioned, Ælfric had studied at Æthelwold's famed school at Winchester and at some point in the mid- to late 980s had joined the fledgling foundation of Æthelmær at Cerne in Dorset (*c.* 987). There Ælfric was placed in charge of the school and at the heart of his substantial literary output lies the need to provide proper instruction and ministry to laymen and religious alike. As with Wulfstan, however, there is a distinctly eschatological tone to this undertaking. In the preface to his First Series of Catholic Homilies (*c.* 990 × 992), Ælfric's first major work, he asserts that orthodox teaching must be made available 'because people need good teaching most urgently in this time, which is the ending of this world' (*for ðam þe menn behofiað godre lare swiðost on þisum timan þe is geendung þyssere worulde*).[177] At the end of this work he then comes back to the theme, riffing on Gregory the Great to the effect that some of the signs of the end of time have already been seen while others are impending.[178] In later writings Ælfric stepped back slightly from such speculation; perhaps like Augustine of Hippo (d. 430), who had witnessed the early stages of the fall of the Western Roman Empire, the calamities of Ælfric's day made him more circumspect in this regard.[179] However, if the homilist became more silent on the topic as the raids began to mount, he seems to have been alone in this respect: by the later 990s Wulfstan was preaching the apocalypse to his flock in London and such sentiments find many echoes elsewhere. Thus, the letter addressed to Bishop Wulfsige of Sherborne by his metropolitan, mentioned at a number of points already, contains a distinctly apocalyptic note, since its author (perhaps Archbishop Ælfric) gives thanks to God that he has been set up to govern the church 'in such dangerous and most difficult times' (*in tam periculosis et laboriosissimis temporibus*), an allusion to the 'dangerous

---

[177] Ælfric, *CH: FS*, prol.57–9 (ed. Clemoes, 174).

[178] Ælfric, *CH: FS* XXXIX.1–17 (ed. Clemoes, 520).

[179] M. Godden, 'The Millennium, Time, and History for the Anglo-Saxons', in *The Apocalyptic Year 1000*, ed. R. Landes, A. Gow and D.C. Van Meter (Oxford, 2003), 155–80, at 158–67. Cf. R.A. Markus, *Saeculum: History and Society in the Theology of St Augustine*, 2nd edn (Cambridge, 1989), 22–44.

times' which were to precede the Last Judgement (II Timothy III.1).[180] That Wulfsige's own pious endeavours were inspired by such concerns is further suggested by the charter issued on the occasion of the reform of Sherborne (998), which explains the necessity of this act by reference to the fact that 'we are those upon whom the ends of the world are come' (*nos sumus in quos fines seculorum deuenerunt*: I Corinthians X.11), another common apocalyptic trope, quoted twice by Ælfric.[181]

An examination of the other charters of these years reveals further evidence for such thoughts. Thus, a diploma forged at Rochester in the 990s includes an allusion to the 'dangerous times' (*tempora periculosa*) in which it was produced; though purportedly a donation of Edgar, this comment can probably be read as a response to developments at the time of its composition.[182] The preamble of a diploma in favour of Westminster Abbey in 998 likewise suggests an active interest in the signs of the end, asserting that 'we know that in the final times dissension grows, discord bubbles up, greed burns, friendship falters, the love of many grows cold and unheard-of evils transpire'.[183] Rather more noteworthy, perhaps, is the charter issued in favour of Shaftesbury in which the cult of Edward the Martyr is first mentioned (1001), whose preamble quotes Luke XXI.31 to the effect that 'when you shall see these things come to pass, know that the kingdom of God is at hand' (*cum uideritis hec fieri, scitote quia prope est regnum Dei*).[184] A document of the following year contains a proem which

---

[180] *Councils*, ed. Whitelock, no. 41, 227–9. See above Chapter 4, pp. 156–7, with n. 64. This allusion may have been inspired by Alcuin, whose letter to Eanbald provided the model for the rest of the epistle, since he frequently had recourse to the phrase elsewhere: W. Brandes, ' "Tempora periculosa sunt". Eschatologisches im Vorfeld der Kaiserkrönung Karls des Großen', in *Das Frankfurter Konzil von 794. Kristallisationspunkt karolingischer Kultur*, ed. R. Berndt, 2 vols. (Mainz, 1997), I, 49–79; M. Garrison, 'The Bible and Alcuin's Interpretation of Current Events', *Peritia* 16 (2002), 68–84.

[181] S 895 (*Sherb* 11). Cf. Ælfric, *CH: SS* XXIII.30 (ed. Godden, 214), and *Supplementary Homilies* XX.392–9 (ed. Pope, 658–9).

[182] S 671 (*Roch* 29). See Keynes, 'Church of Rochester', 334–6.

[183] S 894 (ed. B. Thorpe, *Diplomatarium Anglicum Ævi Saxonici* [London, 1865], 296–8): 'scimus namque ultimis temporibus simultates crebrescere, discordias ebullire, rapacitates inardescere, amicitiam titubare, caritatem refrigescere multorum, et inaudita mala evenire'. Although this document may have been forged on the basis of S 895, the phrase in question was not lifted from its exemplar thus seems to represent an authentic voice of the late 990s: *Charters of Sherborne*, ed. O'Donovan, xix and 42.

[184] S 899 (*Shaft* 29).

opens with a consideration of the Fall of Man, then closes with a quotation from Matthew IV.17 to the effect that mankind must now 'do penance, for the kingdom of heaven is at hand' *(poenitentiam agite, appropinquabit enim regnum coelorum)*, a citation employed two years later by the draftsman of a diploma in favour of Burton.[185] Hints of such thoughts can even be found in the St Frideswide's charter of 1004. As we have seen, this document invokes the tale of the cockles and the wheat to describe recent Scandinavian settlement in England, a parable which itself carried eschatological connotations – it is an allegory of the Day of Judgement, at which the evil will finally face justice, and was cited by both Bede and Ælfric in their discussions of the end times.[186] However, perhaps the most charged apocalyptic utterance is to be found in the Eynsham charter of 1005, whose lengthy preamble alludes to the 'dangerous times' *(tempora periculosa)* in which it is issued and cites the same passage from I Corinthians X.11 ('we are those upon whom the ends of the world are come') found in the Sherborne charter of 998.[187] It emerges from these documents that many at and around court harboured apocalyptic hopes and fears, and we should do well to presume that Æthelred did so too; while divine wrath might be a passing phenomenon, when sufficient signs and portents were present it was often tempting to read a greater cosmic significance into events. Such beliefs may, in turn, explain something of the fever pitch of politics in these years: the king was not only concerned for his nation's material well-being, but also for the fate of humankind.

It is, therefore, clear that many at court shared such thoughts. Though most of these documents were produced after the appointment of Wulfstan to London (996), it would be misleading to see them simply as a reflection of Wulfstanian influence: the letters and charters in question were produced by many different figures, indicating that such beliefs

---

[185] S 904 (KCD 707), S 906 (*Burt* 28). This quotation is found in Bede, *Expositio Apocalypseos*, ch. 8, ed. R. Gryson, CCSL 121A (Turnhout, 2001), 309; and Wulfstan, *Her gongynð be Cristendome*, ll. 115–17 (ed. Bethurum, 206). (As Lionarons, *Homiletic Writings*, 101, notes, Wulfstan inserted an exhortation to receive absolution from a bishop at this point in one of his manuscripts of this work.)

[186] Bede, *Expositio Apocalypseos*, ch. 4 (ed. Gryson, 269–71); Ælfric, *CH: FS* XXXV.122–32 (ed. Clemoes, 480), with Godden, *Ælfric's Catholic Homilies: Introduction*, 289–98.

[187] S 911 (KCD 714). See further above, pp. 204–5.

were widely held. It hardly comes as a surprise that the events of this period should have occasioned such sentiments. In the Middle Ages natural disasters and other misfortunes were frequently interpreted as signs of the end of time (or its proximity) and thus, for example, the Mongol onslaught of the mid-thirteenth century and the Black Death of the mid-fourteenth both provoked similar speculation.[188] More immediate parallels to English experience at this point are offered by the reaction of a group of Lotharingians to the Magyar attacks of the mid-tenth century: they concluded that these invaders were Gog and Magog, the medieval 'horsemen of the apocalypse', whose ravages were said to usher in the reign of Antichrist.[189] What role the turning of the millennium played within this context has been a subject of much controversy, particularly amongst continental scholars.[190] Though we can only scratch the surface of the subject here, the evidence from England suggests that neither extreme can be sustained: clearly, some people were anxious about the turning of this year, but such fears do not seem to have been especially widespread, nor can all eschatological disquiet at this point be attributed to the 'apocalyptic year 1000'. Ælfric was famously cautious when it came to predicting the precise moment of the end, yet was willing to state towards the close of his homily 'On the Prayer of Moses' that 'this time is near to the last times (*is ende-next*) and is the ending of this world, and people will be made unjust amongst themselves, so that father contends against his own son and brother against another to their own destruction'.[191]

---

[188] P. Jackson, 'Medieval Christendom's Encounter with the Alien', *Historical Research* 74 (2001), 347–69; R.E. Lerner, 'The Black Death and Western European Eschatological Mentalities', *American Historical Review* 86 (1981), 533–52.

[189] *Epistola de Hungariis*, ed. R.B.C. Huygens, *Serta mediaevalia. Textus varii saeculorum X–XIII in unum collecti*, CCCM 171A (Turnhout, 2000), 46–55; with J. Fried, 'Endzeiterwartung um die Jahrtausendwende', *DA* 45 (1989), 381–473, at 384–7.

[190] See, e.g., S. Gouguenheim, *Les fausses terreurs de l'an mil. Attente de la fin des temps ou approfondissement de la foi?* (Paris, 1999); R. Landes, 'The Fear of an Apocalyptic Year 1000: Augustinian Historiography, Medieval and Modern', *Speculum* 75 (2000), 97–145; J. Fried, 'Die Endzeit fest im Griff des Positivismus? Zur Auseinandersetzung mit Sylvain Gouguenheim', *HZ* 275 (2002), 281–321; and J. Palmer, *The Apocalypse in the Early Middle Ages* (Cambridge, 2014), 189–226.

[191] Ælfric, *LS* XII.294–7 (ed. Skeat, 304): 'Þes tima is ende-next and ende þyssere þorulde. and menn beoð geworhte wolice him betwynan . swa þæt se fæder wind wið his agenne sunu. and broðor wið oþerne to bealwe him sylfum.' See Godden, 'Apocalypse and Invasion', 136–7.

Wulfstan was more open to speculation and in his fullest eschatological sermon, *Secundum Marcum* ('On Mark'), the archbishop famously remarks that

> great is the depravity that is now coming, let him endure that misery who is to endure it, that Antichrist will be born. Christ was born the best of all children ever born, and Antichrist will be the worst of all children who were born before or will ever be born after in this world. Now it needs must become very evil, because his time approaches quickly, just as it is written and has long been prophesied: *Post mille annos soluetur satanas* [Revelation XX.7]. That is in English, 'after a thousand years Satan will be unbound'. A thousand years and also more have now passed since Christ was amongst people in human form, and now Satan's bonds are very loose, and Antichrist's time is near at hand.[192]

While attempts have been made to read this passage as a sign of Wulfstan's relative lack of interest in the year 1000 and strict orthodoxy where eschatological prediction is concerned (Augustine of Hippo had famously forbad attempts to reckon the precise moment of the end),[193] it is clear that he was indeed open to such thoughts: Wulfstan sees the fact that a thousand years has passed since the incarnation of Christ as a sign that the prophecy in Revelation is about to be fulfilled. Wulfstan was not alone in according the year 1000 some significance. A tract on the six ages of the world, which places the end of the sixth and final age in AD 999 or 1000, is preserved in three English manuscripts of the late tenth or early eleventh century,

---

[192] Wulfstan, *Secundum Marcum* ll. 36–47 (ed. Bethurum, 136–7): 'mycel is seo þwyrnes þe nu is towerd, gebide ðære yrmðe se þe hit gebide, þæt Antecrist geboren beo. Crist wæs ealra bearna betst geboren þe æfre geboren wurde, 7 antecrist bið ealra þæra bearna wyrst on þas woruld geboren þe ær oððe æfter æfre gewurde oððe geweorðe. Nu sceal hit nyde yfelian swyðe, forðam þe hit nealæcð georne his timan, ealswa hit awriten is 7 gefyrn wæs gewitegod: Post mille Annos soluetur satanas; þæt is on englisc, Æfter þusend gearum bið satanas unbunden. Þusend geara 7 eac ma is nu agan syððan crist wæs mid mannum on menniscan hiwe, 7 nu syndon satanases bendas swyðe toslopene, 7 antecristes tima is wel gehende.'

[193] J. Hill, 'Ælfric and Wulfstan: Two Views of the Millennium', in *Essays on Anglo-Saxon and Related Themes in Memory of Lynne Grundy*, ed. J. Roberts and J.[L.] Nelson (Woodbridge, 2000), 213–35, at 234–5; A. Lainé, 'L'Antéchrist dans les homélies eschatologiques de Wulfstan: un mal du siècle', *Historical Reflections/Réflexions Historiques* 26 (2000), 173–87, at 175–6.

suggesting that some people were quite literally counting down to the end of time (despite Augustine's strictures).[194] The draftsmen of three charters produced in the years following the millennium go to considerable lengths to avoid writing the Roman numeral M (1000) – one, for example, is dated 'since the incarnation of Christ 990 years, nine and thrice two, indeed the sixth year in the course of the millennium [i.e. 1005]' (*decursis annis ab incarnatione Christi. dcccc.xc. nouentis terque binis in cursu millenario equidem sexto*) – perhaps suggesting a degree of anxiety about this date.[195]

It is clear, therefore, that some people harboured concerns about the turning of the millennium, concerns which may have been inspired by or found confirmation in the ongoing viking raids. Nevertheless, the evidence does not suggest that these fears were particularly widespread; there are many signs of apocalypticism, only a small range of which make reference to the year 1000.[196] The writings of Wulfstan are a case in point: only once does the venerable prelate mention the turning of the millennium, and even then only as one amongst many factors which he sees as pointing towards the proximity of the end. What is more, Wulfstan's main concern seems to have been that the people of his day were insufficiently prepared for this event, not that they were racked by anxiety; we are dealing with learned speculation, not mass hysteria. Some certainly rejected such thoughts outright: Ælfric was careful to place the events of the Last Times in the indefinite (but near) future, while Byrhtferth of Ramsey refuted attempts to date the end of time (perhaps reflecting the teachings of Abbo of Fleury, who felt similarly).[197] However, rejecting such reckoning is not the same as rejecting

---

[194] *The Liber Vitae of the New Minster and Hyde Abbey, Winchester*, ed. S. Keynes, EEMF 26 (Copenhagen, 1996), 99; D.N. Dumville, *Liturgy and Ecclesiastical History in Late Anglo-Saxon England: Four Studies* (Woodbridge, 1992), 44; *Ælfwine's Prayerbook*, ed. B. Günzel, HBS 108 (Woodbridge, 1993), 72–4 and 143–4.

[195] S 912 (*StAlb* 11). Cf. S 917 (*Burt* 30) and S 1664 (unpublished); with *Charters of Burton*, ed. Sawyer, 57; and *Charters of St Albans*, ed. Crick, 183.

[196] C. Cubitt, 'Apocalyptic and Eschatological Thought in England around the Year 1000', *TRHS* 6th ser. 25 (2015), 27–52. Cf. W. Prideaux-Collins, ' "Satan's Bonds are Extremely Loose": Apocalyptic Expectation in Anglo-Saxon England during the Millennial Era', in *The Apocalyptic Year 1000*, ed. R. Landes, A. Gow and D.C. Van Meter (Oxford, 2003), 289–310.

[197] Byrhtferth, *Enchiridion* IV.2 (ed. Baker and Lapidge, 236–40). On Abbo, see Fried, 'Endzeiterwartung', 422–3; and cf. Byrhtferth, *Enchiridion* IV.1 (ed. Baker and Lapidge, 228–30).

apocalyptic speculation *tout court* and it may be that for many the viking ravages and other misfortunes of this period (murrain in 986, famine in 1005) came to possess a cosmic significance that transcended any interest in the year 1000. The English may have taken their cue from Alcuin, who in letters of the later 790s and early 800s presented the political upheaval of his day as evidence that 'dangerous times' were come.[198]

One might be forgiven for imagining that such thoughts were at odds with the other dominant paradigm for interpreting the Scandinavian attacks, which saw these as a form of divine punishment which might be lifted by appropriate acts of repentance. In a justly famous article Malcolm Godden argued precisely this: that as Wulfstan's career progressed and the millennium receded from sight, the archbishop became less apocalyptic and more penitential in outlook – he moved from seeing the ills of his age as signs of the (inevitable) end of time, to understanding them as (passing) punishments for sin, which would be lifted if the English returned to pious ways.[199] However, more recent work has relativized these claims. For a start, it has become clear that Wulfstan's apocalypticism was not restricted to his early years: his two most developed eschatological homilies were written after 1005 and even at the end of his career the archbishop continued to espouse the belief that the end was nigh, as shown by a sermon he seems to have preached before Cnut and his counsellors (*c.* 1018).[200] Much the same is suggested by the charter material, in which apocalyptic utterances can be found alongside penitential readings of contemporary events throughout these years; the belief that the end is nigh, on the one hand, and the hope that the English might yet obtain mercy through atonement, on the other, were apparently not mutually exclusive. It may be that some were unconcerned by the apparent contradiction between these lines of thought – either way, the solution was much

[198] Garrison, 'The Bible'.

[199] Godden, 'Apocalypse and Invasion', 142–62. See also Godden, 'The Millennium', 167–77.

[200] *Wulfstan*, ed. Napier, no. 50, 266–74; with J.T. Lionarons, 'Napier Homily L: Wulfstan's Eschatology at the Close of his Career', in *Wulfstan, Archbishop of York*, ed. M. Townend (Turnhout, 2004), 413–28. See also M. Godden, 'The Relations of Wulfstan and Ælfric: A Reassessment', in *Wulfstan, Archbishop of York*, ed. M. Townend (Turnhout, 2004), 353–74, at 369–70; S.[M.] Pons-Sanz, *Norse-Derived Vocabulary in Late Old English Texts: Wulfstan's Works, A Case Study* (Odense, 2007), 19–20; and Cubitt, 'Eschatological Thought', 46–50.

the same: to repent and do good while time remained. There may, however, also have been a more intimate association between these concepts. It was expected that sin and iniquity would rise immediately before the end of time, a fact which potentially gave a place to human agency in these developments: if people were especially sinful or pious, they might speed up or slow down the 'final countdown'.[201] This seems to be precisely what Wulfstan had in mind: by neglecting piety the people of his day had brought disaster upon themselves, a disaster which if unchecked threatened to take on cosmic proportions. This may explain why he, despite his pronounced interest in eschatology, shied away from identifying the vikings with Gog and Magog or the other 'peoples of the Endtime' (as his continental counterparts had done in the face of the Magyars); to Wulfstan they are not so much the horsemen of the apocalypse, as signs of sin, which is itself evidence of the end of times.[202] Repentance and reform were thus not only necessary because the end was at hand; they also had the potential to turn back the eschatological clock. This seems to be what the draftsman of the Eynsham charter had in mind too: though 'dangerous times' are come, he clearly hopes that 'good works' might yet offer the English a way out of their bind.

Acknowledging the part played by apocalypticism in the politics of these years throws salient light on many other aspects of Æthelred's regime. The very intensity with which the king pursued his programme of reform and repentance becomes readily understandable if we appreciate that he saw these struggles partly in cosmic terms: by battling sinfulness Æthelred was facing down the precursors of Antichrist who, if successful, might pave the way for the end of time. We have seen that penitential regimes have a tendency to conduct periodic waves of purges, often of increasing scale, and much the same is true of apocalyptic regimes – because these are focused on either preventing or preparing the way for the Last Times, they

---

[201] P. Buc, *Holy War, Martyrdom, and Terror: Christianity, Violence, and the West* (Philadelphia, PA, 2015), 253–61 and 278–9.

[202] Lainé, 'L'Antéchrist', 177–8 and 183–5; Roach, 'Apocalypse and Atonement'. Cf. Palmer, *Apocalypse*, 213–14, noting that the lack of access to Pseudo-Methodius in pre-Conquest England may also explain Wulfstan's reticence where Gog and Magog are concerned.

too show scant regard for traditional *Realpolitik*.[203] Thus, while it has been suggested that the 'immediate reality' of the Scandinavian attacks would have served to push apocalyptic anxieties to the background, the reverse seems if anything to have been the case: the harder the English were pressed, the nearer they felt they were to the end.[204]

Viewed together, the years between the arrival of a large Scandinavian force in 1002 and the programme of reform and refortification inaugurated in 1008 were amongst the busiest of Æthelred's long reign. While the 990s had seen much soul-searching, there is a marked change in tone after the turn of the millennium; as it became clear that early efforts had not borne fruit, the king and his counsellors resorted to ever more drastic solutions to the 'viking problem'. The first sign of desperation is the St Brice's Day Massacre of 1002; the second is the 'palace revolution' of 1005–6. Yet, as the arrival of the 'great fleet' in 1006 demonstrated, even these efforts proved insufficient. After paying a record tribute in 1007, the king and his counsellors spent much of the next year readying themselves for the worst: they ordered helms, coats of armour and had ships prepared, but also issued ordinances about penance and piety. Thus, old approaches were being continued in new guises: the king had receded somewhat from the picture and the focus was now increasingly on the sins of the nation, but the basic principle remained much the same: to repent and reform, purge and pray, while time remained.

---

[203] For different perspectives, see N. Cohn, *The Pursuit of the Millennium: Revolutionary Millenarians and Mystical Anarchists of the Middle Ages*, 2nd edn (London, 1970); and Buc, *Holy War*, esp. 67–89.

[204] Cf. S. Keynes, 'Apocalypse Then: England, A.D. 1000', in *Europe around the Year 1000*, ed. P. Urbańczyk (Warsaw, 2001), 247–70, at 260.

CHAPTER 6

A KINGDOM LOST AND WON
1009–16

As we have seen, the years following the turning of the millennium witnessed something of a mounting crisis in England. Though it would be wrong to suggest that Æthelred was helpless in the face of the viking threat, it is in these years that we first begin to sense real desperation. This period was a harbinger of things to come, and the years between the arrival of Thorkell the Tall's 'immense raiding army' (*ungemætlica unfriðhere*) in 1009 and Æthelred's death in 1016 can only reasonably be described as a period of almost unremitting crisis. It was under the shadow of these years that the author of the main *Chronicle*-account wrote and it was in these years that the seeds of the Danish conquest of 1016 were sown. However, the fact that we know how the story ends does not lessen the drama. Indeed, in these years we can see an intensification of many trends visible over the preceding decade and a half: the viking attacks served to concentrate the collective mind and many measures were undertaken in the hope of overcoming what must have seemed like a grim and increasingly inevitable fate.

To trace these, we will first survey the events of Thorkell the Tall's invasion (1009–12) and then consider the effects of these on the English, which were varied and deep. Thereafter, we will turn our attention to the successive conquests of Swein Forkbeard (1013–14) and Cnut (1015–16), examining the internal divisions and tensions amongst the English which enabled these. The resulting picture is one of failure, but not of an inevitable or unmitigated one, and as elsewhere Æthelred's ongoing efforts to combat these threats deserve a sympathetic hearing.

From crisis to collapse: Thorkell's 'immense raiding army', 1009–12

Much of 1008 had been spent readying the English for the inevitable: the return of the vikings. In this respect, they did not have to wait long. The *Chronicle* reports that the ships whose construction had been ordered in 1008 were prepared and gathered at Sandwich in the following year, where they constituted the greatest naval force in living memory. The intention was clearly to head off would-be attackers, as Sandwich was the vikings' natural first port of call, lying immediately across the Channel from the Low Countries (along whose coast the raiders sailed *en route* to Britain). Yet this was not the centre's only significance: it was also something of an 'outport of London', connected to the future capital by the Wantsum Channel, which before silting up in the later Middle Ages ran from Reculver to Richborough, separating Thanet from the mainland.[1] However, as is so often the case in Æthelred's reign, these good intentions came to naught. Before the vikings appeared, the English forces began to unravel. The chronicler reports that problems started with an accusation raised by Eadric Streona's brother, Brihtric, against Wulfnoth Cild 'the South Saxon'. We are not informed as to the nature of the charges, but Wulfnoth clearly doubted his chances of a fair trial, since he took matters into his own hands, enticing away twenty of the assembled ships from the main force. Thereafter, the South Saxon thegn went on the rampage, ravaging down the south coast and inflicting 'all sorts of damage' (*ælc yfel*). Calamity became catastrophe when the whereabouts of these renegades was made known to Brihtric, who set out with a larger force of eighty ships to surround them; unexpected storms cast his ships ashore, where Wulfnoth proceeded to burn them. When this became known to the main force, the king and his counsellors decided to return home, leaving the remnants to retreat to London. 'And,' so the chronicler reports, with more than a hint of chagrin, 'they thus let the

---

[1] P. Nightingale, 'The Origin of the Court of Husting and the Danish Influence on London's Development into a Capital City', *EHR* 102 (1987), 559–78, at 572.

toil of the entire nation lightly come to naught' (*7 leton ealles þeodscypes geswinc ðus leohtlice forwurðan*).[2] There is much we should like to know about this affair. For a start, it is unclear what the charges were against Wulfnoth (though given the context, one suspects treason). Likewise, it is uncertain what Brihtric's motives were in bringing these accusations forward. It is tempting to see a parallel with the events of 1005–6, which saw Eadric and his associates (including Brihtric) topple much of the old guard at court, apparently by means of similar allegations. Indeed, we may be witnessing the aftershocks of this seismic shift in England's political landscape: one imagines that the 'palace revolution' had not met with universal approbation and Wulfnoth may have been amongst those on the losing end of developments. Particularly telling in this regard is the fact that Wulfnoth's son, Godwine, is later found amongst the beneficiaries to the will of the ætheling Æthelstan (d. 1014), who was himself no friend of Eadric. What is more, this Godwine – apparently the later earl of Wessex, whose son Harold was to fight the Conqueror at Hastings – received an estate from Æthelstan which had once belonged to his father: the accusations against Wulfnoth at this point provide the natural context for the original forfeiture of these lands.[3] Certainly, there seems to have been tension within Æthelred's camp and, as noted, one suspects that Eadric's faction was resorting to a favoured tactic: bringing accusations of faithlessness against their political opponents. The *Chronicle* does not inform us as to the fates of Brihtric and Wulfnoth, but it may be significant that neither is heard of again. Writing in the late eleventh century, Osbern of Canterbury mentions the death of an unnamed brother of Eadric in Kent and it is tempting to identify this figure with Brihtric; however, the episode in question is placed around the time of the sack of Canterbury (1011). What is more, according to Osbern the king showed little sympathy for the murdered magnate, which is hard to square with the situation in the summer of 1009.[4]

---

[2] *ASC* 1009 CDE (ed. O'Brien O'Keeffe, 92–3; ed. Cubbin, 54 [giving the details as to Wulfnoth's origins]).

[3] S 1503 (*CantCC* 142); with S. Keynes, 'Cnut's Earls', in *The Reign of Cnut: King of England, Denmark and Norway*, ed. A.R. Rumble (London, 1994), 43–88, at 70–1. As Keynes notes, the estate in question (Compton in Sussex) is recorded as having belonged to Earl Godwine in the Domesday survey.

[4] Osbern of Canterbury, *Vita S. Elfhegi*, ed. H. Wharton, *Anglia sacra*, 2 vols. (London, 1691), II, 122–48, at 132. See Williams, 'Dangers of Invention', 34–5.

The upshot of these developments is that Æthelred's plans for defence were left in tatters. With the king's depleted naval force back in the safety of London's defences (which, it should be recalled, included a fortified bridge), the Kentish coast was open to attack. News of these developments may have reached Thorkell, who had probably been massing forces for some time; certainly, a large fleet under his command appeared off the Kentish coast soon after 1 August 1009. If the arrival of the 'great fleet' of 1006–7 had witnessed a notable increase in the scale of viking activity, this army represents a further step in this direction: the chronicler describes it as 'the immense raiding army' (*se ungemætlica unfriðhere*) which the English were accustomed to call 'Thorkell's army' (*Ðurkilles here*), a phrase perhaps coined in 1012, when the core of this force entered English employ.[5] The army seems to have been composed of bands previously active in the British Isles, swelled, no doubt, by others hoping to cash in on this increasingly lucrative venture. The Yttergärde rune-stone from Vallentuna, just to the north of modern Stockholm, famously records how a certain Ulf received tribute payments as a part of three successive armies, those of Tosti (1006–7?), Thorketill (i.e. Thorkell: 1009–12) and Cnut (1015–18) (Plate 13).[6] John of Worcester reports that the army was initially composed of two distinct forces: one under Thorkell and another under Hemming and Eilaf, apparently the younger brother of Thorkell and a relative (by marriage) of Swein Forkbeard respectively.[7] Although not mentioned in English sources, skaldic verse (Scandinavian praise-poetry) suggests that Olaf Haraldsson, the later king of Norway, was also part of this army.[8] Below this level, the fleet was more composite, and in 1012 the *Chronicle* tellingly reports that it 'dispersed as widely as it had previously been collected' (*toferde . . . wide swa he ær gegaderod wæs*).[9] Thus, though unusually large, Thorkell's army

---

[5] *ASC* 1009 CDE (ed. O'Brien O'Keeffe, 93–4). See Keynes, 'An Abbot', 155–7.

[6] U 344, ed. E. Wéssen and S.B.F. Jansson. *Upplands runinskrifter*, 4 vols. (Stockholm, 1940–58), II, 79–86; M. Syrett, *The Vikings in England: The Evidence of Runic Inscriptions* (Cambridge, 2002), no. 7, 38–43.

[7] John of Worcester, *Chronicon, s.a.* 1009 (ed. Darlington and McGurk, 462). See Keynes, 'Cnut's Earls', 58–60 (and cf. *ibid.*, 62–4).

[8] *Encomium Emmae*, ed. Campbell, 76–82.

[9] *ASC* 1012 CDE (ed. O'Brien O'Keeffe, 97).

was not structurally different to those of his predecessors.[10] It was in part the amorphousness of such forces which made them so hard to combat: since their leadership was temporary and shifting (Thorkell, Swein and Cnut being the partial exception – and then only in Æthelred's later years), it was difficult to strike lasting deals; the raiders who made an agreement one year might return the next under a new guise, rendering previous arrangements null and void. This might seem disingenuous to modern eyes, but reflects the realities of medieval diplomacy: treaties and alliances were forged between rulers and nations, not informal warbands, and there is little reason to believe that someone like Ulf would have felt bound by the oaths of previous leaders (indeed, one wonders if it is any accident that his three tributes all came under different figures). At a more general level Scandinavian ideals of leadership seem to have differed somewhat from those of the English: skaldic verse is notoriously bloodthirsty (not to mention often overtly pagan), and while this in part reflects the nature of the genre, there is no mistaking the difference between it and verses such as the *Battle of Maldon*; both may glory in bloodshed, but the cardinal Christian virtue of mercy had yet to touch the former.[11]

In any case, Thorkell clearly succeeded in bringing together an unusually large force. The size of such armies was a hot topic of debate in the 1960s and 1970s, but there is now a general consensus that they numbered in the hundreds and thousands, but not tens of thousands.[12] Thorkell's army presumably lay at the upper end of this spectrum and, though speculation is dangerous in the absence of concrete evidence, one imagines that he had something like 5,000–8,000 men at his command – a force perhaps comparable with that led by William the Conqueror in 1066, in other words. Such a figure sits well with the fact that Thorkell's own force –

---

[10] N. Lund, 'The Armies of Swein Forkbeard and Cnut: *Leding* or *lið*?', *ASE* 15 (1986), 105–18. Cf. J. Fried, 'Weshalb die Normannenherrscher für die Franken unvorstellbar waren: um 810', in *Die Macht des Königs. Herrschaft in Europa vom Frühmittelalter bis in die Neuzeit*, ed. B. Jussen (Munich, 2005), 72–82.

[11] Cf. R. Frank, 'Viking Atrocity and Skaldic Verse: The Rite of the Blood-Eagle', *EHR* 99 (1984), 322–43.

[12] Halsall, *Warfare and Society*, 119–33; S. Coupland, 'The Carolingian Army and the Struggle against the Vikings', *Viator* 35 (2004), 49–70, at 56–8. See also Keynes, *Diplomas*, 224–5; and cf. Bachrach, *Warfare*.

which was only a fraction of the entire army – numbered some forty-five ships when it entered Æthelred's employ in 1012. Though estimating ships' crews is itself something of a fraught matter, they seem to have averaged about sixty, meaning that there were something like 2,700 men at Thorkell's personal command.[13] The size and confidence of the army is revealed by its actions: finding the Kentish coast undefended, it immediately proceeded inland towards Canterbury (Map 3). The city, which lay half a day's march from Sandwich, had been left exposed by the departure of Æthelred's naval forces, and the chronicler remarks that it would have fallen had the people of East Kent (a traditional territorial division, which may once have been an independent kingdom) not quickly offered terms; for the price of 3,000 pounds they were able to buy temporary respite.[14] The terms of this agreement were local, however, and the 'immense raiding army' soon headed off to the other favoured viking base: the Isle of Wight.

From there it struck Sussex and Hampshire and made its way inland to Berkshire. In response the king ordered a full national levy – only the second time this is reported to have happened – but, as in 1006–7, this failed to bring the raiders to battle or to terms and the chronicler (predictably) complains that the only time the king did succeed in intercepting Thorkell's force, he was prevented from engaging it by Ealdorman Eadric 'as ever after was the case' (*swa hit gyt æfre wæs*). This account was written in full knowledge of Eadric's later treachery (of which more anon), so we must be wary of its tone; it may be reading the ealdorman's later perfidy back into earlier years. Had he been amongst those who counselled against engaging Thorkell, this need not have been particularly pusillanimous; battles were unpredictable affairs and experienced commanders often sought to avoid them, as John Gillingham observes.[15] We may even be seeing signs of a shift in the manner in which warfare was conducted in these years. As Guy Halsall notes, in the early Middle Ages the aim of campaigns was generally to force

---

[13] N.A.M. Rodger, 'Cnut's Geld and the Size of Danish Ships', *EHR* 110 (1995), 392–403; S. Keynes and R. Love, 'Earl Godwine's Ship', *ASE* 38 (2009), 185–223, at 186–90.

[14] *ASC* CDE 1009 (ed. O'Brien O'Keeffe, 92–4). Cf. B. Yorke, *Kings and Kingdoms of Early Anglo-Saxon England* (London, 1990), 32–6.

[15] J. Gillingham, 'William the Bastard at War', in *Studies in Medieval History Presented to R. Allen Brown*, ed. C. Harper-Bill, C. Holdsworth and J.L. Nelson (Woodbridge, 1989), 141–58.

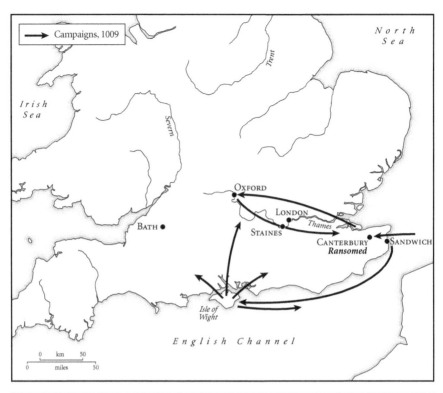

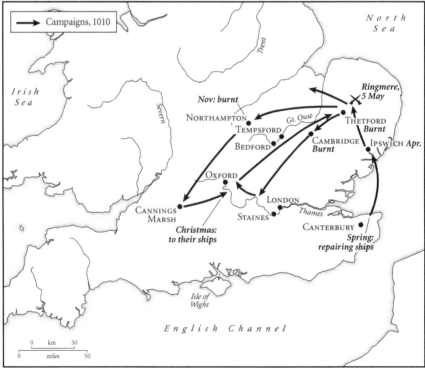

Map 3 Viking activity in England, 1009–10.

a decisive battle, whereas in the eleventh and twelfth centuries this gave way to ravaging, sieges and attrition – the kinds of engagements we seem to be seeing.[16] Certainly, it is clear that Æthelred was leading from the front, even if the result was containment rather than outright victory. In late autumn the viking army returned to Kent (perhaps West Kent, though this is not specified) before moving up to the Thames, ravaging on either side of the river and threatening London. As in 1006–7, the raiders did not stop for winter: they forced a passage through the Chilterns to Oxford, which they proceeded to sack before heading back to their ships, avoiding the host drawn up to meet them at London by crossing over to the south bank of the Thames at Staines. Thorkell's army had apparently taken up where the 'great fleet' left off, striking with impunity into the heartlands of the kingdom – not even Canterbury and London were free from threat. Still, as before, if we read between the lines of the *Chronicle*-account we can see that proactive measures were undertaken in response: the men of East Kent bought a truce, the king led forth a large host, perhaps forcing Thorkell to relocate from the Isle of Wight to the Thames, and in the winter the men of London were able to raise an army sufficiently threatening for Thorkell to avoid engagement by crossing over to the south side of the river. Nevertheless, it is hard to see the events of this year as anything but an abject failure: the king's plan to hinder a landing at Sandwich was brought to naught by squabbles amongst his men and thereafter he seems to have constantly been playing catch-up.

The impression of general collapse is strengthened when we turn to the events of the next three years. At the start of 1010 Thorkell and his army turned their attentions from the Thames Valley and the south to East Anglia, which had largely been spared in recent years. Landing at Ipswich, not far to the north of the mouth of the Thames, they proceeded inland to where they knew the local leader, Ulfcytel, would be gathering forces: Ringmere Heath, a strategic site north-east of Thetford, which may have

[16] Halsall, *Warfare and Society*, 156–62. See further *ibid.*, 177–214 and 229; and T. Reuter, 'Carolingian and Ottonian Warfare', in *Medieval Warfare: A History*, ed. M. Keen (Oxford, 1999), 13–35, at 35; and cf. P. Contamine, *War in the Middle Ages*, trans. M. Jones (Oxford, 1984), 219–37; and J. France, *Western Warfare in the Age of the Crusades, 1000–1300* (London, 1999), 96–127.

been the customary mustering point for the East Anglian levies.[17] Ulfcytel was an experienced commander: he had fought a Scandinavian force near Thetford – perhaps at the same site – six years earlier, an encounter which even the chronicler admits was not entirely hopeless.[18] Since Thorkell's men seem to have been unusually well-informed – they knew where Ulfcytel would be gathering his forces, just as in the previous year they may have known that Sandwich had been left undefended – they must have been aware that they were in for a fight. This time, however, they were able to make quicker work of it. Battle was joined, but the result was a resounding defeat for the English: the men of East Anglia fled, led by the wonderfully named Thurcetel 'Mare's Head', leaving only the men of Cambridgeshire to fight on. Amongst the fallen were Æthelstan, a royal relative (either Æthelred's son-in-law or brother-in-law), and a number of other local notables. Thorkell's army was left in *de facto* control of the region and took the opportunity to ravage near and far, putting Thetford and Cambridge to the torch, before turning its gaze southwards. The memory of this event clearly resonated amongst the victors and it is mentioned a number of times in skaldic verse.[19] At this point the vikings went back to the Thames Valley, whence they headed north-west into Oxfordshire and then east into Buckinghamshire, following the Ouse to Bedford and Tempsford, burning all the way. Thereafter, they returned to their ships and were apparently left free to continue their ravages. At this point the chronicler offers one of his most famous set pieces: he laments that throughout the year the English forces were always at the wrong place at the wrong time, in the west when the vikings were in the east, and in the north when they were in the south. Though Æthelred met with his counsellors in order to formulate plans, they consistently failed to implement them. In the end, local leaders were left unable to raise forces and simply fled as best they could. The basic bonds of society were starting to burst and even local shire levies would not

---

[17] John of Worcester, *Chronicon*, s.a. 1010 (ed. Darlington and McGurk, 464–6); W.H. Stevenson, 'Notes on Old-English Historical Geography', *EHR* 11 (1896), 301–4, at 301–2; R.[G.] Poole, 'Skaldic Verse and Anglo-Saxon History: Some Aspects of the Period 1009–1016', *Speculum* 62 (1987), 265–98, at 278–80.

[18] *ASC* 1004 CDE (ed. O'Brien O'Keeffe, 90–1).

[19] Poole, 'Skaldic Verse', 277–8.

come to the aid of their immediate neighbours.[20] Though full of rhetorical flourish, this extraordinary indictment is hard to ignore; Æthelred and his advisers had indeed proven incapable of matching the speed, organization and ferocity of their foes. The impression is that Thorkell and his men could more or less come and go as they pleased. Thus, for example, in autumn they are reported to have taken Northampton and razed the town and surrounding countryside before ravaging back through Wessex.[21] For Christmas, they finally returned to their ships.

Clearly, matters were starting to come to a head. The *Chronicle*-entry for the following year, 1011, opens by noting that the king and his counsellors decided to sue for peace, offering tribute and provisions if the raiding force would cease its attacks. The account then goes on to list those counties and regions which had been overrun by Thorkell's army: to the north of the Thames these included East Anglia, Essex, Middlesex, Oxfordshire, Cambridgeshire, Hertfordshire, Buckinghamshire, Bedfordshire, half of Huntingdonshire and much of Northamptonshire; and to the south all of Kent, Sussex, Hastings (the region, not the town), Surrey, Berkshire, Hampshire and much of Wiltshire. This list maps closely on to the reported attacks of the previous years. The chronicler goes on to bemoan once more the inefficacy of the English against the vikings, lamenting specifically that 'they were not offered tribute on time, nor fought against' (*man nolde him a timan gafol beodon oþþe wið gefeohtan*). (Note that it is not the payment of tribute *per se* that is criticized, but rather its application: it has only been offered once the worst is over.) Whether tribute was paid at this point is not entirely clear. The chronicler states that despite the 'truce and tribute' (*grið 7 gafol*) the raiders broke up into smaller bands and continued their attacks undeterred, a complaint which would seem to suggest that a sum was indeed offered up. Nevertheless, it is strange that he does not give the figure, as he had in previous years. Perhaps he did not know the amount, or perhaps it was just a small sum for a brief respite. Alternatively, the English may only have promised tribute at this point, which they were then

---

[20] *ASC* 1010 CDE (ed. O'Brien O'Keeffe, 94–5).

[21] Cf. John of Worcester, *Chronicon*, *s.a.* 1010 (ed. Darlington and McGurk, 466), specifying that it was Northampton which was sacked. See further Howard, *Swein Forkbeard's Invasions*, 90.

in the process of collecting when further attacks transpired (it could take up to a year or more to raise such sums, as later events testify).[22] In any case, despite the actions of a few smaller bands, we do not hear of any major engagements, and one is inclined to believe that the truce was largely kept. By September 1011, however, Thorkell's army was up to its old tricks again: it turned on Canterbury which it besieged between the feasts of the Nativity of Mary (8 September) and Michaelmas (29 September). What had gone wrong is unclear. Ian Howard suggests that Thorkell departed from England at this point and arrangements broke down in his absence, but the evidence he adduces is late and largely circumstantial.[23] A more likely scenario is that tribute was taking longer to raise than anticipated; a quick strike by Thorkell and his men might have been intended to spur the English into action. The terms of the truce may themselves have been a cause of tension: large military forces were hard to supply and keep in check, especially in hostile territory, and it is conceivable that the small-scale raiding recorded in the *Chronicle* got out of hand after months of inactivity.[24] Whatever the cause, there is every reason to believe that a substantial part of Thorkell's army was involved in this attack: Canterbury was no mean prize and the city had hitherto been spared the vikings' attention. The result was a siege of some scale, perhaps lasting the entire three weeks between the Nativity of Mary and Michaelmas. As in previous conflicts, the Scandinavian raiders emerged the victors: they took the city, thanks to the treachery of a certain Ælfmær, 'whose life Archbishop Ælfheah had previously saved' (*þe se arcebisceop Ælfeah ær generede æt his life*) – perhaps the abbot of St Augustine's, though conceivably an archdeacon of Christ Church cathedral itself. They went on to capture the archbishop, the

<hr>

[22] John of Worcester, *Chronicon, s.a.* 1011 (ed. Darlington and McGurk, 468), mentions the payment of tribute, but he simply expands on the *Chronicle*-report, which only alludes to the possibility. See further Lavelle, *Aethelred II*, 161, stating that tribute was paid, but noting that 'the Chronicle, for once, does not tell us how much'; and cf. Lawson, 'Levels of Taxation', 394–5, on the times taken to raise such sums.

[23] Howard, *Swein Forkbeard's Invasions*, 91–4. Howard places a great deal of faith on the chronology of *Heimskringla* (cf. *ibid.*, 147–62), a work compiled in the thirteenth century (!) at the earliest, perhaps by the chieftain Snorri Sturluson. See P.P. Boulhosa, *Icelanders and the Kings of Norway: Mediaeval Sagas and Legal Texts* (Leiden, 2005), esp. 5–42, for the problems which attach to this work.

[24] Cf. Halsall, *Warfare and Society*, 152–3.

local reeve Ælfweard, Abbess Leofrun of St Mildred's in Thanet and Bishop Godwine of Rochester, then sacked the city before returning to their ships with the archbishop in tow.[25]

These events sent shockwaves throughout the nation. Though the attacks of 1005–6 and 1009–10 had already been wide-ranging, they had not resulted in the sack of such a major centre: central Wessex had been largely spared and London had resisted successfully. Canterbury itself was a wealthy and well-established city: the traditional 'capital' of Kent, it was also the spiritual heart of the realm, where St Augustine had founded the first English bishopric in 597.[26] Yet it was not just the city that was taken – Ælfheah, the nation's senior metropolitan, fell into enemy hands. The fact that the raiders took the archbishop captive may say something of their motives: had they been looking to renegotiate the truce or speed up payment, Ælfheah would have provided them with just the leverage they needed. These events certainly spurred the English into action: early in the following year Eadric Streona is reported to have met with the nation's leading counsellors at London, where they remained till 48,000 pounds were raised. The fact that no mention is made of new negotiations or offers of peace is surprising and may indicate that what was now delivered was simply the tribute promised in the previous year – perhaps with interest. Indeed, this may be why Eadric took the lead: if the ealdorman was merely implementing an existing agreement, the king's absence becomes more readily understandable. In any case, Eadric's prominence is certainly significant and is a sign of things to come. It was while tribute was being gathered that the most infamous event of these years transpired: the killing of Archbishop Ælfheah at Greenwich, where the Scandinavian force was based, on 19 April 1012. Most accounts of this act are late and embellished, but it is clear even from what the *Chronicle* has to offer that this was especially shocking. According to this report, what happened is that as tribute was being collected the vikings demanded additional sums from

---

[25] *ASC* 1011 CDE (ed. O'Brien O'Keeffe, 95–6). See John of Worcester, *Chronicon, s.a.* 1011 (ed. Darlington and McGurk, 468), for the suggestion that Ælfmær was archdeacon.

[26] See N. Brooks, 'Canterbury, Rome and the Construction of English Identity', in *Early Medieval Rome and the Christian West: Essays in Honour of Donald A. Bullough*, ed. J.M.H. Smith (Leiden, 2000), 221–47.

the archbishop, requests which Ælfheah rebuffed.[27] These demands were probably informed by the role played by previous archbishops in the raising of tribute: as we have seen, Sigeric had been involved in collecting an initial sum for the forces of Olaf and Swein in 994, for which purposes he was forced to sell off church lands, and it stands to reason that Ælfheah had likewise been involved in the payment made by the men of East Kent in 1009.[28] Thorkell's men were thus seeing how far they could play their hand and Ælfheah called their bluff; whether out of frustration with his captors, or an awareness of the financial strains on his see, is hard to know. In response the vikings, who were reportedly drunk at the time, brought the archbishop before an assembly at which they put him to death by hurling bones and ox-heads at him – his soul, however (so the chronicler), went straight to heaven to dwell amongst the saints. The following day the raiders passed the body on to Eadnoth and Ælfhun, the bishops of Dorchester-on-Thames and London (the most local sees), who saw to it that Ælfheah was interred with due reverence at St Paul's.[29]

If the sack of Canterbury had been a first shock, the death of Ælfheah at the hands of his captors must have been an even greater one. News of this event travelled far and wide, and even Thietmar of Merseburg, writing in eastern Saxony *c.* 1016, had heard tell of it (albeit in garbled form): the Saxon bishop reports that he had been informed by a man 'known for truthfulness' (*pro veritate sibi cognitus*) of how Thorkell and his men had captured Archbishop 'Dunstan' (for which, read: Ælfheah) and when the latter was unable to produce the tribute he had promised they went on to execute him, despite the objections of their leader. There are differences in emphasis between this and the *Chronicle*-account: Thietmar has the prelate promise tribute, but unable to produce it (a not entirely improbable proposition, given the sum paid by the men of East Kent only two years earlier), and the story has also grown somewhat in the telling, with Thorkell (here

---

[27] The *Chronicle* does not state the amount, but John of Worcester records that it was 3,000 pounds, a plausible sum for a centre such as Canterbury: *Chronicon, s.a.* 1012 (ed. Darlington and McGurk, 470). John's source is probably Osbern, *Vita S. Elfegi* (ed. Wharton, 137–8); see Williams, 'Dangers of Invention', 38.

[28] N. Brooks, *The Early History of the Church of Canterbury* (Leicester, 1984), 282–5.

[29] *ASC* 1012 CDE (ed. O'Brien O'Keeffe, 96–7). See I. McDougall, 'Serious Entertainments: An Examination of a Peculiar Type of Viking Atrocity', *ASE* 22 (1993), 201–25.

unnamed) now offering resistance and Ælfheah being swapped for the more famous Dunstan.[30] Still, the broad brushstrokes remain much the same and it is clear that Ælfheah's death was becoming something of a *cause célèbre*. What made this so shocking was the mistreatment of an anointed bishop (and not just any bishop at that!); as the spiritual leader of the English, one of the Lord's chosen shepherds, Ælfheah should have been spared such outrages. While Scandinavia was by no means fully Christianized, the church had made substantial inroads in Denmark and to a lesser extent Norway. A number of Thorkell's men will therefore have been Christian (at least in name), making their behaviour all the more shocking.[31] Though complaints about viking treachery and brutality had been common in the eighth and ninth centuries, the raiders of the so-called 'Second Viking Age' in the late tenth and early eleventh seem to have broadly conformed to the established norms of Christian warfare: they generally kept their treaties and truces – the actions of Swein's army in 1004 and a few overly zealous groups in 1011 notwithstanding – and did not make a habit of plundering churches, as had their forebears.[32] For those acquainted with tales of earlier atrocities, however, Ælfheah's death must have conjured up unwelcome memories. Indeed, though Scandinavia was increasingly integrated into mainstream European culture, the vikings retained an association with paganism and brutality; 'heathen' (Old English: *hæðen*) and 'pagan' (Latin: *paganus*) remained synonyms for 'Dane', and stories about earlier outrages continued to find an interested audience.[33] A particular interest in earlier Danish atrocities may be indicated by the popularity of the cult of

---

[30] Thietmar of Merseburg, *Chronicon* VII.42–3 (ed. Holtzmann, 448–51). Cf. *ibid.* VII.39 (ed. Holtzmann, 446–7), on the informant's truthfulness. See most recently A. Bihrer, 'Verwobene Konstellationen, verknüpfte Erfahrungen. England und das Reich in der Ottonen- und Salierzeit. Thietmar von Merseburg und die Angelsachsen', in *Identität und Krise? Zur Deutung vormoderner Selbst-, Welt- und Fremderfahrungen*, ed. C. Dartmann and C. Meyer (Münster, 2007), 45–59, at 56.

[31] For a recent synthesis, see A. Winroth, *The Conversion of Scandinavia: Vikings, Merchants, and Missionaries in the Remaking of Northern Europe* (New Haven, CT, 2011).

[32] P.H. Sawyer, *The Age of the Vikings*, 2nd edn (London, 1971), 137. On burning churches: S. Coupland, 'Holy Ground? The Plundering and Burning of Churches by Vikings and Franks in the Ninth Century', *Viator* 45.i (2014), 73–97; more generally: G. Halsall, 'Playing by Whose Rules? A Further Look at Viking Atrocity in the Ninth Century', *Medieval History* 2.ii (1992), 3–12.

[33] See, e.g., *Battle of Maldon*, ll. 55a, 181b (ed. Scragg, 58, 62); and S 911 (KCD 714).

St Edmund, who had died at the hands of the 'Great Army' in 869: a first (Latin) *Life* was composed by Abbo of Fleury during the reformer's sojourn at Ramsey (985–7) and this was then translated by Ælfric a few years later in his *Lives of Saints* (*c.* 992 × 998) (a work which, it should be recalled, was dedicated to Ealdorman Æthelweard and written with an eye to contemporary ills).[34] The killing of Ælfheah thus conformed to – and doubtless reinforced – existing stereotypes. Past form aside, even elements of Thorkell's army seem to have thought that they had overstepped the mark: not only did killing Ælfheah render him useless as collateral, but for those who were Christian (possibly including Thorkell himself), this would hardly have been acceptable. Thietmar, whose account, though garbled, was written within less than a decade of the events, reports that Thorkell sought to prevent Ælfheah's death and his testimony deserves respect here. This event may even have thrown the proposed peace into question; it would have been in the interest of all that amends be made. Thus, unlike Edmund in 869, whose decapitated head was discarded by his killers and miraculously called out to those searching for him, Ælfheah's corpse was handed over to the local bishops, who saw to it that he was buried with appropriate dignity at St Paul's, the oldest and most respected foundation in London. That the body was not taken back to Canterbury reveals the urgency of the situation: both sides evidently wished to lay the issue to rest as quickly as possible.[35]

As with the burial of Edward in 979, the interment of England's newest martyr paved the way for another ritual: the making of peace. Whatever ill will was in the air, Thorkell's forces were still keen on tribute, while the English were keener yet to see their backs. The chronicler reports in lapidary fashion that the sum was paid and oaths were sworn, after which Thorkell's army dispersed 'as widely as it had previously been collected'. Some forty-five ships, however, entered into royal service – presumably those which constituted Thorkell's personal force – and swore to defend the

---

[34] Abbo of Fleury, *Passio S. Eadmundi*, ed. M. Winterbottom, *Three Lives of English Saints* (Toronto, 1972), 67–87; Ælfric, *LS* XXXII (ed. Skeat, II, 314–34). See Denton, 'Hagiography', 63–90 and 115 (noting, *inter alia*, Abbo's connections with Æthelred's court); and Marafioti, *King's Body*, 184–8.

[35] Cf. S. Keynes, 'The Burial of King Æthelred the Unready at St Paul's', in *The English and their Legacy, 900–1200: Essays in Honour of Ann Williams*, ed. D. Roffe (Woodbridge, 2012), 129–48, at 139.

country so long as Æthelred would feed and clothe (and presumably also pay!) them. This was evidently modelled on earlier agreements, though on a larger scale. Indeed, it seems to be at this point that regular taxation was first put in place in order to pay the mercenaries, the so-called *heregeld* or 'army tax'. Though the *Chronicle* makes no note of this – in fact, the work says nothing about how Thorkell's forces were to be remunerated – payments of tax (*geld*) are mentioned in subsequent years, and when this much-resented exaction was abolished (probably temporarily) in 1051, it is stated that this was the thirty-ninth year since it had been instituted, neatly giving 1012 as its date of origin.[36] It is important to distinguish this from earlier tribute arrangements: unlike these, it was an annual affair, and is consistently called tax (*geld*) not tribute (*gafol*). It is the *heregeld* which eventually gave its name to the 'Danegeld', a term which first appears in the twelfth century to refer to these dues and has rather unfortunately come to be used as a short-hand for all forms of payment in these years.[37]

Calamity and response, 1009–12

So far we have focused on the main events of 1009–12, as laid out in the *Chronicle*. From this it emerges that Æthelred and the English were facing a challenge of unprecedented proportions. However, if we are to get a real sense for the impact of these events we must go beyond the bare bones of the *Chronicle*-narrative; reactions to Thorkell's ravages were many and varied, only a fraction of which are echoed in the *Chronicle*. We must, therefore, turn our attention once more to the strictly contemporary evidence – the decrees, charters, coins and literary works of the period.

Perhaps the most famous response to Thorkell's attacks are the ordinances known as *VII Æthelred*, which survive in two versions: a Latin text, translated from a lost Old English original and preserved in the post-Conquest legal compendium known as *Quadripartitus*; and an Old English

---

[36] *ASC* 1052 D (=1051) (ed. Cubbin, 69–70); with Stafford, 'Royal Government', 182–4; and Keynes, *Diplomas*, 221.

[37] J.A. Green, 'The Last Century of Danegeld', *EHR* 96 (1981), 241–58; D. Roffe, *Domesday: The Inquest and the Book* (Oxford, 2000), 58–64. See further above, Chapter 5, pp. 223–5.

text, preserved in a mid-eleventh-century manuscript containing both homilies and legal ordinances. The version in *Quadripartitus*, though not in the vernacular, is clearly closer to the original, while the Old English redaction was apparently produced by Wulfstan at a somewhat later date; it is shorn of certain details, perhaps because they were no longer deemed relevant.[38] Although the text is not dated, there is good reason to believe that the original decrees were issued in 1009: the injunctions suggest that they were produced in a year in which Monday, Tuesday and Wednesday fell immediately before Michaelmas (29 September), leaving 1009 as the only workable date.[39] *VII Æthelred* is shorter than most of Æthelred's previous ordinances and is clearly a product of the moment: drawn up at Bath in late summer, it consists not so much of general rules and norms as temporary measures to be implemented – as the final clause puts it – 'in order that God almighty might take mercy on us and grant us victory over our enemies and peace' (*ut Deus omnipotens misericordiam nobis faciat et de hostibus triumphum nobis et pacem indulgeat*: chapter 7.1).[40] This was clearly a response to Thorkell's arrival and the choice of site makes good sense within this context: Bath lay not only near the border between the northern and southern halves of Æthelred's kingdom, but also a safe distance from Kent and the southern coast, where the vikings had been most active in recent years. What is more, the site was of great symbolic significance: it was at Bath that Edgar had received his second coronation, a ceremony which marked the high point of his reign (and at which Æthelred himself may have been present) – as at Enham a year earlier, the king was channelling his father's example.[41]

The Bath ordinances must have been issued in late August or early September if they were to stand a chance of implementation before Michaelmas and all indications are that Æthelred called the assembly as soon as he heard of the arrival of Thorkell's forces. The decrees themselves open in

---

[38] Wormald, *Making of English Law*, 330–2; Keynes, 'An Abbot', 179–80; Rabin, *Political Writings*, 184–5.

[39] Keynes, *Diplomas*, 217, n. 224; Wormald, *Making of English Law*, 331, n. 314.

[40] *VII Atr* (ed. Liebermann, I, 260–1; ed. Whitelock, *Councils*, no. 50.i, 375–8). Cf. *VIIa Atr* (ed. Liebermann, I, 262; ed. Whitelock, *Councils*, no. 50.ii, 379–82).

[41] See above, Chapter 2, p. 29, and Chapter 5, pp. 234–5.

typical Wulfstanian fashion, urging all to love and honour one God, to defend the realm and to invoke divine mercy through fasting, alms-giving, confession and abstention from wrongdoing and injustice (chapter 1). More precise requirements follow: a penny is to be given in alms from every hide of land (chapter 1.1); every member of a household is also to give one penny in alms and every thegn is to give a tenth of what he owns (chapter 1.2). Likewise, all adult Christians are required to fast on bread, water and herbs on the Monday, Tuesday and Wednesday preceding Michaelmas (26–28 September) and to process barefoot to church and make confession (chapter 2.1). Priests, for their part, are to join in this procession and sing thirty masses, while deacons and clerics in lower orders are to sing thirty psalms (chapter 2.2). Yet this is not all: the food which would otherwise have been consumed is to be distributed to the poor and slaves are to be exempted from work so that they too can participate (chapters 2.2–3). Hefty fines are laid out for those who do not comply, profits from which are also to be distributed amongst the poor (chapter 2.4). Further undertakings are requested from religious houses 'as long as the present need continues' (*quamdiu necessitas ista nobis est in manibus*): each morning the mass *contra paganos* ('against the pagans') is to be sung for the king and all the people; and at each of the canonical hours (when the Divine Office – a set of psalms, hymns and prayers – was celebrated) members of the community are to prostrate themselves before the altar and sing Psalm 3 ('Oh Lord, how they are multiplied that trouble us'), along with the prayer (or 'collect') *contra paganos* (chapter 3). Every priest, moreover, is to say thirty masses for the king and nation and every monk to recite the psalter – that is, the entire 150 psalms – thirty times (chapter 3.2). Church dues are to be paid correctly and the sale of men into slavery in other countries and theft are both prohibited (chapters 4–5). Finally, the text ends by enjoining that any alms money in arrears should be paid before Michaelmas (chapter 7). All of this, as we have seen, is said to have been decreed so that the English might earn divine mercy and victory over their foes (chapter 7.1).

This is a truly extraordinary text. Drafted by Archbishop Wulfstan with the counsel of the kingdom's great and good, the ordinances represent a concerted effort to confront the nation's ills. The contents conform to what we have already seen of Æthelred's regime: while they acknowledge the military threat presented by the vikings – the first clause demands that all the English participate (with God) in defending the realm – the ultimate aim is less to prepare the kingdom's defence in practical terms, than to entreat the favour of an angered deity. The measures enjoined were nothing new, as Simon Keynes notes: processions were a well-established feature of church life and every year on the three days before Ascension (the so-called rogation days – what would later be known as 'minor rogations') the people were accustomed to go out and entreat divine favour in this fashion.[42] Particular similarities can be seen with Edgar's *Wihtbordesstan* ordinances, which as we have seen were probably issued in response to a visitation of plague in 962–3: there as here piety was entreated in response to calamity.[43] Elements of the programme elaborated are also anticipated by the decision taken by a group of bishops in the late 990s or early 1000s that the mass *contra paganos* should be celebrated on Wednesdays at the larger religious foundations of the realm.[44] More specific inspiration may have come from earlier Carolingian practice. In particular, a set of decrees issued by Charlemagne and his bishops in response to famine in 778–9 anticipates the Bath ordinances in many respects: here every bishop is required to sing three masses and three psalters, one for the king, one for the army, and one 'for the present tribulation' (*pro presente tribulatione*); every priest is to say three masses, and monks, nuns and clerics of lower orders are to sing three psalters; all the population is to engage in two days of fasting; and every bishop, abbot and abbess who can afford it is to give a pound of silver in alms.[45] In subsequent years this combination of alms-giving, procession and prayer, often lasting three days, became the standard response to misfortune; and the basic principle of entreating divine favour through pious

---

[42] Keynes, 'An Abbot', 181–4. See further J. Hill, 'The *Litaniae maiores* and *minores* in Rome, Francia and Anglo-Saxon England: Terminology, Texts and Traditions', *EME* 9 (2000), 211–46; and B. Bedingfield, *The Dramatic Liturgy of Anglo-Saxon England* (Woodbridge, 2002), 191–209.

[43] See above, Chapter 1, p. 41.

[44] See above, Chapter 5, p. 190.

[45] H. Mordek, 'Karls des Großen zweites Kapitular von Herstal und die Hungersnot der Jahre 778/779', *DA* 61 (2005), 1–52; S. Patzold, 'Human Security, fragile Staatlichkeit und Governance im Frühmittelalter. Zur Fragwürdigkeit der Scheidung von Vormoderne und Moderne', *Geschichte und Gesellschaft* 38 (2012), 406–22.

gestures is spelled out in the ordinances of Thionville (805), which thanks to their inclusion in Ansegis of St-Wandrille's collection of decrees found wide circulation, not least in England, where they survive in a manuscript annotated by Archbishop Wulfstan himself.[46] Faced with a large viking force (possibly including elements of Thorkell's army), Æthelred's Aquitanian contemporary, Duke William V (990–1030), is likewise said to have requested the monasteries of his realm to entreat divine mercy through fasts and litanies.[47] Similar practices can be seen to east of the Rhine, where the year before his final showdown with the Magyars Henry I held synods in Dingolfing (for Bavaria) and Erfurt (for the rest of the kingdom) at which he and his bishops instructed the people to observe the fasts and feasts of the apostles and other saints, and to give a penny each (or its equivalent) to the local diocesan bishop; here too divine favour was courted in the face of external threat.[48] Æthelred and his advisers were thus working within an existing tradition, but one which in this precise form was probably new to the English.

One imagines that the resulting efforts were quite the spectacle. Though historians have become wary of reading too much into royal ordinances and other normative texts – these present society as it ought to be, not as it necessarily was – such concerns do not apply to the Bath decrees: issued at a moment of genuine crisis, when the entire nation looked to its king and his counsellors for guidance, it would have been in the interests of all to see that these were implemented. That the ordinances did indeed find wide reception is suggested by their inclusion in *Quadripartitus*, an early twelfth-century compilation and translation (into Latin) of pre-Conquest law; the compiler of this work did not have access to much in the way of

---

[46] Ansegis, *Collectio capitularium* I.112, ed. G. Schmitz, MGH: Cap. n.s. 1 (Hannover, 1996), 499. See Ker, 'Handwriting', 328–30; and M.D. Elliot, 'Canon Law Collections in England *ca* 600–1066: The Manuscript Evidence' (PhD diss., Univ. of Toronto, 2013), 133–8. More generally: M. McCormick, 'The Liturgy of War in the Early Middle Ages: Crisis, Litanies and the Carolingian Monarchy', *Viator* 15 (1984), 1–23, esp. 6–15.

[47] Adémar of Chabannes, *Chronicon* III.53, ed. P. Bourgain with R. Landes and G. Pon, CCCM 129 (Turnhout, 1999), 172. Cf. the fuller account in the α-recension: *ibid.*, 12.

[48] *Die Konzilien Deutschlands und Reichsitaliens 916–1001*, I, *916–960*, ed. E.-D. Hehl, MGH: Conc. 6.i (Hannover, 1987), 106–13 and 120–4; with G. Althoff, *Amicitiae und pacta. Bündnis, Einung, Politik und Gebetsgedenken im beginnenden 10. Jahrhundert*, MGH: Schriften 37 (Hannover, 1992), 75–81.

early Wulfstanian material and the Bath decrees stand apart by their inclusion.[49] We would, therefore, do well to presume that these ordinances found widespread circulation and implementation, and the result would have been something to behold: across England in late September 1009 all those who could be mustered would have made their way to church. There they would have processed around the neighbourhood barefoot, led by a cross-bearer and accompanied by a priest with any relics to hand, before returning to the church to confess their sins. During the procession they would have called upon the mercy of Christ and his saints (perhaps including Edward the Martyr) by chanting litanies – prayers, that is, invoking the intercession of these figures.[50] Most litanies include a request that the king and his army be preserved – a pertinent matter in the face of Thorkell's host – and a few of these show signs of being adjusted to their specific English context (perhaps around this time): one speaks of the king 'of the English' and another of the army 'of the English', while the supplication in the mid-eleventh-century Winchester Troper specifically requests 'that You might see fit to preserve King Æthelred and the army of the English' (*ut Æthelredum regem et exercitum Anglorum conseruare digneris*); a clearer sign of the urgency felt by Æthelred's people at this point would be hard to find.[51] Most litanies close with the three-fold invocation of the Lamb of God, who is asked to take away the sins of the world, spare the suppliants, heed their call and take pity upon them (or 'grant them peace', according to a variant version gaining ground around this time).[52] All this prayer and procession must have represented an impressive show of unity in the face of a common foe: less a 'nation in arms' than a 'nation in prayer', these supplications were a last-ditch attempt to assuage God's wrath. As Simon Keynes remarks, anyone seeking to understand the effects

---

[49] Wormald, *Making of English Law*, 236–44 (esp. the table at 240–1) and 330–1; Keynes, 'An Abbot', 180, n. 139. On *Quadripartitus*, see further Wormald, *Making of English Law*, 465–73.

[50] On litanies, see *Anglo-Saxon Litanies*, ed. Lapidge, 1–61; on Edward's appearances therein, see above, Chapter 4, p. 171, n. 114.

[51] *Litanies*, ed. Lapidge, 233. See also *Leofric Missal*, ed. Orchard, I, 156, and II, 379; and *Litanies*, ed. Lapidge, 239; with Keynes, 'An Abbot', 187–8.

[52] J.A. Jungmann, *Missarum sollemnia. Eine genetische Erklärung der Römischen Messe*, II, *Opfermesse*, rev. ed. (Vienna, 1962), 420–2.

of the viking attacks at this point 'would do well, in their historical imagi-
nations, to join the procession'.[53]

However, the measures do not stop with fasting and processions, as we
have seen: alms were to be distributed and a range of demands was made of
the kingdom's churches. The prayers and psalms requested were also nothing
new: Æthelwulf, the father of Alfred the Great, had requested the singing of
psalms in response to a reduction of secular burdens on religious houses in
854 (immediately before his own departure on pilgrimage to Rome), while
Æthelstan had stipulated that psalms and masses be said for his soul in a
series of unusual diplomas issued over Christmas 932–3.[54] The *Regularis
concordia* (*c.* 970) had regularized such arrangements amongst monastic
circles, establishing that the Morrow Mass should be said 'for the king or
any pressing need' (*pro rege vel quacumque imminente necessitate*); and, as we
have seen, at some point in the late 990s or early 1000s the English bishops
had determined that the mass *contra paganos* should be celebrated weekly.[55]
However, while the principle was well established, the Bath ordinances go
notably further, requiring that the mass *contra paganos* be said at the Morrow
Mass, reflecting the 'pressing need' mentioned in the *Concordia*, the psalm
'Oh Lord, how they are multiplied' and the special prayer (or 'collect')
contra paganos be added to the Divine Office, and the priests and monks
celebrate masses and sing psalters 'for the king and the entire nation' (*pro
rege et omni populo*). All of this liturgical activity must also have been most
impressive; it turned the religious houses of the realm into powerhouses of
prayer. Indeed, the text of the mass *contra paganos* was almost tailor-made
for the situation faced by the English: this invokes the mercy of an offended
deity upon a people suffering 'from the oppression of the pagans' (*de
oppressione paganorum*), which has been brought on account of their sins
(*pro peccatis nostris*).[56] By means of such celebrations the kingdom's monks
and priests fulfilled their obligations as 'those who prayed', a role discussed

---

[53] Keynes, 'An Abbot', 188.

[54] See J.L. Nelson, 'England and the Continent in the Ninth Century: III, Rights and
Rituals', *TRHS* 6th ser. 14 (2004), 1–24, at 14–24; and Foxhall Forbes, *Heaven and Earth*,
232–6, respectively.

[55] *Regularis concordia*, ch. 25 (ed. Spath and Symons, 86). See also above, Chapter 5, p. 190.

[56] *Leofric Missal*, ed. Orchard, II, 341–2.

by both Ælfric of Eynsham and Wulfstan of York in these years; they too were doing their bit for the nation's defence.[57] The Bath decrees thus seek not only to purify the nation, but also to marshal the spiritual weapons at its disposal. The extraordinary nature of the demands speaks of the severity of the situation. Æthelred and his advisers (above all Wulfstan) were starting to become exasperated; for all the efforts of previous years, the viking threat showed no signs of abating.

It has often been noted that this activity bears comparison with the Peace of God movement which was starting to gain ground in France, Catalonia and the Low Countries in these years.[58] Less of a coherent programme than the name suggests, the Peace constituted a series of loosely related efforts undertaken by secular and (in particular) ecclesiastical authorities with the aim of stamping out lawlessness, oppression of the weak and plundering of the church. It took the form of local gatherings at which relics were brought forward and the people swore oaths that they would desist from a variety of unchristian activities, from theft (especially of church goods), to attacks on the defenceless, to the seizure of livestock.[59] These certainly bear a resemblance to Æthelred's legislation of 1008 and 1009, especially insofar as the aim was to stamp out a range of 'unchristian' and 'unlawful' activities. However, one should not press the similarities too far. The Bath ordinances, like the Enham decrees of the previous year, were a national affair, while the Peace of God was a fundamentally local phenomenon: introduced by bishops, sometimes (though by no means always) in conjunction with local secular lords, it reflects above all the interests and concerns of these prelates. Moreover, while the English initiatives of 1008 and 1009 were occasioned by external threats, the Peace of God was in most cases a response to violence and aggression within West Frankish society: it was aimed at its more lawless elements.

---

[57] T.E. Powell, 'The "Three Orders" of Society in Anglo-Saxon England', *ASE* 23 (1994), 103–32.

[58] Lawson, 'Archbishop Wulfstan', 577; Wormald, 'Eleventh-Century State Builder', 17.

[59] J. Bowman, 'Councils, Memory and Mills: The Early Development of the Peace of God in Catalonia', *EME* 8 (1999), 99–129; T. Head, 'Peace and Power in France around the Year 1000', *Essays in Medieval Studies* 23 (2006), 1–17; S. Hamilton, *Church and People in the Medieval West, 900–1200* (London, 2013), 268–70.

As Michael Dolley first noted, the Bath decrees take on their full signif-icance when viewed alongside an extraordinary issue of coins introduced around this time, probably at the same gathering: the so-called *Agnus Dei*, which bears an image of the Lamb of God on the obverse and a bird, prob-ably a dove (though conceivably an eagle), on the reverse (Plate 2).[60] Since the mid-eighth century it had been common for English coins to bear an image of the ruler on the obverse (whence the modern designation 'heads'), and since Edgar's reform this custom had become the rule; by replacing this with an image of the Lamb of God these coins thus broke strongly with convention.[61] Yet this is not the only unusual feature of the type. The place-ment of a dove on the reverse is also something of a novelty, as is the form of the royal style, which in most cases is spelled out fully (rather than abbre-viated), harking back to practices of the pre-reform era. Perhaps most note-worthy of all is the small scale and unusual mint distribution of the issue: to date only twenty-one full specimens have been found (as well as two so-called 'mules'), produced at nine mints, mostly of minor to middling standing; it would seem that large parts of the country did not witness the minting of these coins, while it must have been brief in those that did. Given the close royal oversight of coinage in this period, the introduction (and discontinuation) of this issue must have been decided upon by the king and his counsellors, and there is every reason to believe that the Bath assembly of 1009 played a central role in this regard. Indeed, though it is rarely possible to date a coin issue firmly, in this case various factors speak in favour of 1009, and probably the second half of this year. Thus, of the thirteen moneyers known to have struck the type, three were first active in the *Helmet* issue (*c.* 1003/5–9) and five are last attested in the *Last Small Cross* (*c.* 1009–17), suggesting that the *Agnus Dei* falls between these two. The existence of two 'mules' – that is, coins bearing 'heads' from one issue

---

[60] [R.H.]M. Dolley, 'The Nummular Brooch from Sulgrave', in *England Before the Conquest: Studies in Primary Sources Presented to Dorothy Whitelock*, ed. P. Clemoes and K. Hughes (Cambridge, 1971), 333–49, esp. 338–41. A substantial unpublished typescript of Michael Dolley on the subject (*c.* 1960) survives amongst his papers in the Fitzwilliam Museum, Cambridge (Dolley archive, no. 667). See also S. Keynes and R. Naismith, 'The *Agnus Dei* Pennies of King Æthelred the Unready', *ASE* 40 (2011), 175–223; and cf. D. Woods, 'The *Agnus Dei* Penny of King Æthelred II: A Call to Hope in the Lord (Isaiah XL)?', *ASE* 42 (2013), 299–309.

[61] Naismith, *Money and Power*, 53–69 and 87–127. See also Keynes, 'An Abbot', 190.

and 'tails' from another – combining the image of the Agnus Dei with a reverse of the *Last Small Cross* also points in this direction, since such coins occur during shifts between types, generally involving an older obverse and a newer reverse.[62] We have, moreover, good reason to believe that the *Last Small Cross* was introduced in late 1009, since it was only produced briefly at Oxford and Wallingford before these mints ceased operating, a development which has been plausibly associated with the sack of the former in the winter of 1009–10.[63] All evidence, therefore, points to a date in mid- to late 1009 for the *Agnus Dei*, shortly before the introduction of the *Last Small Cross*.[64]

The imagery of the issue makes good sense within this context: as we have seen, the Bath gathering produced a series of initiatives designed to propitiate God and a short-lived coin issue would sit well alongside these. Indeed, in the three days running up to Michaelmas 1009 the people of England would have been collectively invoking the Lamb of God in their prayers and litanies – what better way, so it must have seemed, to express this than in an issue of coins bearing the Lamb of God's image. Yet the Agnus Dei was not only a symbol of peace: it was also the symbol of Christ at the Last Judgement, the figure who according to Revelation leads his followers to triumph over the forces of evil (Revelation XVII.16, XXI.23, etc.). The dove, the symbol of the Holy Spirit and Christ's peaceful nature, was a natural accompaniment. Though it has been proposed that the *Agnus Dei* was intended as a full (or 'substantive') type, which would last some four to eight years, the small number of coins and unusual range of mints involved suggests a rather more specific purpose: a 'special issue' of sorts, designed as a visual counterpart to the acts of prayer and penitence

---

[62] Keynes and Naismith, '*Agnus Dei* Pennies', 217 (*a*) (description) and 223 (image). Cf. [R.H.]M. Dolley, 'The Coins', in *The Archaeology of Anglo-Saxon England*, ed. D.M. Wilson (London, 1976), 349–72, at 366. I am grateful to Rory Naismith for information regarding the second of these mules, the full details of which have yet to be published.

[63] C.S.S. Lyon, 'The Significance of the Sack of Oxford in 1009/10 for the Chronology of the Coinage of Æthelred II', *BNJ* 35 (1966), 34–7; Allen, *Mints and Money*, 19–21.

[64] J.C. Moesgaard and S.Å. Tornbjerg, 'A Sixteenth Agnus Dei Penny of Æthelred II', *NC* 159 (1999), 327–32, at 331; Keynes, 'An Abbot', 198–9. Cf. Lawson, 'Archbishop Wulfstan', 575–6; and P. Dalton, 'Sites and Occasions of Peacemaking in England and Normandy, c. 900–c. 1150', *HSJ* 16 (2005), 12–26, at 22–3.

undertaken at this point.[65] Though one cannot be certain that the coinage was instituted in time for Michaelmas, it is a nice (if rather wistful) thought that the alms-giving instituted at Bath was undertaken in this distinctive new currency. Indeed, Dolley argued that recoinages generally took place at Michaelmas, and while this, like much of his 'system', must be treated with caution, in this case he may well have been right: coins of the *Last Small Cross* type were being struck at Oxford before winter, so the *Agnus Dei* must have given way to it in the late summer or early autumn. The care that went into the production of these coins, whose dies were cut to as high a standard as those of other substantive issues, has surprised some, but can be readily explained by the circumstances of their production: as an invocation of divine mercy at a critical point, it was natural that they should be given the same care as those of any other major type (the process was, in any case, not particularly difficult or time-consuming). In fact, the *Agnus Dei* may from the start have been intended as a prelude to the *Last Small Cross*, which was initially struck at the same weight standard. The latter issue may in a sense have taken forward the same message: as Dolley observed on many occasions, this type looks back iconographically to the reform coinage of Edgar, perhaps representing a further attempt to invoke this earlier 'Golden Age'.[66] In any case, a brief issue sits well with the distribution of mints: dies were normally sent to the more remote minting places first and there may not have been time to produce sufficient quantities for more major centres such as London and Winchester.[67] It may also be significant that the mints in question were in regions spared Scandinavian activity in 1009: they cluster around central Wessex (Malmesbury, Salisbury) and the

[65] Keynes and Naismith, '*Agnus Dei* Pennies', 196–201. See also B. Malmer, 'Agnus Dei i Bath år 1009', *Myntkontakt* 4/5 (1984), 126–7, at 127; Blackburn, 'Æthelred's Coinage', 160; Stewart, 'Coinage and Recoinage', 477; Keynes, 'An Abbot', 190–9; and Allen, *Mints and Money*, 38; and cf. Lyon, 'Sack of Oxford', 34; Dolley, 'Nummular Brooch', 339; [R.H.]M. Dolley and T. Talvio, 'The Twelfth of the Agnus Dei Pennies of Æthelred II', *BNJ* 47 (1977), 131–3, at 133; [R.H.]M. Dolley and T. Talvio, 'A Thirteenth Agnus Dei Penny of Æthelred II', *BNJ* 49 (1979), 122–5, at 124; B. Kluge, 'Das älteste Exemplar vom Agnus Dei-Typ', in *Studies in Late Anglo-Saxon Coinage in Memory of Bror Emil Hildebrand*, ed. K. Jonsson (Stockholm, 1990), 139–56, at 150; I. Leimus, 'A Fourteenth Agnus Dei Penny of Æthelred II', in *ibid.*, 159–63, at 161; and Woods, '*Agnus Dei* Penny', 307–8.

[66] Dolley, 'Introduction', 127. See similarly P. Stafford, 'Historical Implications of the Regional Production of Dies under Æthelred II', *BNJ* 48 (1978), 35–51, at 49.

[67] Keynes and Naismith, '*Agnus Dei* Pennies', 199–200.

Midlands (Hereford, Stafford, Derby, Nottingham, Leicester, Northampton, Stamford), perhaps reflecting the effective reach of royal authority.[68] Late Anglo-Saxon society was highly monetized, at least by early medieval standards, and there is every reason to believe that these coins, even produced on a restricted scale, would have reached a wide audience. Their iconography would have been readily understandable: the Lamb of God was a well-established biblical figure (known not least from the mass and litanies of saints), as was the dove, even if their appearance on coins was something new. The high value of the Anglo-Saxon penny, which according to one recent assessment would have 'had the buying power of a substantial number of modern US dollars, euros or pounds sterling',[69] means that we can be confident that attention was given to the finer details of such objects. In fact, there seems to have been something of a vogue for 'Lamb of God' and 'Dove' imagery in the metalwork of subsequent years, indicating that this issue made quite a stir.[70] The type was also to have something of a legacy, as a number of later continental coinages were to employ the iconography of the Lamb of God (in most cases without direct knowledge of Æthelred's type, however).[71] The *Agnus Dei* is, in a sense, the numismatic equivalent of the charters of restitution of the 990s: it breaks all the rules and is all the more significant for this fact. While Dolley thought that its iconographic innovations – particularly the replacement of the royal bust with the Lamb of God – were undertaken without royal fiat, leading to its swift recall, this is most improbable; such a striking break with convention would only have been conceivable with royal approval and everything about the issue suggests an intimate association with the king's other undertakings at this point. Thus, like the Bath ordinances, the *Agnus Dei* speaks of Æthelred's steely determination to set the affairs of his realm to rights: the king was calling upon Christ (in the guise of the Lamb of God) to wash away the nation's sins and grant it peace. There may also have been darker undertones. As

[68] Kluge, 'Agnus Dei-Typ', 149; Keynes, 'An Abbot', 197.

[69] Naismith, *Money and Power*, 288.

[70] Dolley, 'Nummular Brooch', 333–6; Keynes and Naismith, '*Agnus Dei* Pennies', 203–6.

[71] M. Dhenin, 'L'"Agnus Dei" thème monétaire', in *Le bestiaire: des monnaies, des sceaux et des médailles*, ed. P. Dehaye (Paris, 1974), 163–77; E. Cavalié, 'Le type numismatique de Saint-Gilles', *Revue numismatique* 6th ser. 162 (2006), 417–42.

noted, the lamb was also the symbol of Christ at the Last Judgement, who would come to judge the age with fire; to Æthelred and his advisers (above all Wulfstan), it might have seemed that this time had come.

There are a number of further indications of the impact of Thorkell's army in these years. Pride of place must go to Wulfstan's *Sermo Lupi ad Anglos* ('Sermon of the Wolf to the English'), the best-known literary work of Æthelred's reign and possibly the most famous prose text in the entire Old English corpus. The *Sermo* survives in three different versions – 'short', 'medium' and 'long' – and was clearly a favoured work of the archbishop, which he continued to revise and re-preach over the course of many years.[72] Each of the versions survives in only one or two manuscripts and we should imagine that they represent snapshots of a constantly evolving text: this was not so much a finished sermon for circulation in the manner of modern works of printed literature, as a performance piece which might be brought out, dusted off and declaimed whenever Wulfstan saw fit. Opinions divide as to which – if any – of the surviving versions represents the 'original', but until recently it was generally agreed that whichever was to be favoured, its composition was to be placed in 1014.[73] The key evidence comes from the fact that all three versions share a phrase referring to how the two greatest acts of treachery, betraying one's lord to death and betraying one's lord into exile, have *both* transpired 'in this land' (*on þysan earde*). Only the shorter version of the sermon goes on to give examples of both of these acts (the murder of Edward the Martyr and the exile of Æthelred), but it is clear that all three must originally have had a phrase to this effect; and since Æthelred's exile took place in the winter of 1013–14, this has served as a convenient date after which the sermon must have been preached (or *terminus post quem*).[74] This seems to find confirmation in

---

[72] On Wulfstan's approach to composition, see A. Orchard, 'Wulfstan as Reader, Writer, and Rewriter', in *The Old English Homily: Precedent, Practice, and Appropriation*, ed. A.J. Kleist (Turnhout, 2007), 311–40.

[73] See, e.g., *Sermo Lupi*, ed. Whitelock, 6; *Homilies of Wulfstan*, ed. Bethurum, 104; S. Dien, '*Sermo Lupi ad Anglos*: The Order and Date of the Three Versions', *Neuphilologische Mitteilungen* 76 (1975), 561–70, at 562; Godden, 'Apocalypse and Invasion', 151–2; and J. Wilcox, 'Wulfstan's *Sermo Lupi ad Anglos* as Political Performance: 16 February 1014 and Beyond', in *Wulfstan, Archbishop of York*, ed. M. Townend (Turnhout, 2004), 375–96.

[74] Wulfstan, *Sermo Lupi*, (BH) ll. 64–71, (C) ll. 77–83, (EI) ll. 71–8 (ed. Bethurum, 257–8, 263, 270).

one of the manuscript witnesses to the longer version, whose rubrics place the *Sermo*'s preaching in 1014.

Impeccable though such logic is, it has its limitations, and there are hints within the text itself that the sermon may have had a life before it reached its present (i.e. post-1014) state. For a start, the manuscript containing the medium version dates this work to 1009, introducing it as 'the sermon of the wolf [i.e. Wulfstan] to the English at the time when the Danes persecuted them most greatly, which was the ninth year of the millennium since the incarnation of our Lord Jesus Christ [i.e. 1009]' (*Sermo Lupi ad Anglos quando Dani maxime persecuti sunt eos, quid fuit anno millesimo. VIIII. ab incarnatione domini nostri Iesu Cristi*) (Plate 14). This might be dismissed as a simple textual error – the Roman numeral VIIII could easily enough be misread for XIIII[75] – were it not for the fact that there is a separate statement within the opening section of the text to the effect that it was 'composed in the days of Æthelred, four years before he died' (*on Æðelredes cyninges dagum gediht, feower geara fæce ær he forferde*), that is, in 1012. Though emendation is also possible here – Whitelock and Pope suggested that 'few' (*feaw(e)ra*) was misread as 'four' (*feower*) by a later scribe[76] – as the coincidences mount it seems best to keep an open mind. The apparent inconsistency between these two dates (1009 and 1012) need not concern us overly much: if, like most of Wulfstan's writings, this sermon was reworked over many years, both might in some sense be 'correct'. In fact, an early modern annotation to one of the texts of the long version, whose rubrics merely state that it was preached 'in the days of King Æthelred' (*in dies Æþelredi regis*), baldly states 'Anno Christi 1009' ('the year of Christ 1009').[77] Though we cannot be sure of the annotator's source – it is conceivable that he had seen the text of the medium version – it would be foolish to ignore such varied traditions associating this work with 1009–12. More importantly, perhaps, the 'canonical' date of 1014 is itself far less secure than we might like to think. Though the authority of

---

[75] *Sermo Lupi*, ed. Whitelock, 6. See also Wilcox, 'Wulfstan's *Sermo Lupi*', 377.

[76] J.C. Pope, Review of Bethurum, *Homilies of Wulfstan*, *Modern Language Notes* 74 (1959), 333–40, at 338; *Sermo Lupi*, ed. Whitelock, 6.

[77] Oxford, Bodleian Library, Hatton 113, fol. 84v.

the manuscript containing this date is considerable – it was produced within Wulfstan's circles and is annotated by the archbishop himself – at the crucial point in the rubrication 'XIIII' (i.e. 14) has been written over an erasure in lighter ink (Plate 15).[78] This number was, in other words, a correction, and while it is impossible to know what originally stood there, it is tempting to suggest that it was XIIII, in which case the rubrics would have read 1009, like those of the manuscript of the medium version (which otherwise match these word-for-word). We know that Wulfstan frequently revisited and reworked his writings and these traditions associating a text clearly completed in 1014 or later with the period between 1009 and 1012 would seem to represent textual barnacles, witnesses to now-lost earlier versions of the text. On this basis, Simon Keynes argues that the initial composition of the *Sermo* took place during the period of Thorkell's raids, perhaps in 1009.[79] The description of the sermon in the two rubrics to bear dates (1009 and 1014), which are probably authorial, points in this direction: both state that this work was preached to the English 'when the Danes persecuted them most greatly', a description which is difficult to square with 1014, when after a brief but calm few months of Danish rule an unusual turn of good fortune landed Æthelred back on the English throne, but might well apply to the years between 1009 and 1012, which as we have seen witnessed almost constant ravaging, culminating in the sack of Canterbury and the death of Archbishop Ælfheah.

Though we cannot be certain of the form of this hypothetical earlier sermon preached by Wulfstan, it perhaps most closely resembled the long version preserved in manuscripts bearing the archbishop's own annotations (and probably revised and re-preached in 1014).[80] Here the prelate opens by impressing upon his listeners the proximity of the end of time, then goes on

---

[78] BL, Cotton Nero A. i, fol. 110r; with N.R. Ker, *Catalogue of Manuscripts Containing Anglo-Saxon* (Oxford, 1957), 213; and Keynes, 'An Abbot', 209, n. 270.

[79] Keynes, 'An Abbot', 203–13. See also *Homilies of Wulfstan*, ed. Bethurum, 356, who already entertained the possibility; and cf. A. Lemke, 'Fear-Mongering, Political Shrewdness or Setting the Stage for a "Holy Society"? – Wulfstan's *Sermo Lupi ad Anglos*', *English Studies* 95 (2014), 758–76, at 760–3, who is too swift to dismiss the evidence of manuscript rubrics.

[80] Keynes, 'An Abbot', 211–13. Cf. Lionarons, *Homiletic Writings*, 155–6, for the alternative possibility that the medium version comes closest to the original. The only substantial difference is the final section in which the example of Gildas is invoked, which the medium version lacks, but fits the context of 1009–12 well (cf. Dien, 'Sermo', 562–3).

to note the various signs of suffering and iniquity amongst the English which have brought them to this sorry state: they have neglected religion, infringed upon church rights, oppressed the poor and helpless, betrayed their lords (including Edward – here the key phrase mentioned above) and sold each other into slavery in foreign lands. All of these and other misfortunes, so Wulfstan continues, have come to pass on account of sin. The very bonds of society are bursting: men are ravaging female slaves before selling them abroad, and kinsmen and neighbours are selling one another into slavery for base profit. This is no wonder, since the English have been guilty of perjury, fornication, treachery and many other heinous offences, which Wulfstan lists and discusses at length. Worst of all, despite their manifest sins, they have not sought repentance on account of their pride. The archbishop notes that there is a precedent for such developments: Gildas had warned the British of their moral turpitude long ago, but because they would not heed his monition they were conquered by the English; now the English faced the prospect of a similar fate. The *Sermo* is certainly an impressive indictment of the society of Wulfstan's day. It should not, however, be read too literally: it is a hortatory work, not a piece of detached observation, and large sections read like a catalogue of every conceivable form of wrongdoing. Yet, if the *Sermo* is a treacherous guide to the social and political realities of Wulfstan's day, it remains an invaluable barometer of feeling at and around the English court: to the archbishop, as to many others, it must have seemed as if society was coming apart at the very seams. Wulfstan's statements would certainly have resonated with his audience. As we have seen, the cult of Edward was a major concern in these years, and the mention of his mistreatment is surely no accident. The extended discussion of the crimes of the nation, ranging from violating church sanctuary to oppression of the poor and from disloyalty to rape, will also have chimed with the experiences of many, as would the belief – expressed in many other contemporary sources – that the ongoing viking raids were divine punishment for such iniquity. The reference to the 'excessive taxes' (*ungyldas*) which had oppressed the nation, leading to the stripping of churches, will also have sounded familiar, as would the mention of crop failure (1005). The description of the oppression of the church is more formulaic, but the mention of 'persecutors of monasteries' (*mynsterhatan*) will doubtless have conjured up memories of Æthelred's actions in the 980s. The final peroration must have struck a particular chord: the parallels between the situation of the English, tottering on the brink of collapse, and their British forebears were bound to give pause. Here Wulfstan took inspiration from the letters of his earlier countryman, Alcuin, who in the wake of the viking sack of Lindisfarne (791) drew a similar analogy between the fate of the English of his day and that of the earlier Britons.[81] The *Sermo Lupi* is thus in a sense a more impassioned version of the kind of ideas we have seen expressed in charters, letters and legal ordinances since the 990s: the archbishop sees the vikings above all as a moral threat, which can only be confronted (if it is to be confronted at all) by a return to pious ways. That the king felt similarly stands to reason; indeed, it is possible that he was amongst the original audience to this most extraordinary of sermons.

Wulfstan's voice may be the loudest, but it is not the only one in these years. As Kathryn Powell has shown, a series of annotations on a manu-script containing homiletic works (mainly by Ælfric) produced in the early eleventh century, was also a reaction to the viking raids of this period.[82] The annotator was probably operating in Kent (perhaps at St Augustine's in Canterbury), a region which had suffered especially heavily between 1009 and 1012. The first of his additions is to Ælfric's homily on Ash Wednesday, where within a list of worldly cares he inserts an aside to the effect that the English are afflicted daily 'by either invasions or various other misfortunes' (*ægðer ge on heregangum ge on oðrum mislicum unbelimpum*) (perhaps he had the famine of 1005 in mind); clearly, these were the cares which weighed most on the mind. To an anonymous homily for the fourth week of Lent later on in the same manuscript he then extends the list of horrors against which the preacher exhorts his audience to pray for protection; inspired by the mention of 'heathens', he inserts a subclause to the effect that it is these people 'who have afflicted us most greatly with excessive taxes and terrible invasion' (*þe us ormætlice swiðe mid [un]gylde 7 mid*

---

[81] Alcuin, *Epistola* 129 (ed. Dümmler, 191–2); with G. Mann, 'The Development of Wulfstan's Alcuin Manuscript', in *Wulfstan, Archbishop of York*, ed. M. Townend (Turnhout, 2004), 235–78. See also N. Howe, *Migration and Mythmaking in Anglo-Saxon England* (New Haven, CT, 1989), 8–32.

[82] K. Powell, 'Viking Invasions and Marginal Annotations in Cambridge, Corpus Christi College 162', *ASE* 37 (2008), 151–71.

weridgryre offset habbað). Such annotations provide a vivid sense of the concern and consternation felt in the face of the viking threat. Moreover, if Powell is correct, these annotations were made for the purpose of preaching; such sentiments would thus not have remained a dead letter. There is other evidence that the kingdom was under pressure at this point. As we have noted, following the sack of Oxford in early 1010 the moneyers there and at nearby Wallingford (which may also have suffered) ceased to operate.[83] Several other mints were relocated around this time: that at Chichester, which given its proximity to the Channel and the Isle of Wight may have been particularly exposed, seems to have been transferred to *Sith[m]estebyri* (probably the hillfort at Cissbury) during the *Last Small Cross* and first part of the *Quatrefoil* issues (c. 1009–23), and that at Ilchester was relocated to the fortified site at South Cadbury for the *Last Small Cross* (c. 1009–18).[84] These latter transfers were clearly precautionary, perhaps reflecting lessons learned from the sack of Wilton six years earlier. What is more, the sites in question may well have been refortified as part of the process (at Cadbury, at least, there is evidence of this). As previously, it would seem that the king's calls for purity and penitence did not preclude more hardnosed strategic planning.

Hints of similar strains can be found in royal charters of these years. As we have seen, a diploma issued in 1009 in favour of Athelney requests prayers 'for our frailty' (*pro nostra fragilitate*), a line which may well reflect the sombre atmosphere at court.[85] Thereafter, the charter record goes remarkably quiet, as it had in 991–2: a further diploma was issued in late 1009 (perhaps at or around Christmas) to the influential Midland thegn Morcar, but no further ones are known till 1011.[86] At this point a trickle

[83] See above, p. 276.

[84] R.H.M. Dolley, 'Three Late Anglo-Saxon Notes', *BNJ* 28 (1955–7), 88–105, at 99–105; R.H.M. Dolley and F. Elmore Jones, 'The Mints "aet Gothabyrig" and "aet Sith(m)estebyrig"', *BNJ* 28 (1955–7), 270–82, at 277–82; Allen, *Mints and Money*, 4, 19–21 and 378. Note, however, that there is only one moneyer from Chichester who shares a name with those later attested at Cissbury (Leofwine), and this is a very common one, so the identification is less certain than some of the earlier literature suggests. (I am grateful to Rory Naismith for guidance on this point.)

[85] S 921 (KCD 1306).

[86] S 922 (*Burt* 32). On the dating, see Keynes, *Diplomas*, 263–4.

returns with two charters, probably issued between the decision to pay off Thorkell's army (made soon after Christmas) and the sack of Canterbury in late September (Archbishop Ælfheah attests both). The first of these grants Æthelmod two hides in Derbyshire in return for twenty-one pounds of gold – a hefty price, perhaps designed to fill royal coffers in the face of new demands for tribute.[87] The second, for the same Morcar favoured in 1009, makes no mention of a payment, perhaps indicating the favour in which the thegn was held.[88] Indeed, Morcar was something of a man of the moment: he is one of the most prominent thegns in diploma witness-lists at this point and was to receive a further grant in the following year.[89] What is more, Morcar's brother, Sigeferth, who often subscribes beside him and was clearly also a man of considerable means, attests the first of these diplomas (in 1009) – the only to survive as an original – with his name written in ALL CAPS (or uncial script, to be precise).[90] It is striking that all three of these charters come from the same archive, Burton, one of the few Anglo-Saxon archives to survive intact from the north Midlands. This, coupled with the repeated appearance of Morcar in these documents, raises the possibility that Æthelred and his court spent much of these years in the region, which was largely spared Thorkell's ravages. If so, this would represent a stark break with established practice: as we have seen, earlier West Saxon kings rarely spent much time north of the Thames Valley and Æthelred seems to have spent most of his time around London, Oxfordshire and the West Saxon heartlands.[91] This region also happened to be the stomping ground of Eadric Streona, who rose to further prominence in these years. These documents bear witness to other signs of strain too. The diploma for Æthelmod in 1011 opens with an unusual chrismon – a symbol representing Christ, often found at the start of such documents – which is composed not only of the Greek letters *chi* (X) and *rho* (P) (the first two

---

[87] S 923 (*Burt* 33).

[88] S 924 (*Burt* 34).

[89] S 928 (*Burt* 37).

[90] *Facsimiles of Anglo-Saxon Charters*, ed. S. Keynes, Anglo-Saxon Charters: Suppl. Series 1 (London, 1991), no. 17. The other diplomas in favour of Morcar only survive in the thirteenth-century Burton cartulary, where their witness-lists have been truncated; it is possible that Sigeferth was accorded similar treatment there.

[91] See above, Chapter 3, pp. 98–9; and Hill, *Atlas*, 91.

letters of 'Christ' in Greek), but also integrates the Roman letter 'A' into the arrangement, allowing the device to be deciphered as both 'Christ' and 'PAX' (the Latin for 'peace').[92] This was not a one-off: a diploma of 1012 in favour of Bishop Godwine of Rochester – the same prelate to whom Æthelred had made tearful amends in 998 – contains a similar device, and it may be that other charters of these years were similarly adorned.[93] Clearly, peace was on the mind of many at court and it is easy to see a connection between such symbolism and the iconography of the *Agnus Dei* type. The second diploma in favour of Morcar (1011) is similarly revealing, albeit on different grounds. This opens with a unique preamble meditating on Creation and its splendours, all of which were brought to naught by the short-sighted weakness of mankind. On account of this, so the document continues, man has lost his immortality and will receive what befits him, and so too 'kingdom after kingdom advances and declines rapidly' (*regnumque post regnum mobiliter uadit et perniciter recedit*).[94] While earthly transience is a popular theme for such documents and the final part of this phrase had been used in two earlier diplomas, it is hard not to see herein a deeper reflection upon the state of the English realm: in early 1011 there can have been little doubt that this was 'declining rapidly'. The effect of this material is cumulative; it shows that peace and stability were on the mind; the entire nation, led by Æthelred himself, now strove to obtain divine mercy through whatever means possible.

Though the events of 1009–12 left deep scars, they also acted as a catalyst. The most obvious result was the rise in status of Ealdorman Eadric: after almost half a decade of attesting towards the bottom of the lists of ealdormen, in 1012 he suddenly leapfrogs his more senior colleagues and this new-found prominence finds expression in the important role accorded to him in negotiations with Thorkell in early 1011. In the following years Eadric would be Æthelred's right-hand man. His freedom of operation is revealed in Welsh reports that he attacked St David's in 1012 (though he

---

[92] S. Keynes, 'An Interpretation of the *Pacs, Pax* and *Paxs* Pennies', *ASE* 7 (1978), 165–73, at 169. See also *Charters of Burton*, ed. Sawyer, pl. 1, for an image.

[93] S 926 (*Roch* 33). For the device, see *Textus Roffensis*, ed. P.H. Sawyer, 2 pts, EEMF 7, 11 (Copenhagen, 1957–62), fol. 159v; with Keynes, '*Pacs, Pax* and *Paxs* Pennies', 169.

[94] S 924 (*Burt* 34). Cf. S 784 (BCS 1285), S 890 (unpublished).

was not the first marcher lord to act thus) and his dominant position also occasioned comment in a late eleventh-century Worcester source, which remarks that he 'ruled like sub-king' (*quasi subregulus dominabatur*).[95] Such power and influence finds little immediate precedent and looks forward to the kind of position enjoyed by Earl Godwine and his sons in the second half of the eleventh century.[96] It was also in late 1012 or early 1013 that Æthelmær, who had retired to Eynsham in 1005, seems to have returned to political life, attaining his father's post of ealdorman of the western shires. What led to his return is unclear. Perhaps Æthelmær's promotion was an olive branch to those who disapproved of Eadric's meteoric rise (Æthelmær had, after all, belonged to the group side-lined in the 'palace revolution'). Alternatively, Æthelred may have hoped that the West Country magnate's return would help restore order in the south-west; there had not been an ealdorman in the region since the death of Æthelmær's father, and this might have seemed an opportune moment to strengthen the region's defensive capabilities. It was, therefore, a notably different court which emerged out of the crucible of these years: one dominated by Eadric, but one in which Æthelmær could also find a place.

Faction, friction and conquest, 1013–16

Once peace had been made in 1012 the English must have let out a collective sigh of relief; after decades of intermittent raiding and three years of non-stop ravaging, there was finally the prospect of peace, however brief. Though wiser heads at court probably had their doubts as to how long the agreement would hold, there was no reason to believe that the English would face further attacks as soon as they did: Thorkell had carved out a fearsome reputation for himself in previous years and it was not unreasonable to

---

[95] See *Brut y Tywysogyon: Peniarth MS. 20*, *s.a.* 1011 (= 1012), ed. T. Jones (Cardiff, 1941), 13; *Brut y Tywysogyon: Red Book of Hergest Version*, *s.a.* 1011 (= 1012), ed. and trans. T. Jones, 2nd edn (Cardiff, 1973), 18–19; *Brenhinedd y Saesson*, *s.a.* 1011 (= 1012), ed. and trans. T. Jones (Cardiff, 1971), 48–9; with K.L. Maund, *Ireland, Wales, and England in the Eleventh Century* (Woodbridge, 1991), 121–2; and *Hemingi chartularium*, ed. Hearne, I, 280–1, respectively.

[96] Keynes, 'Cnut's Earls', 78–88, esp. 78–9. See also Fleming, *Kings and Lords*, 53–103; and cf. Baxter, *Earls of Mercia*, esp. 61–151, for important caveats.

expect that his presence would deter further raids, at least for a time.[97] Such policies had proven successful elsewhere and there was nothing to say they could not work here: Thorkell may have been little more than a hired sword, but so long as the English kept paying, he had every reason to keep his word (as, indeed, he largely seems to have done).[98] The king himself seems to have been spending an increasing amount of time in London, which had escaped the worst of the recent ravages; it was to be his safe haven right up until his death. It was probably here in mid-April 1013 that two charters were issued in favour of a thegn called Sigered. The documents in question are distinctively worded and the attestation of Bishop Ælfhun in the second of these – 'I, Ælfhun, bishop of London, dictating in accordance with the king and his instructions, ordered that this charter and the other two, namely those for Tottenham [which does not survive] and Hatfield [which does], should be written' – suggests that the prelate may have been responsible for their production.[99] If so, this would be a further sign of the king's growing reliance on London and its redoubtable bishop, who was later to accompany him into exile in Normandy and whom John of Worcester identifies as 'tutor' (*magister*) to the young princes Edward and Alfred.[100] Ælfhun himself enjoyed connections to the circles of monastic reform and may have previously been abbot of Milton in Dorset.[101] Given this, these documents may reveal something about the atmosphere at court. The first, in particular, is worthy of note: it opens with a preamble meditating on the vicissitudes of this world, noting that these are signs that the end is nigh; the king's fortunes may have been saved by the previous year's negotiations, but foreboding was apparently still the order of the day.

As it turned out, such concerns were well-founded: in August 1013 Swein Forkbeard arrived off the coast of Sandwich with a large fleet. Swein

[97] A. Williams, 'Thorkell the Tall and the Bubble of Reputation: The Vicissitudes of Fame', in *Danes in Wessex: The Scandinavian Impact on Southern England, c. 800–c. 1100*, ed. R. Lavelle and S. Roffey (Oxford, 2015), 144–57.

[98] See above, Chapter 4, p. 176, with literature cited at n. 128.

[99] S 931a (unpublished), S 931b (unpublished): 'Ego Elfhun Lundonie ciuitatis presul hanc cartulam aliasque duas scilicet at Totanham et at Hatfeld dictitans rege suiusque precipientibus perscribere iussi'. See Keynes, 'Regenbald', 186, n. 7.

[100] John of Worcester, *Chronicon*, *s.a.* 1013 (ed. Darlington and McGurk, 474).

[101] Keynes, *Atlas*, table LXI; Rabin, 'Wulfstan at London', 191.

was by this point at the height of his powers: he had seen off the challenge of Olaf Tryggvason *c.* 999 and enjoyed control not only over the increasingly wealthy and powerful kingdom of Denmark (which stretched well into Skåne in modern Sweden), but also over much of Norway and perhaps also parts of southern Sweden. Indeed, if there was any threat to his position, it probably came from Thorkell: also of Danish descent, Swein may have feared that the viking leader harboured similar ambitions to Olaf, who had used wealth and experience gained in England to win a kingdom for himself back at home.[102] This may explain why this expedition differed from Swein's previous forays: it was an invasion of conquest, not pillage and plunder. That this was so was clear from the start: rather than ravaging the southern heartlands of Æthelred's realm as he had in the past, the Danish monarch headed straight north to Gainsborough in Lincolnshire, where he accepted the submission of Uhtred and the Northumbrians, the men of Lindsey (roughly modern-day Lincolnshire) and the people of the 'Five Boroughs' of the north Midlands.

Soon thereafter, the remaining men north of Watling Street (the traditional dividing line between 'English' and 'Danish' parts of the realm) joined him.[103] Swein was clearly exploiting divisions within the English realm: though the 'Danelaw' had been ruled by southern kings since 954, it remained culturally and politically distinct. Royal authority was more distant and mediatized in these regions and they had been hardest hit by the 'palace revolution' of 1005–6 (Ælfhelm was ealdorman of Northumbria and his sons were based in the north Midlands). They were, therefore, probably more open to 'foreign' rule. In addition to this distinctive regional identity may also have come a sense of common 'Scandinavian-ness': though we should not suppose that 'English' and 'Danish' identity were mutually exclusive (any more than are 'English', 'Welsh', 'Scottish' and 'British' within the modern UK), one imagines that areas of earlier Scandinavian settlement were more open to the prospect of a Danish king.[104] Whatever the precise

---

[102] P.H. Sawyer, 'Swein (*d.* 1014)', *ODNB*, LIII, 453–5. See also Sawyer, 'Cnut's Scandinavian Empire', 17.

[103] *ASC* 1013 CDE (ed. O'Brien O'Keeffe, 97–8).

[104] Stafford, *Unification and Conquest*, 65–7; Innes, 'Danelaw Identities', 73–5. Cf. Reynolds, 'What do we mean by "Anglo-Saxon"', 408–13.

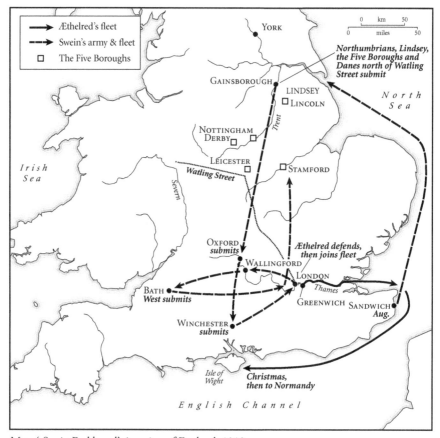

Map 4 Swein Forkbeard's invasion of England, 1013.

grounds, the rapid capitulation of the region serves as a salutary reminder that despite Edgar's efforts, English unity was not to be taken for granted. That Swein was indeed exploiting such divisions is shown by his subsequent actions: he carefully waited till he had crossed Watling Street before allowing his forces to start ravaging.[105] Having crossed this early English Rubicon, the Danish ruler then marched on Oxford, where he quickly accepted the submission of the townsfolk, who may have wished to avoid a repeat of 1010. Oxford was a centre of some note and its rapid capitulation must have come as an unpleasant surprise. The worst was yet to come, however. Swein pushed on to Winchester, the traditional heart of the West Saxon realm,

[105] Whitelock, 'Dealings', 87–8.

which had stood firm in the face of the 'great fleet' in 1006. But this time, the city offered no such resistance: it submitted and offered hostages. Buoyed by these successes, Swein then tried for the one prize which had evaded all previous fleets: London. Here resistance proved too great: Thorkell and Æthelred were present and able to repel the attacks, inflicting notable losses on the Danes. An assemblage of weapons and other implements found at the north end of London Bridge in the 1920s provides a sense of the grim reality behind these conflicts: the weapons are late-tenth-century and of Scandinavian manufacture, representing precisely the sort of gear one imagines Swein and his men would have brought in tow (Plate 16).[106] Still, this reverse did not turn the tide. Swein headed west to Bath where he accepted the submission of the men of this region, led by Æthelmær. Although the ealdorman had had his differences with Æthelred, there is no need to presume that he was motivated by resentment; the writing was on the wall for the king and his regime and submission was merely the path of least resistance. With almost all of England behind him, Swein was now able to prevail upon the people of London to submit. He demanded 'full payment and provisions' (*ful gyld 7 metsunge*: note the use of *gyld*) for his army over the winter, presumably an extension of the *heregeld* already paid to Thorkell. It is hard to be certain of Thorkell's own movements at this point: the *Chronicle* mentions him alongside Swein demanding payment and provisions from the Londoners, which would seem to suggest that the two had come to an arrangement of sorts; however, it then goes on to state that Æthelred was 'with the fleet which lay on the Thames' (*mid þam flotan þe on Temese læg*), which is generally taken as a reference to Thorkell's force.[107] Perhaps Thorkell did indeed stay true; however, it may be that the chronicler is trying to distinguish two forces here: the (foreign) army (*here*) under Thorkell's command at Greenwich, now reconciled to Swein, and the (English) fleet (*flota*) elsewhere on the Thames, still loyal to Æthelred (certainly, Thorkell's was not the only naval force at Æthelred's disposal). In

---

[106] R.E. Mortimer Wheeler, *London and the Vikings* (London, 1927), 18–23. Cf. A. Reynolds and S. Semple, 'Anglo-Saxon Non-Funerary Weapon Depositions', in *Studies in Early Anglo-Saxon Art and Archaeology: Papers in Honour of Martin G. Welch*, ed. S. Brookes, S. Harrington and A. Reynolds (Oxford, 2011), 40–8, esp. 43–5.

[107] *ASC* 1013 CDE (ed. O'Brien O'Keeffe, 98). Cf. Lavelle, *Aethelred II*, 167; Williams, *Æthelred*, 121–2.

any case, abandoned by London and possibly also Thorkell, Æthelred sent his wife Emma across the sea to her brother Richard in Normandy, accompanied by Abbot Ælfsige of Peterborough. The decision to reach out to Richard indicates that the pact of 1002 had held; it also speaks of Æthelred's faith in his second wife, who is depicted playing a key role as intermediary. Indeed, though the sources shed little direct light on their relationship, all indications are of a close one: as noted, Emma attests the king's charters periodically (unlike her predecessor); moreover, the part she later played in legitimating Cnut's fledgling regime – the Danish ruler married her in 1017 in order to help cement his conquest – speaks of her power and influence (not to mention her association with the preceding regime).[108] In any case, once Emma and Ælfsige had ensured that a warm welcome was awaiting, Bishop Ælfhun of London followed with the two princes, Edward and Alfred (and presumably also their sister, Godgifu). In a rather strange role reversal, Æthelred himself went with his fleet to spend Christmas on the Isle of Wight before joining his wife and sons in Norman exile.

The speed of Swein's conquest is perhaps the clearest sign of the damage done by Thorkell's army; the English were now a spent force, more than happy to come to terms with a foreign ruler in exchange for peace and stability. The mid-eleventh-century *Encomium Emmae* claims that Thorkell had been Swein's deputy in the 1010s, preparing the ground for the Danish king's later conquests, but there are reasons to doubt the accuracy of this report: contemporary sources give no sense that Swein and Thorkell were working in tandem and the encomiast, who was writing for the court of Swein's grandson Harthacnut (1040–2), had every reason to exaggerate the power of his patron's grandfather (and, for that matter, to downplay that of Thorkell).[109] The only contemporary evidence of co-operation between Thorkell and his later lords comes from *Liðsmannaflokkr*, an anonymous poem composed following Cnut's conquest. This praises Thorkell alongside Cnut, giving the former a key role in the latter's take-over of England. However, the poem was composed at a time when

---

[108] Stafford, *Queen Emma*, 225–36.

[109] *Encomium Emmae* I.2 (ed. Campbell, 10). See S. Keynes, 'Introduction to the 1998 Reprint', in *Encomium Emmae reginae*, ed. A. Campbell, Camden Classics Reprints 4 (Cambridge, 1998), [xi]–[lxxx]; and cf. Howard, *Swein Forkbeard's Invasions*, 83–4 and 92–4.

Thorkell and Cnut were indeed allied, by a joint force incorporating both of their troops; under these circumstances, there was every reason to paper over earlier disagreements.[110] There is, therefore, no reason to presume direct co-operation before 1016, and there are several factors which speak against this. But while Thorkell does not seem to have been in Swein's employ, this does not mean that the Danish king was unaware of his exploits, and it is perhaps no accident that the latter arrived in England only a year after Thorkell had come to terms with Æthelred: it must have seemed like the country was ripe for the picking. Whatever his precise motives, Swein's actions left the English in disarray and Æthelred was left no choice but to go into exile. As Pauline Stafford notes, it is striking that the king is only reported to have taken his younger sons with him, apparently leaving their elder half-brothers behind.[111] It may be that this reflects fundamental divisions within the royal family, as Stafford suggests; Æthelred's would not be the first family to turn on itself in times of trouble and, as we have seen, second marriages often served to create or exacerbate familial tensions. Nevertheless, we must be cautious of reading too much into the *Chronicle*'s silences: while it is unlikely that his elder sons accompanied Æthelred to Normandy – this would have occasioned note – we cannot exclude the possibility that they found refuge elsewhere, perhaps at the courts of Brian Boru (Bóruma) in Ireland, who had his own qualms with the vikings, or Malcolm (Maíl Coluim) II in Alba (Scotland). Indeed, it might have seemed sensible not to put all one's eggs into one basket and it is interesting to note that when Godwine and his sons went into exile in 1051 they chose to divide their forces.[112] In any case, Edward and Alfred were much younger than their half-brothers, all of whom were now in their late teens or early twenties and thus more than capable of fending for themselves, wherever they might be. This was, therefore, perhaps less a case of gross paternal negligence, than political

---

[110] *Liðsmannaflokkr*, ed. R. Poole, *Poetry from the Kings' Sagas*, I, *From Mythical Times to c. 1035*, ed. D. Whaley, 2 pts (Turnhout, 2012), 1014–28. See further R.G. Poole, *Viking Poems on War and Peace: A Study in Skaldic Narrative* (Toronto, 1991), 86–115.

[111] Stafford, *Queen Emma*, 223. See also S. Keynes, 'The Æthelings in Normandy', *ANS* 13 (1991), 173–205.

[112] Barlow, *Edward*, 118–34.

pragmatism: it was Edward and Alfred who were in need of the most protection and it was they who were likely to receive the warmest welcome at their uncle's court in Normandy. In fact, leaving behind their elder half-siblings might have been the best way for Æthelred to threaten Swein's new regime.

One imagines that Christmas 1013 was one of the loneliest of Æthelred's life: expelled from his kingdom and left with only a fraction of his forces, he was forced to celebrate the second most holy festival of the year on the very island which had often offered shelter to his enemies. One imagines that the irony was not lost on him. Honour was the watchword of medieval politics, and Æthelred's exile could not be seen as anything but ignominious. However, just as Æthelred's star seemed to reach its nadir, fate saw fit to shine upon him: at Gainsborough, where Swein had first staked his claim to England in the previous year, the Danish conqueror was overtaken by illness and died on the Feast of the Purification of Mary (Candlemas: 3 February) 1014. Later legend would hold that St Edmund struck him down, but whatever the cause, this was just the opportunity for which Æthelred had been waiting (and doubtless also praying).[113] His chances of making a successful return may have been buoyed by the presence of Olaf Haraldsson, a quondam member of Thorkell's army, in Normandy; William of Jumièges places Olaf in the region around this time and Óttar svarti's later praise-poem claims (plausibly enough) that the future king of Norway assisted Æthelred in his return from exile.[114] Æthelred's restoration was not entirely unproblematic, as the main Danish army had elected Swein's son, Cnut, in his father's stead. Still, with Olaf's (and perhaps also Thorkell's) backing, Æthelred was in a strong position and it comes as little surprise that the English counsellors now sent

---

[113] *ASC* 1014 CDE (ed. O'Brien O'Keeffe, 98–9). Cf. Herman, *De miraculis S. Edmundi*, chs. 7–9 (ed. Licence, 18–24); William of Malmesbury, *Gesta regum Anglorum* II.179 (ed. Mynors, 308).

[114] William of Jumièges, *Gesta Normannorum Ducum* II.11–12 (ed. van Houts, II, 24–8); Óttar svarti, *Hǫfuðlausn*, 13, ed. M. Townend, *Poetry from the Kings' Sagas*, I, *From Mythical Times to c. 1035*, ed. D. Whaley, 2 pts (Turnhout, 2012), 739–67, at 756–8. See J. Grove, 'Recreating Tradition: Signatr Þórðarson's *Víkingarvísur* and Óttar svarti's *Hǫfuðlausn*', in *Á austrvega: Saga and East Scandinavia*, ed. A. Ney, H. Williams and F.C. Ljungqvist, 2 pts (Gävle, 2009), 327–35.

for him, reportedly saying that 'no lord would be more dear to them than their natural lord, if he would rule them more justly than he had before' (*þæt him nan hlaford leofra nære þonne hiora gecynda hlaford gif he hi riht-licor healdan wolde þonne he ær dyde*). Much has been made of this state-ment, recorded in the *Chronicle* but probably echoing a letter sent to the king at this point. It would seem to represent an early precursor to Magna Carta – so bad was Æthelred's rule that he would only be accepted back begrudgingly.[115] However, we must be wary of taking this statement out of context. The election of Swein in the previous year had severed the bonds of loyalty and obligation between Æthelred and his people first forged by his coronation; at the heart of these negotiations thus lay the need to re-establish the mutual trust and fidelity on which medieval rulership was founded. While there can be little doubt that the strains of the last decade had left their mark and searching questions were now asked of Æthelred's ability to rule, what is striking is not so much that the English sought reas-surances from their king, as that they recalled him at all; clearly, Æthelred's rule was not so bad as to make them look seriously for alternatives. Indeed, as important as the demands of the English – and it is certainly note-worthy that they took this opportunity to place constraints on the king – is the first half of the phrase, which emphasizes their enduring affection for Æthelred. That this was not empty rhetoric is suggested by the delicate situation in which they found themselves: having abandoned their 'natural lord' less than sixth months earlier, the English counsellors were now left with the proposition of his return. They were thus not only making demands, but also trying to convince Æthelred, despite evidence to the contrary, that they were indeed his loyal subjects. It was not only Æthelred who had erred, but also his people (as Wulfstan would note when revising the *Sermo Lupi* around this time), a fact which the king acknowledged in his response: he sent Edward, the elder of the two sons who were with him in exile, with the promise that he would mend his ways and forgive all that

---

[115] See, e.g., M.K. Lawson, *Cnut: The Danes in England in the Early Eleventh Century* (London, 1993), 43–7. For more nuanced treatment, see P. Stafford, 'The Laws of Cnut and the History of Anglo-Saxon Royal Promises' (1982), repr. in and cited from her *Gender, Family and the Legitimation of Power: England from the Ninth to the Early Twelfth Century* (Aldershot, 2006), no. VI; and J.R. Maddicott, *The Origins of the English Parliament, 924–1327* (Oxford, 2010), 36–40.

had been done against him. It was this that the English were really afraid of: recriminations. Æthelred, for his part, seems to have been in a concili-atory mood. Indeed, though he had to eat humble pie, this need not have been against his wishes (or at least not entirely): in previous years Æthelred had consistently presented the viking attacks as the wages of sin, and it would not have taken much to see recent reverses as a ringing indictment of his regime. He had, in a sense, been hoisted by his own petard, and probably felt that some amends were in order.[116]

After this was agreed and pledges were exchanged, Æthelred returned to England during Lent, the traditional period of fasting and repentance. Though the timing was dictated by political rather than religious consid-erations, the coincidence must have added poignancy to the reconciliation between the king and his people, both of whom had reason to regret their recent actions. Upon arrival, Æthelred probably proceeded first to London, the one centre which had shown him consistent loyalty in recent years. From here he raised a force and headed north, where he caught Cnut ill-prepared and drove him out around Easter (25 April). En route back to Denmark, however, the young Dane stopped off at Sandwich where he ordered the hands, ears and noses of the hostages he and his father had taken in the previous year removed. The effects of this gruesome act seem to be reflected in a late eleventh-century Worcester record, which mentions that Æthelwine, a nephew of the later Earl Leofric (d. 1057), had lost both hands as a hostage to the Danes.[117] This was certainly harsh treatment, but well within the medieval 'rules of war': hostages were meant to act as insur-ance and could face brutal punishment if their friends and relatives reneged on deals.[118] Thietmar of Merseburg recalls a group of Saxon hostages facing a similar fate at the hands of a viking band in the mid-990s after one of the captives escaped, while Otto III is reported to have ordered the mutilation of John Philagathos, a close associate of his mother (and perhaps his

[116] Cf. Booker, *Past Convictions*, 129–82.

[117] *Hemingi chartularium*, ed. Hearne I, 259–60; with Baxter, *Earls of Mercia*, 298.

[118] R. Lavelle, 'The Use and Abuse of Hostages in Later Anglo-Saxon England', *EME* 14 (2006), 269–96, at 292–5. However, see A.J. Kosto, *Hostages in the Middle Ages* (Oxford, 2012), esp. 25–52, for caveats.

own godfather), after the prelate had turned coat in 997–8.[119] Much like Thietmar's vikings and Emperor Otto, Cnut was making a statement, one with an eye to his imminent return – he wanted the English to know that he meant business.

In any case, with the Danes temporarily out of the way, Æthelred could set about re-establishing his rule. He began by coming to terms with Thorkell's army and the chronicler notes that a new tax (*gyld*) of 21,000 pounds was paid 'to the army based at Greenwich' (*ðam here þe læg æt Grenawic*). It is around this time that Thorkell's ally Olaf returned to Norway. This decision was probably prompted by the prospect of riper pickings at home, but may also represent a continuation of English efforts to divide their opponents: like his earlier namesake, Olaf Haraldsson was to prove a thorn in the side of the Danish kings, ruling Norway independently till 1029 and contesting the region up to his death in 1030. Further efforts to re-establish Æthelred's regime can be seen in the ordinances known as *VIII Æthelred*, probably issued at the first assembly upon his return. These are amongst the most detailed royal decrees since the time of Alfred the Great and bear unmistakable signs of Wulfstan's influence. Core themes include church sanctuary (chapters 1–5), the payment of tithes and other church dues (chapters 6–15) and the legal status of those in clerical orders (chapters 18–30, 33–4). The overall aim is to purify (*clænsian*) the realm, as one of the later clauses puts it (chapter 40).[120] Though on one level these ordinances represent a continuation of earlier attempts to court divine favour, they are clearly also a response to Æthelred's promise to rule better, upon which his return had been predicated – they place the king within the best traditions of his forebears, above all Edgar, who is named no fewer than three times in the text. The decrees are strongly ecclesiastical in focus and since they are introduced as '*one* of the ordinances which the king of the English disposed with the counsel of his advisers' (*an ðara gerædnessa þe Engla cyninge gedihte mid his witena geþeahte*), it has been suggested that there was originally a secular

---

[119] Thietmar, *Chronicon* IV.23–5 (ed. Holtzmann, 158–63); G. Althoff, *Otto III*, trans. P.G. Jestice (University Park, PA, 2003), 72–81.

[120] *VIII Atr* (ed. Liebermann, I, 263–8); with Wormald, 'Æthelred the Lawmaker', 59–60, and *Making of English Law*, 336 and 457.

counterpart, some of whose contents later flowed into Cnut's ordinances. If so, we can perhaps tease out the nature of the complaints against Æthelred: Cnut's decrees offer a number of concessions regarding the payment of royal dues and rights of forfeiture and confiscation, rights which Æthelred may well have been guilty of exploiting to the full.[121] It is perhaps also on this occasion that the short vernacular work known as the *Promissio regis* was preached. Probably composed by Wulfstan, this brief homiletic text renders into English the promise made by the king on the occasion of his coronation, then goes on to consider the consequences of not living up to this (failure in this world), before finally exhorting the monarch to justice and wisdom. This would certainly have been a fitting moment to remind Æthelred of his duties and no-one would have been better placed to do so than Wulfstan.[122] Indeed, this was something of a fresh start for the king and it may be that Æthelred and his leading magnates renewed their oaths of fidelity at this point, re-establishing the bonds of trust and obligation forged at his coronation.[123] How Æthelred felt about this is a good question. The connection drawn in the *Promissio* between just rule and material success cannot have reflected well on him and it may be that this work was intended as critique of his regime (as its editor suggests). Nevertheless, Æthelred seems to have embraced correction and admonition as an essential part of a healthy regime, as diplomas and decrees since the 990s show, and it may be that such remarks were accepted or even encouraged; just as David had need of Nathan, whose stern warnings inspired the Israelite king's repentance, so too Æthelred had need of advisers such as Wulfstan who were willing to speak truth to power.[124]

If Swein's downfall and Cnut's expulsion seemed to indicate that things were finally going Æthelred's way, the death of his eldest son and

---

[121] *II Cn* 69–83 (ed. Liebermann, I, 356–67); with Keynes, *Diplomas*, 226–7, n. 361; Stafford, 'Laws of Cnut'; and Wormald, *Making of English Law*, 362, n. 442. Cf. Lawson, 'Archbishop Wulfstan', 581, n. 6.

[122] *Promissio regis*, ed. Clayton, '*Promissio regis*', 148–9 (cf. *ibid.*, 145–7, on dating). Note, however, that an earlier date is also conceivable; see above, Chapter 4, p. 155, n. 61.

[123] Keynes, 'Edward the Ætheling', 51–3.

[124] Interestingly, Edgar's own reforming efforts are said to have been inspired by the 'diligent admonition' (*assiduo monente*) of a certain abbot (almost certainly Æthelwold): *Regularis concordia*, ch. 1 (ed. Symons and Spath, 69). Cf. de Jong, *Penitential State*, 112–47.

presumptive heir, Æthelstan, in June 1014 must have put a damper on things. Æthelstan's will survives in its original format, giving us a sense of his standing and associations. The text opens with typically pious gestures: the prince frees those slaves who entered his service through litigation (i.e. were declared unfree through judicial process), then goes on to grant two particularly valuable estates along with a silver-hilted sword, a golden belt and an arm-ring to the Old Minster at Winchester, where his body is to be laid to rest.[125] There follow bequests to Christ Church, Canterbury, the Nunnaminster and New Minster in Winchester, and Shaftesbury (where his uncle Edward the Martyr's presence is noted). Other prominent beneficiaries include Æthelstan's father, Æthelred, Æthelwold's fenland foundation at Ely (which is henceforth to receive dues from an estate bequeathed to the ætheling's brother Edmund), Bishop Ælfsige of Winchester, Æthelstan's household retinue (including a priest, seneschal and various other retainers), the midland magnate Sigeferth, and a certain Godwine (probably the later earl of Wessex). The prince also takes the opportunity to express his affection for his foster-mother Ælfswith, to whom he bequeaths an estate worth 250 mancuses, and finally he underscores that these bequests are all to be undertaken for the souls of his 'dear father, King Æthelred' (*leofan fæder . . . Æþelredes cyncges*) and 'Ælfthryth, my grandmother, who brought me up' (*Ælfþryðe minre ealdemodor þe me afedde*). (Interestingly, no mention is made of his mother, nor of any wife.) Bishop Ælfsige clearly played a key role behind the scenes and is noted amongst the witnesses to the act. The figure who bulks largest, however, is Edmund, the eldest of Æthelstan's brothers and Æthelred's presumptive heir following the ætheling's demise: alongside an East Anglian estate and lands at *Peacesdele* (apparently in the Peak District), he receives a sword said to have belonged to Offa (probably Offa of Mercia, whose reputation was starting to take on legendary proportions in these years),[126] other valuable weapons and a silver trumpet; moreover, it is Edmund who is charged

---

[125] S 1503 (*CantCC* 142). See further *Charters of Christ Church*, ed. Brooks and Kelly, 1041–50. On the dating, see also Keynes, 'Cnut's Earls', 71, n. 156.

[126] On Offa's reputation, see J. Crick, 'Insular History? Forgery and the English Past in the Tenth Century', in *England and the Continent in the Tenth Century: Studies in Honour of Wilhelm Levison (1876–1947)*, ed. D.[W.] Rollason, C. Leyser and H. Williams (Turnhout, 2010), 515–44, at 522 and 525–6.

with fulfilling a number of the more specific bequests. This document places Æthelstan within the best traditions of West Saxon royal piety: the religious centres favoured are all known to have enjoyed close links to the dynasty, either through foundation or through the circles of reform (sometimes both). Yet his associations also go beyond the traditional West Saxon corridors of power: Æthelstan owned lands in East Anglia, Derbyshire, Kent, Sussex and the Midlands, some of which may have come to him through his mother's family. Most interesting of all are the hints that the prince belonged to a different political camp to Eadric Streona, the other main power at court. Thus, Sigeferth, the brother of Morcar and a prominent magnate in his own right, is amongst the will's beneficiaries, while Morcar is said to have been in possession of the ætheling's mail coat at the time of his demise; these were clearly close associates. Sigeferth himself was married to Ealdgyth, a relative of Wulfric Spot (perhaps his niece), and thus related to those who had fallen in the 'palace revolution' (indeed, Ealdorman Ælfhelm may have been his father-in-law).[127] In this respect, it is also significant that Godwine appears amongst the recipients, since he can probably be identified with the son of Wulfnoth, who had come into conflict with Eadric's brother Brihtric in 1009. One imagines that there was little love lost between such figures and the Mercian magnate. Thus, while it would be going too far to see this document as an expression of an anti-Eadric alliance, it provides tantalizing evidence that something like this was in the works.[128]

How Æthelred himself reacted to these developments is hard to say. From the will we know that he acknowledged his son's bequests. Though it was once thought that medieval parents cared less for their children than their modern counterparts, recent work has done much to challenge this notion: while mortality rates were higher and parents more often had to face the prospect of interring their own offspring, there is no reason to believe that they felt the loss any less keenly.[129] Æthelstan was not the first

---

[127] S 1536 (*Burt* 29). See *Charters of Burton*, ed. Sawyer, xxii.

[128] Williams, *Æthelred*, 115–17; Insley, 'Politics, Conflict and Kinship', 32–4.

[129] See most recently C. Bowie, *The Daughters of Henry II and Eleanor of Aquitaine* (Turnhout, 2014), 29–64; and cf. J. Bailey, *Parenting in England 1760–1830: Emotion, Identity, and Generation* (Oxford, 2012).

son Æthelred had lost: Ecgberht ceases attesting diplomas in 1005, Edgar disappears in 1008, and Eadred makes his last appearance in 1012 – in all of these cases the most likely cause being death. The difference, however, is that none of these was first in line to the throne. One imagines that particular hopes were placed on Æthelstan's shoulders – hopes expressed not least by his possession of the sword of Offa, a valued family heirloom (perhaps the 'Avar sword' Charlemagne is said to have sent to the Mercian king in 796).[130] Thus, whatever factional rivalries were present behind the scenes, one imagines that Æthelred was troubled by the death of his eldest son. He was, however, fortunate to have been blessed with many male offspring, and Edmund almost immediately stepped into his elder brother's shoes: he takes over Æthelstan's place in the witness-lists of royal diplomas and in future years was to go on to organize the defence of the realm against Cnut (wielding the sword of Offa, one should like to think). Yet Æthelstan's death was not the only setback Æthelred had to face at this juncture: in late September the *Chronicle* records that a great tide flooded much of the country, leading to the destruction of many villages and the death of countless people.[131] Fate, it would seem, was starting once more to show Æthelred the cold shoulder. One imagines that after the stunning successes of the New Year, these came as a hard blow; success had proven fleeting.

If the will of Æthelstan gives us a sense of some of the rivalries emerging at court, it is the events of the following year which were to give these full expression. At an assembly at Oxford in early 1015 Eadric is reported to have tricked Morcar and Sigeferth into his quarters and then had them executed. This act represents the fulfilment of a process which had begun in 1005–6: then, Eadric had orchestrated Ælfhelm's fall, perhaps arranging for the ealdorman's death; now he oversaw the removal of the last elements of the Midlands magnate's extended family. As before, accusations of treachery were involved (or invoked), since the lands of the thegns were declared forfeit and Sigeferth's wife was forced to retire to the monastery at Malmesbury.[132] Æthelred is not said to have been an active party, but he

---

[130] Keynes, 'King Alfred and the Mercians', 1.

[131] *ASC* 1014 CDE (ed. O'Brien O'Keeffe, 99).

[132] *ASC* 1015 CDE (ed. O'Brien O'Keeffe, 99–100).

may have been more involved than the *Chronicle* suggests; the chronicler writes with the benefit of hindsight and clearly has it in for Eadric, who is given chief responsibility for the later Danish conquest. Certainly, in approving these forfeitures Æthelred rubber-stamped Eadric's actions *post factum*. The Five Boroughs, where the two brothers' power base lay, were amongst the first regions to submit to Swein in 1013 and it may be that this was an act of reckoning. If so, then it was a striking break with the previous year's accord. The impression, however, is that it was above all Eadric's interests which dictated this move; any accusations of treachery are therefore likely to have been little more than a smokescreen. Sigeferth and Morcar were the most prominent magnates in the north Midlands and their star had been on the rise in recent years: since 1009 they had attested amongst the top ranks of the thegns (often second only to Ulfcytel, who for some time had enjoyed an elevated position in East Anglia) and Morcar had received a string of generous grants during the troubled years of Thorkell's ravages, as we have seen.[133] What is more, the brothers were on good terms with the ageing (and possibly already ailing) king's eldest sons, Eadric's main rivals at court; it must have seemed prudent to strike while the iron was hot.

Whatever the justification for these acts, they suggest that Æthelred was increasingly a pawn in Eadric's powerful and grasping hands: weakened by defeat and exile, and deprived of the counsel of his eldest son, the king now came to rely almost entirely upon his senior ealdorman to conduct the business of state. We seem to be witnessing a return to a situation something like that seen in the later 980s: a shift away from broad, consensus-based politics towards dependence on a favoured few. This may already have been a concern at Æthelred's return in 1014 – indeed, if the justness of the king's rule was in question, one suspects that Eadric was amongst the leading culprits. There may, therefore, have been a particular edge to the comment in the *Promissio regis* that the king should keep as counsellors the 'old and wise and temperate' (*eald and wise and syfre*), adjectives which one hesitates to apply to Eadric.[134] In any case, it is clear that Æthelstan's death had served to bring matters to a head: the prince was a close associate of Sigeferth and

---

[133] Keynes, *Atlas*, table LXIII. See Keynes, 'Tale of Two Kings', 215, n. 74.

[134] *Promissio regis* (ed. Clayton, '*Promissio*', 149).

Morcar and his disappearance left the two dangerously exposed. In going after them, however, Eadric had overplayed his hand. Almost immediately Edmund took up his brother's cause: he took Sigeferth's widow from Malmesbury and married her against the king's will, then marched north, where he staked his claim to the brothers' estates and accepted the submission of the surrounding peoples. There has been much speculation as to Edmund's motives. Pauline Stafford, in particular, argues that divisions within the royal family played a decisive part. She believes that Æthelstan and Edmund had considered (and perhaps even attempted) a bid for the kingship following Swein's death in 1014, and that Edmund's revolt in 1015 was a further attempt to wrest the reins of power from an ageing father who now favoured the succession of the sons of his second marriage.[135] The possibility of intra-dynastic conflict should not be ignored; as we have seen, Æthelred was put forward as a rival candidate to his half-brother in 975, and it may be that Emma had similar plans in the works (certainly, she was later to insist that her children with Cnut should accede over his previous offspring). Be that as it may, there is little evidence to this effect: whereas in the case of Ælfthryth there are a number of signs that the queen was working towards the accession of her sons, there are no comparable indications in the case of Emma. What is more, there is evidence of co-operation between the two halves of the royal family in these years: Emma's stepsons (including Æthelstan and Edmund) attest a grant in her favour in 1012 and they also attest alongside (and above) Edward and Alfred on a number of occasions.[136] Though the later *Life* of Edward the Confessor, Emma's first son with Æthelred, claims that the queen had exacted a promise that her firstborn with Æthelred should succeed to the realm, the relevant oath is worded in such a way as not to exclude Edward's elder half-brothers, so it is by no means certain that it can be taken as evidence of such ambitions. In any case, the *Life* itself was written over half a century after these events, in full knowledge of Edward's eventual succession (which must have seemed nothing less than miraculous after over two decades of Norman exile); it presents the monarch as providentially ordained, drawing particular attention to the

---

[135] Stafford, *Queen Emma*, 222–4. See also Stafford, 'Reign of Æthelred', 36; and N.J. Higham, *The Death of Anglo-Saxon England* (Stroud, 1997), 61.

[136] S 925 (KCD 720); Keynes, *Atlas*, table LIX.

biblical example of Jeremiah.[137] In the absence of concrete evidence to the contrary, the witness-lists of Æthelred's charters would seem to put paid to the matter: his sons with his first wife consistently attest above their younger half-brothers, indicating that they remained first in line for the throne. Indeed, we should perhaps resist the temptation of according Emma too much power and influence at this point: although she went on to be the lynchpin of Cnut's regime, the queen does not seem to have enjoyed quite the same prominence under her first husband (to judge by diploma witness-lists, she was rather less of a presence at court than her stepsons).[138]

Still, Stafford is right to note that the bonds which held royal families together often frayed under pressure and Edmund's actions are certainly a sign of this: unhappy with his father's governance (or at least with his growing reliance on Eadric), and perhaps also unconvinced as to Æthelred's ability to defend the realm, the ætheling decided to take matters into his own hands. It was common for medieval princes to rebel against their fathers: royal progeny acted as a beacon for the disgruntled, while for their part kings' sons often found their ambitions stymied by their fathers.[139] This tendency is particularly pronounced amongst the families of long-lived rulers such as Æthelred. One might call this the 'Prince Charles effect': a monarch who reproduced young and lived to a ripe old age had to deal with the prospect of adult sons who had grown up with every expectation of inheriting the realm. The presence of rival branches of the royal family was thus symptomatic of a broader problem: that of balancing the interests of different generations. The Carolingian rulers of the eighth and ninth centuries sought to resolve this by appointing their sons to sub-kingdoms, but this often just provided them with a base from which to rebel.[140] The move towards 'indivisible' realms in the tenth century may have eased some of these strains, but tensions often

---

[137] *Vita Ædwardi regis* I.1, ed. F. Barlow, *The Life of King Edward who rests at Westminster*, 2nd edn (Oxford, 1992), 12. See Keynes, 'Edward the Ætheling', 57; and G. Garnett, *The Norman Conquest: A Very Short Introduction* (Oxford, 2009), 32–3.

[138] Keynes, *Atlas*, table LIX; with Keynes, 'Introduction', [xvi]–[xviii].

[139] K.-H. Krüger, 'Herrschaftsnachfolge als Vater-Sohn-Konflikt', *FMSt* 36 (2002), 225–40; B. Weiler, 'Rebellious Sons: Revolt, Succession, and the Culture of Kingship in Western Europe, c.1170–c.1280', *Historical Research* 82 (2009), 17–40.

[140] B. Kasten, *Königssöhne und Königsherrschaft. Untersuchungen zur Teilhabe am Reich in der Merowinger- und Karolingerzeit*, MGH: Schriften 44 (Hannover, 1997), esp. 199–238.

continued to bubble beneath the surface: Liudolf of East Francia (d. 957) had a notoriously rocky relationship with Otto I (936–73), while later reports suggest that the latter's eventual successor, Otto II (973–83), also felt stifled by this powerful *paterfamilias*.[141] In France, Æthelred's immediate counterpart, Robert the Pious, faced rebellion from his eldest son, Hugh, in his later years.[142] Similar trends can be seen in Anglo-Norman and Angevin England, where they are typified by Henry II (1154–89), who – as those who have seen *The Lion in Winter* will know only too well – spent much of his later years dealing with rebellious offspring.[143] Perhaps the closest parallel to Æthelred's experiences, however, is offered by Henry IV of Germany (1056–1106): another long-lived child monarch, Henry faced uprisings from both of his sons in later years, eventually being toppled by the younger, Henry V, in 1105.[144] As a new generation came of age it was natural for it to define itself against the old and these revolts are in a sense the most extreme expression of this process; Edmund was thus behaving much as Æthelred had in the later 980s. Some rulers tried to prevent their sons from marrying and setting up households in order to preclude such development, and it may be that we are witnessing this here.[145] Certainly, it is noteworthy that Æthelstan did not have a wife at the time of his death, despite being in his mid- to late twenties, and it is striking that his younger brother's first move upon rebelling was to marry against his father's wishes. Whether Edmund really wanted to topple Æthelred should be doubted, however: most rebellious sons were out to make a point and were happy enough to come to terms once concessions were made. Here one imagines that these would have included the acknowledgement of Edmund's marriage, his succession to the lands of Morcar and Sigeferth and an end to the dominance of Eadric. None of the surviving sources mentions Æthelred's response to this, but it may have been

---

[141] On Liudolf, see above, Chapter 1, p. 53; on Otto II, see R. Schieffer, 'Otto II. und sein Vater', *FMSt* 36 (2002), 255–69, esp. 255.

[142] Raoul Glaber, *Libri quinque historiarum* III.33 (ed. France, 152–4).

[143] W.L. Warren, *Henry II* (Berkeley, CA, 1973), 559–632.

[144] Robinson, *Henry IV*, 286–344; Althoff, *Heinrich IV.*, 209–53.

[145] Stafford, 'Royal Government', 155–9. See also Stafford, 'Sons and Mothers', 94–6; and W.M. Aird, 'Frustrated Masculinity: The Relationship between William the Conqueror and his Eldest Son', in *Masculinity in Medieval Europe*, ed. D.M. Hadley (London, 1999), 39–55, esp. 46–7.

something like that of Henry IV in 1105: a mix of shock and horror that opposition was to be found in his midst.[146] Like Henry, Æthelred may have been reminded of the example of David and Absalom: soon after David's penance – which, as we have seen, may have inspired Æthelred's earlier actions – the Israelite ruler's son is reported to have rebelled, temporarily depriving him of the kingship; this is what now threatened Æthelred.

It was, however, at this precise juncture that Cnut reappeared. Whether Edmund knew of the latter's plans seems unlikely: the prince's actions were a response to the execution of Morcar and Sigeferth earlier in the year, not (at least in the first instance) to his father's failed defensive measures. In any case, the return of a large Danish force complicated the situation considerably. Cnut first came to Sandwich, but thereafter turned west and ravaged Dorset, Somerset and Wiltshire. His decision not to head north, as his father had two years earlier, may have been informed by the knowledge that Edmund had established himself there. Incapacitated by illness, Æthelred initially remained at Cosham in Hampshire while Eadric collected an army on his behalf. Edmund, for his part, raised a force in the north. There seems to have been uncertainty as to how the English should then proceed: Edmund was formally in revolt, but the arrival of Cnut made it expedient to join forces against the common foe. This was attempted, but according to the *Chronicle* these efforts foundered on the duplicity of Eadric, who promptly went over to Cnut, taking with him forty ships, identified by John of Worcester as those manned by Danes (presumably Thorkell's force).[147] The Mercian ealdorman was stuck between a proverbial rock and a hard place, as Stafford notes: Æthelred lay ill and his presumptive heir had every reason to resent the influence Eadric had exerted in previous years. Defecting to Cnut, the son of the king to whom Eadric had submitted back in 1013, must have seemed the only viable option; certainly, the Mercian ealdorman was not one to stay on a sinking ship, and it may already have been clear that Æthelred's regime was springing leaks.[148] Whatever his

---

[146] *Briefe Heinrichs IV.*, nos. 37, 39–40 (ed. Erdmann, 46–51, 52–60).

[147] John of Worcester, *Chronicon, s.a.* 1015 (ed. Darlington and McGurk, 480). See Keynes, 'Cnut's Earls', 55; and cf. *Encomium Emmae*, ed. Campbell, 74–5.

[148] Stafford, 'Royal Government', 155–7 and 411–12, and 'Reign of Æthelred', 36–7. See also Keynes, 'Tale of Two Kings', 213–17, and 'Eadric Streona'.

motives, shortly thereafter the rest of the West Saxons submitted, offering hostages and supplying Cnut with horses. The speed with which the young Danish ruler was able to take Wessex reveals the disastrous effects of Æthelred's illness and recent infighting amongst the English. It also serves as a salutary reminder that loyalties did not run simply along ethnic lines: 1015 ended with Edmund, the representative of the West Saxon royal house, in control of the Danelaw and parts of Mercia, while his Danish opponent enjoyed the backing of the men of central Wessex.

Internal divisions continued to hamper English defensive efforts over the winter of 1015–16. Shortly before Christmas Edmund raised an army, but the troops refused to march without the backing of the king and the men of London (where Æthelred had sought refuge following the loss of Wessex); clearly, their presence was deemed necessary if the endeavour were to be legitimate (and perhaps also stand a chance of success).[149] Shortly after Christmas Edmund attempted a second muster: this time he threatened penalties on those who did not appear and made entreaties to his father to lead out the men of London. This met with partial success: Æthelred did indeed join forces with his son, but departed soon after, apparently due to rumours that the latter and his men wished to betray him; evidently there was still much suspicion and ill will between father and son. This is understandable: from Æthelred's perspective Edmund's revolt was an act of betrayal of the highest order, while from Edmund's his father's behaviour was increasingly erratic and tyrannical. In response to these difficulties, Edmund headed north and sought support from Earl Uhtred of York, to whom he was related by marriage (Uhtred's wife being the prince's sister) and who as Ælfhelm's successor may also have been inclined towards the interests of Sigeferth and Morcar. The two joined forces and proceeded to ravage Staffordshire and Shropshire, presumably in a strike against Eadric. Cnut and Eadric responded by heading northwards, pillaging through Buckinghamshire, Bedfordshire, Huntingdonshire, Northamptonshire and Lincolnshire – a counterstrike against those regions loyal to Edmund and Uhtred. It is these attacks which seem to be celebrated in the opening strophes of Óttarr svarti's *Knútsdrápa*, a praise-poem in honour of Cnut, perhaps composed in his early years on the

---

[149] *ASC* CDE 1016 (ed. O'Brien O'Keeffe, 100–3).

English throne.[150] In any case, when Uhtred heard of their approach, he abandoned Edmund's cause and submitted to the Danish prince. But Cnut was apparently in no mood for compromise and, at the advice of Eadric, he executed the earl, replacing him with the Norwegian Erik of Hlaðir (Lade).[151]

Edmund was now forced to abandon the north and sought shelter in London with his father, who may still have been suffering from the illness which had incapacitated him in the previous year. Indeed, it was in London, with his eldest living son by his side, that Æthelred left this mortal coil on St George's Day (23 April) 1016. George was a long way from being adopted as the kingdom's patron saint, but it is a pleasing coincidence that one of England's longest-ruling kings should have died on his feast day. There is no mistaking the sympathy with which the chronicler reports this event, noting that Æthelred 'held his kingdom with great toil and hardship for the length of his life' (*geheold his rice mid myclum geswince 7 earfoðnessum þa hwile ðe his lif wæs*). Edmund then arranged for his father's burial at St-Paul's. As Nicole Marafioti observes, speed was of the essence: by overseeing the funeral of his father, the ætheling was able to strengthen his own claims to the throne in the face of the Danish usurper.[152] However, while Æthelred's burial at St Paul's may have been in part a practical expedient, it was also an appropriate gesture for a king who had spent more time at London than any of his predecessors. Indeed, London had been at the centre of English resistance in recent years and one imagines that Æthelred himself would have wished to find his final rest in the city.[153] For the English, Æthelred's loss must have weighed heavily. Though the king's star had been low in recent years, and though he was certainly not universally loved, Æthelred remained the living and breathing symbol of the body politic; as the demands of the English army before Christmas 1015 had made clear, there was to be no resistance without him.

---

[150] Óttarr svarti, *Knútsdrápa*, ed. M. Townend, *Poetry from the Kings' Sagas*, I, *From Mythical Times to c. 1035*, ed. D. Whaley, 2 pts (Turnhout, 2012), 767–83; with Poole, 'Skaldic Verse', 271–4; and M. Townend, 'Contextualizing the *Knútsdrápur*: Skaldic Praise-Poetry at the Court of Cnut', *ASE* 30 (2001), 145–79, at 159–61 (on dating issues).

[151] On whom: Keynes, 'Cnut's Earls', 57–8.

[152] Marafioti, *King's Body*, 84–6.

[153] Keynes, 'Burial of King Æthelred', 137–144. See also Nightingale, 'Court of Husting'.

In the Middle Ages it was important to die a 'good death'.[154] By modern standards, there can be little doubt that Æthelred's would qualify as 'bad'. He went out with a whimper, not with a bang. At the time of his passing, Æthelred controlled little more than London and its immediate hinterland and his kingdom faced the prospect of a second foreign conquest in only four years. It is not hard to paint these events as a tragedy, as indeed a few years later the London-based chronicler would. Nevertheless, a 'good death' by medieval standards meant something rather different: it meant passing calmly and peacefully, having received the all-important Last Rites. By these standards, it is harder to be certain about Æthelred's demise: the chronicler, ever one to see clouds beside silver linings, has little to say about the event, which may itself be significant. Indeed, though this was hardly a glorious end, there were grounds for hope: despite recent reverses, the resolve of the English was not entirely broken and in Edmund they had a young prince ready to step out from behind his father's shadow. That Æthelred had been reconciled to his eldest son before death must have given him succour; Edmund was not Absalom after all, and had sought conciliation in the end (under what terms, we sadly know not). Still, it is hard to imagine Æthelred being entirely confident as he went to meet his maker. Throughout his reign the king's actions suggest that he was introspective, given to self-criticism, if not self-doubt. He strongly believed that divine favour was reflected in earthly success and must have been aware that his track record was rather mixed in this respect (to put it mildly). Æthelred must, therefore, have had serious concerns about the fate of his soul, concerns which will have outweighed any immediate anxieties about his earthly legacy. Still, here too there were grounds for optimism: though Æthelred could not hope to understand the intricacies of divine providence, he could rest assured that he had done a great deal in the second half of his reign to court God's favour. If this had been for naught, it was not entirely his own fault. Thus, while it can never be more than a matter

---

[154] H. Fuhrmann, 'Vom "schlimmen Tod" oder wie das Mittelalter einen "guten Tod" herbeiwünschte', in his *Überall ist Mittelalter. Von der Gegenwart einer vergangenen Zeit* (Munich, 1996), 205–24 and 296–9; P. Binski, *Medieval Death: Ritual and Representation* (London, 1996), 33–50. On later Anglo-Saxon England, see V. Thompson, *Dying and Death in Later Anglo-Saxon England* (Woodbridge, 2004), 57–90.

of idle speculation, I should like to imagine Æthelred's final hours as being characterized by apprehension, but not panic: a degree of concern, lest he had not done enough, soon enough, but tinged with the hope that he might well have, and informed by a steely conviction that the present state of England was not to be laid entirely at his door.

Æthelred's last years on the throne are those for which more traditional 'doom and gloom' assessments of his reign are most appropriate. From the arrival of Thorkell's army onwards the kingdom found itself in an almost constant state of crisis: Æthelred struggled to mount any serious resistance to the viking attacks and his efforts – valiant though they may at times have been – were seriously undermined by divisions within his own camp. It is hard not to feel that he was reaping what he had sown here: since the 'palace revolution' factionalism had been rife and the death of the ætheling Æthelstan in 1014 gave this full rein. As the situation deteriorated, the king became ever more dependent on the grey eminence that was Eadric Streona, a dependence which became absolute following Æthelstan's death. The king's own worsening health probably also had a part to play, and it is notable that after a swift but successful campaign in the summer of 1014 Æthelred is not recorded undertaking any further 'acts of state' (his brief presence with the men of London in early 1016 notwithstanding). By this point the king was at least forty-six and perhaps as old as fifty – older, that is, than any male member of his family had lived since his great-great-grandfather Alfred the Great (who only just made it to fifty himself). As in earlier years, the kingdom's misfortunes find expression in the documentary and material record: only two diplomas survive in Æthelred's name for 1014, only one for the following year, and none at all for 1016; meanwhile, whereas one might have expected a recoinage in 1015 or 1016, it was to be Cnut's reign before the *Quatrefoil* type replaced *Last Small Cross*, later coins of which were struck at notably lower weights (though this trend is more evident at some mints than others).[155] All indications are that

---

[155] S 932 (ed. H.P.R. Finberg, *The Early Charters of the West Midlands*, 2nd edn [Leicester, 1972], 143–4); S 933 (*Sherb* 15); S 934 (*Abing* 137); Dolley, 'Introduction', 128–9; [C.S.]S. Lyon, 'Die-Cutting Styles in the *Last Small Cross* Issue of *c.* 1009–1017 and Some Problematic East Anglian Dies and Die-links', *BNJ* 68 (1998), 21–41, esp. 22 and 30.

the situation was shaky in these years and it is perhaps not surprising that no coins were struck in Edmund's name: in the face of political turmoil, the kingdom's moneyers seem to have decided to stick with the existing type and await the outcome of the conflict.

However, Æthelred's own demise did not mark the end of English resistance. His son Edmund was indeed to prove a worthy successor, fighting Cnut to a standstill in the summer of 1016 and earning a truce towards the end of that year. Still, fortune was to shine on the son no more than it had the father and Edmund died – apparently succumbing to injuries received in the course of this conflict – in late November. His death left the way free for Cnut, who acceded to the entire kingdom in 1017 and set about establishing an Anglo-Danish regime which was to dominate English politics for the next quarter-century. But that is a story for a different book.[156] Here it is time to take stock and to consider more fully Æthelred's life, death and legacy.

---

[156] Cf. Lawson, *Cnut*; T. Bolton, *The Empire of Cnut the Great: Conquest and the Consolidation of Power in Northern Europe in the Early Eleventh Century* (Leiden, 2009).

AN AGE OF ILL COUNSEL?

As the preceding chapters have shown, Æthelred's life was a long and eventful one. Though it ended on a low note, this was not so much a product of gross incompetence – though there was some of this on show in his later years – as of a series of more contingent factors, some of which Æthelred might have been able to confront more effectively, but many of which lay beyond his control. However, if we are to go beyond simply exonerating Æthelred from the charges frequently laid at his door by posterity, we must reflect further upon his reign, considering how it measures up to those of other rulers of the early and central Middle Ages. No amount of special pleading will make Æthelred into a 'successful' or even 'good' king (though one might well question how helpful such designations are); the aim is to appreciate what he was up against and the reasons for his ultimate downfall.

Æthelred's reign has, of course, often invited comparison with those of other rulers, rarely to his benefit. His illustrious West Saxon predecessor, Alfred the Great, has been an especially popular choice: like Æthelred, Alfred faced a major viking onslaught, yet unlike his great-great-grandson Alfred's defensive efforts were crowned with success, setting his kingdom on the course that would lead to the formation of a unified English realm in the later tenth century. However, close consideration of these rulers reveals rather more similarity than we might anticipate.[1] Both employed remark-ably similar tactics: they resorted to paying tribute to buy time, then attempted to shore up the kingdom's defences by undertaking fortification and strengthening its naval capabilities. Though there can be little doubt that Alfred was on balance the better general, it would be too simple to see in him the great monarch and in Æthelred the incompetent fool. Indeed, it must be borne in mind that our source base skews our view of both of these kings considerably: our knowledge of Alfred depends heavily on the 'Common Stock' of the *Anglo-Saxon Chronicle*, a highly partisan account composed after Alfred's greatest victories, probably at or around his court; meanwhile, the main account of Æthelred's reign was written following Cnut's conquest, in full knowledge of his eventual downfall. Beyond source-critical issues, we must ask the more fundamental question of whether we are really comparing like with like. As Peter Sawyer has observed, the forces of the so-called 'Second Viking Age', starting in Æthelred's reign, were a different kettle of fish to those of the eighth and ninth centuries: they were led by kings and would-be kings and were more than happy to offer battle and besiege major centres such as Canterbury and London.[2] Though the 'Great Army' faced by Alfred looks forward to these forces in many respects, there remains a logic to Sawyer's arguments: Æthelred's opponents had a much firmer territorial base than their ninth-century predecessors and it stands to reason that they were in a position to raise larger, better armed forces. Indeed, it should be recalled that the 'Great Army' itself had fought its way through Northumbria, East Anglia and Mercia before it reached Wessex. These conquests not only sapped its numbers, but also offered Alfred a strategic advantage rarely enjoyed by Æthelred: he could strike back at his enemies in their new power base. As important as the differences between their opponents, however, are developments within the English kingdom itself. While Alfred ruled a compact and largely rural realm, Æthelred's kingdom was not only much larger, but also more urban and

---

[1] Keynes, 'Tale of Two Kings'. See also R. Abels, 'From Alfred to Harold II: The Military Failure of the Late Anglo-Saxon State', in *The Normans and their Adversaries at War: Essays in Memory of C. Warren Hollister*, ed. R. Abels and B.S. Bachrach (Woodbridge, 2001), 15–30.

[2] P.H. Sawyer, 'The Two Viking Ages of Britain', *Mediaeval Scandinavia* 2 (1969), 163–76, at 175–6. See also Sawyer, *Age of the Vikings*, 123–38 and 215–17; and cf. Brooks, 'England in the Ninth Century'.

administratively centralized.[3] Though these might seem like advantages, they were actually something of a double-edged sword: towns proved vulnerable to attack, as the sack of Canterbury reveals, while administrative centralization might facilitate conquest, since it allowed the kingdom to be taken over in one fell swoop.[4] This is not to say that Æthelred's failure was any more inevitable than Alfred's success, but the story is certainly more complex than one of Alfredian brilliance and Æthelredian incompetence.

Indeed, though Æthelred's reign was certainly more troubled than that of his cake-burning forebear, we must also consider whether his problems were really of his own making.[5] As we have seen, Æthelred not only inherited a more centralized kingdom, but also one riven by rivalries, many of which can be traced back to the reigns of his uncle and father. The very strength with which Edgar ruled England in the 960s and 970s was thus part of the problem; tensions had been building up for some time, as the 'anti-monastic reaction' of the 970s and the 'youthful indiscretions' of the 980s attest. To place the blame for these on Edward and Æthelred would therefore be mistaken; they are the fruit of earlier policies. At a deeper level Edgar's reign may also have paved the way for the difficulties faced by his son. As we have seen, Edgar and the reformers had propagated the message that success in this world was dependent upon religious purity and reforming zeal; any misfortune or reverse might thus be seen as the wages of sin. Such teachings worked well in mobilizing support in the relative calm of Edgar's years, but started to backfire when faced with military defeat and natural disaster in Æthelred's reign: they encouraged finger-pointing and mutual recrimination, not solidarity and co-operation.[6] As a result of his own fateful experiences in the 980s, Æthelred came to make these teachings his own in the 990s, and much of the king's activity in his later years is to be understood as an effort to mend his and his nation's

---

[3] A. Reynolds, 'Archaeological Correlates for Anglo-Saxon Military Activity in a Comparative Perspective', in *Landscapes of Defence in Early Medieval Europe*, ed. J. Baker, S. Brookes and A. Reynolds (Turnhout, 2013), 1–38, at 21–3. See also R. Fleming, 'Rural Elites and Urban Communities in Late-Saxon England', *P & P* 141 (1993), 3–37.

[4] S. Baxter, 'The Limits of the Late Anglo-Saxon State', in *Der frühmittelalterliche Staat – europäische Perspektiven*, ed. W. Pohl and V. Wieser (Vienna, 2009), 503–14.

[5] See Stafford, 'Reign of Æthelred', esp. 21–7.

[6] See above, Chapter 5, pp. 209–10.

errant ways. When initial measures did not bear fruit, the result was a series of ever more drastic purges, as Æthelred and his advisers attempted, with increasing desperation, to identify and remove those sinful elements within society. That these efforts did little to assist in the defence of the realm in practical terms is beyond question; they deprived the king of his most experienced counsellors at key moments and sowed the seeds of dissension which were to undermine all subsequent defensive efforts. Be that as it may, we must be careful not to fall victim to what Marc Bloch memorably called an 'inability to lay aside the spectacles of men of the nineteenth and twentieth centuries'.[7] Schooled by Æthelwold and his associates and raised on texts such as the 'Twelve Abuses', to Æthelred and his advisers victory without piety was not only impossible, but inconceivable; the vikings were only a symptom, never the cause. Viewed in this light, the king's close attention to prayer, penitence and reform was perfectly pragmatic: it was the best defensive strategy.[8] We are, in a sense, observing a perfect storm: reformist ideals combined with a legacy of familial faction in ways that were to prove fateful from the 990s onwards.

If we judge Æthelred by the strictly contemporary sources, what emerges is a picture of a rocky reign, but one not without successes. After a period of youthful rebellion against the teachings of his guardians, Æthelred returned to the best traditions of consensus rule in the 990s. The next decade and a half was the high point of his reign: though the viking attacks were a cause for concern, they were not yet making major inroads, and there was every reason to believe that the king's pious undertakings would soon put paid to them. It is only after the turn of the millennium that we start to see signs of panic. Continued failure in battle and new tribute payments revealed that these initial efforts had not achieved the desired effect and more radical solutions were now essayed: first a cull of Scandinavian mercenaries (1002), then a purge of the king's own counsellors (1005–6). Though these acts were inspired by the same ideas about sin and society which had been at the forefront of politics since the early 990s,

---

[7] M. Bloch, *Feudal Society*, trans. L.A. Manyon, 2 pts (London, 1961), 84.

[8] Cf. R. Abels, 'The Costs and Consequences of Anglo-Saxon Civil Defence, 878–1066', in *Landscapes of Defence in Early Medieval Europe*, ed. J. Baker, S. Brookes and A. Reynolds (Turnhout, 2013), 195–222, at 208–10.

they paradoxically led to the dissolution of the consensus regime established at that point. The king's growing paranoia – as it can only fairly be termed – played into the hands of Eadric Streona and a new group of favourites, who were able to exploit this to effect a rapid rise. Nevertheless, elements of the old guard remained and it was only after the death of Æthelred's eldest son, Æthelstan, in 1014 that the king fell fully under Eadric's spell. The latter's overweening influence created tensions within the royal family and the kingdom at large and it was at this point that Æthelred's next eldest son (and presumptive heir), Edmund, led a revolt which was to divide the English in the face of the renewed Danish onslaught. The result was catastrophic, eventually leading to a quarter-century of Anglo-Danish rule. It was in the wake of these years that the main *Chronicle*-account of Æthelred's reign was written and, tendentious though it may be, it probably gives an accurate representation of feelings at this point.

From this bald summary it is clear that Æthelred's reign was fraught with difficulties, but these clustered around his last decade on the throne, and only became acute in his final two years. The king was, therefore, at least in part a victim of his own longevity; long reigns were not always happy ones, and we can but wonder what our impression of Æthelred might be had he died *c.* 1000, at the same age as his father.[9] Certainly, none of the problems Æthelred faced was unique. As we have seen, sons rebelling against their fathers was a common phenomenon throughout the Middle Ages, one which troubled even powerful rulers such as Charlemagne and Henry II. Likewise, aristocratic factionalism was not unique to Æthelredian England. Medieval courts were often places of intrigue, and though this may have reached unusual heights in Æthelred's later years, rulers such as Louis the Pious and Henry IV of Germany faced similar – if not more pronounced – difficulties with their leading nobles. The similarities here may not be entirely coincidental: like Æthelred's, Louis's reign was preceded by that of a powerful and rather overbearing father, and his own years on the throne were characterized by a deep commitment to monastic and moral reform, the result being a uniquely penitential brand of kingship;

---

[9] Cf. G. Tellenbach, ' "Ungeschehene Geschichte" und ihre heuristische Funktion', *HZ* 258 (1994), 297–316.

meanwhile, as another long-lived child monarch, Henry faced similar experiences of minority rule and familial faction. Indeed, though Robin Fleming has identified a decisive break in Æthelred's final years, when the tenth-century ruling elite began to fracture, she perhaps paints a too irenic picture of the earlier years of the century: factional divisions were nothing new and under Eadwig similar developments can be observed, with similar tensions resulting.[10] It may even be that Æthelred was confronted with structural problems not faced by his predecessors: until his father's time the West Saxon realm had been rapidly expanding, bringing with it a stream of new lands and offices with which to reward faithful followers; as these started to dry up, it must have proven tougher to balance the demands of different aristocratic factions, and it is not surprising that infighting was the consequence.[11]

The charge which has weighed most heavily on Æthelred, however, is not incompetence but cruelty: Sir Frank Stenton wrote of his 'acts of spasmodic violence' and more recently James Campbell has characterized him as 'an impulsive, and at times cruel, ruler'.[12] There can be no doubt that Æthelred was willing to impose stern punishments: Ælfgar was blinded in 993, Ælfhelm was executed and his sons blinded in 1006, and in 1014 Morcar and Sigeferth were killed. The question is whether such acts were truly 'impulsive' and 'cruel' by the standards of Æthelred's day. As noted, judicial mutilation lay at the heart of Anglo-Saxon law, a practice which Wulfstan Cantor praised in no uncertain terms and of which Wulfstan of York also famously approved.[13] Æthelred was thus not the first king to mete out such punishments, nor would he be the last. Paradoxical though it may sound to modern ears, mutilation was understood to be a humane

---

[10] Fleming, *Kings and Lords*, 39–52. See above, Chapter 1, pp. 42–3.

[11] Cf. T. Reuter, 'The End of Carolingian Military Expansion' (1990), repr. in and cited from his *Medieval Polities and Modern Mentalities*, ed. J.L. Nelson (Cambridge, 2006), 251–67.

[12] Stenton, *Anglo-Saxon England*, 374; J. Campbell, Review of *Essays on Anglo-Saxon and Related Themes in Memory of Lynne Grundy*, *EHR* 120 (2005), 188.

[13] Wulfstan Cantor, *Narratio metrica de S. Swithuno* II.9, ll. 453–65 (ed. Lapidge, 514–16); *V Atr* 3, *VI Atr* 10, *II Cn* 30.4–5 (ed. Liebermann, I, 238–9, 250, 332–5); with K. O'Brien O'Keeffe, 'Body and Law in Late Anglo-Saxon England', *ASE* 27 (1998), 209–32, esp. 216–28; and Denton, 'Hagiography', 134–5. Cf. C.W. Hollister, 'Royal Acts of Mutilation: The Case against Henry I', *Albion* 10 (1978), 330–40.

penalty, since it allowed the malefactor opportunity to repent his misdeeds before death. This was, moreover, by no means an English peculiarity: the Carolingians frequently sentenced rebellious magnates to blinding, while Æthelred's German counterpart, Otto III, had the rebel (anti-)pope John Philagathos blinded and mutilated in 998. Much the same can be said of the Massacre of St Brice's Day, which as we have seen was less an act of ethnic cleansing than a targeted strike against those elements of society which had proven faithless in recent years. As such, it bears comparison with Charlemagne's execution of 4,500 Saxon captives at Verden in 782, which as Janet Nelson notes was motivated by similar concerns about faithlessness (the Saxons having rebelled repeatedly in previous years).[14] Indeed, while one hesitates to slip into the kind of moral relativism which makes these acts acceptable, one must acknowledge that they were part and parcel of medieval society. If the rhetoric of purity and pollution invoked to justify the St Brice's Day Massacre smacks of a new-found assertiveness on the part of the king and his advisers, it is not alone. As R.I. Moore has shown, the central Middle Ages saw the formation of a veritable 'persecuting society' within western Europe: it was in these years that religious and social intolerance first became systematic.[15] The events of St Brice's Day 1002 are thus part of a broader trend, one also exemplified by Robert the Pious's suppression of the heresy of Orleans in 1022 (the first recorded case of the burning of heretics) and the attacks on Jews in southern France which followed the sack of the Holy Sepulchre in 1009 (the first Jewish pogroms in European history).[16] Four generations later the First Crusade witnessed even more shocking acts in the name of religious

---

[14] Nelson, 'Religion and Politics'.

[15] R.I. Moore, *The Formation of a Persecuting Society*, 2nd edn (Malden, MA, 2007).

[16] R.-H. Bautier, 'L'hérésie d'Orléans et le mouvement intellectuel au début du XIᵉ siècle: Documents et hypothèses' (1975), repr. in and cited from his *Recherches sur l'histoire de la France médiévale: Des Mérovingiens aux premiers Capétiens* (Aldershot, 1991), no. VIII; M.D. Barbezat, 'The Fires of Hell and the Burning of Heretics in the Accounts of the Executions at Orleans in 1022', *Journal of Medieval History* 40 (2014), 399–420; J. Fried, '"999 Jahre nach Christi Geburt: der Antichrist". Wie die Zerstörung des Heiligen Grabes zum apokalyptischen Zeichen wurde und die Denkfigur universaler Judenverfolgung hervorbrachte', in *Konflikt und Bewältigung: die Zerstörung der Grabeskirche zu Jerusalem im Jahre 1009*, ed. T. Pratsch (Berlin, 2011), 97–136.

purity.[17] Such behaviour was especially common when apocalyptic hopes and fears were running high, as was the case in Æthelredian England: those involved often saw themselves as instruments of the divine, the elect few who would purge society of sin before the end.[18] That in England as elsewhere these ideals were developed within the circles of religious reform may seem surprising, but makes perfect sense; the flip side of reformist calls for religious unity was often a more pointed intolerance towards those who did not conform.[19]

However, if Æthelred's more violent acts were not unique, this does not mean that they were universally accepted. As comparison with the reign of Louis the Pious reveals, within penitential regimes there was much scope for discussion and debate regarding who was to blame for misfortunes – one group's scapegoat was often another's paragon of virtue. Though the evidence for Æthelred's court is not nearly so rich, the impression is that a similar dynamic was at work: accusations of treachery were common in Æthelred's later years, when finger-pointing and mutual recrimination seem to have been the order of the day. The fact that the king's interventions at this point almost always worked to the benefit of Eadric and his associates cannot have been lost on contemporaries, and one imagines that the demands for greater justice in 1014 were informed by these experiences. Thus, if Æthelred was guilty of any of the charges often laid at his feet, it is that he had a tendency to favour certain 'in' groups, especially in his earlier and later years. That hints of criticism can be detected in the writings of this period is therefore not surprising; in fact, the real surprise is that we do not hear rather more. Thus, though it has become almost axiomatic that writers such as Ælfric and Wulfstan were critical of the king,[20] the question arises as to whether modern scholarly ingenuity has not at times manufactured

---

[17] J. Rubenstein, *Armies of Heaven: The First Crusade and the Quest for Apocalypse* (New York, 2011), esp. 45–53 and 199–203.

[18] Buc, *Holy War*, 84–9 and 253–61.

[19] D. Iogna-Prat, *Order and Exclusion: Cluny and Christendom Face Heresy, Judaism, and Islam, 1000–1150*, trans. G.R. Edwards (Ithaca, NY, 2002).

[20] Amongst others, see Lawson, 'Wulfstan'; Clayton, 'Of Mice and Men', and 'Ælfric and Æthelred'; Upchurch, 'A Big Dog Barks'; and *Letter*, ed. Jones, 42–9. Where Wulfstan's present editor stands on such matters is not entirely clear: Orchard, 'Wulfstan as Reader', 312–15.

censure where none was intended. Indeed, the purported criticism is often veiled to the point of obscurity, a fact which cannot be explained by Æthelred's influence alone; as the troubled reigns of Louis the Pious and Henry IV demonstrate, it was by no means impossible to criticize a ruling monarch.[21] This is not to say that there was no criticism of the king. There certainly was and there are, as we have seen, a number of points at which Æthelred seems to have responded to accusations of misrule: the politics of the 990s were clearly an answer to charges of ill rule in the later 980s, and the promise to rule more justly in 1014 must be viewed against the backdrop of the 'palace revolution' and the rising star of Eadric Streona in the preceding years. Nevertheless, the impression created by the rich and varied literature of Æthelred's reign is that while many were concerned – often very deeply – about the state of England, few laid this directly at the door of the king. Even the later London-based chronicler did not think that the responsibility for Cnut's conquest lay with Æthelred alone; in his eyes, it was the king's leading advisers who had failed the nation. There were also more positive traditions about Æthelred. When the author of the *Encomium Emmae* came to produce a revised version of his text upon the accession of Edward the Confessor (1042), he praised the latter's father as 'the foremost king – foremost because of all those of his time the most outstanding' (*primus rex – primus autem quia omnium sui temporis prestantissimus*).[22] This is the stuff of courtly praise, but it is not the only sign of more positive views of Æthelred: a prayer entered into a collection of private devotional texts in Cnut's reign wishes 'everlasting rest' (*requiem sempiternam*) for the king's soul, while as late as the 1120s William of Malmesbury remarks that he had heard from his elders that Æthelred 'was neither very foolish nor excessively cowardly' (*neque multum fatuus, neque nimis ignavus*) – though in this case William is quick to set the record straight.[23] Contemporary and

---

[21] See M. de Jong, '*Admonitio* and Criticism of the Ruler at the Court of Louis the Pious', in *La culture du haut Moyen Âge, une question d'élites?*, ed. F. Bougard, R. Le Jan and R. McKitterick (Turnhout, 2009), 315–38; and I.S. Robinson, *Authority and Resistance in the Investiture Contest* (Manchester, 1978), respectively.

[22] Keynes and Love, 'Godwine's Ship', 196 and 198.

[23] *A Pre-Conquest English Prayer-Book (BL MSS Cotton Glaba A.xiv and Nero A.ii [ff.3–13])*, ed. B.J. Muir, HBS 103 (Woodbridge, 1988), 122; William of Malmesbury, *Gesta regum Anglorum* II.165 (ed. Mynors, 276).

near-contemporary observers were clearly less convinced than their modern counterparts of Æthelred's incompetence.

Many of the more unusual features of Æthelred's reign find parallels amongst those of his immediate French and German counterparts, Robert the Pious and Otto III. Indeed, though these rulers have generally received more positive treatment from posterity, their reigns were not without difficulties: much of Robert's was driven by the need to produce a viable heir, a need which led to three marriages in quick succession, in one case in the face of concerted papal opposition; meanwhile in Otto III's the emperor's love of Rome and Italy served to ruffle feathers north of the Alps, while his harsh treatment of political opponents upset many in the peninsula.[24] There are more specific similarities, some of which must be put down to the prevailing *Zeitgeist*. Thus, all three of these rulers enjoyed close ties to the circles of monastic reform, and all three showed a pronounced interest in sin and repentance: Otto III undertook a penitential pilgrimage for his treatment of John Philagathos (and possibly also the Roman city prefect Crescentius) in Lent 999 and is reported to have frequently spent time in private weeping over his sins; while Robert undertook penance for his incestuous marriage to Bertha and is said to have spent much of his time giving alms and caring for the poor.[25] Eschatological interests have also been identified at the courts of all of these rulers: Robert was apparently disturbed by a bout of blood rain in Aquitaine in 1027 (blood rain being a classic apocalyptic sign), while Otto III showed a pronounced interest in Charlemagne and the figure of the Last Emperor, whose reign was expected to precede the coming of Antichrist.[26] It is easy to see parallels here with Æthelred's repentant acts in the 990s and his concerns about the declining state of the age. However, if on one level these comparisons reveal Æthelred

---

[24] Duby, *The Knight*, 75–85; J. Fried, *Der Weg in die Geschichte. Die Ursprünge Deutschlands bis 1024* (Berlin, 1994), 561–602; L. Roach, 'The Legacy of a Late Antique Prophecy: The Tiburtine Sibyl and the Italian Opposition to Otto III', *The Mediaeval Journal* 5.i (2015), 9–32.

[25] S. Hamilton, 'Otto III's Penance: A Case Study of Unity and Diversity in the Eleventh-Century Church', *SCH* 32 (1996), 83–94, and 'A New Model for Royal Penance? Helgaud of Fleury's *Life of Robert the Pious*', *EME* 6 (1997), 189–200.

[26] Fried, 'Endzeiterwartung', 381–94, 427–32 and 434–6; L. Roach, 'Emperor Otto III and the End of Time', *TRHS* 6th ser. 23 (2013), 75–102.

to have been rather less extraordinary, they also highlight much that is unique. Thus, while in Robert's case royal penance was deeply entwined with the king's complex marital politics, and in Otto III's it was a product of the emperor's attempts to assert imperial authority in the teeth of Roman opposition, in England it was the king's own youthful actions and the legacy of his father, mother and guardians which were decisive. Likewise, while Robert's eschatological concerns seem to have focused on natural phenomena and Otto's on Rome and empire (the 'Roman' empire being intimately associated with ideas about the end of time), Æthelred's were a response to foreign invasion, murrain and famine. Indeed, for all the similarities with Robert and Otto, Æthelred's reign finds its closest analogues with two other continental rulers: Louis the Pious and Henry IV. As we have noted, both Louis and Henry faced fierce internal struggles, and while the former's 'penitential state' offers the closest similarities with ideological developments under Æthelred, it is Henry's experiences of regency rule and unruly sons which offer the best parallels to the challenges Æthelred encountered in his earlier and later years. Analogies can also be observed with England's next child monarch, Henry III: a deeply religious ruler, but one given to sudden changes of direction and rather too easily influenced by the loudest voice at court at any given moment.[27] Nevertheless, we should not expect any of these comparisons to be complete: they provide a sense of the problems and possibilities with which Æthelred was confronted, and an idea of how well he fared in the face of these. Not all child monarchs struggled with aristocratic factionalism, nor did all long-lived kings alienate their sons; these were specific problems, which emerged from very specific sets of circumstances.

On balance, Æthelred certainly measures up better to contemporary expectations of rule than his popular image would lead one to believe. Though his later years cannot but be considered a fiasco (if not an unmitigated one), to view his reign purely in terms of collapse and catastrophe would not only be to overlook many positive developments in these years (administrative and otherwise), but also to ignore his successes, ranging from

---

[27] For introductory sketches, see N. Vincent, 'King Henry III', *History Today* 52.vi (2002), 11–17; and D.[A.] Carpenter, *The Struggle for Mastery: Britain, 1066–1284* (London, 2003), 338–91.

helping to establish two successive kings in Norway, to driving Cnut and the Danes from Lindsey in 1014. Yet it is important to go beyond the simple task of seeking silver linings beside clouds. The contention of the present book is less that Æthelred was a 'good' king than that he is too complex and interesting to be dismissed as a 'bad' or 'weak' one. Or, in other words, if Æthelred failed – and in some sense he clearly did – it is our task to understand why. As we have seen, Æthelred's politics from 993 onwards cannot be understood without reference to the legacy of his mother, Bishop Æthelwold and the reformers: the king had grown up on their teachings and after a brief dalliance with new ideas and new favourites in the 980s, he embraced these wholeheartedly in his later years. When faced by reverses and misfortunes, Æthelred initially identified himself and his counsellors as the guilty parties and set about remedying his ways, restoring church lands, promoting new figures, fostering reform and making amends. This also coincided with his reconciliation with his mother, who was to remain his guiding hand till her death (999 × 1001). When these initial efforts did not have the desired effect, Æthelred moved on to rooting out other sinful elements within society, ranging from the (purportedly) faithless Danish mercenaries in his employ (1002) to his own leading advisers (1005–6). As the viking threat mounted, these measures became more extreme and the results were predictably disastrous. However, if the policies failed, that does not mean that they were ill-conceived. As noted, the ideas which guided Æthelred were in many respects perfectly rational. They are reminiscent of the attitudes studied by the anthropologist Mary Douglas in the 1960s and '70s: Douglas noted that anxieties about purity and pollution are particularly pronounced in societies in which hierarchical and group bonds are strong (Æthelredian England would qualify); in such contexts purges become the natural response to mishap.[28] To blame the king and his counsellors is therefore beside the point: their actions may not accord with what a modern armchair general would advocate, but they possessed an elegant logic of their own, one which was not lost on contemporaries, who wrote profusely about sin, repentance and the

---

[28] M. Douglas, *Natural Symbols: Explorations in Cosmology*, rev. edn (New York, 1982), 99–106. See also M. Douglas, *Purity and Danger: An Analysis of Concepts of Pollution and Taboo* (London, 1966); and B. Moore, *Moral Purity and Persecution in History* (Princeton, NJ, 2000).

Last Judgement. That this line of thought damaged the kingdom's defensive capabilities in the long run, depriving the king of his senior advisers and generals in the face of the 'great fleet' of 1006 and eventually leading to the dominance of Eadric Streona, should not be denied. Nonetheless, if Æthelred's court became a place of conspiracy and intrigue, it was primarily as a result of this mind-set, not the personal failings of the king. In this respect, Æthelred's experiences in the 980s and 990s had created something of a perfect storm, leading him and his counsellors to embrace reformist teachings about sin and repentance to an unprecedented degree.

Æthelred was therefore neither 'unready' – a simple misunderstanding of his later moniker – nor especially ill-advised. If anything, he was rather too active and availed himself rather too willingly of counsel: it was his determination to root out sin and purify society which sowed the seeds of his downfall. Given this, it may be no accident that Æthelred's Anglo-Danish successors – who were themselves relatively recent converts – did not embrace such ideas about sin and repentance to the same degree: as in the aftermath of Louis the Pious's reign in Francia, in post-Æthelredian England it must have seemed like a good idea to tone down such teachings.[29] Still, the penitent ruler was not consigned to oblivion: Cnut too took counsel from Archbishop Wulfstan and on at least one occasion took the opportunity to restore lands to the church, expressing regret for his earlier mistakes in the process.[30]

Of course, the incompetent, ill-tempered and resolutely ill-prepared Æthelred found in popular narratives from the twelfth century to the present day makes for better entertainment than the troubled, resourceful, but ultimately unsuccessful ruler presented here. For this reason, it is likely that a degree of unreadiness will always plague Æthelred. As recently as 2001 a one-act opera about the king opened in New York, in which Æthelred and his wife Emma appeal to Clio, the muse of history, to change his sobriquet from 'the Unready' to 'the Resourceful', a project which goes well enough until Dunstan intervenes, reminding the king of how he had

---

[29] Cf. de Jong, *Penitential State*, 260–70.

[30] S 956 (*WinchNM* 33). Cf. John of Worcester, *Chronicon*, *s.a.* 1031 (ed. Darlington and McGurk, 512–18), preserving Cnut's 'Letter of 1027', in which the king promises, *inter alia*, to amend any earlier misdeeds he had committed as a result of his youthful intemperance.

defiled himself in the font at his baptism.[31] Good entertainment – and perhaps good opera – this may be, and the plot at least gives a nod to more recent reassessments of Æthelred's reign; nonetheless, the impression of incompetence of comic proportions remains. The true story of Æthelred's life, however, is a tragedy, not a comedy, as the London-based chronicler already understood: a tale of a ruler who despite energetic – and at times resourceful – efforts could not succeed in bringing his nation the 'peace and victory' (to quote the Bath ordinances of 1009) they so desperately desired. Whether an Alfred the Great or a Charlemagne would have fared better in his shoes is an interesting question, but ultimately beside the point. What we can say is that Æthelred's reign was too long, too complex and too dynamic to dismiss him as 'incompetent' or even 'unready'; he deserves better, and so do we. Æthelred may not have been a great or even a good king, but he was not a hopeless one, and the *Chronicle*'s own epitaph perhaps best sums up his reign: 'he held his kingdom with great toil and hardship for the length of his life' (*he geheold his rice mid myclum geswince 7 earfoðnessum þa hwile ðe his lif wæs*).[32]

---

[31] For a recording, see R. Wilson (conductor and composer), *Aethelred the Unready* (Albany Records, 2002).

[32] *ASC* CDE 1016 (ed. O'Brien O'Keeffe, 101).

BIBLIOGRAPHY

Manuscripts

Cambridge, Corpus Christi College, MS 162
Cambridge, Corpus Christi, College, MS 201
Exeter Cathedral, D.C., MS 2070
London, British Library, MS Cotton Nero A. i
London, British Library, MS Cotton Otho A. xii
London, British Library, MS Cotton Tiberius B. v
London, British Library, MS Cotton Vespasian A. viii
London, British Library, MS Stowe 944 (New Minster *Liber vitae*)
Oxford, Bodleian Library, MS Hatton 113
Paris, Bibliothèque nationale, MS lat. 943 (The Dunstan Pontifical)

Primary sources

Abbo of Fleury, *Passio S. Eadmundi*, ed. M. Winterbottom, *Three Lives of English Saints* (Toronto, 1972), 67–87
Adelard of Ghent, *Lectiones in depositione S. Dunstani*, ed. M. Winterbottom and M. Lapidge, *The Early Lives of St Dunstan* (Oxford, 2012), 111–44
Adémar of Chabannes, *Chronicon*, ed. P. Bourgain with R. Landes and G. Pon, CCCM 129 (Turnhout, 1999)
Adso, *De ortu et tempore Antichristi*, ed. D. Verhelst, CCCM 45 (Turnhout, 1976)
Ailred of Rivaulx, *Vita S. Eadwardi*, PL 195, cols. 737–90
Alcuin of York, *Epistolae*, ed. E. Dümmler, *Epistolae Karolingi aevi*, II, MGH: Epp. 4 (Berlin, 1895), 1–481
Ælfric, *Catholic Homilies: The First Series*, ed. P. Clemoes, EETS s.s. 17 (Oxford, 1997)
Ælfric, *Catholic Homilies: The Second Series*, ed. M. Godden, EETS s.s. 5 (Oxford 1979)
Ælfric, *Letter to the Monks at Eynsham*, ed. C.A. Jones (Cambridge, 1998)
Ælfric, *Lives of Saints*, ed. W.W. Skeat, EETS o.s. 76, 82, 94, 114 (Oxford, 1881–1900; repr. as 2 vols., Oxford, 1966)
Ælfwine's Prayerbook, ed. B. Günzel, HBS 108 (Woodbridge, 1993)
Angelsächsische Homilien und Heiligenleben, ed. B. Assmann with a supplementary introduction by P. Clemoes (Darmstadt, 1964)

Anglo-Saxon Charters: An Annotated List and Bibliography, ed. P.H. Sawyer, Royal Historical Society Guides and Handbooks 8 (London, 1968); rev. S. Kelly and R. Rushforth *et al.* online at http://www.esawyer.org.uk/ (see 'Electronic resources')

The Anglo-Saxon Chronicle MS A, ed. J.M. Bately, The Anglo-Saxon Chronicle: A Collaborative Edition 3 (Cambridge, 1986)

The Anglo-Saxon Chronicle MS B, ed. S. Taylor, The Anglo-Saxon Chronicle: A Collaborative Edition 4 (Cambridge, 1983)

The Anglo-Saxon Chronicle MS C, ed. K. O'Brien O'Keeffe, The Anglo-Saxon Chronicle: A Collaborative Edition 5 (Cambridge, 2001)

The Anglo-Saxon Chronicle MS D, The Anglo-Saxon Chronicle: A Collaborative Edition 6, ed. G P. Cubbin (Cambridge, 1996)

The Anglo-Saxon Chronicle MS E, ed. S. Irvine, The Anglo-Saxon Chronicle: A Collaborative Edition 7 (Cambridge, 2004)

Anglo-Saxon Litanies of the Saints, ed. M. Lapidge, HBS 106 (London, 1991)

Anglo-Saxon Wills, ed. D. Whitelock (Cambridge, 1930)

Anglo-Saxon Writs, ed. F.E. Harmer (Manchester, 1952)

Ansegis, *Collectio capitularium*, ed. G. Schmitz, MGH: Cap. N.S. 1 (Hannover, 1996)

Asser, *Vita Alfredi regis*, ed. W.H. Stevenson with an introduction by D. Whitelock, *Asser's Life of King Alfred* (Oxford, 1959)

Æthelweard, *Chronicon*, ed. A. Campbell (London, 1962)

An Atlas of Attestations in Anglo-Saxon Charters, c. 670–1066, ed. S. Keynes, rev. edn (Cambridge, 2002); also online at http://www.kemble.asnc.cam.ac.uk/ (see 'Electronic resources')

B., *Vita S. Dunstani*, ed. M. Winterbottom and M. Lapidge, *The Early Lives of St Dunstan* (Oxford, 2012), 1–108

Bede, *De natura rerum*, ed. C.W. Jones, CCSL 123A (Turnhout, 1975), 189–234

Bede, *Expositio Apocalypseos*, ed. R. Gryson, CCSL 121A (Turnhout, 2001)

Bede, *Historia ecclesiastica gentis Anglorum*, ed. B. Colgrave and R.A.B. Mynors (Oxford, 1969)

The Benedictional of Archbishop Robert, ed. H.A. Wilson, HBS 24 (London, 1903)

The Blickling Homilies, ed. R. Morris, EETS o.s. 58, 63, 73 (Oxford, 1874–80; repr. as 1 vol. Oxford, 1967)

Brenhinedd y Saesson, ed. and trans. T. Jones (Cardiff, 1971)

Die Briefe Heinrichs IV., ed. C. Erdmann, MGH: Deutsches Mittelalter 1 (Leipzig, 1937)

Brut y Tywysogyon: Peniarth MS. 20, ed. T. Jones (Cardiff, 1941)

Brut y Tywysogyon: Red Book of Hergest Version, ed. and trans. T. Jones, 2nd edn (Cardiff, 1973)

Byrhtferth of Ramsey, *Enchiridion*, ed. P.S. Baker and M. Lapidge, EETS s.s. 15 (Oxford, 1995)

Byrhtferth of Ramsey, *Vita S. Oswaldi*, ed. M. Lapidge, *Byrhtferth of Ramsey: The Lives of St Oswald and St Ecgwine* (Oxford, 2009), 1–202

Charters of Abingdon Abbey, ed. S.E. Kelly, 2 pts, Anglo-Saxon Charters 7–8 (Oxford, 2000–1)

Charters of Burton, ed. P.H. Sawyer, Anglo-Saxon Charters 2 (Oxford, 1979)

Charters of Christ Church, Canterbury, ed. N. Brooks and S.E. Kelly, 2 pts, Anglo-Saxon Charters 17–18 (Oxford, 2013)

Charters of Glastonbury Abbey, ed. S.E. Kelly, Anglo-Saxon Charters 15 (Oxford, 2012)

Charters of Malmesbury Abbey, ed. S.E. Kelly, Anglo-Saxon Charters 11 (Oxford, 2005)

Charters of Peterborough Abbey, ed. S.E. Kelly, Anglo-Saxon Charters 14 (Oxford, 2009)

Charters of Rochester, ed. A. Campbell, Anglo-Saxon Charters 1 (London, 1973)

Charters of St Albans, ed. J. Crick, Anglo-Saxon Charters 12 (Oxford, 2007)

Charters of St Paul's, London, ed. S.E. Kelly, Anglo-Saxon Charters 10 (Oxford, 2004)

Charters of Sherborne, ed. M.A. O'Donovan, Anglo-Saxon Charters 3 (Oxford, 1988)

The Claudius Pontificals (from Cotton MS. Claudius A.iii in the British Museum), ed. D.H. Turner, HBS 97 (Chichester, 1971)

Collectio canonum Hibernensis, ed. H. Wasserschleben, *Die irische Kanonensammlung*, 2nd edn (Leipzig, 1885)

Councils and Ecclesiastical Documents Relating to the English Church, I, *A.D. 871–1204*, ed. D. Whitelock, M. Brett and C.N.L. Brooke (Oxford, 1981)

The Cult of Saint Swithun, ed. M. Lapidge, Winchester Studies 4.ii (Oxford, 2003)

Eadmer of Canterbury, *Vita S. Dunstani*, ed. A.J. Turner and B.J. Muir, *Eadmer of Canterbury: Lives and Miracles of Saints Oda, Dunstan, and Oswald* (Oxford, 2006), 41–158

The Early Lives of St Dunstan, ed. M. Winterbottom and M. Lapidge (Oxford, 2012)

Encomium Emmae reginae, ed. A. Campbell, Camden Classics Reprints 4 (Cambridge, 1998)

Epistola de Hungariis, ed. R.B.C. Huygens, *Serta mediaevalia. Textus varii saeculorum X–XIII in unum collecti*, CCCM 171A (Turnhout, 2000), 46–55

Facsimiles of Ancient Charters in the British Museum, ed. E.A. Bond *et al.*, 4 vols. (London, 1873–8)

Facsimiles of Anglo-Saxon Charters, ed. S. Keynes, Anglo-Saxon Charters: Suppl. Series 1 (London, 1991)

Folcuin of St-Bertin, *Gesta abbatum S. Bertini Sithiensium*, ed. O. Holder-Egger, MGH: SS 13 (Hannover, 1881), 607–73

Geffrei Gaimar, *L'Estoire des Engleis*, ed. I. Short (Oxford, 2009)

Die Gesetze der Angelsachsen, ed. F. Liebermann, 3 vols. (Halle, 1903–16)

Goscelin of St-Bertin, *Vita S. Yvonis*, PL 155, cols. 79–90

A Hand-Book of the Land-Charters and other Saxonic Documents, ed. J. Earle (Oxford, 1888)

Hemingi chartularium ecclesiæ Wigorniensis, ed. T. Hearne, 2 vols. (Oxford, 1723)

Herman, *De miraculis S. Edmundi*, ed. T. Licence, *Herman the Archdeacon and Goscelin of Saint-Bertin: Miracles of St Edmund* (Oxford, 2014), 1–124

Historia ecclesie Abbendonensis, ed. J. Hudson, 2 vols. (Oxford, 2002–7)

Homilies of Ælfric: A Supplementary Collection, ed. J.C. Pope, 2 pts, EETS o.s. 259–60 (London, 1967–8)

The Homilies of Wulfstan, ed. D. Bethurum (Oxford, 1957)

Isidore of Seville, *Etymologiae*, ed. W.M. Linsay (Oxford, 1911)

John of Worcester, *Chronicon*, ed. R.R. Darlington and P. McGurk (Oxford, 1995)

Die Konzilien Deutschlands und Reichsitaliens 916–1001, I, *916–960*, ed. E.-D. Hehl, MGH: Conc. 6.i (Hannover, 1987)

Lampert of Hersfeld, *Annales*, ed. O. Holder-Egger, MGH: SS rer. Germ. 38 (Hannover, 1894)

Lantfred of Winchester, *Translatio et miracula S. Swithuni*, ed. M. Lapidge, *The Cult of Saint Swithun*, Winchester Studies 4.ii (Oxford, 2003), 252–332

Leges Eadwardi Confessoris, ed. B. O'Brien, *God's Peace and King's Peace: The Laws of Edward the Confessor* (Philadelphia, PA, 1999), 158–202

The Leofric Missal, ed. N. Orchard, 2 vols., HBS 113 (Woodbridge, 2002)

Liber Eliensis, ed. E.O. Blake, Camden Society 3rd ser. 92 (London, 1962)

The Liber Vitae of the New Minster and Hyde Abbey, Winchester, ed. S. Keynes, EEMF 26 (Copenhagen, 1996)

Liðsmannaflokkr, ed. R. Poole, *Poetry from the Kings' Sagas*, I, *From Mythical Times to c. 1035*, ed. D. Whaley, 2 pts (Turnhout, 2012), 1014–28

Matthew Paris, *Chronica majora: additamenta*, ed. H.R. Luard, Rolls Series (London, 1882)

The Old English Boethius: An Edition of the Old English Versions of Boethius's De Consolatione Philosophiae, ed. M. Godden and S. Irvine, 2 vols. (Oxford, 2009)

Old English Version of the Heptateuch, ed. S. Crawford, EETS o.s. 160 (London, 1922)

Osbern of Canterbury, *Vita S. Dunstani*, ed. W. Stubbs, *Memorials of Saint Dunstan*, Rolls Series (London, 1874), 69–128

Osbern of Canterbury, *Vita S. Elfhegi*, ed. H. Wharton, *Anglia sacra*, 2 vols. (London, 1691), II, 122–48

Óttarr svarti, *Hǫfuðlausn*, ed. M. Townend, *Poetry from the Kings' Sagas*, I, *From Mythical Times to c. 1035*, ed. D. Whaley, 2 pts (Turnhout, 2012), 739–67

Óttarr svarti, *Knútsdrápa*, ed. M. Townend, *Poetry from the Kings' Sagas*, I, *From Mythical Times to c. 1035*, ed. D. Whaley, 2 pts (Turnhout, 2012), 767–83

Papsturkunden 896–1046, ed. H. Zimmermann, 2 vols. (Vienna, 1984–5)

Passio S. Eadwardi regis et martyris, ed. C.E. Fell, *Edward, King and Martyr* (Leeds, 1971)

A Pre-Conquest English Prayer-Book (BL MSS Cotton Glaba A.xiv and Nero A.ii [ff.3–13]), ed. B.J. Muir, HBS 103 (Woodbridge, 1988)

Pseudo-Cyprian, *De XII abusivis saeculi*, ed. S. Hellmann (Leipzig, 1910)

Raoul Glaber, *Historiarum libri quinque*, ed. J. France, *Rodulfus Glaber Opera* (Oxford, 1989), 1–252

Regula Benedicti, ed. J. Neufville with notes and an introduction by A. de Vogüé, 2 pts, Sources Chrétiennes 181–2 (Paris, 1972)

Regularis concordia, ed. T. Symons and S. Spath, *Consuetudinem saeculi X/XI/XII monumenta non-cluniacensa*, ed. K. Hallinger, Corpus Consuetudinum Monasticarum 7.iii (Siegburg, 1984), 61–147

Scriftboc, ed. A. Frantzen, 'The Anglo-Saxon Penitentials: A Cultural Database' (http://www.anglo-saxon.net/penance/, accessed 13 January 2016)

Sulcard of Westminster, *Prologus de construccione Westmonasterii*, ed. B.W. Scholz, *Traditio* 20 (1964), 59–91

Textus Roffensis, ed. P.H. Sawyer, 2 pts, EEMF 7, 11 (Copenhagen, 1957–62)

Thietmar of Merseburg, *Chronicon*, ed. R. Holtzmann, MGH: SS rer. Germ. n.s. 9 (Berlin, 1935)

Two Ælfric Texts: 'The Twelve Abuses' and 'The Vices and Virtues', ed. M. Clayton (Woodbridge, 2013)

Two Cartularies of the Benedictine Abbeys of Muchelney and Athelney in the County of Somerset, ed. E.H. Bates (London, 1899)

Upplands runinskrifter, ed. E. Wéssen and S.B.F. Jansson, 4 vols. (Stockholm, 1940–58)

Vita Ædwardi regis, ed. F. Barlow, *The Life of King Edward who rests at Westminster*, 2nd edn (Oxford, 1992)

Walter Map, *De nugis curialum*, ed. M.R. James, rev. C.N.L. Brooke and R.A.B. Mynors (Oxford, 1983)

Widukind of Corvey, *Res gestae Saxonicae*, ed. H.-E. Lohmann and P. Hirsch, MGH: SS rer. Germ. 60 (Hannover, 1935)

William of Malmesbury, *De antiquitate Glastonie ecclesie*, ed. J. Scott (Woodbridge, 1981)

William of Malmesbury, *Gesta regum Anglorum*, ed. R.A.B. Mynors with R.M. Thomson and M. Winterbottom (Oxford, 1998)

William of Malmesbury, *Vita S. Dunstani*, ed. M. Winterbottom and R.M. Thomson, *William of Malmesbury: Saints' Lives* (Oxford, 2002), 8–302

Wulfstan Cantor, *Vita S. Æthelwoldi*, ed. M. Lapidge and M. Winterbottom, *Wulfstan of Winchester: Life of St Æthelwold* (Oxford, 1991)

Wulfstan Cantor, *Narratio metrica de S. Swithuno*, ed. M. Lapidge, *The Cult of Saint Swithun*, Winchester Studies 4.ii (Oxford, 2003), 372–550

Wulfstan. Sammlung der ihm zugeschriebenen Homilien nebst Untersuchungen über ihre Echtheit, I, *Text und Varianten*, ed. A.S. Napier (Berlin, 1883)

Wulfstan of York, *Institutes of Polity*, ed. K. Jost (Bern, 1959)

Wulfstan of York, *Sermo Lupi ad Anglos*, D. Whitelock, 3rd edn (Exeter, 1976)

Secondary literature

Abels, R., 'English Logistics and Military Administration 871–1066: The Impact of the Viking Wars', in *Military Aspects of Scandinavian Society in a European Perspective, AD 1–1300*, ed. A.N. Jørgensen and B.L. Clausen (Copenhagen, 1997), 257–65

Abels, R., 'From Alfred to Harold II: The Military Failure of the Late Anglo-Saxon State', in *The Normans and their Adversaries at War: Essays in Memory of C. Warren Hollister*, ed. R. Abels and B.S. Bachrach (Woodbridge, 2001), 15–30

Abels, R., 'Byrhtnoth (d. 991)', in *ODNB*, IX, 333–5

Abels, R., 'Cowardice and Duty in Anglo-Saxon England', *Journal of Medieval Military History* 6 (2006), 29–48

Abels, R., 'Paying the Danegeld: Anglo-Saxon Peacemaking with the Vikings', in *War and Peace in Ancient and Medieval History*, ed. P. de Souza and J. France (Cambridge, 2008), 173–92

Abels, R., 'The Costs and Consequences of Anglo-Saxon Civil Defence, 878–1066', in *Landscapes of Defence in Early Medieval Europe*, ed. J. Baker, S. Brookes and A. Reynolds (Turnhout, 2013), 195–222

Abels, R., ' "The Crimes by which Wulfbald Ruined Himself with His Lord": The Limits of State Action in Late Anglo-Saxon England', *Reading Medieval Studies* 40 (2014), 42–53

Abrams, L., 'The Anglo-Saxons and the Christianization of Scandinavia', *ASE* 24 (1995), 213–49

Abrams, L., 'King Edgar and the Men of the Danelaw', in *Edgar, King of the English 959–75: New Interpretations*, ed. D. Scragg (Woodbridge, 2008), 171–91

Abrams, L., 'Early Normandy', *ANS* 35 (2013), 45–64

Aird, W.M., 'Frustrated Masculinity: The Relationship between William the Conqueror and his Eldest Son', in *Masculinity in Medieval Europe*, ed. D.M. Hadley (London, 1999), 39–55

Airlie, S., 'The Palace of Memory: The Carolingian Court as Political Centre', in *Courts and Regions in Medieval Europe*, ed. S.R. Jones, R. Marks and A.J. Minnis (York, 2000), 1–20

Alcock, L., *Cadbury Castle: The Early Medieval Archaeology* (Cardiff, 1995)

Allen, M., *Mints and Money in Medieval England* (Cambridge, 2012)

Althoff, G., 'Der frieden-, bündnis-, und gemeinschaftsstiftende Charakter des Mahles im frühen Mittelalter', in *Essen und Trinken in Mittelalter und Neuzeit*, ed. I. Bitsch, T. Ehlert and X. von Ertzdorff (Sigmaringen, 1990), 13–25

Althoff, G., *Amicitiae und pacta. Bündnis, Einung, Politik und Gebetsgedenken im beginnenden 10. Jahrhundert*, MGH: Schriften 37 (Hannover, 1992)

Althoff, G., *Otto III*, trans. P.G. Jestice (University Park, PA, 2003)

Althoff, G., *Heinrich IV.* (Darmstadt, 2006)

Althoff G., and C. Witthöft, 'Les services symboliques entre dignité et contrainte', *Annales* 58 (2003), 1293–1318

Anderson, E.R., '*The Battle of Maldon*: A Reappraisal of Possible Sources, Date, and Theme', in *Modes of Interpretation in Old English Literature: Essays in Honour of Stanley B. Greenfield*, ed. P.R. Brown, G.R. Crampton and F.C. Robinson (Toronto, 1986), 247–72

Andersson, T.M., 'The Viking Policy of Ethelred the Unready', *Scandinavian Studies* 53 (1987), 284–95

Angenendt, A., *Kaiserherrschaft und Königstaufe. Kaiser, Könige und Päpste als geistliche Patrone in der abendländischen Missionsgeschichte*, Arbeiten zur Frühmittelalterforschung 15 (Berlin, 1984)

Ashley, S., 'The Lay Intellectual in Anglo-Saxon England: Ealdorman Æthelweard and the Politics of History', in *Lay Intellectuals in the Carolingian World*, ed. P. Wormald and J.L. Nelson (Cambridge, 2007), 218–44

Atkinson, R.J.C., 'Silbury Hill, 1969–70', *Antiquity* 44 (1970), 313–14

Bachrach, B.S., and D.[S.] Bachrach, 'Saxon Military Revolution, 912–973?: Myth and Reality', *EME* 15 (2007), 186–222

Bachrach, D.S., *Warfare in Tenth-Century Germany* (Woodbridge, 2012)

Bailey, J., *Parenting in England 1760–1830: Emotion, Identity, and Generation* (Oxford, 2012)

Baker, J., and S. Brookes, *Beyond the Burghal Hidage: Anglo-Saxon Civil Defence in the Viking Ages* (Leiden 2013)

Baker, J., S. Brookes and A. Reynolds, ed., *Landscapes of Defence in Early Medieval Europe* (Turnhout, 2013)

Banton, N., 'Monastic Reform and the Unification of Tenth-Century England', *SCH* 18 (1982), 71–86

Barbezat, M.D., 'The Fires of Hell and the Burning of Heretics in the Accounts of the Executions at Orleans in 1022', *Journal of Medieval History* 40 (2014), 399–420

Barlow, F., *Edward the Confessor*, rev. edn (New Haven, CT, 1997)

Barlow, F., *Thomas Becket*, rev. edn (London, 1997)

Barlow, F., *William Rufus*, rev. edn (New Haven, CT, 2000)

Barrow, J., 'Chester's Earliest Regatta? Edgar's Dee-Rowing Revisited', *EME* 10 (2001), 81–93

Barrow, J., 'The Chronology of the Benedictine "Reform"', in *Edgar, King of the English 959–75: New Interpretations*, ed. D. Scragg (Woodbridge, 2008), 211–23

Barrow, J., 'The Ideology of the Tenth-Century English Benedictine "Reform"', in *Challenging the Boundaries of Medieval History: The Legacy of Timothy Reuter*, ed. P. Skinner (Turnhout, 2009), 141–54

Bartlett, R., *The Making of Europe: Conquest, Colonization and Cultural Change, 950–1350* (London, 1993)

Bately, J., 'The *Anglo-Saxon Chronicle*', in *The Battle of Maldon, AD 991*, ed. D. Scragg (Oxford, 1991), 37–50

Bately, J., 'Did King Alfred Actually Translate Anything? The Integrity of the Alfredian Canon Revisited', *Medium Ævum* 78 (2009), 189–215

Bately, J., and A. Englert, ed., *Ohthere's Voyages: A Late 9th-Century Account of Voyages along the Coasts of Norway and Denmark and its Cultural Context* (Roskilde, 2007)

Bates, D., J. Crick and S. Hamilton, ed., *Writing Medieval Biography, 750–1250: Essays in Honour of Professor Frank Barlow* (Woodbridge, 2006)

Bauduin, P., 'La papauté, les Vikings et les relations anglo-normandes: autour du traité de 991', in *Échanges, communications et réseaux dans le Haut Moyen Âge. Études offertes à Stéphane Lebecq*, ed. A. Gautier and C. Martin (Turnhout, 2011), 197–210

Bautier, R.-H., 'L'hérésie d'Orléans et le mouvement intellectuel au début du XIe siècle: Documents et hypothèses' (1975), repr. in and cited from his *Recherches sur l'histoire de la France médiévale: Des Mérovingiens aux premiers Capétiens* (Aldershot, 1991), no. VIII

Bautier, R.-H., 'Anne de Kiev, reine de France, et la politique royale au XIe siècle' (1985), repr. in and cited from his *Recherches sur l'histoire de la France médiévale: Des Mérovingiens aux premiers Capétiens* (Aldershot, 1991), no. X

Baxter, S., *The Earls of Mercia: Lordship and Power in Late Anglo-Saxon England* (Oxford, 2007)

Baxter, S., 'The Limits of the Late Anglo-Saxon State', in *Der frühmittelalterliche Staat – europäische Perspektiven*, ed. W. Pohl and V. Wieser (Vienna, 2009), 503–14

Baxter, S. *et al.*, ed., *Early Medieval Studies in Memory of Patrick Wormald* (Farnham, 2009)

Becher, M., *Otto der Große. Kaiser und Reich: Eine Biographie* (Munich, 2012)

Bedingfield, B., 'Public Penance in Anglo-Saxon England', *ASE* 31 (2002)

Bedingfield, B., *The Dramatic Liturgy of Anglo-Saxon England* (Woodbridge, 2002)

Benham, J., 'Law or Treaty? Defining the Edge of Legal Studies in the Early and High Medieval Periods', *Historical Research* 86 (2013), 487–97

Bihrer, A., 'Verwobene Konstellationen, verknüpfte Erfahrungen. England und das Reich in der Ottonen- und Salierzeit. Thietmar von Merseburg und die Angelsachsen', in *Identität und Krise? Zur Deutung vormoderner Selbst-, Welt- und Fremderfahrungen*, ed. C. Dartmann and C. Meyer (Münster, 2007), 45–59

Binski, P., *Medieval Death: Ritual and Representation* (London, 1996)

Bishop, T.A.M., *English Caroline Minuscule* (Oxford, 1971)

Blackburn, M., 'Æthelred's Coinage and the Payment of Tribute', in *The Battle of Maldon, AD 991*, ed. D. Scragg (Oxford, 1991), 156–69

Blackburn, M., 'Currency under the Vikings, Part 4: The Dublin Coinage *c.* 995–1050', *BNJ* 78 (2008), 111–37

Blackburn, M.A.S., and K. Jonsson, 'The Anglo-Saxon and Anglo-Norman Element of North European Coin Finds', in *Viking-Age Coinage in the Northern Lands*, ed. M.A.S. Blackburn and D.M. Metcalf, 2 pts (Oxford, 1981), 147–255

Blair, J., *Anglo-Saxon Oxfordshire* (Stroud, 1997)

Blake, N.F., 'The Battle of Maldon', *Neophilologus* 49 (1965), 332–45

Blake, N.F., 'The Genesis of *The Battle of Maldon*', *ASE* 7 (1978), 119–29

Blattmann, M., ' "Ein Unglück für sein Volk": der Zusammenhang zwischen Fehlverhalten des Königs und Volkswohl in Quellen des 7.–12. Jahrhunderts', *FMSt* 30 (1996), 80–102

Bloch, M., *Feudal Society*, trans. L.A. Manyon, 2 pts (London, 1961)

Blunt, C.E., and C.S.S. Lyon, 'Some Notes on the Mints of Wilton and Salisbury', in *Studies in Late Anglo-Saxon Coinage in Memory of Bror Emil Hildebrand*, ed. K. Jonsson (Stockholm, 1990), 25–34

Bolton, T., *The Empire of Cnut the Great: Conquest and the Consolidation of Power in Northern Europe in the Early Eleventh Century* (Leiden, 2009)

Bonassie, P., 'Consommation d'aliments immondes et cannibalisme de survie dans l'Occident du haut Moyen Âge' (1989), repr. in and cited from his *Les sociétés de l'an mil. Un monde entre deux âges* (Brussels, 2001), 143–68

Booker, C., *Past Convictions: The Penance of Louis the Pious and the Decline of the Carolingians* (Philadelphia, PA, 2009)

Bornholdt Collins, K., and E. Screen, 'New Moneyers in Æthelred II's Benediction Hand Type', *BNJ* 77 (2007), 270–6

Bornscheuer, L., *Miseriae regum. Untersuchungen zum Krisen- und Todesgedanken in den herrschaftstheologischen Vorstellungen der ottonisch-salischen Zeit*, Arbeiten zur Frühmittelalterforschung 4 (Berlin, 1968)

Bouchard, C.B., *'Those of My Blood': Constructing Noble Families in Medieval Francia* (Philadelphia, PA, 2001)

Bouchard, C.B., *Rewriting Saints and Ancestors: Memory and Forgetting in France, 500–1200* (Philadelphia, PA, 2015)

Boulhosa, P.P., *Icelanders and the Kings of Norway: Mediaeval Sagas and Legal Texts* (Leiden, 2005)

Bourdieu, P., 'The Biographical Illusion', in *Identity: A Reader*, ed. P. du Gay, J. Evans and P. Redman (London, 2000), 297–303

Bowie, C., *The Daughters of Henry II and Eleanor of Aquitaine* (Turnhout, 2014)

Boyle, A., 'Death on the Dorset Ridgeway: A Viking Murder Mystery', *HSJ* 25 (2013), 19–33

Boyle, E., 'A Welsh Record of an Anglo-Saxon Political Mutilation', *ASE* 35 (2006), 245–9

Braekman, W., 'Wyrdwriteras: An Unpublished Ælfrician Text in Manuscript Hatton 115', *Revue belge de philologie et d'histoire* 44 (1966), 959–70

Brandes, W., ' "Tempora periculosa sunt". Eschatologisches im Vorfeld der Kaiserkrönung Karls des Großen', in *Das Frankfurter Konzil von 794. Kristallisationspunkt karolingischer Kultur*, ed. R. Berndt, 2 vols. (Mainz, 1997), I, 49–79

Brooks, N., *The Early History of the Church of Canterbury* (Leicester, 1984)

Brooks, N., 'Canterbury, Rome and the Construction of English Identity', in *Early Medieval Rome and the Christian West: Essays in Honour of Donald A. Bullough*, ed. J.M.H. Smith (Leiden, 2000), 221–47

Brooks, N., 'The Development of Military Obligations in Eighth- and Ninth-Century England' (1971), repr. in and cited from his *Communities and Warfare, 700–1400* (London, 2000), 32–47

Brooks, N., 'England in the Ninth Century: The Crucible of Defeat' (1978), repr. in and cited from his *Communities and Warfare, 700–1400* (London, 2000), 48–68

Brooks, N., 'Weapons and Armour in the *Battle of Maldon*' (1991), repr. in and cited from his *Communities and Warfare, 700–1400* (London, 2000), 162–74

Brooks, N., 'The Career of St Dunstan' (1992), repr. in and cited from his *Anglo-Saxon Myths: State and Church 400–1066* (London, 2000), 154–80

Brooks, N., 'Why is the *Anglo-Saxon Chronicle* about Kings?', *ASE* 39 (2010), 43–70

Brooks, N., and C. Cubitt, ed., *St Oswald of Worcester: Life and Influence* (London, 1996)

Brown, P., *The Cult of Saints: Its Rise and Function in Latin Christianity*, rev. edn (Chicago, IL, 2014)

Buc, P., *Holy War, Martyrdom, and Terror: Christianity, Violence, and the West* (Philadelphia, PA, 2015)

Budny, M., 'Byrhtferth's Tapestry or Embroidery', in *The Battle of Maldon, AD 991*, ed. D. Scragg (Oxford, 1991), 263–78

Bührer-Thierry, G., '"Just Anger" or "Vengeful Anger"? The Punishment of Blinding in the Early Medieval West', in *Anger's Past: The Social Uses of an Emotion in the Middle Ages*, ed. B.H. Rosenwein (Ithaca, NY, 1998), 75–91

Bullough, D.A., 'St Oswald: Monk, Bishop and Archbishop', in *St Oswald of Worcester: Life and Influence*, ed. N. Brooks and C. Cubitt (London, 1996), 1–22

Campbell, J., 'England, France, Flanders and Germany in the Reign of Ethelred II' (1978), repr. in and cited from his *Essays in Anglo-Saxon History* (London, 1986), 191–207

Campbell, J., 'England, *c.* 991' (1993), repr. in and cited from his *The Anglo-Saxon State* (London, 2000), 157–78

Campbell, J., 'The Late Anglo-Saxon State: A Maximum View' (1994), repr. in and cited from his *The Anglo-Saxon State* (London, 2000), 1–30

Campbell, J., 'Anglo-Saxon Courts', in *Court Culture in the Early Middle Ages: The Proceedings of the First Alcuin Conference*, ed. C. Cubitt (Turnhout, 2003), 155–69

Campbell, J., Review of *Essays on Anglo-Saxon and Related Themes in Memory of Lynne Grundy*, ed. J. Roberts and J.[L.] Nelson, *EHR* 120 (2005), 188

Carpenter, D.A., *The Minority of Henry III* (Berkeley, CA, 1990)

Carpenter, D.[A.], *The Struggle for Mastery: Britain, 1066–1284* (London, 2003)

Cavalié, E., 'Le type numismatique de Saint-Gilles', *Revue numismatique* 6th ser. 162 (2006), 417–42

Chaplais, P., 'The Origin and Authenticity of the Royal Anglo-Saxon Diploma' (1965), repr. in and cited from *Prisca Munimenta: Studies in Archival and Administrative History Presented to Dr A.E.J. Hollander*, ed. F. Ranger (London, 1973), 28–42

Chaplais, P., 'The Authenticity of the Royal Anglo-Saxon Diplomas of Exeter' (1966), repr. in and cited from his *Essays in Medieval Diplomacy and Administration* (London, 1981), no. XV

Clark, C., 'The Narrative Mode of *The Anglo-Saxon Chronicle* before the Conquest' (1971), repr. in and cited from her *Words, Names, and History: Selected Writings of Cecily Clark* (Cambridge, 1995), 3–19

Clark, C., 'On Dating *The Battle of Maldon*: Certain Evidence Reviewed' (1983), repr. in and cited from her *Words, Names, and History: Selected Writings of Cecily Clark* (Cambridge, 1995), 20–36

Clark, G., 'The Hero of *Maldon*: Vir Pius et Strenuus', *Speculum* 54 (1979), 257–82

Clayton, M., *The Cult of the Virgin Mary in Anglo-Saxon England* (Cambridge, 1990)

Clayton, M., 'Of Mice and Men: Ælfric's Second Homily for the Feast of a Confessor', *Leeds Studies in English* n.s. 24 (1993), 1–26

Clayton, M., 'Ælfric and Æthelred', in *Essays on Anglo-Saxon and Related Themes in Memory of Lynne Grundy*, ed. J. Roberts and J.[L.] Nelson (Woodbridge, 2000), 65–88

Clayton, M., 'The Old English *Promissio regis*', *ASE* 37 (2008), 90–150

Clayton, M., '*De Duodecim Abusiuis*, Lordship and Kingship in Anglo-Saxon England', in *Saints and Scholars: New Perspectives on Anglo-Saxon Literature and Culture in Honour of Hugh Magennis*, ed. S. McWilliams (Woodbridge, 2012), 141–63

Clemoes, P.A.M., 'The Chronology of Ælfric's Works', in *The Anglo-Saxons: Studies in Some Aspects of their History and Culture Presented to Bruce Dickens*, ed. P.A.M. Clemoes (London, 1959), 212–47

Clemoes, P.[A.M.], and K. Hughes, ed., *England Before the Conquest: Studies in Primary Sources Presented to Dorothy Whitelock* (Cambridge, 1971)

Cohn, N., *The Pursuit of the Millennium: Revolutionary Millenarians and Mystical Anarchists of the Middle Ages*, 2nd edn (London, 1970)

Contamine, P., *War in the Middle Ages*, trans. M. Jones (Oxford, 1984)

Cooper, J., ed., *The Battle of Maldon: Fiction and Fact* (London, 1993)

Cooper, T.-A., 'The Shedding of Tears in Late Anglo-Saxon England', in *Crying in the Middle Ages: Tears of History*, ed. E. Gertisman (London, 2011), 175–92

Corbet, P., *Autour de Burchard de Worms. L'Église allemande et les interdits de parenté (IXème–XIIème siècle)* (Frankfurt, 2001)

Coupland, S., 'The Fortified Bridges of Charles the Bald', *Journal of Medieval History* 17 (1991), 1–12

Coupland, S., 'From Poachers to Gamekeepers: Scandinavian Warlords and Carolingian Kings', *EME* 7 (1998), 85–114

Coupland, S., 'Frankish Tribute Payments to the Vikings and their Consequences', *Francia* 26.i (1999), 57–75

Coupland, S., 'The Carolingian Army and the Struggle against the Vikings', *Viator* 35 (2004), 49–70

Coupland, S., 'Holy Ground? The Plundering and Burning of Churches by Vikings and Franks in the Ninth Century', *Viator* 45.i (2014), 73–97

Crawford, S., *Childhood in Anglo-Saxon England* (Stroud, 1999)

Crick, J., 'The Wealth, Patronage, and Connections of Women's Houses in Late Anglo-Saxon England', *Revue Bénédictine* 109 (1999), 154–85

Crick, J., 'Insular History? Forgery and the English Past in the Tenth Century', in *England and the Continent in the Tenth Century: Studies in Honour of Wilhelm Levison (1876–1947)*, ed. D.[W.] Rollason, C. Leyser and H. Williams (Turnhout, 2010), 515–44

Cross, J.E., 'Mainly on Philology and the Interpretive Criticism of *Maldon*', in *Old English Studies in Honour of John C. Pope*, ed. R.B. Burlin and E.B. Irving, Jr, (Toronto, 1974), 235–53

Cubitt, C., 'The Tenth-Century Benedictine Reform in England', *EME* 6 (1997), 77–94

Cubitt, C., 'Sites and Sanctity: Revisiting the Cult of Murdered and Martyred Anglo-Saxon Royal Saints', *EME* 9 (2000), 53–83

Cubitt, C., 'Bishops, Priests and Penance in Late Saxon England', *EME* 14 (2006), 41–63

Cubitt, C., 'Archbishop Dunstan: A Prophet in Politics', in *Myth, Rulership, Church and Charters: Essays in Honour of Nicholas Brooks*, ed. J. Barrow and A. Wareham (Aldershot, 2008), 145–66

Cubitt, C., ' "As the Lawbook Teaches": Reeves, Lawbooks and Urban Life in the Anonymous Old English Legend of the Seven Sleepers', *EHR* 124 (2009), 1021–49

Cubitt, C., 'Ælfric's Lay Patrons', in *A Companion to Ælfric*, ed. H. Magennis and M. Swan (Leiden, 2009), 165–92

Cubitt, C., 'Bishops and Succession Crises in Tenth- and Eleventh-Century England', in *Patterns of Episcopal Power: Bishops in Tenth and Eleventh Century Western Europe*, ed. L. Körntgen and D. Waßenhoven (Berlin, 2011), 111–26

Cubitt, C., 'The Politics of Remorse: Penance and Royal Piety in the Reign of Æthelred the Unready', *Historical Research* 85 (2012), 179–92

Cubitt, C., 'Personal Names, Identity and Family in Benedictine Reform England', in *Verwandschaft, Name und soziale Ordnung (300–1000)*, ed. S. Patzold and K. Ubl (Berlin, 2014), 223–42

Cubitt, C., 'Reading Tenth- and Eleventh-Century Latin Hagiography in the Context of the Reign of Æthelred II "the Unready" ', in *Hagiography in Anglo-Saxon-England: Adopting and Adapting Saints' Lives into Old English Prose (c. 950–1150)*, ed. L. Lazzari, P. Lendinara, C. Di Sciacco (Turnhout, 2014), 345–64

Cubitt, C., 'Apocalyptic and Eschatological Thought in England around the Year 1000', *TRHS* 6th ser. 25 (2015), 27–52

Cubitt, C., and M. Costambeys, 'Oda (*d.* 958)', in *ODNB*, XLI, 484–7

Curschmann, F., *Hungersnöte im Mittelalter. Ein Beitrag zur deutschen Wirtschaftsgeschichte des 8. bis 13. Jahrhunderts* (Leipzig, 1900)

Dale, J., *Kingship in Comparison: Inauguration and Liturgical Kingship in England, France and the Empire c.1050–c.1250* (Woodbridge, forthcoming)

Dalton, P., 'Sites and Occasions of Peacemaking in England and Normandy, c. 900–c. 1150', *HSJ* 16 (2005), 12–26

d'Avray, D.L., *Medieval Marriage: Symbolism and Society* (Oxford, 2005)

Deshman, R., '*Christus rex et magi reges*: Kingship and Christology in Ottonian and Anglo-Saxon Art' (1976), repr. in and cited from his *Eye and Mind: Collected Essays in Anglo-Saxon and Early Medieval Art*, ed. A. Cohen (Kalamazoo, MI, 2010), 104–36

Deshman, R., '*Benedictus monarcha et monachus*: Early Medieval Ruler Theology and the Anglo-Saxon Reform' (1988), repr. in and cited from his *Eye and Mind: Collected Essays in Anglo-Saxon and Early Medieval Art*, ed. A. Cohen (Kalamazoo, MI, 2010), 137–71

Dhenin, M., 'L'"Agnus Dei" thème monétaire', in *Le bestiaire: des monnaies, des sceaux et des médailles*, ed. P. Dehaye (Paris, 1974), 163–77

Dien, S., '*Sermo Lupi ad Anglos*: The Order and Date of the Three Versions', *Neuphilologische Mitteilungen* 76 (1975), 561–70

Dierkens, A., *Abbayes et chapitres entre Sambre et Meuse (VIIᵉ–XIᵉ siècles). Contribution à l'histoire religieuse des campagnes du Haut Moyen Âge* (Sigmaringen, 1985)

Dolley, R.H.M., 'The Sack of Wilton in 1003 and the Chronology of the "Long Cross" and "Helmet" Types of Æthelræd II', *Nordisk Numismatisk Unions Medlemsblad* 5 (May 1954), 152–6

Dolley, R.H.M., 'Three Late Anglo-Saxon Notes', *BNJ* 28 (1955–7), 88–105

Dolley, R.H.M. 'Æthelræd's Rochester Ravaging of 986: An Intriguing Numismatic Sidelight', *Spink's Numismatic Circular* 75 (1967), 33–4

Dolley, [R.H.]M., 'The Nummular Brooch from Sulgrave', in *England Before the Conquest: Studies in Primary Sources Presented to Dorothy Whitelock*, ed. P. Clemoes and K. Hughes (Cambridge, 1971), 333–49

Dolley, [R.H.]M., 'The Coins', in *The Archaeology of Anglo-Saxon England*, ed. D.M. Wilson (London, 1976), 349–72

Dolley, [R.H.]M., 'An Introduction to the Coinage of Æthelred II', in *Ethelred the Unready*, ed. D.[H.] Hill (London, 1978), 115–33

Dolley, R.H.M., and F. Elmore Jones, 'The mints "aet Gothabyrig" and "aet Sith(m)esteb-yrig"', *BNJ* 28 (1955–7), 270–82

Dolley, R.H.M., and D.M. Metcalf, 'The Reform of the English Coinage under Edgar', in *Anglo-Saxon Coins: Studies Presented to F.M. Stenton on the Occasion of his 80th Birthday, 17 May 1960*, ed. R.H.M. Dolley (London, 1961), 136–68

Dolley, [R.H.]M., and T. Talvio, 'The Twelfth of the Agnus Dei Pennies of Æthelred II', *BNJ* 47 (1977), 131–3

Dolley, [R.H.]M., and T. Talvio, 'A Thirteenth Agnus Dei Penny of Æthelred II', *BNJ* 49 (1979), 122–5

Douglas, M., *Purity and Danger: An Analysis of Concepts of Pollution and Taboo* (London, 1966)

Douglas, M., *Natural Symbols: Explorations in Cosmology*, rev. edn (New York, 1982)

Downham, C. 'England and the Irish Sea Zone in the Eleventh Century', *ANS* 26 (2003), 55–73

Downham, C., *Viking Kings of Britain and Ireland: The Dynasty of Ívarr to A.D. 1014* (Edinburgh, 2007)

Duby, G., *The Knight, the Lady and the Priest: The Making of Marriage in Medieval France*, trans. B. Bray (New York, 1983)

Duggan, A., *Thomas Becket* (London, 2004)

Dumville, D.N., 'The Ætheling: A Study in Anglo-Saxon Constitutional History', *ASE* 8 (1979), 1–33

Dumville, D.N., *Liturgy and Ecclesiastical History in Late Anglo-Saxon England: Four Studies* (Woodbridge, 1992)

Dumville, D.N., *Wessex and England from Alfred to Edgar: Six Essays on Political, Cultural, and Ecclesiastical Revival* (Woodbridge, 1992)

Dumville, D.N., *English Caroline Script and Monastic History: Studies in Benedictinism, A.D. 950–1030* (Woodbridge, 1993)

Dumville, D.N., 'English Square Minuscule Script: The Mid-Century Phases', *ASE* 23 (1994), 133–64

Dumville, D.N., 'The Death of King Edward the Martyr – 18 March, 979?', *Anglo-Saxon* 1 (2007), 269–83

Dunn, M., *The Emergence of Monasticism: From the Desert Fathers to the Early Middle Ages* (Oxford, 2003)

Earle, J.W., ' "The Battle of Maldon", line 86: OE *lytegian* = Lat. *litigare*', in *Old English and New: Studies in Language and Linguistics in Honour of Frederic G. Cassidy*, ed. J.H. Hall, N. Doane and D. Ringler (New York, 1992), 77–82

Emerson, R.K., 'From *epistola* to *sermo*: The Old English Version of Adso's *Libellus de Antichristo*', *JEGP* 83 (1983), 1–10

Englert, A., and A. Trakadas, ed., *Wulfstan's Voyage: The Baltic Sea Region in the Early Viking Age as Seen from Shipboard* (Roskilde, 2008)

Erkens, F.-R., '. . . *more Grecorum conregnantem instituere vultis*? Zur Legitimation der Regentschaft Heinrichs des Zänkers im Thronstreit von 984', *FMSt* 27 (1993), 273–89

Erkens, F.-R., ' "Sicut Esther regina". Die westfränkische Königin als *consors regni*', *Francia* 20.i (1993), 15–38

Fernández del Pozo, J.M., 'Alfonso V, rey de León. Estudio histórico-documental', in *León y su historia. Miscelánea histórica*, V (León, 1984), 11–262

Finberg, H.P.R., *The Early Charters of the West Midlands*, 2nd edn (Leicester, 1972)

Fisher, D.J.V., 'The Anti-Monastic Reaction in the Reign of Edward the Martyr', *Cambridge Historical Journal* 10 (1952), 254–70

Fleming, R., *Kings and Lords in Conquest England* (Cambridge, 1991)

Fleming, R., 'Rural Elites and Urban Communities in Late-Saxon England', *P & P* 141 (1993), 3–37

Foot, S., 'Anglo-Saxon Minsters: A Review of Terminology', in *Pastoral Care before the Parish*, ed. J. Blair and R. Sharpe (Leicester, 1992), 212–25

Foot, S., 'The Making of *Angelcynn*: English Identity before the Norman Conquest', *TRHS* 6th ser. 6 (1996), 25–49

Foot, S., *Veiled Women*, 2 vols. (Aldershot, 2000)

Foot, S., *Monastic Life in Anglo-Saxon England, c. 600–900* (Cambridge, 2006)

Foot, S., 'Dynastic Strategies: The West Saxon Royal Family in Europe', in *England and the Continent in the Tenth Century: Studies in Honour of Wilhelm Levison (1876–1947)*, ed. D.[W.] Rollason, C. Leyser and H. Williams (Turnhout, 2010), 237–53

Foot, S., *Æthelstan: The First King of England* (New Haven, CT, 2011)

Fouracre, P., 'The Context of the OHG *Ludwigslied*' (1985), repr. in and cited from his *Frankish History: Studies in the Construction of Power* (Aldershot, 2012), no. IX

Foxhall Forbes, H., *Heaven and Earth in Anglo-Saxon England: Theology and Society in an Age of Faith* (Farnham, 2013)

France, J., *Western Warfare in the Age of the Crusades, 1000–1300* (London, 1999)

Frank, R., 'Viking Atrocity and Skaldic Verse: The Rite of the Blood-Eagle', *EHR* 99 (1984), 322–43

Frank, R., 'The Ideal of Men Dying with their Lord in *The Battle of Maldon*: Anachronism or *nouvelle vague*', in *People and Places in Northern Europe 500–1600: Essays in Honour of Peter Hayes Sawyer*, ed. I.N. Wood and N. Lund (Woodbridge, 1991), 95–106

Freeman, E.A., *The History of the Norman Conquest of England: Its Causes and its Results*, I, *The Preliminary History to the Election of Eadward the Confessor*, 3rd edn (Oxford, 1877)

Fried, J., 'Endzeiterwartung um die Jahrtausendwende', *DA* 45 (1989), 381–473

Fried, J., 'Kaiserin Theophanu und das Reich', in *Köln: Stadt und Bistum in Kirche und Reich des Mittelalters. Festschrift für Odilo Engels zum 65. Geburtstag*, ed. H. Vollrath and S. Weinfurter (Cologne, 1993), 139–85

Fried, J., *Der Weg in die Geschichte. Die Ursprünge Deutschlands bis 1024* (Berlin, 1994)

Fried, J., 'Wissenschaft und Phantasie. Das Beispiel der Geschichte', *HZ* 263 (1996), 291–316

Fried, J., 'Die Endzeit fest im Griff des Positivismus? Zur Auseinandersetzung mit Sylvain Gouguenheim', *HZ* 275 (2002), 281–321

Fried, J., 'Weshalb die Normannenherrscher für die Franken unvorstellbar waren: um 810', in *Die Macht des Königs. Herrschaft in Europa vom Frühmittelalter bis in die Neuzeit*, ed. B. Jussen (Munich, 2005), 72–82

Fried, J., '"999 Jahre nach Christi Geburt: der Antichrist". Wie die Zerstörung des Heiligen Grabes zum apokalyptischen Zeichen wurde und die Denkfigur universaler Judenverfolgung hervorbrachte', in *Konflikt und Bewältigung: die Zerstörung der Grabeskirche zu Jerusalem im Jahre 1009*, ed. T. Pratsch (Berlin, 2011), 97–136

Fuhrmann, H., 'Fälschungen im Dienste der Wahrheit', in his *Überall ist Mittelalter. Von der Gegenwart einer vergangenen Zeit* (Munich, 1996), 48–62 and 277–8

Fuhrmann, H., 'Vom "schlimmen Tod" oder wie das Mittelalter einen "guten Tod" herbeiwünschte', in his *Überall ist Mittelalter. Von der Gegenwart einer vergangenen Zeit* (Munich, 1996), 205–24 and 296–9

Gameson, R., 'The Origin of the Exeter Book of Old English Poetry', *ASE* 25 (1996), 135–85

Gameson, R., ed., *The Cambridge History of the Book in Britain*, I, *c.400–1100* (Cambridge, 2012)

Gannon, A., *The Iconography of Early Anglo-Saxon Coinage: Sixth to Eighth Centuries* (Oxford, 2003)

Garrison, M., 'The Bible and Alcuin's Interpretation of Current Events', *Peritia* 16 (2002), 68–84

Gatch, M.McC., *Preaching and Theology in Anglo-Saxon England: Ælfric and Wulfstan* (Toronto, 1977)

Gautier, A., *Le festin dans l'Angleterre anglo-saxonne (V*e*–XI*e *siècle)* (Rennes, 2006)

Gautier, A., 'Butlers and Dish-Bearers in Anglo-Saxon Courts: Household Officers at the Royal Table', *Historical Research* (forthcoming)

Gazzoli, P., '*Denemearc, Tanmaurk ala*, and *Confinia nordmannorum*: The *Annales regni francorum* and the Origins of Denmark', *Viking and Medieval Scandinavia* 7 (2011), 29–43

Geary, P.J., *Phantoms of Remembrance: Memory and Oblivion at the End of the First Millennium* (Princeton, NJ, 1994)

Gelling, M., *Signposts to the Past: Place Names and the History of England*, 2nd edn (Chichester, 1988)

Gillingham, J., 'William the Bastard at War', in *Studies in Medieval History Presented to R. Allen Brown*, ed. C. Harper-Bill, C. Holdsworth and J.L. Nelson (Woodbridge, 1989), 141–58

Gillingham, J., '"The Most Precious Jewel in the English Crown": Levels of Danegeld and Heregeld in the Early Eleventh Century', *EHR* 104 (1989), 373–84

Gillingham, J., 'Chronicles and Coins as Evidence for Levels of Tribute and Taxation in Late Tenth- and Early Eleventh-Century England', *EHR* 105 (1990), 939–50

Gneuss, H., '*The Battle of Maldon* 89: Byrhtnoð's *ofermod* Once Again' (1976), repr. in and cited from his *Language and History in Early England* (Aldershot, 1996), no. X

Godden, M., 'Ælfric's Saints' Lives and the Problem of Miracles', *Leeds Studies in English* n.s. 16 (1985), 83–100

Godden, M., 'Ælfric and Anglo-Saxon Kingship', *EHR* 102 (1987), 911–15

Godden, M., 'Money, Power and Morality in Late Anglo-Saxon England', *ASE* 19 (1990), 41–65

Godden, M., 'Apocalypse and Invasion in Late Anglo-Saxon England', in *From Anglo-Saxon to Early Middle English: Studies Presented to E.G. Stanley*, ed. M. Godden, D. Gray and T.F. Hoad (Oxford, 1994), 130–62

Godden, M., *Ælfric's Catholic Homilies: Introduction, Commentary and Glossary*, EETS s.s. 18 (Oxford, 2000)

Godden, M., 'The Millennium, Time, and History for the Anglo-Saxons', in *The Apocalyptic Year 1000*, ed. R. Landes, A. Gow and D.C. Van Meter (Oxford, 2003), 155–80

Godden, M., 'The Relations of Wulfstan and Ælfric: A Reassessment', in *Wulfstan, Archbishop of York*, ed. M. Townend (Turnhout, 2004), 353–74

Godden, M., 'Did King Alfred Write Anything?', *Medium Ævum* 76 (2007), 1–23

Gore, D., *The Vikings in the West Country* (Exeter, 2015)

Görich, K., 'Versuch zur Rettung von Kontingenz – Oder: Über Schwierigkeiten beim Schreiben einer Biographie Friedrich Barbarossas', *FMSt* 43 (2009), 179–97

Gouguenheim, S., *Les fausses terreurs de l'an mil. Attente de la fin des temps ou approfondissement de la foi?* (Paris, 1999)

Green, J.A., 'The Last Century of Danegeld', *EHR* 96 (1981), 241–58

Gretsch, M., *The Intellectual Foundations of the English Benedictine Reform* (Cambridge, 1999)

Gretsch, M., 'Historiography and Literary Patronage in Late Anglo-Saxon England: The Evidence of Æthelweard's *Chronicon*', *ASE* 41 (2012), 205–48

Grierson, P., 'Numismatics and the Historian', *NC* 7th ser. 2 (1962), i–xiv

Hadley, D.W., '"Cockle amongst the Wheat": The Scandinavian Settlement of England', in *Social Identity in Early Medieval Britain*, ed. W.O. Frazer and A. Tyrell (London, 2000), 111–35

Halbrooks, J., 'Byrhtnoth's Great-Hearted Mirth, or Praise and Blame in *The Battle of Maldon*', *Philological Quarterly* 82 (2004), 235–55

Halsall, G., 'Anthropology and the Study of pre-Conquest Warfare and Society: The Ritual War in Anglo-Saxon England', in *Weapons and Warfare in Anglo-Saxon England*, ed. S.C. Hawkes (Oxford, 1989), 155–77

Halsall, G., 'Playing by Whose Rules? A Further Look at Viking Atrocity in the Ninth Century', *Medieval History* 2.ii (1992), 3–12

Halsall, G., *Warfare and Society in the Barbarian West, 450–900* (London, 2003)

Hamilton, S., 'Otto III's Penance: A Case Study of Unity and Diversity in the Eleventh-Century Church', *SCH* 32 (1996), 83–94

Hamilton, S., 'A New Model for Royal Penance? Helgaud of Fleury's *Life of Robert the Pious*', *EME* 6 (1997), 189–200

Hamilton, S., *The Practice of Penance, 900–1050* (Woodbridge, 2001)

Hamilton, S., 'Rites for Public Penance in Late Anglo-Saxon England', in *The Liturgy of the Late Anglo-Saxon Church*, ed. H. Gittos and M.B. Bedingfield (Woodbridge, 2005), 65–103

Hamilton, S., *Church and People in the Medieval West, 900–1200* (London, 2013)

Harrison, K., *The Framework of Anglo-Saxon History to AD 900* (Cambridge, 1976)

Hart, C.R., *The Early Charters of Eastern England* (Leicester, 1966)

Hart, C.R., *The Early Charters of Northern England and the Midlands* (Leicester, 1975)

Hart, C.R., 'Athelstan "Half King" and his Family' (1973), rev. and repr. in his *The Danelaw* (London, 1992), 569–604

Hart, C.[R.], 'Edward (*c.*962–978)', in *ODNB*, XVII, 783–5

Haslam, J., 'Daws Castle, Somerset, and Civil Defence Measures in Southern and Midland England in the Ninth to Eleventh Centuries', *Archaeological Journal* 168 (2011), 195–227

Haslam, J., 'The Unfinished Chapel at Bradford on Avon, Wiltshire, and Ecclesiastical Politics in the Early Eleventh Century', *Archaeological Journal* 170 (2013), 272–301

Hawkes, S.C., ed., *Weapons and Warfare in Anglo-Saxon England* (Oxford, 1989)

Hayward, P.A., 'The Idea of Innocent Martyrdom in Late Tenth- and Eleventh-Century English Hagiology', *SCH* 30 (1993), 81–92

Hayward, P.A., 'Translation-Narratives in Post-Conquest Hagiography and English Resistance to the Norman Conquest', *ANS* 21 (1999), 67–93

Head, T., 'Peace and Power in France around the Year 1000', *Essays in Medieval Studies* 23 (2006), 1–17

Heather, P.J., '*Foedera* and *foederati* of the Fourth Century', in *Kingdoms of the Empire: The Integration of Barbarians in Late Antiquity*, ed. W. Pohl (Leiden, 1997), 57–74

Heidecker, K., *The Divorce of Lothar II: Christian Marriage and Political Power in the Carolingian World*, trans. T.M Guest (Ithaca, NY, 2010)

Higham, N.J., *The Death of Anglo-Saxon England* (Stroud, 1997)

Higham, N.J., and D.H. Hill, ed., *Edward the Elder, 899–924* (London, 2001)

Higham N.J., and M. Ryan, *The Anglo-Saxon World* (New Haven, CT, 2013)

Hill, D.[H.], 'Trends in the Development of Towns in the Reign of Ethelred II', in *Ethelred the Unready*, ed. D.[H.] Hill (London, 1978), 213–26

Hill, D.[H.], ed., *Ethelred the Unready* (London, 1978)

Hill, D.[H.], *An Atlas of Anglo-Saxon England* (Oxford, 1981)

Hill, D.[H.], 'Gazetteer of Burghal Hidages Sites', in *The Defence of Wessex: The Burghal Hidage and Anglo-Saxon Fortifications*, ed. D.[H.] Hill and A.R. Rumble (Manchester, 1996), 189–231

Hill, D.H., 'The Shiring of Mercia – Again', in *Edward the Elder, 899–924*, ed. N. Higham and D.H. Hill (London, 2001), 144–59

Hill, J., 'Ælfric and Wulfstan: Two Views of the Millennium', in *Essays on Anglo-Saxon and Related Themes in Memory of Lynne Grundy*, ed. J. Roberts and J.[L.] Nelson (Woodbridge, 2000), 213–35

Hill, J., 'The *Litaniae maiores* and *minores* in Rome, Francia and Anglo-Saxon England: Terminology, Texts and Traditions', *EME* 9 (2000), 211–46

Hill, T.D., 'The *Liber Eliensis* "Historical Selections" and the Old English *Battle of Maldon*', *JEGP* 96 (1997), 1–12

Hillen, C., 'Minority Governments of Henry III, Henry (VII) and Louis IX Compared', *Thirteenth Century England* 11 (2007), 46–60

Hoffmann, H., 'Eigendiktat in den Urkunden Ottos III. und Heinrichs II.', *DA* 44 (1988), 390–423

Hoffmann, H., *Mönchskönig und rex idiota. Studien zur Kirchenpolitik Heinrichs II. und Konrads II.*, MGH: Studien und Texte 8 (Hannover, 1993)

Holdsworth, C., 'Tavistock Abbey in its Late Tenth Century Context', *Report and Transactions of the Devonshire Association for the Advancement of Science* 135 (2003), 31–58

Hollister, C.W., 'Royal Acts of Mutilation: The Case against Henry I', *Albion* 10 (1978), 330–40

van Houts, E.[M.C.], 'Normandy's View of the Anglo-Saxon Past in the Twelfth Century', in *The Long Twelfth-Century View of the Anglo-Saxon Past*, ed. M. Brett and D.A. Woodman (Farnham, 2015), 123–40

Howard, I., *Swein Forkbeard's Invasions and the Danish Conquest of England, 991–1017* (Woodbridge, 2003)

Howard, I., *The Reign of Æthelred II: The King of the English, Emperor of All the Peoples of Britain, 978–1016* (Oxford, 2010)

Howe, J., 'The Laity's Reform of the Church', *American Historical Review* 93 (1988), 317–39

Howe, N., *Migration and Mythmaking in Anglo-Saxon England* (New Haven, CT, 1989)

Hudson, J., 'L'écrit, les archives et le droit en Angleterre (IXᵉ–XIIᵉ siècle)', *Revue historique* 308 (2006), 3–35

Hudson, J., *The Oxford History of the Laws of England*, II, *871–1216* (Oxford, 2012)

Huschner, W., *Transalpine Kommunikation im Mittelalter. Diplomatische, kulturelle und politische Wechselwirkungen zwischen Italien und dem nordalpinen Reich (9.–11. Jahrhundert)*, 3 pts, MGH: Schriften 52 (Hannover, 2003)

Insley, C., 'Charters and Episcopal Scriptoria in the Anglo-Saxon South-West', *EME* 7 (1998), 173–97

Insley, C., 'Politics, Conflict and Kinship in Early Eleventh-Century Mercia', *Midland History* 26 (2001), 28–42

Insley, C., 'Where did All the Charters Go? Anglo-Saxon Charters and the New Politics of the Eleventh Century', *ANS* 24 (2002), 109–27

339

Insley, C., 'Charters, Ritual and Late Tenth-Century Kingship', in *Gender and Historiography: Studies in the Earlier Middle Ages in Honour of Pauline Stafford*, ed. J.L. Nelson, S. Reynolds and S.M. Johns (London, 2012), 75–89

Insley, C., 'The Family of Wulfric Spott: An Anglo-Saxon Marcher Dynasty?', in *The English and their Legacy, 900–1200: Essays in Honour of Ann Williams*, ed. D. Roffe (Woodbridge, 2012), 115–28

Iogna-Prat, D., *Order and Exclusion: Cluny and Christendom Face Heresy, Judaism, and Islam, 1000–1150*, trans. G.R. Edwards (Ithaca, NY, 2002)

Jackson, P., 'Medieval Christendom's Encounter with the Alien', *Historical Research* 74 (2001), 347–69

Jäschke, K.-U., *Burgenbau und Landesverteidigung um 900. Überlegungen zu Beispielen aus Deutschland, Frankreich und England*, Vorträge und Forschungen: Sonderband 16 (Sigmaringen, 1975)

Jayakumar, S., 'Reform and Retribution: The "Anti-Monastic Reaction" in the Reign of Edward the Martyr', in *Early Medieval Studies in Memory of Patrick Wormald*, ed. S. Baxter *et al.* (Farnham, 2009), 337–52

John, E., *Orbis Britanniae and Other Studies* (Leicester, 1966)

John, E., 'War and Society in the Tenth Century: The Maldon Campaign', *TRHS* 5th ser. 27 (1977), 173–95

John, E., 'The Return of the Vikings', in *The Anglo-Saxons*, ed. J. Campbell (London, 1982), 192–213

de Jong, M., 'Carolingian Monasticism: The Power of Prayer', in *The New Cambridge Medieval History*, II, *c.700–c.900*, ed. R. McKitterick (Cambridge, 1995), 622–53

de Jong, M., 'What was Public about Public Penance? *Paenitentia publica* and Justice in the Carolingian World', *Settimane* 44 (1997), 863–904

de Jong, M., 'Monastic Prisoners or Opting Out? Political Coercion and Honour in the Frankish Kingdoms', in *Topographies of Power in the Early Middle Ages*, ed. M. de Jong and F. Theuws (Leiden, 2001), 291–328

de Jong, M., '*Admonitio* and Criticism of the Ruler at the Court of Louis the Pious', in *La culture du haut Moyen Âge, une question d'élites?*, ed. F. Bougard, R. Le Jan and R. McKitterick (Turnhout, 2009), 315–38

de Jong, M., *The Penitential State: Authority and Atonement in the Age of Louis the Pious, 814–40* (Cambridge, 2009)

Jonsson, K., *Viking-Age Hoards and Late Anglo-Saxon Coins: A Study in Honour of Bror Emil Hildebrand's Anglosachsiska mynt* (Stockholm, 1987)

Jonsson, K., ed., *Studies in Late Anglo-Saxon Coinage in Memory of Bror Emil Hildebrand* (Stockholm, 1990)

Jost, K., *Wulfstanstudien*, Schweizer anglistische Arbeiten 23 (Bern, 1950)

Jungmann, J.A., *Missarum sollemnia. Eine genetische Erklärung der Römischen Messe*, II, *Opfermesse*, rev. edn (Vienna, 1962)

Karras, R.M., *Unmarriages: Women, Men, and Sexual Unions in the Middle Ages* (Philadelphia, PA, 2012)

Kasten, B., *Königssöhne und Königsherrschaft. Untersuchungen zur Teilhabe am Reich in der Merowinger- und Karolingerzeit*, MGH: Schriften 44 (Hannover, 1997)

Keen, L., ed., *Studies in the Early History of Shaftesbury Abbey* (Dorchester, 1999)

Keller, H., and S. Ast, '*Ostensio cartae*. Italienische Gerichtsurkunden des 10. Jahrhunderts zwischen Schriftlichkeit und Performance', *Archiv für Diplomatik* 53 (2007), 99–121

Ker, N.R., *Catalogue of Manuscripts Containing Anglo-Saxon* (Oxford, 1957)

Ker, N.R., 'The Handwriting of Archbishop Wulfstan', in *England Before the Conquest: Studies in Primary Sources Presented to Dorothy Whitelock*, ed. P.[A.M.] Clemoes and K. Hughes (Cambridge, 1971), 315–31

Keynes, S., 'An Interpretation of the *Pacs*, *Pax* and *Paxs* Pennies', *ASE* 7 (1978), 165–73

Keynes, S., *The Diplomas of King Æthelred 'the Unready', 978–1016: A Study in their Use as Historical Evidence* (Cambridge, 1980)

Keynes, S., 'A Tale of Two Kings: Alfred the Great and Æthelred the Unready', *TRHS* 5th ser. 36 (1986), 195–217

Keynes, S., 'Regenbald the Chancellor (*sic*)', *ANS* 10 (1988), 185–222

Keynes, S., 'The Æthelings in Normandy', *ANS* 13 (1991), 173–205

Keynes, S., 'Crime and Punishment in the Reign of King Æthelred the Unready', in *People and Places in Northern Europe 500–1600: Essays in Honour of Peter Hayes Sawyer*, ed. I.N. Wood and N. Lund (Woodbridge, 1991), 67–81

Keynes, S., 'The Historical Context of the Battle of Maldon', in *The Battle of Maldon, AD 991*, ed. D. Scragg (Oxford, 1991), 81–113

Keynes, S., 'Cnut's Earls', in *The Reign of Cnut: King of England, Denmark and Norway*, ed. A.R. Rumble (London, 1994), 43–88

Keynes, S., 'The "Dunstan B" Charters', *ASE* 23 (1994), 165–93

Keynes, S., 'England, 700–900', in *The New Cambridge Medieval History*, II, *c.700–c.900*, ed. R. McKitterick (Cambridge, 1995), 18–42

Keynes, S., 'King Alfred and the Mercians', in *Kings, Currency and Alliances: History and Coinage of Southern England in the Ninth Century*, ed. M.A.S. Blackburn and D.N. Dumville (Woodbridge, 1998), 1–45

Keynes, S., 'Introduction to the 1998 Reprint', in *Encomium Emmae reginae*, ed. A. Campbell, Camden Classics Reprints 4 (Cambridge, 1998), [xi]–[lxxx]

Keynes, S., 'King Alfred the Great and Shaftesbury Abbey', in *Studies in the Early History of Shaftesbury Abbey*, ed. L. Keen (Dorchester, 1999), 17–72

Keynes, S., 'The Declining Reputation of Æthelred the Unready' (1978), rev. and repr. in *Anglo-Saxon History: Basic Readings*, ed. D. Pelteret (New York, 2000), 157–90

Keynes, S., 'Apocalypse Then: England A.D. 1000', in *Europe around the Year 1000*, ed. P. Urbańczyk (Warsaw, 2001), 247–70

Keynes, S., 'Edward, King of the Anglo-Saxons', in *Edward the Elder, 899–924*, ed. N.J. Higham and D.H. Hill (London, 2001), 40–66

Keynes, S., 'Ely Abbey 672–1109', in *A History of Ely Cathedral*, ed. P. Meadows and N. Ramsay (Woodbridge, 2003), 3–58

Keynes, S., 'Eadric Streona (*d.* 1017)', in *ODNB*, XVII, 538–9

Keynes, S., 'Eadwig (*c.* 940–959)', in *ODNB*, XVII, 539–42

Keynes, S., 'Wulfsige, Monk of Glastonbury, Abbot of Westminster (*c* 990–3), and Bishop of Sherborne (*c* 993–1002)', in *St Wulfsige and Sherborne: Essays to Celebrate the Millennium of the Benedictine Abbey 998–1998*, ed. K. Barker, D.A. Hinton and A. Hunt (Oxford, 2005), 53–94

Keynes, S., 'Re-Reading King Æthelred the Unready', in *Writing Medieval Biography, 750–1250: Essays in Honour of Professor Frank Barlow*, ed. D. Bates, J. Crick and S. Hamilton (Woodbridge, 2006), 77–97

Keynes, S., 'An Abbot, an Archbishop, and the Viking Raids of 1006–7 and 1009–12', *ASE* 36 (2007), 151–220

Keynes, S., 'The Massacre of St Brice's Day (13 November 1002)', in *Beretning fra seksogtyvende tværfaglige vikingesymposium*, ed. N. Lund (Aarhus, 2007), 32–67

Keynes, S., 'Edgar, *rex admirabilis*', in *Edgar, King of the English 959–75: New Interpretations*, ed. D. Scragg (Woodbridge, 2008), 1–58

Keynes, S., 'Edward the Ætheling (*c.* 1005–16)', in *Edward the Confessor: The Man and the Legend*, ed. R. Mortimer (Woodbridge, 2009), 41–62

Keynes, S., 'King Æthelred's Charter for Eynsham Abbey (1005)', in *Early Medieval Studies in Memory of Patrick Wormald*, ed. S. Baxter *et al.* (Farnham, 2009), 451–73

Keynes, S., 'The Burial of King Æthelred the Unready at St Paul's', in *The English and their Legacy, 900–1200: Essays in Honour of Ann Williams*, ed. D. Roffe (Woodbridge, 2012), 129–48

Keynes, S., 'The Cult of King Edward the Martyr', in *Gender and Historiography: Studies in the Earlier Middle Ages in Honour of Pauline Stafford*, ed. J.L. Nelson, S. Reynolds and S.M. Johns (London, 2012), 115–25

Keynes, S., 'Manuscripts of the *Anglo-Saxon Chronicle*', in *The Cambridge History of the Book in Britain*, I, *c.400–1100*, ed. R. Gameson (Cambridge, 2012), 537–52

Keynes, S., 'Church Councils, Royal Assemblies, and Anglo-Saxon Royal Diplomas', in *Kingship, Legislation and Power in Anglo-Saxon England*, ed. G.R. Owen-Crocker and B.W. Schneider (Woodbridge, 2013), 17–182

Keynes, S., 'Shire', in *The Wiley Blackwell Encyclopedia of Anglo-Saxon England*, ed. M. Lapidge *et al.*, 2nd edn (Chichester, 2013), 434–5

Keynes, S., 'King Æthelred the Unready and the Church of Rochester', in *Textus Roffensis: Law, Language, and Libraries in Early Medieval England*, ed. B. O'Brian and B. Bombi (Turnhout, 2015), 315–62

Keynes, S., and R. Love, 'Earl Godwine's Ship', *ASE* 38 (2009), 185–223

Keynes S., and R. Naismith, 'The *Agnus Dei* Pennies of King Æthelred the Unready', *ASE* 40 (2011), 175–223

Kirby, D.P., *The Making of Early England* (London, 1967)

Klein, S., *Ruling Women: Queenship and Gender in Anglo-Saxon Literature* (Notre Dame, IN, 2006)

Kluge, B., 'Das älteste Exemplar vom Agnus Dei-Typ', in *Studies in Late Anglo-Saxon Coinage in Memory of Bror Emil Hildebrand*, ed. K. Jonsson (Stockholm, 1990), 139–56

Kölzer, T., 'Das Königtum Minderjähriger im fränkisch-deutschen Mittelalter. Eine Skizze', *HZ* 251 (1990), 291–332

Konshuh, C., '*Anraed* in their *Unraed*: The Æthelredian Annals (983–1016) and their Presentation of King and Advisors', *English Studies* 97 (2016), 140–62

Kosto, A.J., *Hostages in the Middle Ages* (Oxford, 2012)

Koziol, G., *Begging Pardon and Favor: Ritual and Political Order in Early Medieval France* (Ithaca, NY, 1992)

Koziol, G., 'Is Robert I in Hell? The Diploma for Saint-Denis and the Mind of a Rebel King (Jan. 25, 923)', *EME* 14 (2006), 233–67

Koziol, G., *The Politics of Memory and Identity in Carolingian Royal Diplomas: The West Frankish Kingdom (840–987)* (Turnhout, 2012)

Koziol, G., 'The Conquest of Burgundy, the Peace of God, and the Diplomas of Robert the Pious', *French Historical Studies* 37 (2014), 173–214

Kritsch, K.R., 'Fragments and Reflexes of Kingship Theory in Ælfric's Comments on Royal Authority', *English Studies* 97 (2016), 163–85

Krüger, K.-H., 'Herrschaftsnachfolge als Vater-Sohn-Konflikt', *FMSt* 36 (2002), 225–40

Lainé, A., 'L'Antéchrist dans les homélies eschatologiques de Wulfstan: un mal du siècle', *Historical Reflections/Réflexions Historiques* 26 (2000), 173–87

Landes, R., 'The Fear of an Apocalyptic Year 1000: Augustinian Historiography, Medieval and Modern', *Speculum* 75 (2000), 97–145

Landes, R., A. Gow and D.C. Van Meter, ed., *The Apocalyptic Year 1000* (Oxford, 2003)

Lapidge, M., 'The Life of St Oswald', in *The Battle of Maldon, AD 991*, ed. D. Scragg (Oxford, 1991), 51–8

Lapidge, M., 'The Hermeneutic Style in Tenth-Century Anglo-Latin Literature' (1975), repr. in and cited from his *Anglo-Latin Literature 900–1066* (London, 1993), 105–49

Lapidge, M., 'Æthelwold as Scholar and Teacher' (1988), repr. in and cited from his *Anglo-Latin Literature 900–1066* (London, 1993), 183–211

Lapidge, M., 'Æthelwold and the *Vita S. Eustachii*' (1988), repr. in and cited from his *Anglo-Latin Literature 900–1066* (London, 1993), 213–23

Lapidge, M., 'Abbot Germanus, Winchcombe, Ramsey and the Cambridge Psalter' (1992), repr. in and cited from his *Anglo-Latin Literature 900–1066* (London, 1993), 387–417

Lapidge, M., 'Byrhtferth and Oswald', in *St Oswald of Worcester: Life and Influence*, ed. N. Brooks and C. Cubitt (London, 1996), 64–83

Lapidge, M., *et al.*, ed., *The Wiley Blackwell Encyclopedia of Anglo-Saxon England*, 2nd edn (Chichester, 2013)

Larson, L.M., *The King's Household in England before the Norman Conquest* (Madison, WI, 1904)

Lavelle, R., *Aethelred II: King of the English*, 2nd edn (Stroud, 2008)

Lavelle, R., 'The Use and Abuse of Hostages in Later Anglo-Saxon England', *EME* 14 (2006), 269–96

Lavelle, R., *Royal Estates in Anglo-Saxon Wessex: Land, Politics and Family Strategies* (Oxford, 2007)

Lavelle, R., *Alfred's Wars: Sources and Interpretations of Anglo-Saxon Warfare in the Viking Age* (Woodbridge, 2010)

Lavelle, R., 'Royal Control and the Disposition of Estates in Tenth-Century England: Reflections on the Charters of King Eadwig (955–959)', *HSJ* 23 (2014), 23–49

Lavelle, R., 'Law, Death and Peacemaking in the "Second Viking Age": An Ealdorman, his King, and Some "Danes" in Wessex', in *Danes in Wessex: The Scandinavian Impact on Southern England, c. 800–c. 1100*, ed. R. Lavelle and S. Roffey (Oxford, 2015), 122–43

Lavelle, R., and S. Roffey, ed., *Danes in Wessex: The Scandinavian Impact on Southern England, c. 800–c. 1100* (Oxford, 2015)

Lawson, M.K., 'The Collection of Danegeld and Heregeld in the Reigns of Aethelred II and Cnut', *EHR* 99 (1984), 721–38

Lawson, M.K., '"Those stories look true": Levels of Taxation in the Reigns of Aethelred II and Cnut', *EHR* 104 (1989), 385–406

Lawson, M.K., 'Danegeld and Heregeld Once More', *EHR* 105 (1990), 951–61

Lawson, M.K., 'Archbishop Wulfstan and the Homiletic Element in the Laws of Æthelred II and Cnut', *EHR* 107 (1992), 565–86

Lawson, M.K., *Cnut: The Danes in England in the Early Eleventh Century* (London, 1993)

Leech, R.H., 'Arthur's Acre: A Saxon Bridgehead at Bristol', *Transactions of the Bristol and Gloucestershire Archaeological Society* 127 (2009), 11–20

Le Goff, J., 'The Whys and Ways of Writing a Biography: The Case of Saint Louis', *Exemplaria* 1 (1989), 207–25

Le Goff, J., *Saint Louis*, trans. G.E. Gollrad (Notre Dame, IN, 2009)

Leimus, I., 'A Fourteenth Agnus Dei Penny of Æthelred II', in *Studies in Late Anglo-Saxon Coinage in Memory of Bror Emil Hildebrand*, ed. K. Jonsson (Stockholm, 1990), 159–63

Lemke, A., 'Fear-Mongering, Political Shrewdness or Setting the Stage for a "Holy Society"? – Wulfstan's *Sermo Lupi ad Anglos*', *English Studies* 95 (2014), 758–76

Lerner, R.E., 'The Black Death and Western European Eschatological Mentalities', *American Historical Review* 86 (1981), 533–52

Leyser, K.J., *Rule and Conflict in an Early Medieval Society: Ottonian Saxony* (London, 1979)

Leyser, K.J., 'Ritual, Ceremony and Gesture: Ottonian Germany', in his *Communications and Power in Medieval Europe*, ed. T. Reuter, 2 vols. (London, 1994), I, 189–213

Lintzel, M., 'Die Schlacht von Riade und die Anfänge des deutschen Staates', *Sachsen und Anhalt* 9 (1933), 27–51

Lionarons, J.T., 'Napier Homily L: Wulfstan's Eschatology at the Close of his Career', in *Wulfstan, Archbishop of York*, ed. M. Townend (Turnhout, 2004), 413–28

Lionarons, J.T., *The Homiletic Writings of Archbishop Wulfstan: A Critical Study* (Woodbridge, 2010)

Locherbie-Cameron, M.A.L., 'The Men Named in the Poem', in *The Battle of Maldon, AD 991*, ed. D. Scragg (Oxford, 1991), 238–49

Loe, L., *et al.*, *'Given to the Ground': A Viking Age Mass Grave on Ridgeway Hill, Weymouth* (Oxford, 2014)

Love, R., 'Latin Commentaries on Boethius's *Consolation of Philosophy*', in *The Brill Companion to Alfred the Great*, ed. P. Szarmach and N.G. Discenza (Leiden, 2015), 83–111

Loyn, H.R., 'The Hundred in England in the Tenth and Early Eleventh Centuries' (1974), repr. in and cited from his *Society and Peoples: Studies in the History of England and Wales, c. 600–1200* (London, 1992), 111–34

Lund, N., 'The Armies of Swein Forkbeard and Cnut: *Leding* or *lið*?', *ASE* 15 (1986), 105–18

Lund, N., 'Peace and Non-Peace in the Viking Age – Ottar in Biarmaland, the Rus in Byzantium, and Danes and Norwegians in England', in *Proceedings of the Tenth Viking Conference*, ed. J.E. Knirk (Oslo, 1987), 255–69

Lynch, J.H., *Christianizing Kinship: Ritual Sponsorship in Anglo-Saxon England* (Ithaca, NY, 1998)

Lyon, C.S.S., 'The Significance of the Sack of Oxford in 1009/10 for the Chronology of the Coinage of Æthelred II', *BNJ* 35 (1966), 34–7

Lyon, [C.S.]S., 'Die-Cutting Styles in the *Last Small Cross* Issue of *c.* 1009–1017 and Some Problematic East Anglian Dies and Die-links', *BNJ* 68 (1998), 21–41

McClure, J., 'Bede's Old Testament Kings', in *Ideal and Reality in Frankish and Anglo-Saxon Society*, ed. P. Wormald *et al.* (Oxford, 1983), 76–98

McCormick, M., 'The Liturgy of War in the Early Middle Ages: Crisis, Litanies and the Carolingian Monarchy', *Viator* 15 (1984), 1–23

McDougall, I., 'Serious Entertainments: An Examination of a Peculiar Type of Viking Atrocity', *ASE* 22 (1993), 201–25

McKinnell, J., 'On the Date of *The Battle of Maldon*', *Medium Ævum* 44 (1975), 121–36

McKitterick, R., ed., *The New Cambridge Medieval History*, II, *c.700–c.900* (Cambridge, 1995)

McKitterick, R., *Charlemagne: The Formation of a European Identity* (Cambridge, 2008)

MacLean, S., 'Queenship, Nunneries and Royal Widowhood in Carolingian Europe', *P & P* 178 (2003), 3–38

MacLean, S., 'Ritual, Misunderstanding and the Contest for Meaning: Representations of the Disrupted Royal Assembly at Frankfurt (873)', in *Representations of Power in Medieval Germany, c. 800–1500*, ed. S. MacLean and B. Weiler (Turnhout, 2006), 97–120

MacLean, S., 'Reform, Queenship and the End of the World in Tenth-Century France: Adso's "Letter on the Origin and Time of the Antichrist" Reconsidered', *Revue belge de philologie et d'histoire* 86 (2008), 645–75

MacLean, S., 'Monastic Reform and Royal Ideology in the Late Tenth Century: Ælfthryth and Edgar in Continental Perspective', in *England and the Continent in the Tenth Century: Studies in Honour of Wilhelm Levison (1876–1947)*, ed. D.[W.] Rollason, C. Leyser and H. Williams (Turnhout, 2010), 255–74

MacLean, S., 'Palaces, Itineraries and Political Order in the Post-Carolingian Kingdoms', in *Diverging Paths? The Shape of Power and Institutions in Medieval Christendom and Islam*, ed. A. Rodriguez and J. Hudson (Leiden, 2014), 291–320

McNair, F., 'The Politics of Being Norman in the Reign of Richard the Fearless, Duke of Normandy (r. 942–996)', *EME* 23 (2015), 308–28

Magennis, H., and M. Swan, ed., *A Companion to Ælfric* (Leiden, 2009)

Malmer, B., 'Agnus Dei i Bath år 1009', *Myntkontakt* 4/5 (1984), 126–7

Mann, G., 'The Development of Wulfstan's Alcuin Manuscript', in *Wulfstan, Archbishop of York*, ed. M. Townend (Turnhout, 2004), 235–78

Mansfield, M., *The Humiliation of Sinners: Public Penance in Thirteenth-Century France* (Ithaca, NY, 1995)

Marafioti, N., 'Punishing Bodies and Saving Souls: Capital and Corporal Punishment in Late Anglo-Saxon England', *HSJ* 20 (2008), 39–57

Marafioti, N., *The King's Body: Burial and Succession in Late Anglo-Saxon England* (Toronto, 2014)

Markus, R.A., *Saeculum: History and Society in the Theology of St Augustine*, 2nd edn (Cambridge, 1989)

Markus, R.A., *The End of Ancient Christianity* (Cambridge, 1990)

Marten, L., 'The Shiring of East Anglia: An Alternative Hypothesis', *Historical Research* 81 (2008), 1–27

Maund, K.L., *Ireland, Wales, and England in the Eleventh Century* (Woodbridge, 1991)

Mazel, F., *Féodalités, 888–1180* (Paris, 2010)

Mazel, F., 'Monachisme et aristocratie aux Xe–XIe siècles. Un regard sur l'historiographie récente', in *Ecclesia in medio nationis: Reflections on the Study of Monasticism in the Central Middle Ages*, ed. S. Vanderputten and B. Meijns (Leuven, 2011), 47–75

Meens, R., 'Children and Confession in the Early Middle Ages', *SCH* 31 (1994), 53–65

Meens, R., 'Politics, Mirrors of Princes and the Bible: Sins, Kings and the Well-Being of the Realm', *EME* 7 (1998), 345–57

Meens, R., *Penance in Medieval Europe: 600–1200* (Cambridge, 2014)

Metcalf, D.M., 'Large Danegelds in Relation to War and Kingship: Their Implications for Monetary History, and Some Numismatic Evidence', in *Weapons and Warfare in Anglo-Saxon England*, ed. S.C. Hawkes (Oxford, 1989), 179–89

Metcalf, D.M., and W. Lean, 'The Battle of Maldon and the Minting of Crux Pennies in Essex: *Post hoc propter hoc?*', in *The Battle of Maldon: Fiction and Fact*, ed. J. Cooper (London, 1993), 205–24

Metcalf, D.M., 'Inflows of Anglo-Saxon and German Coins into the Northern Lands *c.* 997–1024: Discerning the Patterns', in *Coinage and History in the North Sea World, c. AD 500–1250: Essays in Honour of Marion Archibald*, ed. B. Cook and G. Williams (Leiden, 2006), 349–88

Misonne, D., 'Gérard de Brogne et sa dévotion aux reliques' (1982), repr. in and cited from *Revue Bénédictine* 111 (2001), 90–110

Misonne, D., 'Gérard de Brogne, moine et réformateur (†959)' (1984), repr. in and cited from *Revue Bénédictine* 111 (2001), 25–49

Moesgaard, J.C., and S.Å. Tornbjerg, 'A Sixteenth Agnus Dei Penny of Æthelred II', *NC* 159 (1999), 327–32

Molyneaux, G., 'Why were Some Tenth-Century English Kings Presented as Rulers of Britain?', *TRHS* 6th ser. 21 (2011), 59–91

Molyneaux, G., *The Formation of the English Kingdom in the Tenth Century* (Oxford, 2015)

Moore, B., *Moral Purity and Persecution in History* (Princeton, NJ, 2000)

Moore, R.I., *The Formation of a Persecuting Society*, 2nd edn (Malden, MA, 2007)

Mordek, H., 'Karls des Großen zweites Kapitular von Herstal und die Hungersnot der Jahre 778/779', *DA* 61 (2005), 1–52

Mortimer Wheeler, R.E., *London and the Vikings* (London, 1927)

Murray, A., *Reason and Society in the Middle Ages* (Oxford, 1978)

Naismith, R., *Money and Power in Anglo-Saxon England: The Southern English Kingdoms, 757–865* (Cambridge, 2012)

Naismith, R. 'Payments for Land and Privilege in Anglo-Saxon England', *ASE* 41 (2012), 277–342

Naismith, R., 'Prelude to Reform: Tenth-Century English Coinage in Perspective', in *Early Medieval Monetary History: Studies in Memory of Mark Blackburn*, ed. M. Allen, R. Naismith and E. Screen (Farnham, 2014), 39–84

Naismith, R., 'The Coinage of Æthelred II: A New Evaluation', *English Studies* 97 (2016), 117–39

Naismith, R., *Medieval European Coinage*, VIII, *Britain and Ireland c.400–1066* (Cambridge, forthcoming)

Neidorf, L., '*II Æthelred* and the Politics of *The Battle of Maldon*', *JEGP* 111 (2012), 451–73

Nelson, J.L., 'Inauguration Rituals' (1977), repr. in and cited from her *Politics and Ritual in Early Medieval Europe* (London, 1986), 283–307

Nelson, J.L., 'The Second English *Ordo*', in her *Politics and Ritual in Early Medieval Europe* (London, 1986), 361–74

Nelson, J.L., *Charles the Bald* (London, 1992)

Nelson, J.L., 'The Frankish Empire', in *The Oxford Illustrated History of the Vikings*, ed. P.[H.] Sawyer (Oxford, 1997), 19–47

Nelson, J.L., 'Rulers and Government', in *The New Cambridge Medieval History*, III, *c. 900–1024*, ed. T. Reuter (Cambridge, 1999), 95–129

Nelson, J.L., 'Writing Early Medieval Biography', *History Workshop Journal* 50 (2000), 129–36

Nelson, J.L., 'Æthelwulf (*d.* 858)', in *ODNB*, I, 438–41

Nelson, J.L., 'England and the Continent in the Ninth Century: III, Rights and Rituals', *TRHS* 6th ser. 14 (2004), 1–24

Nelson, J.L., 'Religion and Politics in the Reign of Charlemagne', in *Religion und Politik im Mittelalter. Deutschland und England im Vergleich*, ed. L. Körntgen and D. Waßenhoven (Berlin, 2013), 17–29

Nelson, J.L., S. Reynolds and S.M. Johns, ed., *Gender and Historiography: Studies in the Earlier Middle Ages in Honour of Pauline Stafford* (London, 2012)

Nightingale, P., 'The Origin of the Court of Husting and the Danish Influence on London's Development into a Capital City', *EHR* 102 (1987), 559–78

Nightingale, J., *Monasteries and Patrons in the Gorze Reform: Lotharingia c. 850–1000* (Oxford, 2001)

Niles, J.D., '*Maldon* and Mythopoesis' (1994), repr. with two addenda in his *Old English Heroic Poems and the Social Life of Texts* (Turnhout, 2007), 203–52

Niles, J.D., 'Byrhtnoth's Laughter and the Poetics of Gesture' (2000), repr. with an addendum in his *Old English Heroic Poems and the Social Life of Texts* (Turnhout, 2007), 253–78

Noble, T.F.X., 'The Monastic Ideal as a Model for Empire: The Case of Louis the Pious', *Revue Bénédictine* 86 (1976), 235–50

O'Brien O'Keeffe, K., 'Body and Law in Late Anglo-Saxon England', *ASE* 27 (1998), 209–32

Oexle, O.-G., 'Memoria und Memorialüberlieferung im früheren Mittelalter', *FMSt* 10 (1976), 70–95

Offergeld, T., *Reges pueri. Das Königtum Minderjähriger im frühen Mittelalter*, MGH: Schriften 50 (Hannover, 2001)

Orchard, A., 'Wulfstan as Reader, Writer, and Rewriter', in *The Old English Homily: Precedent, Practice, and Appropriation*, ed. A.J. Kleist (Turnhout, 2007), 311–40

Owen-Crocker, G.R., and B.W. Schneider, ed., *Kingship, Legislation and Power in Anglo-Saxon England* (Woodbridge, 2013)

Palmer, J., *The Apocalypse in the Early Middle Ages* (Cambridge, 2014)

Patzold, S., *Konflikte im Kloster. Studien zu Auseinandersetzungen in monastischen Gemeinschaften des ottonisch-salischen Reichs*, Historische Studien 463 (Husum, 2000)

Patzold, S., 'Konsens und Konkurrenz. Überlegungen zu einem aktuellen Forschungskonzept der Mediävistik', *FMSt* 41 (2007), 75–103

Patzold, S., 'Human Security, fragile Staatlichkeit und Governance im Frühmittelalter. Zur Fragwürdigkeit der Scheidung von Vormoderne und Moderne', *Geschichte und Gesellschaft* 38 (2012), 406–22

Pestell, T., *Landscapes of Monastic Foundation: The Establishment of Religious Houses in East Anglia, c. 650–1200* (Woodbridge, 2004)

Pollard, A.M. *et al.*, ' "Sprouting like Cockle Amongst the Wheat": The St. Brice's Day Massacre and the Isotopic Analysis of Human Bones from St. John's College, Oxford', *Oxford Journal of Archaeology* 31 (2012), 83–102

Pollard, J., and A. Reynolds, *Avebury: The Biography of a Landscape* (Stroud, 2002)

Pons-Sanz, S.[M.], *Norse-Derived Vocabulary in Late Old English Texts: Wulfstan's Works, A Case Study* (Odense, 2007)

Pons-Sanz, S.M., 'Norse-Derived Terms and Structures in *The Battle of Maldon*', *JEGP* 107 (2008), 421–44

Poole, R.[G.], 'Skaldic Verse and Anglo-Saxon History: Some Aspects of the Period 1009–1016', *Speculum* 62 (1987), 265–98

Poole, R.G., *Viking Poems on War and Peace: A Study in Skaldic Narrative* (Toronto, 1991)

Pope, J.C., Review of Bethurum, *Homilies of Wulfstan*, *Modern Language Notes* 74 (1959), 333–40

Pope, J.M., 'Monks and Nobles in the Anglo-Saxon Monastic Reform', *ANS* 17 (1995), 165–80

Powell, K., 'Meditating on Men and Monsters: A Reconsideration of the Thematic Unity of the *Beowulf* Manuscript', *Review of English Studies* 57 (2006), 1–15

Powell, K., 'Viking Invasions and Marginal Annotations in Cambridge, Corpus Christi College 162', *ASE* 37 (2008), 151–71

Powell, T.E., 'The "Three Orders" of Society in Anglo-Saxon England', *ASE* 23 (1994), 103–32

Pratt, D., *The Political Thought of King Alfred the Great* (Cambridge, 2007)

Pratt, D., 'Written Law and the Communication of Authority in Tenth-Century England', in *England and the Continent in the Tenth Century: Studies in Honour of Wilhelm Levison (1876–1947)*, ed. D.[W.] Rollason, C. Leyser and H. Williams (Turnhout, 2010), 331–50

Pratt, D., 'The Voice of the King in "King Edgar's Establishment of Monasteries"', *ASE* 41 (2012), 145–204

Pratt, D., 'Kings and Books in Anglo-Saxon England', *ASE* 43 (2014), 297–377

Prestwich, M., 'Medieval Biography', *Journal of Interdisciplinary History* 40 (2010), 325–346

Prideaux-Collins, W., '"Satan's Bonds are Extremely Loose": Apocalyptic Expectation in Anglo-Saxon England during the Millennial Era', in *The Apocalyptic Year 1000*, ed. R. Landes, A. Gow and D.C. Van Meter (Oxford, 2003), 289–310

Pulsiano P., '"Danish Men's Words Are Worse than Murder": Viking Guile and *The Battle of Maldon*', *JEGP* 96 (1997), 13–25

Rabin, A., 'Female Advocacy and Royal Protection in Tenth-Century England: The Career of Queen Ælfthryth', *Speculum* 84 (2009), 261–88

Rabin, A., 'Holy Bodies, Legal Matters: Reaction and Reform in Ælfric's *Eugenia* and the Ely Privilege', *Studies in Philology* 110 (2013), 220–65

Rabin, A., *The Political Writings of Archbishop Wulfstan* (Manchester, 2015)

Rabin, A., 'Wulfstan at London: Episcopal Politics in the Reign of Æthelred', *English Studies* 97 (2016), 186–206

Rahtz, P., 'The Bones of St. Edward the Martyr', *British Archaeological News* 4.ii (March 1989), 17–18

Rainbird, P., and D. Druce, 'A Late Saxon Date from Oldaport', *Proceedings of the Devon Archaeological Society* 62 (2004), 177–80

Rambaran-Olm, M.R., 'Trial by History's Jury: Examining II Æthelred's Legislative and Literary Legacy, AD 993–1006', *English Studies* 95 (2014), 777–802

Reuter, T., 'Carolingian and Ottonian Warfare', in *Medieval Warfare: A History*, ed. M. Keen (Oxford, 1999), 13–35

Reuter, T., 'The End of Carolingian Military Expansion' (1990), repr. in and cited from his *Medieval Polities and Modern Mentalities*, ed. J.L. Nelson (Cambridge, 2006), 251–67

Reuter, T., '*Regemque, quem in Francia pene perdidit, in patria magnifice recepit*: Ottonian Ruler Representation in Synchronic and Diachronic Comparison' (1998), repr. in and cited from his *Medieval Polities and Modern Mentalities*, ed. J.L. Nelson (Cambridge, 2006), 127–46

Reuter, T., 'Sex, Lies and Oath-Helpers: The Trial of Queen Uota' (2002), trans. in and cited from his *Medieval Polities and Modern Mentalities*, ed. J.L. Nelson (Cambridge, 2006), 217–30

Reuter, T., 'Contextualising Canossa: Excommunication, Penance, Surrender, Reconciliation', in his *Medieval Polities and Modern Mentalities*, ed. J.L. Nelson (Cambridge, 2006), 147–66

Reuter, T., 'The Ottonians and the Carolingian Tradition', in his *Medieval Polities and Modern Mentalities*, ed. J.L. Nelson (Cambridge, 2006), 268–83

Reynolds, A., *Anglo-Saxon Deviant Burial Customs* (Oxford, 2009)

Reynolds, A., 'Archaeological Correlates for Anglo-Saxon Military Activity in a Comparative Perspective', in *Landscapes of Defence in Early Medieval Europe*, ed. J. Baker, S. Brookes and A. Reynolds (Turnhout, 2013), 1–38

Reynolds, A., and S. Semple, 'Anglo-Saxon Non-Funerary Weapon Depositions', in *Studies in Early Anglo-Saxon Art and Archaeology: Papers in Honour of Martin G. Welch*, ed. S. Brookes, S. Harrington and A. Reynolds (Oxford, 2011), 40–8

Reynolds, S., 'What Do We Mean by "Anglo-Saxon" and "Anglo-Saxons"?', *Journal of British Studies* 24 (1985), 395–414

Reynolds, S., *Kingdoms and Communities in Western Europe, 900–1300*, 2nd edn (Oxford, 1997)

Ridyard, S.J., *The Royal Saints of Anglo-Saxon England: A Study of West Saxon and East Anglian Cults* (Cambridge, 1988)

Roach, L., 'Hosting the King: Hospitality and the Royal *iter* in Tenth-Century England', *Journal of Medieval History* 37 (2011), 34–46

Roach, L., 'Public Rites and Public Wrongs: Ritual Aspects of Diplomas in Tenth- and Eleventh-Century England', *EME* 19 (2011), 182–203

Roach, L., 'Penance, Submission and *deditio*: Religious Influences on Dispute Settlement in Later Anglo-Saxon England, 871–1066', *ASE* 41 (2012), 343–71

Roach, L., 'Emperor Otto III and the End of Time', *TRHS* 6th ser. 23 (2013), 75–102

Roach, L., *Kingship and Consent in Anglo-Saxon England, 871–978: Assemblies and the State in the Early Middle Ages* (Cambridge, 2013)

Roach, L., 'Law Codes and Legal Norms in Later Anglo-Saxon England', *Historical Research* 86 (2013), 465–86

Roach, L., 'Penitential Discourse in the Diplomas of King Æthelred "the Unready"', *Journal of Ecclesiastical History* 64 (2013), 258–76

Roach, L., 'Apocalypse and Atonement in the Politics of Later Æthelredian England', *English Studies* 95 (2014), 733–57

Roach, L., 'The Legacy of a Late Antique Prophecy: The Tiburtine Sibyl and the Italian Opposition to Otto III', *The Mediaeval Journal* 5.i (2015), 1–33

Roach, L., 'A Tale of Two Charters: Diploma Production and Political Performance in Æthelredian England', in *Writing Kingship and Power in Anglo-Saxon England: Studies in Honour of Simon Keynes*, ed. R. Naismith and D.A. Woodman (Cambridge, forthcoming)

Roach, L., 'Wulfstan Cantor', in *The Wiley Blackwell Encyclopedia of Medieval British Literature*, ed. S. Echard and R. Rouse (Chichester, forthcoming)

Roach, L., 'The Privilege of Liberty in Later Anglo-Saxon England', in *Magna Carta: New Interpretations*, ed. S. Ambler and N. Vincent (forthcoming)

Roberts, J., and J.[L.] Nelson, ed., *Essays on Anglo-Saxon and Related Themes in Memory of Lynne Grundy* (Woodbridge, 2000)

Robinson, I.S., *Authority and Resistance in the Investiture Contest* (Manchester, 1978)

Robinson, I.S., *Henry IV of Germany, 1056–1106* (Cambridge, 1999)

Robinson, J.A., *Gilbert Crispin, Abbot of Westminster* (Cambridge, 1911)

Rodger, N.A.M., 'Cnut's Geld and the Size of Danish Ships', *EHR* 110 (1995), 392–403

Roesdahl, E., S.M. Sindbæk, A. Pedersen and D.M. Wilson, *Aggersborg: The Viking-Age Settlement and Fortress* (Moesgaard, 2014)

Roffe, D., *Domesday: The Inquest and the Book* (Oxford, 2000)

Roffe, D., ed., *The English and their Legacy, 900–1200: Essays in Honour of Ann Williams* (Woodbridge, 2012)

Rogers, H.L., '*The Battle of Maldon*: David Casley's Transcript', *Notes and Queries* n.s. 23 (1985), 147–55

Rollason, D.W., 'The Cults of Murdered Royal Saints in Anglo-Saxon England', *ASE* 11 (1982), 1–22

Rollason, D.W., *Saints and Relics in Anglo-Saxon England* (Oxford, 1989)

Rollason, D.[W.], C. Leyser and H. Williams, ed., *England and the Continent in the Tenth Century: Studies in Honour of Wilhelm Levison (1876–1947)* (Turnhout, 2010)

Roller, M.B., 'Exemplarity in Roman Culture: The Cases of Horatius Cocles and Cloelia', *Classical Philology* 99 (2004), 1–56

Rosenwein, B.H., *To Be the Neighbor of Saint Peter: The Social Meaning of Cluny's Property, 909–1049* (Ithaca, NY, 1989)

Rose-Troup, F., 'Crediton Charters of the Tenth Century', *Transactions of the Devonshire Association* 74 (1942), 237–61

Rubenstein, J., *Armies of Heaven: The First Crusade and the Quest for Apocalypse* (New York, 2011)

Rumble, A.R., ed., *The Reign of Cnut: King of England, Denmark and Norway* (London, 1994)

Rumble, A.R., 'Laity and the Monastic Reform in the Reign of Edgar', in *Edgar, King of the English 959–75: New Interpretations*, ed. D. Scragg (Woodbridge, 2008), 242–51

Rushforth, R., 'English Caroline Minuscule', in *The Cambridge History of the Book in Britain*, I, *c.400–1100*, ed. R. Gameson (Cambridge, 2012), 197–210

Salvador-Bello, M., 'The Edgar Panegyrics in the Anglo-Saxon Chronicle', in *Edgar, King of the English 959–75: New Interpretations*, ed. D. Scragg (Woodbridge, 2008), 252–72

Sanmark, A., and S. Semple, 'Places of Assembly: New Discoveries in Sweden and England', *Fornvännen* 103 (2008), 245–59

Sawyer, P.H., 'The Two Viking Ages of Britain', *Mediaeval Scandinavia* 2 (1969), 163–76

Sawyer, P.H., *The Age of the Vikings*, 2nd edn (London, 1971)

Sawyer, P.[H.], 'Ethelred II, Olaf Tryggvason, and the Conversion of Norway', *Scandinavian Studies* 59 (1987), 299–307

Sawyer, P.[H.], 'Cnut's Scandinavian Empire', in *The Reign of Cnut: King of England, Denmark and Norway*, ed. A.R. Rumble (London, 1994), 10–22

Sawyer, P.H., *From Roman Britain to Norman England*, 2nd edn (London, 1998)

Scattergood, J., '*The Battle of Maldon* and History', in *Literature and Learning in Medieval and Renaissance England: Studies Presented to Fitzroy Pyle*, ed. J. Scattergood (Dublin, 1984), 11–24

Scharer, A., 'Herrscherurkunden als Selbstzeugnisse?', *Mitteilungen des Instituts für Österreichische Geschichtsforschung* 119 (2011), 1–13

Schieffer, R., 'Von Mailand nach Canossa. Ein Beitrag zur Geschichte der christlichen Herrscherbuße von Theodosius d. Gr. bis zu Heinrich IV.', *DA* 28 (1972), 333–70

Schieffer, R., 'Otto II. und sein Vater', *FMSt* 36 (2002), 255–69

Schmid, K., and J. Wollasch, ed., *Memoria. Der geschichtliche Zeugniswert des liturgischen Gedenkens im Mittelalter* (Munich, 1984)

Schneider, C., *Prophetisches Sacerdotium und heilsgeschichtliches Regnum im Dialog, 1073–1077. Zur Geschichte Gregors VII. und Heinrichs IV.* (Munich, 1972)

Schneider, J., *Auf der Suche nach dem verlorenen Reich. Lotharingien im 9. und 10. Jahrhundert* (Cologne, 2010)

Schneidmüller, B., *Die Welfen. Herrschaft und Erinnerung* (Stuttgart, 2000)

Schneidmüller, B., 'Rule by Consensus: Forms and Concepts of Political Order in the European Middle Ages', *Medieval History Journal* 16 (2013), 449–71

Schoenfeld, E.J., 'Anglo-Saxon *Burhs* and Continental *Burgen*: Early Medieval Fortifications in Constitutional Perspective', *HSJ* 6 (1994), 49–66

Scott, S.T., 'The Edgar Poems and the Poetics of Failure in the *Anglo-Saxon Chronicle*', *ASE* 39 (2010), 105–37

Scragg, D., ed., *The Battle of Maldon, AD 991* (Oxford, 1991)

Scragg, D., '*The Battle of Maldon*: Fact or Fiction?', in *The Battle of Maldon: Fiction and Fact*, ed. J. Cooper (London, 1993), 19–31

Scragg, D., *The Return of the Vikings: The Battle of Maldon 991* (Stroud, 2006)

Scragg, D., ed., *Edgar, King of the English 959–75: New Interpretations* (Woodbridge, 2008)

Scragg, D., 'Old English Homiliaries and Poetic Manuscripts', in *The Cambridge History of the Book in Britain*, I, *c.400–1100*, ed. R. Gameson (Cambridge, 2012), 553–61

Screen, E., 'Anglo-Saxon Law and Numismatics: A Reassessment in the Light of Patrick Wormald's *The Making of English Law*', *BNJ* 77 (2007), 150–72

Sellar, W.C., and R.J. Yeatman, *1066 and All That* (London, 1931)

Semmler, J., 'Das Erbe der karolingischen Klosterreform im 10. Jahrhundert', in *Monastische Reformen im 9. und 10. Jahrhundert*, ed. R. Kottje and H. Maurer (Sigmaringen, 1989), 29–77

Shahar, S., *Childhood in the Middle Ages* (London, 1990)

Sheerin, D.J., 'The Dedication of the Old Minster, Winchester, in 980', *Revue Bénédictine* 88 (1978), 261–73

Sheppard, A., *Families of the King: Writing Identity in the Anglo-Saxon Chronicle* (Toronto, 2004)

Sisam, K., 'The Relationship of Æthelred's Codes V and VI', in his *Studies in the History of Old English Literature* (Oxford, 1953), 278–87

Smyth, A., *Scandinavian York and Dublin: The History and Archaeology of Two Related Viking Kingdoms*, 2 vols. (Dublin, 1975–9)

Snook, B., *The Anglo-Saxon Chancery: The History, Language and Production of Anglo-Saxon Charters from Alfred to Edgar* (Woodbridge, 2015)

Stafford, P., 'Historical Implications of the Regional Production of Dies under Æthelred II', *BNJ* 48 (1978), 35–51

Stafford, P., 'Sons and Mothers: Family Politics in the Early Middle Ages', in *Medieval Women*, ed. D. Baker (Oxford, 1978), 79–100

Stafford, P., *Unification and Conquest: A Political and Social History of the Tenth and Eleventh Centuries* (London, 1989)

Stafford, P., *Queen Emma and Queen Edith: Queenship and Women's Power in Eleventh-Century England* (Oxford, 1997)

Stafford, P., 'The Reign of Æthelred II: A Study in the Limits of Royal Policy and Action' (1978), repr. in and cited from her *Gender, Family and the Legitimation of Power: England from the Ninth to the Early Twelfth Century* (Aldershot, 2006), no. IV

Stafford, P., 'The King's Wife in Wessex 800–1066' (1981), repr. in and cited from her *Gender, Family and the Legitimation of Power: England from the Ninth to the Early Twelfth Century* (Aldershot, 2006), no. IX

Stafford, P., 'The Laws of Cnut and the History of Anglo-Saxon Royal Promises' (1981), repr. in and cited from her *Gender, Family and the Legitimation of Power: England from the Ninth to the Early Twelfth Century* (Aldershot, 2006), no. VI

Stafford, P., 'Queens, Nunneries and Reforming Churchmen: Gender, Religious Status and Reform in Tenth- and Eleventh-Century England' (1999), repr. in and cited from her *Gender, Family and the Legitimation of Power: England from the Ninth to the Early Twelfth Century* (Aldershot, 2006), no. XI

Stafford, P., '*Cherchez la femme*. Queens, Queens' Lands and Nunneries: Missing Links in the Foundation of Reading Abbey' (2000), repr. in and cited from her *Gender, Family and the Legitimation of Power: England from the Ninth to the Early Twelfth Century* (Aldershot, 2006), no. XII

Stafford, P., 'Political Ideas in Late Tenth-Century England: Charters as Evidence' (2001), repr. in and cited from her *Gender, Family and the Legitimation of Power: England from the Ninth to the Early Twelfth Century* (Aldershot, 2006), no. VII

Stafford, P., 'Reeve', in *The Wiley Blackwell Encyclopedia of Anglo-Saxon England*, ed. M. Lapidge et al., 2nd edn (Chichester, 2013), 397–8

Stenton, F.M., *The Latin Charters of the Anglo-Saxon Period* (Oxford, 1955)

Stenton, F.M., *Anglo-Saxon England*, 3rd edn (Oxford, 1971)

Stevenson, W.H., 'Notes on Old-English Historical Geography', *EHR* 11 (1896), 301–4

Stewart, B.H.I.H., 'Coinage and Recoinage after Edgar's Reform', in *Studies in Late Anglo-Saxon Coinage in Memory of Bror Emil Hildebrand*, ed. K. Jonsson (Stockholm, 1990), 455–85

Syrett, M., *The Vikings in England: The Evidence of Runic Inscriptions* (Cambridge, 2002)

Taylor, C.S., 'The Origin of the Mercian Shires', in *Gloucestershire Studies*, ed. H.P.R. Finberg (Leicester, 1957), 17–45

Tellenbach, G., 'Die Unteilbarkeit des Reiches. Ein Beitrag zur Entstehungsgeschichte Deutschlands und Frankreichs', *HZ* 163 (1941), 20–42

Tellenbach, G., 'Der Charakter Kaiser Heinrichs IV. Zugleich ein Versuch über die Erkennbarkeit menschlicher Individualität im hohen Mittelalter', in *Person und Gemeinschaft im Mittelalter. Festschrift für Karl Schmid zum fünfundsechzigsten Geburtstag*, ed. G. Althoff *et al.* (Sigmaringen, 1988), 345–68

Tellenbach, G., ' "Ungeschehene Geschichte" und ihre heuristische Funktion', *HZ* 258 (1994), 297–316

Thacker, A., 'Cults at Canterbury: Relics and Reform under Dunstan and his Successors', in *St Dunstan: His Life, Times and Cult*, ed. N. Ramsay, M. Sparks and T. Tatton-Brown (Woodbridge, 1992), 221–44

Thacker, A., 'Saint-Making and Relic Collecting by Oswald and His Communities', in *St Oswald of Worcester: Life and Influence*, ed. N. Brooks and C. Cubitt (London, 1996), 244–68

Thompson, S.D., *Royal Anglo-Saxon Diplomas: A Palaeography* (Woodbridge, 2006)

Thompson, V., *Dying and Death in Later Anglo-Saxon England* (Woodbridge, 2004)

Thompson Smith, S., *Land and Book: Literature and Land Tenure in Anglo-Saxon England* (Toronto, 2012)

Thornton, D.E., 'Edgar and the Eight Kings, AD 973: *textus et dramatis personae*', *EME* 10 (2001), 49–79

Tinti, F., 'Benedictine Reform and Pastoral Care in Late Anglo-Saxon England', *EME* 23 (2015), 229–51

Tock, B.-M., 'La mise en scène des actes en France au Haut Moyen Âge', *FMSt* 38 (2004), 287–96

Tollerton, L., *Wills and Will-Making in Anglo-Saxon England* (Woodbridge, 2011)

Townend, M., 'Contextualizing the *Knútsdrápur*: Skaldic Praise-Poetry at the Court of Cnut', *ASE* 30 (2001), 145–79

Townend, M., 'Norse Poets and English Kings: Skaldic Performance in Anglo-Saxon England', *Offa* 58 (2001), 269–75

Townend, M., ed., *Wulfstan, Archbishop of York* (Turnhout, 2004)

Treharne, E., *Living Through Conquest: The Politics of Early English, 1020–1220* (Oxford, 2012)

Turner, R.V., 'Eleanor of Aquitaine and Her Children: An Inquiry into Medieval Family Attachment', *Journal of Medieval History* 14 (1988), 321–35

Ubl, K., *Inzestverbot und Gesetzgebung. Die Konstruktion eines Verbrechens (300–1100)* (Berlin, 2008)

Ubl, K., 'Der kinderlose König. Ein Testfall für die Ausdifferenzierung des Politischen im 11. Jahrhundert', *HZ* 292 (2011), 323–63

Upchurch, R.K., 'A Big Dog Barks: Ælfric of Eynsham's Indictment of the English Pastorate and *Witan*', *Speculum* 85 (2010), 505–33

Vanderputten, S., *Monastic Reform as Process: Realities and Representations in Medieval Flanders, 900–1100* (Ithaca, NY, 2013)

Vincent, N., *Peter des Roches: An Alien in English Politics, 1205–1238* (Cambridge, 1996)

Vincent, N., 'King Henry III', *History Today* 52.vi (2002), 11–17

Vogtherr, T., ' "Weh Dir, Land, dessen König ein Kind ist." Minderjährige Könige um 1200 im europäischen Vergleich', *FMSt* 37 (2003), 291–314

Vollrath, H., *Die Synoden Englands bis 1066* (Paderborn, 1986)

Wallis, S. *et al.*, *The Oxford Henge and Late Saxon Massacre with Medieval and Later Occupation at St John's College, Oxford* (Reading, 2014)

Ward, E.J., 'Anne of Kiev (*c.* 1024–*c.* 1075) and a Reassessment of Maternal Power in the Minority Kingship of Philip I of France', *Historical Research* (forthcoming)

Wareham, A., 'Fiscal Policies and the Institution of a Tax State in Anglo-Saxon England within a Comparative Context', *Economic History Review* 65 (2012), 910–31

Warren, W.L., *Henry II* (Berkeley, CA, 1973)

Waßenhoven, D., 'The Role of Bishops in Anglo-Saxon Succession Struggles, 955–978', in *Leaders of the Anglo-Saxon Church from Bede to Stigand*, ed. A.R. Rumble (Woodbridge, 2012), 97–108

Watson, B., T. Brigham and T. Dyson, *London Bridge: 2000 Years of a River Crossing* (London, 2001)

Weidhagen-Hallerdt, M., 'A Possible Ring Fort from the Late Viking Period in Helsingborg', *Current Swedish Archaeology* 17 (2009), 187–204

Weiler, B., *Kingship, Rebellion and Political Culture: England and Germany, c. 1215–c.1250* (Basingstoke, 2007)

Weiler, B., 'Rebellious Sons: Revolt, Succession, and the Culture of Kingship in Western Europe, *c.* 1170–*c.* 1280', *Historical Research* 82 (2009), 17–40

Weinfurter, S., 'Die Zentralisierung der Herrschaftsgewalt im Reich durch Kaiser Heinrich II.' (1986), repr. in and cited from his *Gelebte Ordnung, gedachte Ordnung. Ausgewählte Beiträge zu König, Kirche und Reich* (Sigmaringen, 2005), 213–64

Weinfurter, S., 'Kaiserin Adelheid und das ottonische Kaisertum' (1999), repr. in and cited from his *Gelebte Ordnung, gedachte Ordnung. Ausgewählte Beiträge zu König, Kirche und Reich* (Sigmaringen, 2005), 189–212

Whitelock, D., 'Foreword', in *Liber Eliensis*, ed. E.O. Blake, Camden Society 3rd ser. 92 (London, 1962), ix–xviii

Whitelock, D., 'Wulfstan and the so-called Laws of Edward and Guthrum' (1941), repr. in and cited from her *History, Law and Literature in 10th–11th Century England* (London, 1981), no. IX

Whitelock, D., 'The Dealings of the Kings of England with Northumbria in the Tenth and Eleventh Centuries' (1959), repr. in and cited from her *History, Law and Literature in 10th–11th Century England* (London, 1981), no. III

Whitelock, D., 'The Appointment of Dunstan as Archbishop of Canterbury' (1973), repr. in and cited from her *History, Law and Literature in 10th–11th Century England* (London, 1981), no. IV

Wilcox, J., 'The St. Brice's Day Massacre and Archbishop Wulfstan', in *Peace and Negotiation: Strategies for Co-Existence in the Middle Ages and the Renaissance*, ed. D. Wolfthal (Turnhout, 2000), 79–91

Wilcox, J., 'Wulfstan's *Sermo Lupi ad Anglos* as Political Performance: 16 February 1014 and Beyond', in *Wulfstan, Archbishop of York*, ed. M. Townend (Turnhout, 2004), 375–96

Williams, A., 'Some Notes and Considerations on Problems Connected with the English Royal Succession, 860–1066', *ANS* 1 (1979), 144–67 and 225–33

Williams, A., '*Princeps Merciorum gentis*: The Family, Career and Connections of Ælfhere, Ealdorman of Mercia, 956–83', *ASE* 10 (1981), 143–72

Williams, A., 'The Battle of Maldon and *The Battle of Maldon*: History, Poetry and Propaganda', *Medieval History* 2.ii (1992), 35–44

Williams, A., *Æthelred: The Ill-Counselled King* (London, 2003)

Williams, A., 'An Outing on the Dee: King Edgar at Chester, A.D. 973', *Mediaeval Scandinavia* 14 (2004), 229–43

Williams, A., 'The Dangers of Invention: The Sack of Canterbury, 1011, and the Theft of Dunstan's Relics', in *Cathedrals, Communities and Conflict in the Anglo-Norman World*, ed. P. Dalton, C. Insley and L.J. Wilkinson (Woodbridge, 2011), 27–40

Williams, A., 'Thorkell the Tall and the Bubble of Reputation: The Vicissitudes of Fame', in *Danes in Wessex: The Scandinavian Impact on Southern England, c. 800–c. 1100*, ed. R. Lavelle and S. Roffey (Oxford, 2015), 144–57

Williams, G., 'Hákon Aðalsteins fóstri: Aspects of Anglo-Saxon Kingship in Tenth-Century Norway', in *The North Sea World in the Middle Ages: Studies in the Cultural History of North-Western Europe*, ed. T.R. Liszka and E.M. Walker (Dublin, 2001), 108–26

Williams, T.J.T., 'Landscape and Warfare in Anglo-Saxon England and the Viking Campaign of 1006', *EME* 23 (2015), 329–59

Winkler, E.A., 'England's Defending Kings in Twelfth-Century Historical Writing', *HSJ* 25 (2013), 147–163

Winroth, A., *The Conversion of Scandinavia: Vikings, Merchants, and Missionaries in the Remaking of Northern Europe* (New Haven, CT, 2011)

Wollasch, J., 'The First Wave of Reform', in *The New Cambridge Medieval History*, III, *c. 900–1024*, ed. T. Reuter (Cambridge, 1999), 163–85

Wood, I.N., and N. Lund, ed., *People and Places in Northern Europe 500–1600: Essays in Honour of Peter Hayes Sawyer* (Woodbridge, 1991)

Wood, S., *The Proprietary Church in the Medieval West* (Oxford, 2006)

Woods, D., 'The *Agnus Dei* Penny of King Æthelred II: A Call to Hope in the Lord (Isaiah XL)?', *ASE* 42 (2013), 299–309

Wormald, P., 'Æthelred the Lawmaker', in *Ethelred the Unready*, ed. D.[H.] Hill (London, 1978), 47–80

Wormald, P., Review of Ridyard, *Royal Saints, Journal of Ecclesiastical History* 42 (1991), 101–2

Wormald, P., *The Making of English Law: King Alfred to the Twelfth Century*, I, *Legislation and its Limits* (Oxford, 1998)

Wormald, P., '*Lex scripta* and *verbum regis*: Legislation and Germanic Kingship from Euric to Cnut' (1977), repr. in and cited from his *Legal Culture in the Early Medieval West: Law as Text, Image and Experience* (London, 1999), 1–43

Wormald, P., 'A Handlist of Anglo-Saxon Lawsuits' (1986), repr. in and cited from his *Legal Culture in the Early Medieval West: Law as Text, Image and Experience* (London, 1999), 253–87

Wormald, P., 'Giving God and King their Due: Conflict and its Regulation in the Early English State' (1997), repr. in and cited from his *Legal Culture in the Early Medieval West: Law as Text, Image and Experience* (London, 1999), 333–57

Wormald, P., 'The Strange Affair of the Selsey Bishopric, 953–963', in *Belief and Culture in the Middle Ages: Studies Presented to Henry Mayr-Harting*, ed. R. Gameson and H. Leyser (Oxford, 2001), 128–41

Wormald, P., 'Germanic Power Structures: The Early English Experience', in *Power and the Nation in European History*, ed. L. Scales and O. Zimmer (Cambridge, 2005), 105–24

Wormald, P., 'Æthelwold and his Continental Counterparts: Contact, Comparison, Contrast' (1988), repr. in and cited from his *The Times of Bede: Studies in Early English Christian Society and its Historian*, ed. S. Baxter (Oxford, 2006), 169–206

Yorke, B., 'Aethelmaer: The Foundation of the Abbey at Cerne and the Politics of the Tenth Century', in *The Cerne Abbey Millennium Lectures*, ed. K. Barker (Cerne Abbas, 1988), 15–25

Yorke, B., 'Æthelwold and the Politics of the Tenth Century', in *Bishop Æthelwold: His Career and Influence*, ed. B. Yorke (Woodbridge, 1988), 65–88

Yorke, B., *Kings and Kingdoms of Early Anglo-Saxon England* (London, 1990)

Yorke, B., 'The Legitimacy of St Edith', *HSJ* 11 (1998), 97–113

Yorke, B., 'Edward, King and Martyr: A Saxon Murder Mystery', in *Studies in the Early History of Shaftesbury Abbey*, ed. L. Keen (Dorchester, 1999), 99–116

Yorke, B., 'The Women in Edgar's Life', in *Edgar, King of the English 959–75: New Interpretations*, ed. D. Scragg (Woodbridge, 2008), 143–57

Yorke, B., 'The Burial of Kings in Anglo-Saxon England', in *Kingship, Legislation and Power in Anglo-Saxon England*, ed. G.R. Owen-Crocker and B.W. Schneider (Woodbridge, 2013), 237–57

Unpublished works

Banton, N., 'Ealdormen and Earls in England from the Reign of Alfred to the Reign of Æthelred II' (DPhil diss., Univ. of Oxford, 1981)

Conn, M.A., 'The Dunstan and Brodie (Anderson) Pontificals: An Edition and Study' (PhD diss., Univ. of Notre Dame, 1993)

Denton, J.E., 'Late Tenth-Century Anglo-Saxon Hagiography: Ramsey and the Old Minster, Winchester' (PhD diss., Univ. of Cambridge, 2012)

Elliot, M.D., 'Canon Law Collections in England *ca* 600–1066: The Manuscript Evidence' (PhD diss., Univ. of Toronto, 2013)

Foxhall Forbes, H., 'The Development of the Notions of Penance, Purgatory and the Afterlife in Anglo-Saxon England' (PhD diss., Univ. of Cambridge, 2008)

Hudson, A., 'Æthelwold's Circle, Saints' Cults, and Monastic Reform, c. 956–1006' (DPhil diss., Univ. of Oxford, 2014)

Jayakumar, S., 'The Politics of the English Kingdom, c. 955–c. 978' (DPhil diss., Univ. of Oxford, 2001)

Keynes, S., 'The Diplomas of King Æðelred II (978–1016)' (PhD diss., Univ. of Cambridge, 1978)

Little, G.R., 'Dynastic Strategies and Regional Loyalties: Wessex, Mercia and Kent, c. 802–939' (PhD diss., Univ. of Sheffield, 2007)

McGuigan, N., 'Neither Scotland nor England: Middle Britain, c.850–1150' (PhD diss., Univ. of St Andrews, 2015)

O'Gorman, D.M., '*Unius regulae ac unius patriae*: A Standardizing Process in Anglo-Saxon England' (PhD diss., Loyola Univ., 2015)

Sprigade, K., 'Die Einweisung ins Kloster und in den geistlichen Stand als politische Maßnahme im frühen Mittelalter' (PhD diss., Univ. of Heidelberg, 1964)

Stafford, P., 'Royal Government in the Reign of Æthelred II, A.D. 979–1016' (DPhil diss., Univ. of Oxford, 1973)

Electronic resources

'Anglo-Saxon Penitentials: A Cultural Database': www.anglo-saxon.net/penance/ (online edition and translation of the Old English penitentials by A. J. Frantzen)

'Electronic Sawyer', ed. S. Kelly and R. Rushforth *et al.*: www.esawyer.org.uk/ (a revised version of *Anglo-Saxon Charters*, ed. P.H. Sawyer, listed under 'Primary sources')

'Kemble': http://www.kemble.asnc.cam.ac.uk/ (guides on various aspects of charter criticism, maps of the Anglo-Saxon period and tables from *An Atlas of Attestations*, ed. S. Keynes, listed under 'Primary sources')

'Monumenta Germaniae Historica digital': www.dmgh.de (digital versions of all primary sources edited in the MGH series, listed under 'Abbreviations')

'ODNB online': www.oxforddnb.com/ (an online version of the *Oxford Dictionary of National Biography*, listed under 'Abbreviations')

"Prosopography of Anglo-Saxon England': www.pase.ac.uk (prosopographical guidance to the Anglo-Saxon period)
'Rundata: The Scandinavian Runic-Text Database': www.nordiska.uu.se/forskn/samnord.htm (an electronic database of runic inscriptions with modern English translations, hosted by the University of Uppsala)

Popular representations

Bracewell, P., *Shadow on the Crown* (New York, 2013)
Bracewell, P., *The Price of Blood* (New York, 2015)
Logue, C., 'An Archaic Jingle', *Times* (17 Nov. 1977), 14
Wilson, R. (conductor and composer), *Aethelred the Unready* (Albany Records, 2002)
Woods, J., *Eadric the Grasper* (Scotts Valley, CA, 2009)

INDEX

INDEX OF CHARTERS